the Post-Secondary LEARNING EXPERIENCE

Marilyn Hadad, Ph.D.
Ryerson University

Maureen J. Reed, Ph.D.
Ryerson University

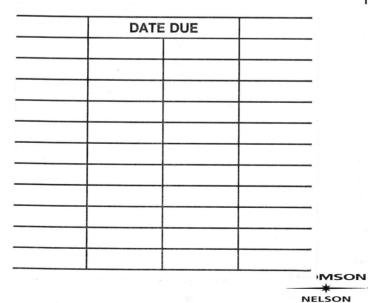

THOMSON
NELSON

Australia   Canada   Mexico   Singapore   Spain   United Kingdom   United States

THOMSON

NELSON

The Post-Secondary Learning Experience

by Marilyn Hadad and Maureen J. Reed

Associate Vice-President, Editorial Director:
Evelyn Veitch

Executive Editor:
Anne Williams

Marketing Manager:
Sandra Green

Developmental Editor:
Natalie Barrington

Permissions Coordinator:
Indu Ghuman

Production Editor:
Lara Caplan

Copy Editor:
Laurel Sparrow

Proofreader:
Mariko Obokata

Indexer:
Belle Wong

Production Coordinator:
Ferial Suleman

Design Director:
Ken Phipps

Interior Design:
Liz Harasymczuk

Cover Design:
Johanna Liburd

Cover Image:
Digital Vision/Getty Images

Compositor:
Integra

Printer:
Transcontinental

Library and Archives Canada Cataloguing in Publication

Hadad, Marilyn, 1950–
The post-secondary learning experience/Marilyn Hadad, Maureen J. Reed.

Includes bibliographical references and index.
ISBN 0-17-640678-6

1. Education, Higher—Canada.
2. Universities and colleges— Canada.
I. Reed, Maureen J. (Maureen Joyce), 1959–
II. Title.

LA417.5.H24 2006   378.71
C2005-906052-2

This book is dedicated to my cousin, Her Worship Kathleen Marilyn Bryant. One is truly blessed when beloved family is also a beloved friend. — *MH*

To Ron Collis, Reed Collis, and The Family — *MR*

CONTENTS

PREFACE

This book carries with it many hopes. Between us, we have nearly half a century of teaching experience and we have been fortunate to work with thousands of students. In addition, we are blessed (or cursed!) with vivid memories of what it was like to be a student. As professors, we have been excited by our students' many accomplishments. At times, however, we have been troubled when bright, hard-working students have found their academic careers to be difficult. Some of these students chose to take other paths. Yet we know that some of these students, even some who failed or dropped out, were capable of success, given the right guidance. These students were not lazy or unmotivated. They just realized too late that they needed to change the ways in which they approached their education. Through talking to many students and through remembering our own experiences, we knew what the real reason for first-year fiascoes was: many students were simply unprepared for the demands and expectations of the post-secondary world. They lacked the skills (*not* the brains or the motivation) to handle the tasks placed before them. We tried to help individual students who approached us, but we were determined to do more.

To that end, Marilyn joined committees at Ryerson University that were designing new degree programs, and proposed to them a compulsory, one-semester credit course, informally known as "University 101." Maureen joined the Ryerson University Success and Retention Committee where she and members of the committee formally investigated the reasons for student attrition and what could be done to retain students in a satisfying, productive, post-secondary experience. Together, we were asked to design and teach a course that would do this, a "University 101" course.

Our experience in designing this course taught us much. The Success and Retention Committee review of the literature revealed that courses teaching skills for post-secondary work were most effective (and taken seriously) if they were given for academic credit. Giving a course for academic credit means that the course must contain solid academic material. But the available books in the area, while being superb as workbooks, lacked much of the theoretical basis we felt was needed to provide the material for a credit course. That is, while these books gave wonderful ideas on how to remember what one studies, for example, they did not explain why these tips work (theory) or how we know they can be effective (empirical research). This is not meant as a criticism of these books: they accomplish their ends admirably. However, we felt that by including both theory and empirical research along with tips and strategies, we could attain two major goals. First, we could provide academic material for a credit course, and second, we could give students a basis for formulating their own techniques or modifying the ideas we present to suit their individuality more effectively. The good people at Thomson Nelson agreed with us, hence this book.

FEATURES OF THIS TEXT

We have chosen to use an informal style in writing this book, a style we feel allows for maximum accessibility and easy readability. We also present theory in a relevant context so students can easily apply it to their own situations. To further augment student engagement, we have included the following features:

- chapter opening case studies, which are carried throughout the chapter
- concrete illustrations to exemplify theory and explanations
- use of common student questions as subheadings
- margin glossaries and end-of-chapter key terms lists

- exercises and self-tests throughout the chapters, many of which are standardized
- feature boxes, which highlight additional explanations and tips
- individual and group end-of-chapter activities
- websites where students can obtain more information and test themselves further
- an online student website (www.postsecondarylearning.nelson.com) with more information and student-involvers; the website will contain links to all URLs listed in the text

We quickly found that, in terms of content, we could easily have written a 700-page book! The choice of what to include in this book was often difficult. We chose the areas that, in our and our reviewers' experience, provided the most and greatest challenges to students. Other areas are sometimes contained in the online study guide (e.g., how to cope with shyness, additional information on how to write a laboratory report), but undoubtedly we have missed areas that some instructors will find important. We hope that instructors will give us feedback on what we have missed (as well as what we did right!).

CHAPTER FEATURES

Below is a very condensed outline of the topics we cover in each chapter:

CHAPTER 1

- How post-secondary school differs from high school
- Resources available to students
- Levels of learning in post-secondary school

CHAPTER 2

- Self-awareness
- Self-concept
- Self-esteem
- Self-efficacy
- Values
- Identity and identity crises

CHAPTER 3

- Sources and effects of stress
- Techniques for stress reduction
- Loneliness
- Relationships
- Romantic breakups

CHAPTER 4

- Time management
- Budgeting
- Test anxiety

- Procrastination
- Decision-making and stress

CHAPTER 5

- How we learn
- Individual learning styles
- Theory of learning
- Modifying your learning for academic success

CHAPTER 6

- How memory works
- Selecting important material and note taking
- Recall techniques such as mnemonics
- Strategies for remembering

CHAPTER 7

- How people think
- The biases and flaws in thinking
- How to evaluate theories
- How to problem-solve using different heuristics
- Decision-making and critical thinking

CHAPTER 8

- Theoretical definition of motivation
- What motivates us
- Why our motivation flags
- What we can do to increase motivation

CHAPTER 9

- Suggestions for reading more effectively
- How to critically evaluate material
- Standards for information literacy at post-secondary institutions
- How to meet these standards when conducting library research

CHAPTER 10

- How to plan and write an essay at the post-secondary level
- Plagiarism
- Referencing with APA and MLA

CHAPTER 11

- How to critically evaluate research and journal articles

CHAPTER 12

- Preparing and giving effective oral presentations
- Managing the fears associated with presentations
- Assertiveness
- How to give and receive criticism
- Effective use of visual aids

CHAPTER 13

- Suggestions for dealing effectively with group problems and conflict
- Roles that arise within a group
- Leadership
- Diversity in a group

CHAPTER 14

- Creativity in the post-secondary setting
- Suggestions for increasing creativity

THE FINAL WORD

- Using these skills in future endeavours
- Career planning and optimism

ACKNOWLEDGMENTS

We mentioned the possibility of writing a book initially to Andy Wellner of Thomson Nelson, almost casually. He, however, was far from casual: he jumped at our suggestion, encouraging us to write a formal book proposal. He took our proposal to Anne Williams who further encouraged us and started the publishing ball rolling. Anne was replaced for a few months by Rod Banister while she took a maternity leave (twins!), and Rod carried on with the same enthusiasm as Anne had shown. Meeting with the whole Thomson Nelson production team was a high point for us: the quality, dedication, and gusto of these professionals are both impressive and inspirational, and they all deserve our heartfelt thanks. Perhaps our heartiest thanks go to our developmental editor, Natalie Barrington. Natalie supported us on a day-to-day basis. She helped us stay organized and focused; she provided us with the information we needed on the technical aspects of writing a book (and there were astoundingly many!); and she put up with and comforted us on our worries and missteps. We would like to thank our research assistant, Milana Drobner, for her many hours of library work. Our sharp-eyed copyeditor, Laurel Sparrow, also deserves our great appreciation for her able and thorough work on preparing our manuscript for printing. Finally and foremost, we would like to thank the many and wonderful reviewers of our chapters. Their suggestions made our material stronger. They allowed us to better understand the perspectives and needs of others who teach similar courses at the post-secondary level.

Deborah Boutilier, Niagara College, OISE/UT

Martin Boyne, Trent University

John Buskard, John Abbott College

Dr. Julie M. Fraser, University of Windsor

John C. Garland, Ph.D. Memorial University

Pamela Idahosa, George Brown College

Dr. Selia Karsten, Seneca College

Dr. R. Kenedy, York University

Dr. Deborah J. Kennett, Trent University

Don Kinder, Ryerson University

Kelly Little, St. Clair College

Alexandra Pawlowsky, University of Manitoba

Barry Pomeroy, University of Winnipeg

Fleurette Simmonds, Durham College

Miriam Unruh, University of Manitoba

To the students who will use this book: you're what this is all about. You have always been and always will be our top priority. Of course we want you to learn, but more than this, we want you to enjoy the learning process. We want you to keep learning throughout your lives and we want you to have the best possible post-secondary experience. Let us know how you're doing. We can be contacted through the website, http://www .postsecondarylearning.nelson.com

Marilyn Hadad and Maureen Reed

ABOUT THE AUTHORS

Marilyn Hadad teaches at Ryerson University, specializing in personal growth and all areas of adjustment. She received her B.Sc. from the University of Toronto and her M.A. and Ph.D. from Queen's University in Kingston, Ontario. She is co-author, with Ryerson professor William Glassman, of the one-semester introductory psychology textbook, *Approaches to Psychology*, 4th ed., Open University Press, and she has also authored the custom publication manuscript, *Models of Personal Growth*, for her popular and dynamic course of the same name. When not teaching, serving on committees, writing, or reviewing textbooks and articles, Marilyn enjoys Toronto's art scene.

Maureen Reed teaches at Ryerson University in the Department of Psychology. Maureen received her B.A. from Queen's University in Kingston, Ontario, and her M.A. and Ph.D. from York University in Toronto. She enjoys teaching numerous courses in psychology and in post-secondary success. She has conducted extensive research in perception, information processing, and post-secondary success, with an emphasis on disabilities. Maureen is also a partner in Collis & Reed Research, where she applies her research skills to business, industry, health, and government groups. Outside work, Maureen enjoys working with Big Sisters of Clarington and spending time with her husband Ron and son Reed.

INTRODUCTION

The Case of Carl

► Carl is 19 years old. He's from a small farming community where he was bused to high school every day. His elementary school and his high school were small. His high school graduating class had only 12 students, and Carl was the one with the top marks. Today, he is entering the world of post-secondary education. He has left his hometown to live in a college residence with people he has never met before. The college is in an unfamiliar large city 500 kilometres from his hometown. He knows no one here.

On the one hand, he's exhilarated: he's been looking forward to post-secondary school and being out on his own in a big city for a long time. But on the other hand, he's scared, and he's reluctant to admit this to anyone, even himself. He knows that he's always wanted to go to college, but now that he's here, he wonders if it wouldn't have been wiser to wait a year or two before entering. If he had waited, he could have worked to save for college, and then money would not have been as tight as it is for him now. If he had waited, perhaps someone else from his high school would have graduated and wanted to go to this college as well.

Apart from the social factor of not knowing anyone, he's excited and pretty confident in himself; he feels that since he managed schoolwork and social life in high school so well, he can handle the academic work and social life of college. One of the upper-year students in his residence warns him very seriously that college is different from high school and that he had better make himself aware of all the resources available to him before a crisis hits. Carl listens carefully to this. He wants to make sure that he is fully ready for the challenges of college.

In this chapter, we will:

- Discuss the differences between secondary and post-secondary schools

- Describe the resources available to you

- Discuss the kinds of work you will be asked to do

Like Carl, you are probably entering the world of post-secondary education for the first time. Welcome! We're so glad that you're here! Many people consider these to be the best days of their lives. But, these great days are mixed with difficult ones. Our aim is to help you make the difficult days into days that you will remember as challenging yet worthwhile, days that will give you knowledge and even wisdom to make the rest of your life satisfied, fulfilled, and productive. This will be up to you, though. We can give you some understanding of how you learn and what gets in the way of your learning. We can give you some tools and suggestions to improve your post-secondary experience. In the long run, however, it's your decision how to run your life, whether you will use what others pass on to you, and what parts of this information best apply to your situation. It's all your call.

THE TRANSITION TO POST-SECONDARY EDUCATION

WHY IS A FORMAL COURSE OR A TEXTBOOK TALKING ABOUT THE TRANSITION TO POST-SECONDARY EDUCATION NECESSARY?

That's a good question. After all, countless numbers of people have muddled through first year on their own and managed to figure out how to deal with this situation. Why can't you? Maybe you can, but why should you go through the process of adapting that many people have gone through with pain, if you can avoid most of the unpleasantness? To use an analogy, you might be able to recover from pneumonia on your own, but why would you try to get along without a physician and antibiotics? For most of us, it would be a big risk that isn't worth taking. Just as some people die of pneumonia without the right treatment, it's by no means certain that everyone can handle the transition to post-secondary education on their own.

The fact is that many students don't complete their post-secondary education, and not because they are failing (Price, 1993). They drop out of school, usually at the end of first year (Matusky, 2001). Some of these people may be dropping out for very good reasons. They may feel that they are in the wrong program and wish to start over in a different program; they may have difficult personal, familial, or financial situations; or they may decide that post-secondary education isn't the path for them, given what they want from life. But many people who drop out do so simply because they are unprepared for the world they have entered, and may feel their sense of self-worth decrease because they think they can't make it in post-secondary education.

Take Mary, for example. She had always done well in high school, and was clearly bright, studious, and motivated. However, during her first term at college she failed two tests. She had never failed before and became discouraged. Why had she failed? Mary decided to visit the academic skills centre at her college, where she was told that she is indeed bright but that studying in college is different from studying in high school. Mary simply needed to learn about these differences and begin to understand how she best learns. Mary has now graduated from college with honours. She remembers her first year at college as a year of discovery. Her grades were not great but she passed, and she learned about living on her own and about both success and failure. In retrospect, first year really helped her to prepare for challenges she would face later in life. Mary, like most students, learned how to do well at college.

Many students have difficulties in their first year and spend a few years figuring out how to do well. We believe that through this book we can show you how to do well in a shorter period of time. Research in the area of education has found that we can decrease the number of people having difficulties in first year if we find a way to prepare them better to cope with the college and university environments (Barefoot & Fidler, 1996). When first-year students are given information about what to expect and how to handle school at this level, they also do better in their classes and they report having a much better post-secondary experience.

WHAT KIND OF PREPARATION DO I NEED FOR POST-SECONDARY EDUCATION?

First, you need to know the differences between high school and college/university. Many students enter university and college with a very rudimentary idea of what to expect. Some people think that post-secondary schools are like high schools, only geared to a higher level of information, and they believe that if they keep doing what they did to get through high school, they will do well. These people are wrong for the most part, and many of them find this out the hard way. Other people think that this is a time to enjoy a new adult status, without really understanding the responsibilities that come along with adulthood. These people often learn the hard way too. But perhaps most people enter post-secondary schools not really knowing what to expect. They wind up pretty surprised and scrambling to figure out ways of coping with the new situation. In many cases, they perform poorly on both a personal and an academic level for a semester or even two semesters before they figure out techniques to make their lives easier. We don't want you to go through much of this. This book is designed to prepare you with information that may help you cope better with post-secondary education.

HOW IS POST-SECONDARY EDUCATION DIFFERENT FROM SECONDARY EDUCATION?

While colleges and universities may differ from each other in some respects, they share many of the same characteristics. To see where mistakes in expectations are often made, let's look at Carl's experiences in his first semester.

Carl walks into his first class and finds, to his amazement, that the classroom is actually a huge amphitheatre in which about 400 students are already seated. He wasn't prepared for the fact that classes in most post-secondary institutions are much larger than high school classes. Post-secondary classes, especially in the first year, tend to range from 100 to over 1000! It's easy for anyone to get lost in the crowd under these conditions, and Carl begins to feel like a number instead of a person. This is very upsetting for him since, in high school, his teachers knew him by name and met with his parents sometimes, and he had a wide circle of people whom he had known for years. In order to cope with this, Carl will need to have a strong sense of who he is and what he wants from his education. He will also need to know how to make friends.

In college, his instructors will not necessarily know his name or who he is from the beginning of the course to the end. Carl should know that this is something that most of his instructors dislike too: they want to know him, but obviously with large numbers, they can't. It will be up to Carl to introduce himself to them by going to their offices during their posted office hours simply to take five minutes to get acquainted. He'll find that most likely the instructors will be welcoming and will remember him from that time on. This will probably make Carl feel more connected to his courses and make it easier for him to go to the instructors for help if it is needed. Of course, it also means that he's more likely to be noticed if he misses classes or comes in late on a continual basis.

One of Carl's instructors is Alvin Klein. Let's look at the job that Instructor Klein does, because college or university instructors' work is different from high school teachers'.

First of all, a post-secondary instructor may not have any formal academic training in teaching, but he probably has years of experience in teaching students at this level. Why wasn't he required to go to a school for training teachers the way teachers in elementary and high school are? One reason is that, at this level, he isn't expected to teach in the way that elementary and high school teachers do. Students like Carl are supposed to be able to learn from anyone, and mainly, on their own. The instructor's role is more to be a guide and a source of information, just as a textbook is a source of information. Instructor Klein is an expert in his field of study. His job, in part, is to transmit the knowledge he has to the students and to acquaint them with the questions that remain unanswered in his field of study. As an adult who has demonstrated himself to be bright, Carl isn't supposed to need an academically trained teacher who will know how to motivate him and how to present concepts at his developmental level.

Carl is lucky that Instructor Klein, like so many of his instructors, is committed to being the best educator he can be, but he may not use the same teaching techniques as elementary and high school teachers do.

Another difference between high school teachers and post-secondary instructors, such as Alvin Klein, is that teaching is typically only one part of the instructor's job, while it is the main job of high school teachers. As is the case in most post-secondary institutions, the college hired Instructor Klein to teach, to conduct research, to write books and articles, and to oversee administration. In the last college at which Instructor Klein worked, teaching was a smaller part of his job than one of the other components. Carl didn't realize that instructors have many other responsibilities, though, and he felt a little resentful that he could not see his instructors at any time other than posted office hours. He complained that the instructor was forgetting that the student is the first priority and that the student is paying a great deal of money for an education. In an ideal world, there would be time for all students (and education would be free!), but Carl must realize that his instructors may be teaching three separate classes with over 200 students in each, writing a book, carrying out research, supervising graduate students, sitting on four or five committees, and so on. All of these elements are *expected* of instructors like Alvin Klein. On a post-secondary level, instructors wear many hats, and each is as important as the next. One of Instructor Klein's pet peeves is that students assume that he has been on vacation from May until September. For him, like the vast majority of other faculty members, these months have been time to review recent publications in his subject areas and prepare new, updated lectures for the classes he will be teaching in the fall semester. He has also been trying to catch up with the research and administration he needs to do as part of his contract with the institution.

Quick tip for Carl: *Go to Instructor Klein's office during the posted office hours to introduce yourself. Ask him questions such as what kind of research he does or what courses he likes to teach, what the area of his work and teaching is and what his greatest interest is, and why he is interested in that area. Instructors typically love to talk about their work, and students often find that their instructors' work is fascinating.*

Another shock for Carl comes after he has attended the first class in each of his courses. He finds that he was given a course outline in each class, detailing what work he is supposed to do, when tests are to be given, how much of his final mark they will be worth, and what course material they will cover. In addition, the outlines contain information on assignments and their due dates. When he has looked at all the course outlines, Carl can see that he already knows all of the test dates and due dates for each course. He also notes that the workload is much heavier than it was in high school. It might surprise Carl to know that many students say that their problem in school is not in the difficulty of the material to be learned, but in the amount of material that is covered. Carl studies the course outlines to see when reviews of material are to be given, but he doesn't find any mention of reviews. Rather, it seems that every minute of class time is devoted to the presentation of new material. Carl will find that, at this level, formal in-class reviews of material are rare. Usually a concept is presented once, and if a student misses it, it is up to him to make up what he has missed, by reading about the concept or by asking the instructor individually for help with that concept (that's a large part of what office hours are for).

Quick tip for Carl: *Note right from the beginning that you are going to need to be very organized about your class attendance and your studying. You may not realize it yet, but you will need to use study techniques that do not rely solely on memorization since there is typically too much material to be memorized, and straight regurgitation of material is generally inadequate as you progress through this level of education. We will discuss time management and methods of studying in later chapters.*

Now for attendance. Carl wasn't required to have an excuse note for non-attendance in his last year of high school, but it was a fair bet that if he cut classes, his family would find out and he would be in trouble. That's not the case at the post-secondary level. Generally, Carl's instructors make it clear that they expect him to miss a class only because of illness or some other unavoidable problem. In one of his classes, though, Carl's instructor tells the class specifically that attendance is not required. In another class, attendance is required and the instructor expects students to inform her of their reason for being absent. The instructor asked that this be done before the class if possible, since she may be planning something that requires a certain number of students to be present, but definitely within a day after the missed class. That seems reasonable to Carl; after all, it is just good manners and he can understand that instructors appreciate courtesy as much as anyone else. What Carl doesn't perhaps realize is that when students show good manners, they are more likely to be remembered favourably, and that can't hurt!

Let's look at an example. Carl's new friends, Martha and Geoffrey, both missed a class because of illness. Since the class has more than 100 people in it, they were sure that they wouldn't be missed. At the next class, as luck would have it, both of them were late, and they slipped in quietly. Martha left the class as soon as it was over, but Geoffrey stayed behind to apologize to the instructor for being late and to explain that he had missed the last class due to illness. The instructor thanked him for his courtesy and told him what to read to catch up with what he missed. The instructor also told Geoffrey to come by his office if he had a problem understanding the missed material. Months later, both Martha and Geoffrey applied for a job as a research assistant with the instructor. Which one do you think stayed in the instructor's mind and got the job?

Quick tip for Carl: *Attend all classes and be on time. If you are unavoidably late, apologize to the instructor. If you have to miss a class in which attendance is required, let the instructor know ahead of time, and in all cases, make sure you get lecture notes from someone else (preferably someone who you know takes good notes).*

In the example above, Martha acted as perhaps most students do. She had a golden opportunity to make herself known and to impress an instructor and she didn't take it. She probably would have, had she been clairvoyant and seen that sometime in the future she would like that instructor to know her! If she feels like a faceless number in the school, we might begin to see why.

Martha realized that in the post-secondary setting, unless attendance in a particular class is mandatory, there will be no penalty for missing a class or being late. No one will inform a student's family. As a matter of fact, even if Martha's mother telephoned the instructor and asked to know how Martha is doing, the instructor could not tell her without Martha's express consent. In academic matters, Martha (even if she is still a minor) is considered an adult, and her marks are confidential. By the same token, it is inappropriate for Martha's mother to ask for her marks or to try to intervene with an instructor to change a class, for example: instructors can only deal with Martha. This is a great change for a number of students. Many students are accustomed to having their parents both monitor their work and make arrangements and intercede for them with the school. Now these students must learn to do this for themselves since in most matters the school can only deal with the student. (In most cases, parents find this a lot more difficult than students do!)

Now let's look at the class itself. In looking around, one of the most notable things that Carl sees (apart from the large number of students) is that there is such a wide cross-section of students from different cultures and different age groups. This is one of the most exciting and educational parts of post-secondary school. For many people, like Carl, this is the first time they have had the opportunity to get to know the viewpoints of people outside their own group.

Quick tip for Carl: *Get acquainted with many people. Everyone is enriched by diversity, and you will find that there are commonalities among people that you might not have expected. Others will be as enriched by knowing you as you are enriched by knowing them.*

When the first tests are given, Carl is again surprised. Many of the questions he is asked are not the ones that he expected. Many questions are from the textbook, not from material the instructor covered in class. Carl's immediate thought is, "That's not fair!" But then he remembers that his instructors warned him that this would be the case. As a student in a post-secondary institution, he is required to be much more independent than he ever was in high school. There is such a large amount of material to cover that there is no way for the instructors to cover all of it in class. The textbook contains information that the instructors don't discuss because (a) they don't have time; (b) it isn't as interesting for them to talk about as some other areas; and (c) they rely on the textbook to teach that material. Now Carl remembers his instructors saying that the material in the textbook would be covered on the tests. He also remembers that he decided not to read the parts in the book that had not been covered by the instructor. Carl thought that if the instructor had not discussed the material, it must be because it wasn't important. Now he realizes that this was a bad assumption: maybe they didn't discuss that material because they thought the textbook did a good job of explaining it and in-class time could be spent more profitably in covering other material.

Carl's new friend Martha gets a shock with her tests too. She had made a different assumption from Carl: Martha assumed that all the material she needed for a test was in the book, so there was no point in going to lectures. When she saw questions that she didn't know the answers to, she also thought, "That's not fair!" Martha even complained to the instructor that the test had covered material not in the textbook. Her instructor raised her eyebrows and responded, "No, that material was in my lectures. Surely you have the material in your class notes." Unfortunately, Martha's assumption meant that she didn't have class notes.

Quick tip for Carl: *Realize that tests and exams generally cover both text and lecture material; in the future, plan on asking the instructor directly about this so you never again base your studying on your perhaps incorrect assumptions.*

Carl gets another shock when his first post-secondary essay is returned to him. He had felt quite confident about his essay because he felt that high school had equipped him well for writing. To his surprise, he finds that he lost 10 percent of his mark for failing the "literacy" component of the essay. The instructor tells the class that many people failed this component, that while in many cases their ideas might have been good, their grammar, punctuation, and word usage were so poor that it was almost impossible to understand what their ideas were. When Carl examines his paper, he finds several errors that he missed when proofreading the paper. First, it seems that Carl had not proofread the paper well: why should he, when his word processing software had tools that could be relied upon to find the errors? What Carl forgot was that the computer program wouldn't catch errors such as writing "fist" instead of "first," or "to" when Carl meant "too." Carl also hadn't paid much attention to the grammar-checking tool in the word processing program; he had just assumed that he knew the right grammar.

Quick tip for Carl: *Don't rely on your word processor's "spell check" to proofread a paper for you. Do it yourself or have a trusted and literate friend do it for you. There will be more about this in Chapter 10.*

Carl finds that in four separate parts of his paper, the instructor has written "Support your opinion." What does that mean? In later chapters, we will discuss more about opinion versus evidence, critical thinking, and writing an essay, so that you won't get the shocks that Carl did.

Carl is very unhappy about that essay because he spent so much time writing it. "Don't I get any credit for all the time I put in on this?" he complains to Martha. Martha has just been through the same experience, and, having spoken to the instructor, she knows the answer to give Carl.

"No," she says, "you get credit for what you produce. It's *expected* that we will all put a lot of time and effort into doing our work. 'A for effort' doesn't work here. Besides, Carl," she continues, "the instructors don't know us: when we say that we've put in a lot of time, how do they know that we really did? As far as they know, our idea of what 'a lot of time' means may be pretty different from theirs. I thought I had put in a lot of time, and I told my instructor that I had spent the weekend before the paper was due working on it. My instructor said that she could see the problem immediately: I hadn't spent enough time!"

As the semester progresses, Carl finds that the biggest difference between post-secondary school and high school is that he is expected to be mature and professional in his approach to his work. Like most young people, Carl has been accorded more responsibilities and granted more adult status as he has grown older, but this is the first time that the whole responsibility for his life has fallen on him. If he succeeds, the success is his. But if he fails, the failure is his too. Carl discovers quickly that no teacher will call him in after school to ask if he's having a problem. If he has a problem, he is expected to deal with it. But, he is thankful to find, he doesn't have to deal with his problems alone. Almost every post-secondary institution has resources to help students deal with whatever problems they may have, but accessing these resources is completely up to them. Most of these are resources that Carl won't need, but there are some that he will find very useful.

RESOURCES FOR POST-SECONDARY STUDENTS

WHAT RESOURCES ARE AVAILABLE TO ME AT SCHOOL?

During the summer, after Carl had accepted the position in his school, he was sent what seemed like reams of paper detailing the resources available to him, as part of an orientation package. He tried to look over this literature, but there was so much of it, and, since he had not yet started school, it frankly didn't have much relevance to him. Unfortunately, he threw all of this literature out instead of putting it away. That was a mistake, since, as it does for most students, the day has come when Carl has some problems with which he could use some help, and he could save time and make his life much easier by taking advantage of the resources the school offers him. The resources available at Carl's school are much the same as those available at other post-secondary institutions.

- *Academic/study skills centre.* Carl is having problems with adapting his studying to the new requirements of the post-secondary level. He has been using trial and error to find a more successful study strategy than the one he had been using, but, sadly, there has been more error than he can absorb. His school employs trained people who specialize in helping students learn how to study more effectively, but Carl doesn't seek them out until his second semester, even though the study skills centre has publicized workshops in such areas as "How to write multiple-choice tests" and "Taking good lecture notes." Even if these workshops don't meet Carl's needs, the people at the study skills centre would be happy to work individually with Carl. But they don't get the chance until Carl is already in academic danger.

- *Subject centres.* Carl's friend Martha has a more specific problem: she has a great deal of difficulty with essay writing. Martha finds out that her school (like most) has a writing centre staffed with people who can help her find a direction and structure for an essay. In discovering this, Martha is also pleased to find that there is a math centre for people having problems in math, and a computer centre for those pesky computer glitches she so often runs into. If Martha explores further, she might find several other centres offering help in specific subjects.

- *Financial centre.* Carl encounters a serious problem as the first semester progresses: he finds that his parents are not able to help him financially as much as expected because of a family emergency. Carl needs to find a job and to apply for grants, scholarships, loans—anything, as quickly as possible. Carl hears about the financial centre at the school and he hurries there, where counsellors help him find ways to get the money he needs and plan how to budget his money. While he is there, he meets another student, who gives him some additional information: she was in an accident and wasn't able to go to her part-time job to make the money she was counting on for textbooks. The financial centre was able to get her some emergency money right away to tide her over until she recovered.

■ *Career counselling centre.* Geoffrey, Carl's roommate, entered his program hoping it would be the right one for him since he really doesn't know what he wants to do with his life. On the advice of an instructor he spoke to, Geoffrey takes advantage of the centre for career counselling at his school to learn more about his aptitudes and interests. The counsellor also shows him the centre's resources for helping students find part-time jobs during the school year, summer jobs, and even full-time jobs once they graduate.

■ *Housing centre.* Carl is a nice person, but Geoffrey is not used to having a roommate and feels that he wants to have a place to himself. After his positive experience with the career counselling centre, he decides to check out the housing centre at the school to see if they can help him in this regard. They can and do. After seeing all of the available accommodations, Geoffrey decides that he really wants a small apartment off campus, and since money is not a problem for him (lucky fellow), he moves within a month.

■ *Athletic centre.* Carl likes sports, but isn't very enthusiastic about being on a team, nor does he feel athletic enough to be accepted on a team. As a matter of fact, with all the studying (and snacking) and eating more junk food than his family would have allowed, Carl finds that he is gaining a little weight and getting out of shape. He mentions this to his counsellor at the study skills centre, who tells him to go to the athletic centre to take a look at the programs available there. Carl finds that the athletic centre offers a wide array of well-supervised "get-fit" programs, and signs up for one immediately. He also finds that the centre offers beginner classes in sports that he has never even considered before. He consults the trainer who is monitoring him in his fitness program, and decides that fencing will meet his needs in increasing his cardiovascular fitness. Besides, it looks like fun.

■ *Health centre.* Carl wakes up with a fever and a very sore throat one morning. He has an immediate resource through the health centre, where a physician diagnoses him and prescribes an antibiotic, and gives him a number to call if his condition becomes worse: the health centre staff will see to it that he is cared for and even hospitalized if necessary. In addition, they remind him that he can come to them for flu shots and health-related counselling on issues such as contraception, weight management, managing specific disorders, etc. Carl gets better quickly, in part because he is reassured that quality medical care is readily available to him.

■ *Psychological counselling centre.* Carl has been feeling very depressed because of his family's emergency situation and the change in his financial status. He mentions this to his physician at the health centre, who tells him about a psychological counselling service available to students. Carl feels a little reluctant to check this out, but the physician finally persuades him that there is no reason to feel embarrassed about getting help for problems such as his, and so he makes an appointment to see a counsellor. The counsellor tells Carl that he is a trained professional in counselling, and that everything Carl says will be confidential between the two of them. There will be no charge for this service since Carl's tuition includes a component that pays for these services.

"Will the fact that I'm coming here appear on my transcript or in my records that might affect getting a job one day?" Carl asks nervously.

"Absolutely not," reassures the counsellor.

"If people see me coming in here, won't they think I'm crazy?" Carl asks further.

"No," says the counsellor, "most people who come here don't have mental disorders; they have problems to solve and they want to grow as individuals."

So Carl stays to talk to the counsellor about his depression. After only five sessions, Carl finds that he feels so much better that he is becoming interested in some of the programs that the centre offers. There are workshops in assertiveness training, social skills, public speaking, meditation, and all sorts of other areas that pertain to his personal growth. In addition, the centre maintains links, and in some cases even hotlines, to Alcoholics Anonymous and Al-Anon (for the families of alcoholics), to drug rehabilitation programs, to suicide prevention programs, and to cult awareness programs.

- *Special needs centre.* Carl's friend Martha has dyslexia, a disorder that makes reading a challenge for her. She learned special techniques for reading much earlier in her life, but she still needs some accommodation (such as using a word processor to write her exams and having extra time to complete a test) to make sure she has the same chance to succeed as other students. Almost every post-secondary institution makes accommodation for students like Martha. While she is at the special needs centre, Martha meets another student, Tim, who has an anxiety disorder that makes it very difficult for him to write a test or exam in the same room as a crowd of people. In conjunction with the psychological counselling centre, the special needs centre is making sure that Tim is allowed to write his tests in a room by himself. These are not major accommodations, but they will be enough to level the playing field for Martha and Tim, so that their success or failure will depend on their own talent and motivation, not on the particular challenges they face that could affect their performance in school.

- *Academic advisors.* Carl's ex-roommate Geoffrey, having worked with the career counselling centre, now has a much better idea of what he wants to do with his life, but he is still somewhat unclear about to how to achieve his goals. He can get more help: there are general academic advisors who can assist with choosing programs and courses, and specialist advisors who are attached to particular programs to help students in that program and to give information to students contemplating entering that program.

- *Special interest groups.* Carl has discovered that his school has plenty of clubs and activity groups catering to the needs and interests of many different people. There are clubs for people with hobbies such as chess or photography; there are clubs based on religious affiliation, such as the Muslim Student Society and the Christian Student Society; there are gay and lesbian groups; single-parent groups; and, of course, there is the student government, which oversees students' needs, and works with the school's administration to meet these needs. Most of these groups also have contacts with counsellors and experts in the field to help students with any problems that are pertinent to the group's interests. These can range from spiritual guidance to advice on what kind of camera to buy.

- *Peer counselling.* One of the most helpful resources that Carl finds in his quest to become a better student is in his peers. There is a whole network of upper-year students who have gone through what Carl is going through, and who are ready, willing, and able to help him in a variety of ways. When counsellors at the other centres told him about peer counselling and put him in touch with some of these people, he found that he had ready access to some of the best advice on the campus. Now he's determined that, one day, he too will be a peer counsellor—after all, he's well aware of the kinds of issues that first-year students face on a regular basis, and now, if he doesn't have the answers, he knows where to go and where to send people to get those answers.

Quick tip for Carl: *Explore your school. Discover the resources available to you and where they are located. Keep a list of these resources handy just in case one day you or a friend needs to use these services.*

Carl and his friends are now well equipped to find help with almost any problem that they might encounter. Their tuition covers many services that they had not expected, and this increases their feeling of confidence in being able to master the post-secondary environment. But Carl still has a slight fear of the level of work that he will be required to do. "Am I up to it?" he wonders.

SCHOOLWORK AT THE POST-SECONDARY LEVEL

IS THE ACADEMIC WORK REALLY HARD?

Well, it's not usually very easy, but you would not have been admitted to a post-secondary institution if you were not able and ready to tackle work at this level. It will help if you understand the levels of learning that you will experience and what is expected of you at each level.

HOW DO THE LEVELS PROGRESS?

Bloom's Taxonomy
a classification system of levels of learning

knowledge level
in Bloom's Taxonomy, the level at which the student learns basic information

factual knowledge
terminology and the basic factors within the area of study

conceptual knowledge
how the elements fit together in concepts, theories, categories, etc.

procedural knowledge
the skill of how to do something

metacognitive knowledge
understanding of oneself in terms of what one knows; knowing what one knows

A group of educational psychologists headed by Benjamin Bloom partitioned learning into six levels, with each succeeding level requiring greater complexity of thought. We call this classification **Bloom's Taxonomy**. We'll look at each level with examples.

The first level is the one encountered most by students. This is the level of **knowledge**. At this level, you will learn information. These are the basic facts and theories that you need to have in order to progress to upper levels. Students often dislike this level because it usually calls for memorization of facts and regurgitation of information at test time. True, memory work alone isn't much fun, but it is a necessary first step. You can't form opinions about economics or sociology until you know the subjects' basic facts and premises. That would be like someone talking about which team is going to win the Stanley Cup without knowing the principles of hockey. An uninformed opinion (i.e., one based on ideas without accurate information to substantiate these ideas) isn't worth much anywhere, but especially in the academic world. At this level, students gain **factual knowledge** in which they learn terminology and the basic factors within the area of study, such as the elements of the periodic table in chemistry (Krathwohl, 2002). Students also gain **conceptual knowledge** of how the elements fit together in concepts, theories, categories, etc. (e.g., the classification hierarchy of biology; the theory of cognitive dissonance; the generalizations of spelling; the principles of grammar). In many cases, students also gain **procedural knowledge**, the skill of how to do something, such as how to use laboratory equipment or how to determine which reference book to use to find information. Arguably the most important type of knowledge that the student gains at this level is **metacognitive knowledge**. Metacognitive knowledge refers to your understanding of yourself in terms of what you know. When you look at a problem and say "I know how to do that!", you are showing metacognitive knowledge; you know what you know. At the knowledge level, it's important for us to find out what we do and do not know. Think about studying: when you know that you understand a concept, you can move on to study something else. But think of the problem you will have if your metacognitive knowledge isn't adequate. Have you ever answered a question incorrectly on a test and been surprised, thinking to yourself, "I thought I knew that!"? It isn't uncommon, but it does show a failure of metacognitive knowledge. Actually this happens to many of us quite often. In studying, we look at the page of the book that we have read so many times and believe that we have committed it to memory, but when asked, we find that we know what part of the page the answer can be found on, but not what the answer is! In Chapter 6, we'll help you sharpen your memory skills.

At the knowledge level, you will get test and exam questions such as these:

- *List* the five most common elements in the human body.
- *Name* the countries in Europe that use the euro as currency.
- *Define* the term *dyad.*
- *Label* this map, showing the major mountain ranges.
- *Arrange* the following developmental stages in their order of occurrence.
- *Relate* the situation that led to the onset of the Hundred Years' War.

comprehension level
in Bloom's Taxonomy, the level at which the student is expected to show understanding of terms, concepts, theories, etc.

The second level of Bloom's Taxonomy is the **comprehension level**. At this level, you are expected to not only have the knowledge of basic facts, theories, etc., but also to show your understanding of these items. Now you are being asked to demonstrate that you are more than just a memorizer, that you can actually explain what the concepts mean, what the theories are getting at, etc. Your test and exam questions at this level will look something like this:

- *Explain* the concept of positive reinforcement.
- *Discuss* what Plato meant by *the allegory of the cave.*
- *Contrast* the interests of a collectivist society with the interests of an individualistic society.
- *Describe* the arguments given by Martin Luther in his break with the Catholic Church.
- *Translate* the term *Weltschmerz* into English. (N.B. There is no direct English equivalent.)
- *Distinguish* between St. Benedict's view of the monastic life and St. Bernard's view of the monastic life.

Once again, the underlined words in the questions should tell you that you need to go beyond the information of the knowledge level, into an explanation or an expansion of the definition of a concept or the basic statement of a theory. Be aware, though, that you still need the information of the first level! Each level of Bloom's Taxonomy incorporates the preceding level, so at each level more complexity and thinking are demanded of you. In subsequent chapters, we will help you with your comprehension of the material you are learning.

application level
in Bloom's Taxonomy, the level at which the student is required to demonstrate that he/she can use basic information

Third is the **application level**. Many people feel that it isn't very meaningful to learn concepts and theories unless you can actually use them. At the application level, you are required to demonstrate that you can do this. Clearly this will require you to have both the knowledge and the comprehension of the material. Questions on tests and exams may look like this:

- *How could* the theory of cognitive dissonance *be used to explain* getting over disappointment at losing an election?
- *Demonstrate* the relevance of the Industrial Revolution to the decrease in interest in the arts.
- *Predict* what would result if African countries entered a union such as that in Europe.
- *How much change* would there be in society if children's sex were not revealed to the public until the child reached puberty?
- *Illustrate* the way that one could test for the presence of iron in water.

The underlined words in these questions indicate that your creativity and ingenuity are called into play to answer these questions. In these cases, you need to search your memory for information, call upon your understanding of that information, and be inventive enough to use that information to solve a particular problem or to make educated guesses (predictions) of hypothetical situations. This is getting much more complex, but also much more interesting and engaging. This is actually where the academic fun starts as you put your own slant on the material you have learned.

In the fourth level of Bloom's Taxonomy, the **analysis level**, you are required to see patterns in the material you have learned, to organize elements into a new and meaningful whole, and to catch subtle meanings and nuances. This level calls for a substantial amount of insight and understanding. It's unlikely that you will be asked to reach this level in introductory courses since these courses are designed to give you knowledge and understanding, and to begin the application process. Introductory-level courses are the foundation courses for the upper-level courses in which analysis is required on a regular basis. Questions may look like this:

analysis level
in Bloom's Taxonomy, the level at which the student is required to see patterns in the material, to organize elements into a new and meaningful whole, and to catch subtle meanings and nuances

- *Compare* Newton's view of gravity with that of Einstein.

- *What assumptions* do you think Durkheim was making in his analysis of suicide?

- *What is the relationship* between the European political situation and the emergence of existential philosophy?

- *Examine* the motives of the United States in its support of the League of Nations.

- *Distinguish* between Sigmund Freud's theory of the unconscious and Carl Jung's theory of the unconscious in terms of their personal views of the nature of the human being.

Questions using words such as those that are underlined above are typically longer essay questions, and may, in fact, be the bases of out-of-class essays and assignments. They certainly require more thinking and reflection on the part of the student, and they give the student the chance to demonstrate a broader understanding of material than before.

synthesis level
in Bloom's Taxonomy, the level at which the student is required to create something new derived from analysis of the material

The fifth level is called the **synthesis level**. It is somewhat similar to application in that it requires you to create something new. But unlike application, the creation is derived from your analysis of the material, not simply your knowledge and understanding of the material. Having seen more connections and meanings in the analysis level, you are now ready to use those new connections and meanings in a novel way. Test and exam (and essay) questions now look like this:

- *Propose an alternative* explanation to that of Stanley Williams for the sudden eruption of volcanoes.

- *Formulate* a compromise theory that utilizes the most relevant and substantiated parts of any two theories of economic growth.

- *Develop a research plan* to test your concept of well-designed space for children.

- *Compose* an answer to Buddha's First Noble Truth, that life is suffering.

- *Create* a series of guidelines to help a student successfully negotiate his or her first semester of post-secondary education.

These are clearly pretty challenging questions, ones that require you to have developed your own understanding of a broad range of material, and to be able to use what you have analyzed in an application that brings new thinking and new patterns to what came before.

evaluation level
in Bloom's Taxonomy, the level at which the student is asked to be critical of what has been learned, and is asked for educated opinions

Having such a deep understanding of material brings the student to the sixth and final level of Bloom's Taxonomy, the **evaluation level**. At previous levels, you may have been asked to give your opinions of concepts and theories, but at this level, you are most fully equipped to be critical of what you have learned. At this level, you are asked for your educated opinions. Rest assured that, if you have done the work of the previous levels, you will be ready for this when the time comes that it is required of you. At this point, you will be able to give valid reasons to substantiate your opinions, and you will most likely stimulate the thinking of your instructors as well. Now you will be asked questions such as these:

■ *Evaluate* the contributions that Michelangelo made to the development of sculpture during the Renaissance.

■ *Criticize* Alfred Adler's premise that all individuals strive for superiority.

■ *What inconsistencies appear* in Shakespeare's use of the concept of mercy in *Twelfth Night* and *Othello*?

■ *Defend* the argument that both creationism and Darwinism should be taught in elementary schools.

■ *In what way* was Stanley Hall's racial theory *based on fallacy*?

Box 1.1 summarizes some of the key words you might see in questions at each level of Bloom's Taxonomy.

Reaching the point at which you are ready to answer these sorts of questions marks you as a truly educated person. This is the end goal of your post-secondary education, as far as educators are concerned. You may have an end-goal of getting trained for a job, and that's fine—we all hope you get a wonderful job when you graduate too. But even more we hope that, whatever you choose to do with your life, you will have the ability to use your intellect to understand your world and solve life's problems. Before you go on with reading this book, take the test in Exercise 1.1. This is a test of what is called *academic self-efficacy. Self-efficacy* simply means how well you think you can handle a task. *Academic self-efficacy* refers to how well you think you can handle schoolwork and the environment at the post-secondary level. It will give you an idea of what you expect of yourself as a student.

Key Words for Bloom's Taxonomy   BOX 1.1

Here are words you may see in questions at each level of Bloom's Taxonomy.

KNOWLEDGE

define	recall	what	relate
list	choose	where	label
who	which one	when	arrange

COMPREHENSION

classify	discuss	state in your own words
show	translate	demonstrate
explain	select	review
describe		

APPLICATION

apply	implement	tell what would happen
predict	sketch	solve
dramatize	calculate	use
illustrate	modify	discover
show		

ANALYSIS

analyze	infer	what is the function of
appraise	connect	what conclusions
compare	test	examine
contrast	criticize	differentiate

SYNTHESIS

create	develop	integrate	formulate
arrange	compose	prepare	organize
categorize	design		

EVALUATION

judge	critique	conclude	determine
evaluate	measure	grade	rank
appraise	support	rate	defend
argue			

Sources: Bloom, Englehart, Furst, Hill, & Krathwohl, 1956; Krathwohl, 2002.

EXERCISE 1.1

▶ *Academic Self-Efficacy Scale*

Based on your thoughts about university, indicate using the following scale how strongly you agree or disagree with each statement. There are no right or wrong answers. We simply want to know how you feel each statement applies to you. Please answer every item, and circle only one answer for each item. Use the following code to **indicate how a statement describes your thinking about you as a student**.

1 = Strongly disagree

2 = Moderately disagree

3 = Mildly disagree

4 = Mildly agree

5 = Moderately agree

6 = Strongly agree

1.	Compared with other students, I expect to do well.	1 2 3 4 5 6
2.	I'm certain I can understand the ideas taught in classes.	1 2 3 4 5 6
3.	I expect to do well.	1 2 3 4 5 6
4.	Compared with other students, I think I'm a good student.	1 2 3 4 5 6
5.	I am sure I can do an excellent job on course assignments and tests.	1 2 3 4 5 6
6.	I think I will receive good grades.	1 2 3 4 5 6
7.	My study skills are excellent compared with other students'.	1 2 3 4 5 6
8.	Compared with other students, I think I know a great deal about the subject matter covered in classes.	1 2 3 4 5 6
9.	I know that I will be able to learn new material.	1 2 3 4 5 6

Scoring:

Sum all the scores of the individual items. The total score of the scale can range from 9 to 54. For normal populations, the score is usually 38. The higher your score, the greater your self-efficacy. Similarly, the lower your score, the lower your self-efficacy.

Source: Reprinted by permission of Dr. Deborah Kennett.

Now take the test in Exercise 1.2 to get more acquainted with where you are right now in terms of your academic habits and skills, and what you may wish to work on in the future. This test measures *academic resourcefulness*, or how skilled you are at figuring out how to handle academic tasks.

EXERCISE 1.2

▶ *Academic Resourcefulness Inventory*

The purpose of this questionnaire is to determine your PRESENT FEELINGS about university/high school, such as your feelings toward coursework, classes, tutorials/seminars, etc. A number of scales or dimensions are given. Each scale is defined by opposing phrases (e.g., optimistic about making friends–pessimistic about making friends). Your task is to circle **one** of the seven scale positions on a particular dimension which you feel best describes your present opinion of yourself as a student.

As a student of university, I see myself as being

	Very	Quite	Some-what	Neutral	Some-what	Quite	Very	
Successful completing exams/tests in the allotted time	7	6	5	4	3	2	1	Unsuccessful completing exams/tests in allotted time
Inclined to utilize quantitative skills (e.g., statistics, computers) when necessary	7	6	5	4	3	2	1	Disinclined to utilize quantitative skills (e.g., statistics, computers) when necessary

Easily confused when taking an exam/test	1	2	3	4	5	6	7	Self-assured when taking an exam/test
Uninspired to do my best	1	2	3	4	5	6	7	Inspired to do my best
Disorganized with my work	1	2	3	4	5	6	7	Organized with my work
Fearful about being wrong in class	1	2	3	4	5	6	7	Unafraid of being wrong in class
Poor at organizing my time	1	2	3	4	5	6	7	Good at organizing my time
Regular tutorial/seminar attendee	7	6	5	4	3	2	1	Irregular tutorial/seminar attendee
Successful at meeting deadlines	7	6	5	4	3	2	1	Unsuccessful at meeting deadlines
Apt to be too tired to study effectively	1	2	3	4	5	6	7	Unlikely to be too tired to study effectively
Likely to benefit from the comments I receive on my written work	7	6	5	4	3	2	1	Unlikely to benefit from the comments I receive on my written work
Timid about expressing my views in class	1	2	3	4	5	6	7	Fearless about expressing my views in class
Lazy	1	2	3	4	5	6	7	Industrious
Eager to use free hours between classes for studying	7	6	5	4	3	2	1	Disinclined to use free hours between classes for studying
Infrequently requesting extensions	7	6	5	4	3	2	1	Frequently requesting extensions
Tardy completing papers and essays	1	2	3	4	5	6	7	Prompt completing papers and essays
Inclined to miss lectures	1	2	3	4	5	6	7	Disinclined to miss lectures
Inclined to take time each day to review my notes to prepare for future exams/tests	7	6	5	4	3	2	1	Disinclined to take time each day to review my notes to prepare for future exams/tests
Apt to work to my full potential	7	6	5	4	3	2	1	Unlikely to work to my full potential
Forgetful of names, dates, formulae, etc., during exams/tests	1	2	3	4	5	6	7	Mindful of names, dates, formulae, etc., during exams/tests
Unlikely to find enough time to thoroughly research topics I am writing on	1	2	3	4	5	6	7	Likely to find enough time to thoroughly research topics I am writing on
Able to do some work in all my courses every day	7	6	5	4	3	2	1	Unable to do some work in all my courses every day
Satisfied with my grades	7	6	5	4	3	2	1	Dissatisfied with my grades

Scoring:

Sum all the scores of the individual items. The total score of the scale can range from 23 to 161. For normal populations, the score is usually 109. Scores higher than this indicate that you feel quite confident of your ability as a student. Scores lower than this suggest that you have feelings of uncertainty about your abilities in some areas.

Source: Reprinted by permission of Dr. Deborah Kennett.

If your score was not as high as you might have liked it to be on the academic resourcefulness scale, don't worry too much: these skills can be learned. Learning these skills will have a big payoff for you: students with academic resourcefulness skills tend to feel more capable and confident in their work and, sure enough, attain higher grades (Kennett, 1994; Kennett & van Gulick, 2001). This book is really about helping you to acquire these skills, so that not only will you have more academic success, but you will enjoy your post-secondary experience more. We would like these to be some of the best days of your life!

Advice for Carl

WHAT TO DO	WHY
Attend the school's orientation sessions	Carl will start to meet people who are also new to the school and will learn to find his way around the campus. He will find out how to access many of the resources that he will need in his academic career, and he will decrease the stress he feels by increasing the amount of information he has.
Introduce himself to other people	Carl needs to become part of the school community, to have friends in his classes to work with and friends outside his classes to socialize with. He might start by introducing himself in places where he will spend a great deal of time, such as his residence and the library.
Since he is new to the city, Carl might take a tour of the city	If Carl talks to upper-year student mentors who are taking part in the orientation of freshmen, or some other people who are more familiar with the city (e.g., upper-year students), he will find that they are happy to share with him what they have found in terms of good places to eat, places to buy things, etc. They will also tell him about places to avoid!
Re-evaluate his ideas about what to expect from a post-secondary school	This would be a good time to talk more to upper-year student mentors, to ask these people about what they think the big surprises are for freshmen, and what they know now that they wish they'd known when they were freshmen. If Carl does this, he will learn more valuable information, he will feel more prepared to meet new challenges, and he will also make stronger connections with peer mentors.
Get organized	Carl's first week of classes will tell him most of what academic work will be required of him, so he needs to start gearing up by getting his books and supplies. Then, perhaps the best advice we can give him is to read on in this book!

CHAPTER SUMMARY

- Students are often unprepared for the transition to post-secondary education, and their marks often drop, leaving them feeling discouraged and sometimes even ready to drop out of school. Knowing what to expect and how to handle the work at this level reduces the difficulty of the problems students may encounter and gives them more tools to make a pleasurable success of their education.

- There are several differences between high school and post-secondary schools, including the size and impersonality of classes, the pace of learning, the role of instructors, and the requirement for independence in scheduling and learning.

■ There are a multitude of resources available to students for help with almost any problem they encounter. These include help in studying, financial help and counselling, medical help, and career planning. Help in many areas is available in most schools both from trained counsellors and from knowledgeable peers who have been through many of the same problems.

■ The schoolwork of post-secondary schools can be described by Bloom's Taxonomy, which outlines levels of understanding and knowledge that the student gains as he or she progresses through school. The general path is one from learning basic facts at the knowledge level, through comprehension of these facts, application, analysis, synthesis of the material, and finally evaluation of what has been learned.

KEY TERMS

analysis level
application level
Bloom's Taxonomy
comprehension level

conceptual knowledge
evaluation level
factual knowledge
knowledge level

metacognitive knowledge
procedural knowledge
synthesis level

INDIVIDUAL ACTIVITIES

1. After reading the section on expectations in university, list the differences you find between the high school you attended and the typical post-secondary school. Are you surprised in any way?

2. Which of the resources that have been discussed do you think might be beneficial for you in your academic career? Which resources might prove useful for you in the future? Check out these resources in your school.

3. Try this exercise on Bloom's Taxonomy. For each of the following questions, indicate which level of the taxonomy is being used. What kind of information would be needed for each question?

   a. Compare and contrast the separation of provinces in Canada with the separation of states in the United States.
   b. Discuss the economic problems of an individual who is unemployed and is new to Canada.
   c. Propose a plan to end traffic snarls in the downtown core of either Montreal or Toronto.

4. What kinds of questions did you receive in high school? Where do they fit in Bloom's Taxonomy? What kinds of questions have you never been required to answer?

ANSWERS TO INDIVIDUAL ACTIVITY 3

a. This question is at the analysis level of Bloom's Taxonomy. It requires the factual and conceptual knowledge of the knowledge level and the understanding of the comprehension level. It will also require the ability to apply (application level) your knowledge and comprehension to being able to pick out similarities and differences between the political situations in two countries.

    b. This question is at the comprehension level of Bloom's Taxonomy. It requires you to have factual and conceptual knowledge of immigration and unemployment, and to be able to comprehend how this will affect the individual.

    c. This question is at the synthesis level of Bloom's Taxonomy. Answering this question will require knowledge, comprehension, application of knowledge to the problem in general, analysis of how the knowledge and information can apply specifically to the two cities, and synthesis to devise a new plan specifically for one of the two cities. In this case, you would probably do some evaluation yourself to determine if your plan is feasible, and certainly your instructor will evaluate your plan as well.

GROUP ACTIVITIES

1. In a group of four or five students, discuss what your expectations of post-secondary school are. How do your expectations differ within the group? Having read this chapter, are there any expectations that you are starting to question?

2. Check out the resources that are available on your campus. Each student or group of students can visit one resource centre, talk to the staff there, and pick up any handouts or pamphlets that may be available. Share the information you have obtained with the other members of the class or group.

3. Look at the levels of Bloom's Taxonomy. In a group of three to six students, make up questions based on the material in this chapter that demonstrate each level. (What level is *this* question on?)

REFERENCES

Barefoot, B. O., & Fidler, P. P. (Eds.) (1996). *The 1994 National Survey of Freshman Seminar Programs: Continuing Innovations in the Collegiate Curriculum.* Columbia, SC: National Resource Center for The Freshman Year Experience, University of South Carolina. (ERIC Document Reproduction Service No. ED393386)

Bloom, B. S. (Ed.), Englehart, M. D., Furst, E. J., Hill, W. H., & Krathwohl, D. R. (1956). *Taxonomy of educational objectives: The classification of educational goals. Handbook I: Cognitive domain.* New York: David McKay.

Kennett, D. J. (1994). Academic self-management counseling: Preliminary evidence for the importance of learned resourcefulness on program success. *Studies in Higher Education, 19(3),* 295–307.

Kennett, D. J., & van Gulick, C. (2001). Dealing with academic success and failure: The association between learned resourcefulness, explanatory style, reported grades and sharing experiences with academic self-control. In D. J. Kennett, & A. M. Young (Eds.), *Notes on applied statistical methods in psychology integrating STATISTICA software, Part 2* (pp. 341–373). Peterborough, ON: Trent University Press.

Krathwohl, D. R. (2002). A revision of Bloom's taxonomy: An overview. *Theory into Practice, 41(4),* 212–218.

Price, L. A. (1993). Characteristics and early student dropouts at Allegany Community College and recommendations for early intervention. (ERIC Document Reproduction Service No. ED 361051)

CHAPTER 2

KNOWING YOURSELF

LEARNING OBJECTIVES

In this chapter, you will learn to:

- Understand what a self-concept is

- Comprehend the need for realistic appraisal of yourself and your values

- Understand the role of self-efficacy in the development of self-esteem

- Become aware of the problems that may arise in the formation of an identity

The Cases of Lenore and Eddie

▶ Lenore is entering her first year in college as a business major. She doesn't feel very sure of her major because her parents chose it. Although she has agonized over it, Lenore doesn't know what she wants to do with her life. Her parents want only the best for her; they love her, and they have always been there for her, helping her with her problems, and encouraging her always to feel good about herself, but they are worried. They suggested that she major in business because it is something in which she will be able to make a good living. Since she doesn't have any better ideas and because she is a respectful and obedient daughter who loves and trusts her parents, Lenore is going along with this, but with serious reservations and with a noticeable lack of enthusiasm. She hopes that the courses will "turn her on" to business and provoke some excitement, or that she will discover some other area that will incite the passion she knows is within her and give her some purpose in life. She believes her parents are wiser and more experienced than she is, and she has always looked to them for guidance in the past, but she isn't sure that they know who she really is. Lenore thinks that if she can find this out for herself, everything will fall into place.

Eddie, on the other hand, has always known what he is going to be when he finishes school: a lawyer. His father and his grandfather are both lawyers, and Eddie knows that a place in the family firm of Mercer and Mercer is waiting for him when he graduates. After all, he is a Mercer too, and all the Mercers become lawyers and live a privileged life. These expectations of his family have been clear to him for his whole life, and he has never seriously questioned them. He doesn't feel that meeting these expectations will be too difficult for him because he was a good student in high school—academic work seemed to come easily for him. But when his girlfriend asks him what it is about law that interests him so much, he is confused. He has never really thought about what the actual work of a lawyer is; he only accepted the idea that he was going to follow the family tradition of entering law. He can see the "future Eddie" very clearly, sitting behind a large, elegant desk in a spacious office, wearing expensive suits and eating lunch in trendy restaurants with glamorous clients. That seems to be as far as his vision of his future goes.

Lenore and Eddie seem to be two very different people. Lenore doesn't know who she is and she wants to find herself and her path in life. Eddie is quite sure that he does know who he is and what sort of path his life will follow, but the reality is that he has never truly thought about it. Lenore and Eddie actually have the same problem: they really don't know who they are. Lenore doesn't know *what* she wants, but she wants it very badly. Eddie avoids the whole painful process of developing a sense of himself. It may well be that business is a good career for Lenore and law is a good career for Eddie, but neither of them has *chosen* the career being pursued—rather, both have fallen into these careers because of their lack of self-awareness. In this chapter, we will examine the problems that Lenore, Eddie, and many other people have in this regard.

SELF-AWARENESS

AM I SELF-AWARE?

self-awareness
the extent to which we know ourselves, including what we are like, what we think, and what we feel

Self-awareness refers to the extent to which we know ourselves, including what we are like, what we think, and what we feel. Getting to know ourselves is not as easy as it seems, and many of us have a real problem in this area. When some of us are asked how we are feeling, we answer either, "I feel good" or "I feel bad." But the words "good" and "bad" can mean many things when we talk about emotions. When we feel "good," are we happy? satisfied? victorious? joyful? serene? relieved? relaxed? pleased? blissful? carefree? All of these words, and many more, indicate a "good" mood. By the same token, when we feel "bad," are we resentful? dissatisfied? in pain? depressed? sad? embarrassed? unsure? insecure? gloomy? disappointed? frustrated? disgruntled? Without the ability to be more specific, we may be revealing a lack of self-awareness.

Sometimes we see a lack of self-awareness in other ways. Take Mr. Patel, who has just lost an important client at work. When he comes home, he sees his sons playing video games. Immediately he starts yelling, "You kids are always playing those games. You need to get your studying done and stop wasting time." Mrs. Patel, however, rolls her eyes and says, "The boys are getting good marks at school, they have finished their homework, and I told them they could play video games until dinner." Maybe Mr. Patel is right and his sons do waste time on video games instead of doing homework, but clearly that isn't the case this time. Maybe Mr. Patel is really taking his miserable feelings about losing the client at work out on the boys. When we ask him about this, his answer is, "No, of course I'm not taking anything out on the boys. I just think they waste too much time on video games." This kind of lack of self-awareness is called **displacement** (Glassman & Hadad, 2004). When we are unaware of our true feelings, we sometimes channel them onto something unrelated, but safe. Mr. Patel, angry about work, yells at his boys. And so, Mr. Patel's sons may now take out their feelings on their dog, who chases the cat, who hunts the bird!

displacement
placing feelings about one person or situation onto a different unrelated person or situation

IS A LACK OF SELF-AWARENESS REALLY A PROBLEM?

When we lack self-awareness, we reduce our choices in life and our control over our own lives. The decisions we make are not based on accurate information, so we may make bad decisions, some of which could be costly and painful. In the above example, not only have Mr. Patel's sons been yelled at unjustly, but Mr. Patel himself has little chance of changing his behaviour in the future if he is unwilling to admit what he is doing in the present. Mr. Patel can't admit what he's doing because he doesn't know what he's doing—he lacks self-awareness, and so instead of being in charge of his feelings, he allows his feelings to be in charge of him.

The lack of self-awareness that can be seen in the examples above is likely to have further repercussions in people's lives. Any decision that we make in life is affected by our sense of who we are and what we want. Without this crucial information, we may not make important decisions, or our decisions may be made for us by other people and often in other people's best interests. Of course, the wants and needs of other people are also part of the information we need in governing our lives, but our awareness of ourselves needs to be at least as great as our awareness of others. Plato (327–347 B.C.E.) credited Socrates as saying that the unexamined life is not worth living. This may be something of an overstatement, but the gist of the message is true: without examining ourselves, we have little chance of maximizing our joy and success in life.

SELF-CONCEPT

WHO AND WHAT AM I?

self-concept
the total of what we think and feel, how we behave, what attitudes we have, everything we believe about ourselves

When we gain self-awareness and try to determine who and what we are, we are really talking about self-concept. **Self-concept** is the total of what we think and feel, how we behave, what attitudes we have, in short, everything we believe about ourselves.

HOW DO WE ARRIVE AT A SELF-CONCEPT?

We get our self-concepts from a variety of sources of information. For example, how did our parents treat us? What message did we get from this—that we were attractive, talented, smart, sweet, aggressive, funny? This is the source of most people's first piece of information about themselves. But more information comes in—from our extended families, from our friends, from people we see on the street, from our teachers, and from our society and culture. All of these are strong influences on our lives, and give us information about ourselves. This information helps to shape our personalities.

Take the example of Eddie, whom we met earlier. He may have grown up in downtown Ottawa with wealthy, doting parents who devoted all their energies to him. The information he has received suggests that he is bright and handsome, the joy of the family who will be a flourishing lawyer and successful in any life endeavour he takes on. It would not be surprising for Eddie to have a self-concept that is of a strong young man with limitless potential. But what if Eddie's parents had been abusive and more concerned with their own problems than with their son? The message they sent might have produced a self-concept that reflected a belief that he is worthless.

What about Lenore, who grew up with very traditional parents who worry constantly about her and the choices she makes? In this case, whether her parents mean to send it or not, Lenore may be receiving a message that suggests that she cannot think for herself. Her self-concept, then, will be very different from Eddie's, as a result of the predominant message sent by the parents.

To complicate this further, imagine that Lenore and Eddie grew up in a war-torn, chaotic country with parents who worried constantly about whether they would be able to protect and feed their children. Lenore and Eddie might have received the message that they are potential victims of a dangerous world in which only the strongest and the most ruthless will survive and prosper. The predominant message about the children's self-concept is sent not only by the parents, but also by the whole culture and historical setting in which they are living.

Think about yourself now. What is your self-concept? Take a look at Exercise 2.1. These are some of the adjectives that have been compiled to describe people. Which of these adjectives apply to you? Try to pick out 10 to 20 that seem to fit you. Which are the adjectives that you feel definitely do not pertain to you? Can you pick out 10 to 20 of these? Now you have an idea of what your self-concept is.

EXERCISE 2.1   ▶ *What Describes You?*

Which of these words apply to you the most? Which apply the least?

sincere	stubborn	prejudiced	independent
pessimistic	naïve	friendly	courageous
broad-minded	sloppy	impulsive	diplomatic
distrustful	grouchy	shy	loyal
patient	trustworthy	short-tempered	unreliable
anxious	influential	obsessive	charming
helpful	nervous	sarcastic	responsible
neat	clumsy	respectful	persistent
logical	rebellious	imaginative	clean
vain	studious	superstitious	energetic
sociable	accepting	industrious	modest
oversensitive	daring	proud	smart
cheerful	immature	optimistic	kind
honest	cynical	caring	easygoing
sensible	efficient	courteous	selfless
forgetful	capable	straightforward	generous
shrewd	insightful	idealistic	boastful
methodical	punctual	warm	

Sources: Bochner & Van Zyl, 1985; Schonbach, 1972.

CAN I CHANGE MY SELF-CONCEPT?

Look back at Exercise 2.1. Are there more adjectives that you feel reflect you, at least a little bit, in some situations? You may have noted that for some adjectives, you couldn't really say "Yes, it reflects me" or "No, it doesn't"; for some adjectives the better answer might have been "Well, sometimes yes and sometimes no. It depends." That's a perfectly valid answer as well. How can that be?

Take Lenore. She is a serious, assertive young woman when arguing for kids in her volunteer community service placement. At home, she is quiet, respectful, and obedient to her parents. With her friends, she is funny and irreverent, the group's clown. Which one is the real Lenore? Sometimes she herself is confused by this. She wonders if she is being untrue to herself in some of these situations. Can she really be all of these contradictory people? The answer is yes, she probably can.

Many of us try to find the "real me" as if there were a single, unchanging personality that should emerge consistently in all situations. But that isn't the case. While we have a core of basic traits and characteristics, we are more like multifaceted diamonds: we show different facets of ourselves in different situations, and this gives us the flexibility to handle the complex world we live in.

This kind of flexibility gives us more information about our self-concepts: self-concepts can change. Certainly we can and do change them, depending on what situation we are in. We also change them as we grow and develop. Think about your self-concept five years ago. Have you changed in your view of yourself since then? Many of us have. We have become stronger, more confident, more experienced, and wiser. Or, sadly, we may have become more cynical, more aggressive, and lonelier. How our self-concept changes depends on the experiences we have had and how we have viewed them.

CAN I CHANGE MY SELF-CONCEPT TO MAKE ME BETTER?

real self
Karen Horney's term for the ideas we have about ourselves as we really are

ideal self
Karen Horney's term for the ideas we have about what we want to be, the self we aspire to be

tyranny of the shoulds
Karen Horney's term for the pressure created by expectations placed upon us

Take one more look at the list of adjectives in Exercise 2.1. You were asked to pick out the adjectives that you believe apply to you. The ideas you have about yourself indicate what you believe is your **real self** (Horney, 1945). But for most of us, the real self isn't quite what we want to be. Instead we have ideas about what we want to be, the self we aspire to be. This is called the **ideal self**. Go back to Exercise 2.1 and pick out the adjectives that apply to your ideal self. Are they very different from the adjectives you used for your real self? Is there much overlap in the two lists? If there isn't, there may be a problem: the farther your ideal self moves away from what you conceive of as your real self, the more alienated you become from yourself, the more you become removed from what you really are and what you can be. But look again at the list of adjectives you have made for your ideal self. Are these attributes that you really want to have? Or are these attributes that you think you *should* have?

Most of us have been raised in families and societies that have had strong ideas about what people should be like and how people should feel in different situations. (Has anyone ever said to you, "You shouldn't feel that way"?) Noted personality theorist Karen Horney (1945) calls this the **tyranny of the shoulds**, for tyranny is exactly what this is. A tyranny exists when conditions are placed on us that are arbitrary and unjust. Sometimes others place these conditions on us, and sometimes we place them on ourselves. In a tyranny, there is no freedom, no compassion, no leeway for spontaneous actions, but there is massive punishment for deviations from what you "should" do. With a tyranny of the shoulds, we feel massive pressure to conform to what we feel we ought to be like or to do or to believe. It becomes harder and harder for us to know what we really are, what we really think, what we really want. And to make matters worse, we wind up not liking ourselves very much.

Take Lenore. She's really a wonderful person, but she doesn't feel that way. She keeps thinking about all the ways in which she fails to live up to the exacting standards of her ideal self. By her account, she "should" be a loving daughter, an adoring and attentive girlfriend, a readily accessible and ever-supportive friend, an *A* student, an employee that her employer wants to keep forever, a caretaker of her younger siblings, a worker who can raise her own tuition, an expert seamstress who designs and sews all her own clothing, and on and on. It's clear that attaining this list of "shoulds" is impossible for the vast majority of us.

Thankfully, the situation doesn't have to be so grim. First, very often we rate our real selves as much worse than we really are, and we rate our ideal self as something so incredibly wonderful that no human being could ever attain it (Horney, 1945). The gap between the real self and the ideal self becomes magnified and distorted. So we need to do two things: have a realistic idea of what we are, and have a realistic idea of what we want to be. "Realistic" is the key word here. Neither of the authors of this book is taller than 5'3" nor very athletically talented—we are never going to be star basketball players, and it would be unrealistic to even contemplate it. And worse still, if we did keep the unattainable idea of being star basketball players firmly in our minds, we would probably stop enjoying playing basketball (against each other!) for fun. We would be so caught up in the realization that our dream can never come true that we would poison our enjoyment and maybe even neglect to find the dream that *is* attainable and worthy for us. So it is with Lenore. She can never maximize all the wonderful things she really is and enjoy her life to the fullest because she is caught up in feeling inadequate about all the things that she is not.

In many ways, people form their self-concepts more by the influences of the outside world than by their own thinking. We hear society's pronouncements of what we "should" be and we become progressively dissatisfied with ourselves, to the point that we no longer even know what it is that we are or what we want. We are ". . . like an elephant who had rather be a rose bush, and a rose bush that tries to be a kangaroo" (Perls, in Fagan & Shepherd, 1970, p. 20). It would be a better idea for the elephant to find out about the wonderful characteristics she has and become the best elephant she is capable of being, and let the rose bush and the kangaroo do the same for themselves.

To find out a little more about yourself, try the personality tests that are given at these weblinks, but remember that no personality test is completely accurate, so take the tests for fun exploration without getting too serious about the results: http://www.healthyplace.com/site/tests/psychological.asp; and http://www.quincyweb.net/quincy/psychology.html.

VALUES

WHAT ARE YOUR VALUES IN LIFE?

value
that which is important to us

Examining your traits in an adjective checklist can give you some idea of what you believe you are, but you are more than just personality characteristics. What do you **value**? That is, what is important to you? What will you fight for, even though you may lose and be punished for it? As this chapter is being written, a copy of the latest edition of a national Canadian newsmagazine, *Maclean's*, is on the desk. This is the week in which the world remembers D-Day of the Second World War, and the thousands of brave people who suffered and died during that time. The caption on the front of the magazine is "What will you die for?" (*Maclean's*, June 7, 2004), a chilling thought, but perhaps one that we need to contemplate, for this may sum up what we are better than any other measure. Ask a parent what he or she will die for, and the answer that tends to pop out of his or her mouth is "My kids." The vast majority of parents are very serious about this. There are countless examples in history of parents' sacrificing themselves for their children, whether it is through running into a burning building to save them or fighting a war to ensure their children's freedom or working two jobs to make sure that their children have financial security.

Most of you are not parents, so what will you die for? Even if you are parents, there are undoubtedly other things that you treasure, if not enough to give your life for, then enough to make sacrifices for. What are these things? What do you stand for? There are no right or wrong answers, but this is another area in which society often imposes "shoulds" on us. For example, many of us feel that we "should" be willing to sacrifice ourselves for freedom in our democratically based society. It surprises us when people in other societies don't seem as enamoured of freedom as we do. How do we account for the feelings of many of those in societies such as the Democratic People's Republic of Korea (North Korea)? It's hard to speculate on what the next few years might bring on the political front, but we may need to understand (if not agree with) those people who believe that the collective good of the group outweighs the rights and freedoms of the individual. Values, then, are very much influenced by the environment in which we were raised, but they are not *dictated* by our environments in ways that make them unchangeable. That is why we find people in the People's Republic of China, for instance, who oppose their government and take enormous risks to change it. History will always remember the protest in Tiananmen Square in June 1989 and the reports of the repercussions on those who chose to make their values known. In a similar fashion, the Western world has seen protests that in some cases led to a change in the way society runs. The anti-war protests of the 1960s and 1970s did not, sadly, lead to an end to war, but they did lead to a serious questioning and removal of the involuntary conscription into the armed forces that was standard procedure at the time in the United States. "Bra-burning" as a form of protest against the relegation of women to an inferior status in Western society seemed silly to many in the 1960s, however, there is no question that protests such as those led to a twenty-first century that is seeing an amazing increase in the opportunities and rights accorded women in Western society. Standing up for one's values, then, can change the world.

On a far less dramatic note, knowing the values we hold dear is important when we make decisions about our futures. For example, if you value family above work, it would be a wise idea for you to avoid careers that are known to entail working 70 hours a week. If you value interpersonal relationships highly, you may be unhappy as a research scientist or in any other career that requires you to work alone for long periods of time. Recognize that if you embark on a career path that is not of your own choosing, there is little chance that you will find your work satisfying or that you will be maximally productive. Think about this as you choose courses as well: there is always at least a little leeway in a student's timetable, a little room for you to take a few courses that reflect your personal values and interests. If you value nature, try a course in biology or astronomy, for instance, even if your major area of study is business. The future engineer whose spiritual life is important to him or her should be encouraged to try a course in theology or comparative religion. In Exercise 2.2, there is a scale in which you can get an idea about what you value, and how much you value it.

EXERCISE 2.2

▶ *What Do You Value?*

Milton Rokeach devised this test to help people clarify what their values are. Listed below are 18 values, in alphabetical order. Which is the most important to you? Which is the next most important? Rank all 18 values this way to determine how relatively important each value is to you.

A comfortable life (a prosperous life)

An exciting life (a stimulating, active life)

A sense of accomplishment (lasting contribution)

A world at peace (free of war and conflict)

A world of beauty (beauty of nature and the arts)

Equality (brotherhood, equal opportunity for all)

Family security (taking care of loved ones)

Freedom (independence, free choice)

Happiness (contentedness)

Inner harmony (freedom from inner conflict)

Mature love (sexual and spiritual intimacy)

National security (protection from attack)

Pleasure (an enjoyable, leisurely life)

Salvation (saved, eternal life)

Self-respect (self-esteem)

Social recognition (respect, admiration)

True friendship (close companionship)

Wisdom (a mature understanding of life)

Are there other values that are important to you? Can you add to this list?

Everyone's ranking is different, and obviously there are no right or wrong answers, but for interest's sake, here are the average rankings of values done in a large sample of American adults in the 1980s:

1. Family security
2. A world at peace
3. Freedom
4. Self-respect
5. Happiness
6. Wisdom
7. A sense of accomplishment
8. A comfortable life

9.   Salvation

10. True friendship

11. National security

12. Equality

13. Inner harmony

14. Mature love

15. An exciting life

16. A world of beauty

17. Pleasure

18. Social recognition

Source: *Public Opinion Quarterly*, Volume 32(4), 1968, p. 554, Values Survey, "The Role of Values in Public Opinion Research" by M. Rokeach. Reprinted by permission of Oxford University Press.

SELF-ESTEEM

WHAT IS SELF-ESTEEM?

self-esteem
the way we feel about ourselves; the emotional level of self-concept that measures how much we like or dislike ourselves, whether we think we are worthwhile or not, whether we value ourselves or not

Self-esteem refers to the way we feel about ourselves. This is the emotional level of self-concept that measures how much we like or dislike ourselves, whether we think we are worthwhile or not, whether we value ourselves or not. We examined this a little in our discussion of the real self and the ideal self, and it appeared that it was very important that we feel good about ourselves, that we like ourselves and believe that we are worthwhile human beings. Research has seemed to support this (see, for example, McFarlin, Baumeister, & Blascovich, 1984; Rosenberg, 1985) and it has been taken for granted by many that it is desirable to have a high level of self-esteem in order to be mentally healthy, to achieve our goals, and to have a good life. The strength of this assumption can be seen in actions taken by the state of California, which in 1986 funded a Task Force on Self-Esteem and Personal and Social Responsibility with a budget of over a quarter of a million dollars per year for several years. The argument was that raising self-esteem in the young would reduce crime, drug use, teen pregnancy, academic underachievement, and even pollution! While this sounds rather incredible and not a little far-fetched, the underlying reasoning was that having a high self-esteem would help people cope with the problems of life without resorting to counterproductive and self-destructive behaviours. Is this true? Let's take a more critical view of self-esteem.

ISN'T HAVING A HIGH SELF-ESTEEM ALWAYS A GOOD THING?

While there is much truth in the idea that it is important to value ourselves, a re-examination of the relationship between self-esteem and positive outcomes in life indicates that there is a very large catch that we must be aware of. The studies that are supposed to show that people with high self-esteem do better in life rely mainly on self-report data. This means that people are asked how they *think* they are doing (see Baumeister, Campbell, Krueger, & Vohs, 2003). So when we ask Eddie, who has high self-esteem, if many people find him attractive, he says yes. Is this because there really are many people who find Eddie attractive? Or does Eddie say yes because he *believes* that people find him attractive when they really don't? That is, is Eddie's interpretation of his social world accurate, or is it a distortion based on his high self-esteem? When we test this (i.e., ask people around Eddie how attractive they find him), we find that Eddie is seen as average looking. It seems that people with high self-esteem see themselves as beautiful, but the rest of us may see them as pretty ordinary (Diener, Wolsic, & Fujita, 1995). The same sorts of results are found when we look at attributes other than physical attractiveness. For example, people with high self-esteem think that they are more intelligent than they really are (Gabriel, Critelli, & Ee, 1994). Because of a wide variety of studies such as these, we are now beginning to believe that we have been a little too uncritical of the benefits of self-esteem. For example, do we really think that it would be a good thing for an individual who robs people for a living to believe that he or she is a fine person? Doesn't this imply that this individual will make no attempt even to contemplate the notion that perhaps robbing others is not an acceptable action and to change his or her behaviour? This is clearly an extreme example, so let's take a look at some other examples.

Lenore's parents wanted her to always feel good about herself; that is, to have high self-esteem. One of the things they did to encourage this was to raise their daughter with praise and encouragement for every drawing, every moulded figurine, every creation the child made. By the time Lenore entered school, her self-esteem in terms of her artistic ability was very high indeed. For the primary years, all went well: the teachers rewarded every child's attempts, and Lenore's self-esteem remained intact. But when she got to Grade 4, she started to recognize that her drawings were not as good as those of some of the other children. In fact, hers were pretty poor, and now the art teacher was suggesting that her parents consider enrolling her in music instead of art! Lenore was devastated. Suddenly her self-esteem plummeted. What she had thought about herself and what she had valued about herself were not being confirmed by outside sources who seemed to be expert in the area. She started wondering what else about herself wasn't true, and whether she could trust any of the things her parents had told her about herself: maybe they were just biased by their love for her, she thought. Lenore became a person plagued by self-doubt and a low self-esteem, with the hunch that her parents don't really know her.

Eddie had a different problem as he experienced his first year of college. He's a smart fellow: with minimal studying, he achieved the marks in high school that got him admittance to a number of fine post-secondary schools. In fact, his marks were almost all *A*s and high *B*s. Essay-writing was his real strength, so when he found out that he would be required to write several essays for college, he groaned a little, but thought that at least the heavy workload would tap his area of greatest self-esteem. Imagine his horror when his first essay was returned with a grade of *D*, with marks off for poor spelling and grammar! Eddie was totally shaken. "The instructor must be unfair," he thought. "He probably didn't agree with what I wrote, so he marked me lower than I deserved just because I didn't regurgitate his opinions. My writing is really excellent."

The example of Eddie, unfortunately, is not so far-fetched. Most instructors at post-secondary schools have had experiences with students who are given instructions about how to improve their written work but who decline to follow these instructions because they "didn't agree with the instructor's comments." While we can't get inside these students' heads, we may surmise that at least some of them may have been suffering from the same problem as Eddie. Their self-esteem in terms of writing papers may have been so high that they refused to contemplate the possibility that they might not have been as good as they thought they were, at least not at the higher education level.

What went wrong in Lenore's and Eddie's cases? Certainly Lenore's parents had every intention of supporting and strengthening their child; nothing but love motivated them to tell Lenore that she was artistically talented. The problem was that it wasn't true. In Eddie's case, his high school teachers had been marking him on his effort as well as on his product and in comparison with all the other high school students. At post-secondary schools, marks are not generally given for effort and the comparison group is other very bright students. Eddie never realized this: his self-esteem was also based on something that wasn't completely true. The dangers for these two people are plentiful. Lenore may have a very difficult time seeing herself as a valuable person now, and she may have an even more difficult time believing that her parents value her for the person she really is. If he convinces himself that the instructors are biased, Eddie may not use the feedback he has received to make corrections in the way he approaches writing, and so, he will go on getting poorer grades than he is capable of, and living an academic life of frustration and anger. It might even happen that Eddie will drop out of school rather than become the lawyer of his future vision.

In the real-life example of students' declining to follow instructions to improve their written work, we may surmise that somewhere along the line, some of these students picked up the message that their opinions are "as good as anyone else's" and that instructors have no right to impose their opinions on students. That doesn't sound so bad until we realize that, in the case of some students, it is possible that two mistakes are being made. First, it may be that the students do not realize that the instructors are not trying to change their students' opinions—they are trying to show them how to express their opinions more clearly, logically, and powerfully. Second, the students who believe their opinions to be as valid as the instructors' are forgetting that anybody's opinions, in truth, are only valid when they are based on information. If there is no supporting evidence of any kind, the opinions resemble bigotries and biases. One of the functions of post-secondary education is to give students more information on which to base opinions. The instructors have already acquired the information and, on the basis of this, have *informed* opinions. Students are always welcome to disagree with the instructor's opinion, but in order to do so effectively, the student must present the information on which to base a different opinion and indicate to the instructor how the opinion was arrived at and how it is supported. That is usually the aim of writing post-secondary essays—to show the evidence and derive a conclusion or opinion from this evidence.

So the assumption that high self-esteem is always a good thing may not be valid. Of course, there are many situations in which high self-esteem is good. Certainly people with high self-esteem feel better, and people with low self-esteem have a harder time bouncing back from disappointments and traumas (Steele, 1988). This is intuitively obvious: if we feel bad about ourselves in the first place, a setback of some sort seems like the world is confirming the negative opinion we already have of ourselves. But if we feel good about ourselves, a setback is more likely to appear to be just a momentary glitch in an otherwise smooth path. For this reason most likely, people with a high self-esteem tend to persist in the face of adversity, while their friends with a lower self-esteem give up (Lane, Lane, & Kyprianou, 2004; Shrauger & Sorman, 1977). In a similar fashion, people with low self-esteem have more social anxiety and depression. Feeling that they have little worth in the first place, they are less likely to make appropriate overtures to others or to be skilled socially.

So with a low self-esteem, these people may create a self-fulfilling prophecy: because they believe that they won't be liked, they act in ways that ensure that they are not liked.

But at times, socially, high self-esteem may not be so desirable either. In their high sense of worth, some people may simply assume that everyone will like them and so will not learn to be socially adept. In fact, they may come across as so arrogant and conceited that the rest of us want nothing to do with them, as they monopolize the conversation, talking about themselves because they are sure that everyone is just as interested in them as they are.

Both high and low self-esteem individuals may have a distorted view of reality.

Another area where unrealistic self-esteem can lead to problems occurs when the individual has an experience that suggests that he/she is not totally wonderful. Both Lenore and Eddie received grades of *C* on presentations they gave in their classes. Lenore, with an unrealistically low self-esteem, feels depressed in this situation ("I'm never going to be able to present my work well.") and drops out of any course that requires a presentation, while Eddie, with an unrealistically high self-esteem, reacts angrily, irrationally ("How dare the instructor not appreciate my superior work?"), and refuses to change, which leads him to fail even more (Baumeister, Heatherton, & Tice, 1993). The lesson we are learning here is about the need for honesty and realism. The person who appreciates his or her good points, is aware of and is working to correct his/her flaws, and values himself/herself as a growing and developing human being is showing both high self-esteem and humility. This person is more likely to cope well with the world. Achieving this balanced and accurate view of oneself is difficult, though. It requires a great deal of courage to face one's flaws without trying to rationalize them away. It takes commitment to work on these flaws without demanding an impossible perfection from oneself. What is truly inspiring is that so many of us show this courage and commitment without really thinking about it.

It may take even more courage, wisdom, and sensitivity for people like Lenore's parents to learn how to encourage their daughter while telling her the truth about her artistic ability. Perhaps that's another lesson we need to learn: do we really support our friends when we lie to them? Is telling your friend that she's wonderful at public speaking when in fact she speaks in a sleep-inducing monotone really doing her a favour? Or do we tell our friend this lie because it's easier for us and we want our friend to feel good and like us? This is not to suggest that we need to be brutal in our honesty (do *not* tell Aunt Penelope that the new haircut she loves makes her look like a pinhead, even if it does!). What it suggests is that we need to learn to both give and take criticism appropriately so that our self-esteem will reflect reality and we can learn to correct our mistakes, overcome our flaws, and grow as human beings.

SELF-EFFICACY

HOW CAN WE REALISTICALLY INCREASE OUR SELF-ESTEEM?

self-efficacy
Albert Bandura's term for our judgment regarding how well we can do a certain action or task

In 1986 Albert Bandura wrote a groundbreaking book that proposed a concept called **self-efficacy**, which refers to our judgment regarding how well we can do a certain action or task. Can you write your name? You probably scoff and say, "Of course." That means your self-efficacy is very high in this area. You *know* that you can write your name, and do it well. You may not place much value on being able to do this task, though. This is because you are so accustomed to being able to do it, and because other people you know can do this task as well. But if you could recall being five or six years old and learning to do this task for the first time and having the realization dawn on you that you could actually write your name, you would recall the thrill of pride that went through you as you developed the beginnings of your self-efficacy in this area. As you practised writing your name over and over, your sense of self-efficacy increased, until, perhaps, you took your ability for granted. Over time, you have become supremely confident of your ability to execute the task of writing your name to the point that you no longer even think about it. Be aware, though, that someone else, who is just learning this, is still thrilled.

So self-efficacy develops from learning a task, becoming good at it, and feeling competent in your ability to execute the task. Take a more complex task. In elementary and high school, you learned how to study and perform well on tests and assignments. Your marks reflected this, probably putting you in the top half of your class. You probably developed a self-efficacy about this: you knew that you could apply yourself to academic material and master it. You may have watched friends in school who had not mastered this task as well as you, and you may have recognized that this is a skill that is not to be taken for granted. Being able to study and perform well is valuable and not common to everyone. With this sense of self-efficacy, you progressed to post-secondary education, confident that you were a top performer who knew how to deal with the academic demands of college or university.

For many of you, however, a shock may set in as your marks drop substantially in the first semester. Your sense of self-efficacy may plummet quite dramatically as you now think that you do not, in fact, have the skills to do the work required. Increasing your self-efficacy in response to the demands of post-secondary education and keeping your grades from dropping so radically is what this book is about. As we saw in Chapter 1, it can be a major shock to realize that the skills you developed earlier in your academic career are not the same skills that will get you through post-secondary work. It may also be shock to see that, in college and university, the high school above-average student *is* the average student: everyone at this level was a top scorer in high school or they would not have been admitted to higher education.

Let's take a hypothetical example of what might happen to Eddie. He was in the top 10 percent of his high school graduating class, and he felt confident in coming to college that he would be able to handle the work (i.e., his sense of self-efficacy was high). His first test was a disaster: he scored in the bottom half of the class. There are essentially three possibilities for Eddie now.

1. Eddie's sense of self-efficacy, his belief in his ability to do well at the post-secondary level, could be shattered. He could feel that he had been wrong all along, that his marks in high school were either flukes or the result of teachers' being kind to him. He could become convinced that he can't do college-level work, and promptly drop out of school.

2. Eddie could decide that the results of *this* test were the fluke, that his skills were excellent and that undoubtedly the instructor was at fault for his poor mark. In this case, Eddie might persist in studying the way he had in high school since he had faith in his study skills (i.e., his sense of self-efficacy is still high but is being maintained unrealistically). Unfortunately, this strategy will probably lead to subsequent tests revealing the same lower-level performance from Eddie.

3. On the other hand, Eddie might question his self-efficacy. His reasoning could be that while his study skills had served him well in high school, they might not be appropriate for work on a higher academic level. He might now request an interview with his instructor for help in how to modify his studying to be more effective, he might join a study group with people who did well in the test to improve his own skills by watching how they study, and he will probably develop a new, more refined skill in studying. The results of this might lead Eddie to get an *A* on his next test. This would indicate to him that his new skill was appropriate and valuable in this setting, and he may now have confidence that he can apply this skill to the rest of his studying and get good marks. He has developed a new, realistic self-efficacy. We hope that Eddie also realizes that he showed self-efficacy in knowing what to do when he received his test back: confronting the problem and searching for a workable solution shows that Eddie has skill in problem-solving. If he realizes this about himself, his sense of self-efficacy about his ability to handle problems should be high.

If we know we can do a particular task well, we have a high self-efficacy in that area. If we value that area, this self-efficacy feeds into our self-esteem and makes us feel good about ourselves. If we do not value that area (e.g., as adults, being able to sign our names), our self-esteem may be untouched by our self-efficacy. And if we are unrealistic, thinking that we are skilled in some area when we really are not, we may have an enhanced self-esteem, but one that is not valid and reveals more about our grandiose beliefs about ourselves than about our true worth.

We develop a sense of self-efficacy by trying techniques aimed at effectively performing a task and listening to the feedback we get, to see if we, in fact, have been effective or not. Some of these techniques have been obtained by observing others perform a task effectively and imitating their actions; for example, learning how to make new friends by watching how popular people approach and interact with others at a party. Some techniques have been obtained by having been specifically trained in their performance; for example, being taught how to operate equipment in a photography lab. And some techniques are ones that we devise for ourselves, often through a process of trial and error. Examples of this can be seen when we try to figure out for ourselves how to work the new CD player without looking at the instruction manual, or how to make our feelings known to someone we care about without offending the person, or perhaps even how to study for a subject that is totally different from any that we have ever studied before. In all these cases, the important part is to note the results of our actions. If the consequences of our behaviour are positive, we may feel that we are developing a valuable new skill, and our self-esteem increases with our sense of self-efficacy. If the consequences are clearly not positive, though, we may feel that we have to go back to the drawing board and try another technique. Our self-esteem is not enhanced, but we may have faith that we will eventually master the problem. Note that in this case, our self-efficacy is high in the area of learning: we know that we *don't* know how to do Task A (low self-efficacy for A), but we also know that we *can* learn how to do it (high self-efficacy for learning in general).

Self-efficacy, then, can increase our self-esteem when it is realistic. If we can do complex tasks well, and we know it, we feel good about ourselves, and so we should. If we have the belief that we can *learn* to do new tasks, we feel good about ourselves, and this is probably even better than feeling self-efficacy about specific tasks, because this more general self-efficacy is the knowledge that we can grow and develop, learn more and more, and be successful at what we undertake. The danger comes, again, from being unrealistic. Take a moment to reflect on your own self-efficacy. In what areas do you feel competent and sure of your ability to accomplish your goal? In what areas do you feel less sure of your ability? What do you need to do to increase your self-efficacy in these areas?

This brings us to a tricky and sensitive question: is the feedback we get always accurate? More pointedly, are our instructors always right? No. Sometimes our instructors misunderstand what we are saying. Sometimes they, being fallible human beings, mark lower than they might on another day. This is unlikely because there are usually fixed standards for marking (and of course, this problem doesn't arise in areas with clear right or wrong answers). But it is possible. These situations are extremely rare, contrary to student belief. Almost always the instructor is right in his/her feedback: after all, the instructor is a professional who has a great deal of experience and training in the area. If instructors are not always accurate in their feedback, what about other people? Can we always trust others to give us honest feedback? Perhaps not. We need to learn how to evaluate feedback to form a realistic understanding of ourselves. Have we heard this feedback more than once? Is the person giving us this feedback a reliable and knowledgeable source? If we can answer "yes" to both of these questions, we have reason to suspect that the feedback may be accurate, and we should at least seriously consider what is being told to us.

We need to be able to face what we really are, warts and all. This doesn't mean that we have to *like* every facet of ourselves; we can work to change what we don't like. But we can't even identify these areas until we can accept ourselves as we are. Exercise 2.3 is a test to determine your level of self-acceptance. Are you a high scorer who feels freedom to be yourself and to interact spontaneously with others? Or are you a low scorer who is often touchy and tentative in dealing with others?

EXERCISE 2.3   ▶ *Self-Acceptance Scale*

Using the following scale, indicate the extent to which each statement is true or false for you.

1 = Completely true

2 = Mostly true

3 = Half true, half false

4 = Mostly false

5 = Completely false

1. I would like it if I could find someone who would tell me how to solve my personal problems.

2. I don't question my worth as a person, even if I think others do.

3. When people say nice things about me, I find it difficult to believe they really mean it. I think maybe they're kidding me or just aren't being sincere.

4. If there is any criticism or anyone says anything about me, I just can't take it.

5. I don't say much at social affairs because I'm afraid people will criticize me or laugh if I say the wrong thing.

6. I realize that I'm not living very effectively, but I don't believe I've got it in me to use my energy in better ways.

7. I look on most of the feelings and impulses I have toward people as being quite natural and acceptable.

8. Something inside me just won't let me be satisfied with any job I've done—if it turns out well, I get a very smug feeling that this is beneath me, I shouldn't be satisfied with this, this isn't a fair test.

9. I feel different from others. I'd like to have the security that comes from knowing I'm not too different.

10. I'm afraid for people that I like to find out what I'm really like, for fear they'd be disappointed in me.

11. I'm frequently bothered by feelings of inferiority.

12. Because of other people, I haven't been able to achieve as much as I should have.

13. I am quite shy and self-conscious in social situations.

14. In order to get along and be liked, I tend to be what people expect me to be rather than anything else.

15. I seem to have an inner strength in handling things. I'm on a solid foundation and it makes me sure of myself.

16. I feel self-conscious when I'm with people who have a superior position to mine in business or at school.

17. I think I'm neurotic or something.

18. Very often, I don't try to be friendly with people because I think they won't like me.

19. I feel that I'm a person of worth, on an equal plane with others.

20. I can't avoid feeling guilty about the way I feel toward certain people in my life.

21. I'm not afraid to meet new people. I feel that I'm worthwhile and there's no reason why they should dislike me.

22. I sort of only half believe in myself.

23. I'm very sensitive. People say things and I have a tendency to think they're criticizing me or insulting me in some way and later when I think of it, they may not have meant anything like that at all.

24. I think I have certain abilities and other people say so too. I wonder if I'm not giving them an importance way beyond what they deserve.

25. I feel confident that I can do something about the problems that may arise in the future.

26. I guess I put on a show to impress people. I know I'm not the person I pretend to be.

27. I do not worry or condemn myself if other people pass judgement against me.

28. I don't feel very normal, but I want to feel normal.

29. When I'm in a group, I usually don't say much for fear of saying the wrong thing.

30. I have a tendency to sidestep my problems.

31. Even when people do think well of me, I feel sort of guilty because I know I must be fooling them—that if I were really to be myself, they wouldn't think well of me.

32. I feel that I'm on the same level as other people and that helps to establish good relations with them.

33. I feel that people are apt to react differently to me than they would normally react to other people.

34. I live too much by other people's standards.

35. When I have to address a group, I get self-conscious and have difficulty saying things well.

36. If I didn't always have such hard luck, I'd accomplish much more than I have.

Reverse your scores on items 2, 7, 15, 19, 21, 25, 27 and 32 (i.e., 1 becomes 5, 2 becomes 4, 3 remains the same, 4 becomes 2, and 5 becomes 1). Add all the scores. Your score will vary from 36 to 180.

■ 36–110: If you scored in this range, this suggests that you don't accept yourself very well. You seem to have a negative view of yourself, as if something is wrong with you. You likely are also shy and lack confidence in social situations, feeling that others have a negative view of you too. This tends to have an adverse effect on your work and on your relationships with family and friends.

■ 111–150: These are average scores, but your self-acceptance may vary from situation to situation, and you may feel more comfortable with some people than with others. In general though, you are accurate in your perceptions of when you are doing well and when you could have done better.

■ 151–180: This range of scores reflects high levels of self-acceptance and confidence in the ability to handle any problems or challenges that arise, and a generally good feeling toward life.

Source: Berger, Emanuel M. (1955). "Relationships among acceptance of self, acceptance of others, and MMPI [Minnesota Multiphasic Personality Inventory] scores." *Journal of Counseling Psychology*, Vol. 2, Issue 4, pp. 279–283, [Winter]. Reprinted with permission of American Psychological Association.

IDENTITY

WHAT IS IDENTITY?

identity
a sense of who we are, especially in our relationship with the outside world

Identity is related to, but not exactly the same as, self-concept. Identity refers more to our relationship with the outside world. If you are asked, "Who are you?" your answer will include some components of your self-concept, but it will include other components that relate to your roles in society. So you may answer, "I'm a student in social work. I'm Jack's girlfriend. I'm a volunteer at the community youth centre. I'm an honest person. I'm a believer in recycling," and so on. Your identity changes somewhat over time, as your situation changes (for example, you won't be a student forever), but for the most part, there is a continuity about your identity because, in spite of the changes that have occurred in you, you see yourself as basically the same person you were yesterday and the same person you will be tomorrow. By the same token, your identity also reveals that you are someone who is different from everyone else; you are unique, having a mixture of components to your identity that is different from others' identities.

The idea of identity seems quite straightforward, but in fact, forming and retaining an identity are often difficult in modern Western society. Identity formation is enhanced by stability in one's family, one's community, and one's work (Baumeister, 1986). In modern Western society, however, such stability is often lacking: we move around a lot, we can live in the same apartment for years yet never meet our neighbours, and we may change jobs and careers several times during our lives. This is very different from the way society used to be, when most of us lived in the same community that we were born in, surrounded by people whose acquaintance went back several generations, and worked in the same profession as our parents, grandparents, and even great-grandparents. In modern society, it is a common experience to have an identity crisis.

WHAT IS AN IDENTITY CRISIS?

identity crisis
a problem in forming a stable sense of self, a difficulty in answering the question "Who am I?"

identity achieved
a sense of who one is, after having struggled with an identity crisis and having committed oneself to personal values and a code of behaviour

moratorium
an identity state in which we are having an identity crisis and we have not been able to form the commitments that would solve the crisis

foreclosure
an identity state in which we have committed to actions and a code of behaviour without having experienced an identity crisis or questioned our identities

identity diffusion
an identity state in which we have never had an identity crisis, nor have we formed any commitment to a career or a set of values or code of behaviour

In the 1940s, theorist Erik Erikson first used the term **identity crisis** as a potential problem in adolescence (see Glassman & Hadad, 2004). The term caught on, and other researchers began conducting studies that indicated that an identity crisis could occur at other points in a person's life. An identity crisis is a problem in forming a stable sense of self, a difficulty in answering the question "Who am I?"

There are four possible classifications for people with identity crises (Marcia, 1966, 1967, 1980). Let's look at these classifications with examples. First, recall Lenore, who has experienced a crisis, not knowing who she is or what she believes in. If she is successful in committing herself to studying business or any other area of her choice, and to her own set of personal values and ethical code of conduct, she will be regarded as mature and well adjusted. This classification is called **identity achieved**.

Second, there is Claude, who has also experienced an identity crisis but has not been able to form the commitments that would solve the crisis. Claude, in the category of **moratorium**, still seems to be in this crisis: he jumps from job to job and from role to role, as if trying to "find" himself. One day he appears in a very conservative business suit, convinced that the corporate world is the one for him, and the next day he wears overalls, as he attempts to fulfill himself by becoming a farmer. Claude isn't really flighty or flaky; rather, he is trying out a variety of options to find one that works best for him.

In the third category, **foreclosure**, we find Eddie. He doesn't seem to have ever had a crisis. He plans on studying law, just as his parents wanted. He certainly seems competent and stable, no one would question his emotional maturity when first meeting him. But as one gets to know Eddie a little better, one finds that he tends to be rigid in his views and insists on things being done his way. It seems that his maturity, like his views on life and his career, is something he adopted from his parents rather than something he developed for himself. For Eddie, his identity is not really a part of him; it's more like an overcoat someone has given him to put on. Eddie is going to have a hard time in forming intimate relationships. Poor Eddie *can't* be right for himself, or for anyone else, when he really doesn't know who "himself" is!

Finally, meet Fatima, who has **identity diffusion.** She has never had an identity crisis, but she's never formed any commitment to a career or a set of values either. Fatima is a little like Peter Pan; she never seems quite grown-up as she flits from job to job and relationship to relationship. She's not like Claude, who is actively exploring different paths; Fatima isn't looking for any path or coherence in her life.

Types of identity states, then, are determined by two factors: (1) whether or not there is, or has been, a crisis, and (2) whether the individual has formed any commitment to a career or code of values. This is shown in Table 2.1.

TABLE 2.1   Identity States

		Commitment	
		Yes	**No**
Crisis	**Yes**	Identity achieved	Moratorium
	No	Identity foreclosure	Identity diffusion

As tough as identity crises seem to be to resolve, there is evidence that they do not harm us. In fact, they may actually be good for us, if we can successfully resolve them. There are many positive effects for people who came through the crisis and reached an achieved identity (Bernard, 1981; Bourne, 1978). These people have more motivation and ambition, they perform better under stress, and they have a greater ability to form mature, intimate relationships. They were also found to have higher grades in post-secondary education.

ARE THERE OTHER TYPES OF IDENTITY CRISES?

identity deficit
having little of our own identity, which makes major decisions in life very difficult

Yes. Not all identity crises are alike. Lenore and Eddie may be expected to go through an identity crisis fueled by **identity deficit**: that is, they don't have enough of their own identity to make the major decisions of life. In Lenore's case, there never was much information about herself inside her to know what she wanted. In Eddie's case, the information he had about himself came from his environment and its expectations of him. If Lenore wants to know herself, she is going to have to search in, what is to her, unknown waters. Eddie has an extra step, though: if he wants to know himself, first he has to reject many of the things he thought he knew. Eddie has to recognize that many of the long-held beliefs he has lived by are not, in fact, his own. Only then will he be able to discover what he truly is and what he believes. (Note that Eddie may come through the process of finding his identity successfully and wind up believing exactly the same information that he had been taught all along. The difference will be that this time, Eddie will know the beliefs are his own, not just reflections of his family.)

For some people, identity crises are fueled by having almost too much identity. Let's look again at the case of Eddie. If Eddie finds himself to be someone who likes expensive clothing, cars, and exotic vacations, but at the same time is also a person who is committed to civil liberties and the belief that everyone should have equal rights, he may find himself in conflict. These two facets of his identity may result in **identity conflict**; that is, two parts of himself are inconsistent with each other, a problem when it comes time for Eddie to make a firm decision about his future career. Should he take the "money" route and go into law, as his family expects him to do? Or should he take the "poverty" route and become a social worker, satisfying his need to work for the welfare of others? Of course, this is an extreme simplification. In reality, lawyers are not necessarily rich, and social workers do not necessarily live in poverty. Nor is it necessarily the case that Eddie cannot find a way to satisfy both aspects of his personality (e.g., he can go into law professionally, spending part of his time working on civil rights issues and volunteering his expertise to those without the funds to hire a lawyer).

identity conflict
a state in which two or more parts of ourselves are inconsistent with each other

People like Lenore and Eddie who are going through an identity deficit crisis usually experience wild fluctuations in their moods, sometimes feeling despair that they will ever "find" themselves, and sometimes feeling completely exhilarated in their discoveries about themselves. If Eddie does wind up with an identity conflict, though, he may not have too many of these fluctuations. His predominant feeling is more likely to be guilt for betraying a part of himself, and helplessness in being able to find a path that will satisfy all facets of his personality. If you are a parent, you probably know exactly what these feelings are like. Your role as parent is extremely important to you, but so is your role as student or worker. How do you decide how to allot your time? As one mother in our class said, "You just can't win—if you spend time with the kids, you feel guilty about not studying, and if you study, you feel guilty for neglecting the kids! Damned if you do and damned if you don't!"

One of the most difficult identity crises is found in the case of children whose parents are from a culture different from the one in which they are raising their children. For example, Indira was born and raised in Canada and thinks of herself, rightly, as a Canadian. But her parents were raised in a traditional manner in Pakistan. While they too are proud of their Canadian citizenship, they also love their Pakistani heritage and they have tried to raise their children with this heritage as well. However, this heritage is often in conflict with the beliefs of the environment that they live in. As Indira grows older, she experiences more of this environment; going to college, for example, she is exposed to many more divergent ideas that make her question many of the traditional beliefs her family has taught her. Indira is in an identity conflict: she loves her family and her Pakistani heritage, but she also loves Canadian culture and its more liberal belief systems. She is a young woman torn between two cultures. How Indira will resolve this conflict will depend on many factors, including her family's ability to tolerate the possibility that she may believe differently from them and wish to live her life differently from their chosen path. Indira may renounce one side of her identity, becoming either "wholly Canadian" or "wholly Pakistani"; or she may try to compartmentalize her life, choosing, for example, to be "Canadian" professionally but "Pakistani" at home. Or she may be able to find a compromise in some areas. In any case, Indira's challenges are great, but if she can come through them successfully, the rewards will also be great.

In summary, then, self-awareness leads us to form a self-concept. Valuing this self-concept means having self-esteem based on self-efficacy, a realistic appraisal of our abilities and traits. From this, we devise an identity in our lives, an understanding of who we are, what we stand for, what roles we fulfill and how valuable we are. Armed with this knowledge, we can make wise choices, develop a happy, fulfilled, and productive life, and make a difference by being on this earth. Box 2.1 lists some ways in which you can increase your self-esteem realistically.

How to Increase Your Self-Esteem Realistically!   BOX 2.1

1. Recognize that you are in control of how you see yourself. You are not trapped by how others see you; rather, you determine how you feel about yourself.

2. Increase your self-awareness. Take stock of your thoughts, feelings, ideas, and behaviours just as if you were examining a stranger whom you wanted to know better. Keep a journal, if you wish, of what you discover about yourself.

3. Set your own goals and aspirations. The world will undoubtedly have great ideas about what you should be and what you should do. But your life is yours to choose and make decisions about. Don't wantonly hurt others, but don't let the tyranny of the shoulds rule you either.

4. Make sure that what you want is realistic. If your goals and aspirations are unrealistic (e.g., if only perfection seems worthwhile), you will doom yourself to a life of frustration and disappointment. Strive for excellence, not for perfection and the unattainable.

5. Stop telling yourself you're not good enough. You didn't fail the test because you're stupid; you failed because you didn't study enough or you didn't study the right way for that particular test. Your girlfriend/boyfriend didn't dump you because you're a loser; he/she dumped you because this relationship was simply not one that was working out for both of you in the long haul. You didn't get the job because someone else was more qualified, not because you're inept. And so on.

6. Build on your strengths. You have a lot going for you that you may not be paying sufficient attention to. For example, the very fact that you're in a post-secondary educational institution suggests that you're bright, motivated, and determined. Do you give yourself credit for this?

7. Be positive with other people. Approach others with the assumption that they will like you and want to have a rewarding interaction with you. You lose nothing by this attitude, and you maximize the chances that your interactions will be mutually satisfying.

Source: Adapted from *Psychology Applied to Modern Life, Adjustment in the 21st Century* (With InfoTrac), 7th edition, by Weiten. © 2003. Reprinted with permission of Wadsworth, a division of Thomson Learning: www.thomsonrights.com. Fax 800 730-2215.

What of Lenore and Eddie, whom we met at the beginning of the chapter? We have returned to their problems throughout this chapter, but to sum up, we must suggest to both of them that they begin to explore themselves. They need to learn what they truly are, apart from expectations put upon them. They need to learn what they truly believe in. They need to learn what they are good at and what they feel good doing. There are many personality tests that can help them discover more about themselves (e.g., online personality tests at http://www.healthyplace.com/site/tests/psychological.asp and http://www.quincyweb.net/quincy/psychology.html), but as a first step, Exercises 2.1 and 2.2 would be useful. They should remember, however, that some tests are more valid than others, even the best tests are sometimes wrong, and that no personality test will ever capture anyone's whole personality. Lenore and Eddie should also remember that, as we discussed in Chapter 1, if they need honest feedback, advice, or even an objective knowledgeable person to bounce their ideas and feelings off of, their own post-secondary schools have counsellors who are experienced in this area and are caring about the often confusing world of a student.

Advice for Lenore and Eddie

WHAT LENORE AND EDDIE CAN DO	OUTCOME
Acknowledge that they don't know themselves very well.	Now they can take steps to know themselves better.
Try Exercise 2.1.	This will give them a better idea of what they believe they are and are not, and what they would like to be.
Try Exercise 2.2.	This will indicate to them what they value or hold dear in their lives.
Go to the suggested websites and try some other personality tests.	This will increase their understanding of who they are and what they believe in.
Try Exercise 2.3.	This will indicate whether they accept themselves as they are or whether they wish they were different. This is an indication of how high their self-esteem is.
List the things that they feel competent or skilled at doing. They might also ask people whom they trust to be honest about what others see as their greatest strengths.	This will indicate the areas in which they have self-efficacy, and a high self-esteem would be realistic in these areas.
List the things that they do not feel competent at, or that they have been unsuccessful at in the past. They might also ask people whom they trust to be honest about what others see as areas they might want to work on.	This will indicate the areas in which they have little self-efficacy, and their self-esteem might be realistically lower.
Put together all the information that they have amassed so far.	This will give them a broader picture of their self-concept and will allow them to see the areas in which their self-esteem is or is not realistic.
Take the suggestions in Box 2.1.	This will increase their self-esteem realistically and allow them to make better choices in a more satisfying life.
Go to their school's counselling centre.	If Lenore and Eddie find that they need help in determining what their self-concepts are, or in developing realistic self-esteem, the counsellors at the counselling centre are trained and eager to help.

CHAPTER SUMMARY

■ Self-awareness refers to the extent to which we know ourselves, including what we are like, what we think, and what we feel. When we are unaware of our true feelings, we sometimes channel them onto something unrelated, but safe (displacement). When we lack self-awareness, we reduce our choices in life and our control over our own lives. The decisions we make are not based on accurate information, so we may make bad decisions.

■ When we gain self-awareness and try to determine who and what we are, we gain a self-concept. Self-concept is the total of what we think and feel, how we behave, what attitudes we have, in short, everything we believe about ourselves. We derive our self-concepts from all the information about ourselves that we have received from outside sources (parents, teachers, society).

■ In different situations we may show different facets of ourselves, that is, different parts of our self-concepts, and our self-concepts may change over time as well.

■ Karen Horney differentiated between what we think we really are (the real self) and what we want to be (the ideal self). If the gap between the real self and the ideal self is too great, we feel unhappy with ourselves, and sometimes tell ourselves that we are not what we should be. This is called the tyranny of the shoulds. In most cases, when there is a large gap, it is because we are unrealistically making our real selves seem much worse than they are, and we are aspiring to an unattainably high goal for our ideal selves.

■ Part of knowing ourselves comes from knowing what we value, what is important to us in life. Knowing the values we hold dear is important when we make decisions about our futures.

■ Self-esteem refers to the way we feel about ourselves. This is the emotional level of self-concept that measures how much we like or dislike ourselves, whether we think we are worthwhile or not, whether we value ourselves or not. It is desirable to have a high level of self-esteem in order to be mentally healthy, to achieve our goals, and to have a good life, since having a low self-esteem may lead us to create a self-fulfilling prophecy. It is important that our self-esteem be realistic, though; not undeservedly too high or too low. We are unable to make good judgments about whether we need to change our behaviour if we don't have an accurate and balanced view of ourselves.

■ Self-efficacy refers to our judgment regarding how well we can do a certain action or task. We develop a sense of self-efficacy by trying techniques aimed at effectively performing a task and listening to the feedback we get to see if we have, in fact, been effective or not. If we know we can do a particular task well, we have a high self-efficacy in that area. If we value that area, this self-efficacy feeds into our self-esteem and makes us feel good about ourselves. Self-efficacy, then, can increase our self-esteem when it is realistic.

■ Identity refers to our self-concept in relationship with the outside world. Your identity changes somewhat over time, as your situation changes, but for the most part, there is a continuity about your identity because, in spite of the changes that have occurred in you, you see yourself as basically the same person you were yesterday and the same person you will be tomorrow. By the same token, your identity also reveals that you are someone who is different from everyone else; you are unique, having a mixture of components to your identity that is different from others'.

■ An identity crisis is a problem in forming a stable sense of self, a difficulty in answering the question "Who am I?" When we have an identity achieved, we have a sense of who we are after having struggled with an identity crisis and having committed ourselves to personal values and a code of behaviour. When we have a moratorium, we have an identity state in which we are having an identity crisis and we have not been able to form the commitments that would solve the crisis. With foreclosure, we have an identity state in which we have committed to actions and a code of behaviour without having experienced an identity crisis or questioned our identities. Finally, with identity diffusion, we have an identity state in which we have never had an identity crisis, nor have we formed any commitment to a career or a set of values or code of behaviour either.

■ In some cases, we may have identity deficit in which we have little of our own identity, which makes major decisions in life very difficult. Or we may have identity conflict, a state in which two or more parts of ourselves are inconsistent with each other.

KEY TERMS

displacement	identity crisis	self-concept
foreclosure	identity deficit	self-efficacy
ideal self	identity diffusion	self-esteem
identity	moratorium	tyranny of the shoulds
identity achieved	real self	value
identity conflict	self-awareness	

INDIVIDUAL ACTIVITIES

1. Think about the sources in your early years that gave you messages about yourself. What messages did they give you? Do you think these were the messages they intended to give you? What messages do you wish they had not given you? What messages do you wish they had given you?

2. Many Native Peoples expect that changes will happen in every individual, and they give new names to reflect these changes. Think back on the child you were at age five. If you were deciding on a name for this child to reflect the child's personality, what would it be? The name does not need to be a commonly accepted first name; rather, it should be descriptive. Were you "Little Thumb-sucker"? Or "Shy One"? Or "Kitten-lover"? Or "Nightmare-haunted"? The possibilities are infinite. Repeat this exercise, thinking of yourself at ages 10, 15, 20, and so on to your present age. Now imagine yourself at an age 5, 10, 15, and 20 years from now. What name do you hope you will have then?

3. What values do you share with your family? In what ways are your values different from some of theirs? How do you think you developed these different values?

4. Think of one area of your present life (e.g., the academic program or school you're in, a relationship you have, where you live, your job, the clothes you wear, the food you eat, etc.). Now create as many alternatives as you can, imagining yourself in each alternative. For example, if you normally dress in jeans and a T-shirt, imagine yourself dressing in a suit and tie every day. Or in peasant skirts and blouses. How would you feel? What difference would it make in how you see yourself or how others see you? Are there any alternatives you find rather appealing? Is it possible for you to incorporate any of these appealing alternatives into your life? If not, why not? Are these alternatives really not viable? Or do you choose not to incorporate any changes in this area?

5. Hopefully you have some idea of what quality or features of life you value. Now think of ways in which you can recognize and incorporate these values into your daily life. For example, if you value humour, look at the number of times per day you laugh or make

others laugh. Increase this (you don't have to become a clown!). Become the person who clips out the newspaper's joke of the day and shows it to others. Plan a party around a potluck meal and renting a couple of the best comedy movies you know of. If compassion is a value you hold dear, increase your compassionate responses to others, and to yourself.

6. Start to develop a personal mission statement for yourself. How do you plan on growing and developing over the next 5 years? 10 years? 20 years? Consider what you want your identity to be and where you need to increase your self-efficacy. What will you do to attain your goals?

GROUP ACTIVITIES

1. In pairs, Person A faces Person B and asks "Who are you?" Person B gives one response (e.g., "I'm Anna."), which Person A writes down. Person A repeats, "Who are you?" and Person B replies. Continue this until Person B is unable to give any further responses. Then switch places, with Person B asking "Who are you?" and recording Person A's responses. Give each other the list that has been compiled of each individual's responses. Examine the list that your responses have generated. On reflection, have you left anything out? Which were the most important responses you gave? Did they come first in your list?

2. Form groups of males and females, about three or four of each gender and with as much mixture of racial, religious, and ethnic groups as possible. Take a question, such as "What is the most important characteristic a person can have in a romantic relationship?" or "What is the most important characteristic for a parent to instill in a child?" Each member of the group writes down his/her answer. Then each member writes down the answer that he/she thinks a member of the opposite sex would give. Then, as a group, compare the answers. Are there differences between what males say they value in a relationship and what females say they value? How well did each sex predict what the opposite sex would say? Also note the characteristics given by members of different racial, religious, and ethnic groups. Do different values emerge in these cases?

3. Form groups of five or six with as much mixture of racial, religious, and ethnic groups as possible. Each person acts as a "spokesperson" for his/her group, answering the question, "How would your group regard an identity crisis? How would your group deal with such a crisis in a teenager?" Note that the answers should reflect the values of the group regarding this issue (if there aren't, this in itself is interesting), not stereotypes that may be applied to a group.

REFERENCES

Bandura, A. (1986). *Social foundations of thought and action: A social-cognitive theory.* Englewood Cliffs, NJ: Prentice-Hall.

Baumeister, R. F. (1986). *Identity: Cultural change and the struggle for self.* New York: Oxford University Press.

Baumeister, R. F., Campbell, J. D., Krueger, J. I., & Vohs, K. D. (2003). Does high self-esteem cause better performance, interpersonal success, happiness, or healthier lifestyles? *Psychological Science in the Public Interest, 4(1),* 1–44.

Baumeister, R. F., Heatherton, T. F., & Tice, D. M. (1993). When ego threats lead to self-regulation failure: Negative consequences of high self-esteem. *Journal of Personality and Social Psychology, 64,* 141–156.

Bernard, H. S. (1981). Identity formation during late adolescence: A review of some empirical findings. *Adolescence, 16,* 349–357.

Bochner, S., & Van Zyl, T. (1985). Desirability ratings of 110 personality-trait words. *Journal of Social Psychology, 125(4),* 459–465.

Bourne, E. (1978). The state of research on ego identity: A review and appraisal. Part II. *Journal of Youth and Adolescence, 7,* 371–391.

Diener, E., Wolsic, B., & Fujita, F. (1995). Physical attractiveness and subjective well-being. *Journal of Personality and Social Psychology, 69,* 120–129.

Fagan, J., & Shepherd, I. L. (1970). *Gestalt therapy now: Theory, techniques, applications*. Palo Alto, CA: Science and Behavior Books.

Gabriel, M. T., Critelli, J. W., & Ee, J. S. (1994). Narcissistic illusions in self-evaluations of intelligence and attractiveness. *Journal of Personality, 62*, 142–155.

Glassman, W. E., & Hadad, M. (2004). *Approaches to psychology*. (4th ed.). Berkshire, UK: Open University Press.

Horney, K. (1945). *Our inner conflicts*. New York: Norton.

Lane, J., Lane, A. M., & Kyprianou, A. (2004). Self-efficacy, self-esteem and their impact on academic performance. *Social Behavior and Personality, 32(3)*, 247–256.

Maclean's, (June 7, 2004). Cover. Toronto: Rogers Publishing.

Marcia, J. E. (1966). Development and validation of ego-identity status. *Journal of Personality and Social Psychology, 3*, 551–558.

Marcia, J. E. (1967). Ego-identity status: Relationship to change in self-esteem, "general maladjustment," and authoritarianism. *Journal of Personality, 35*, 118–133.

Marcia, J. E. (1980). Identity in adolescence. In R. M. Lerner, A. C. Petersen, & J. Brooks-Gunn (Eds.), *Encyclopedia of adolescence* (Vol. 1). New York: Garland.

McFarlin, D. B., Baumeister, R. F., & Blascovich, J. (1984). On knowing when to quit: Task failure, self-esteem, advice, and non-productive persistence. *Journal of Personality, 52*, 138–155.

Rosenberg, M. (1985). Self-concept and psychological well-being in adolescence. In R. L. Leahy (Ed.), *The development of the self*. Orlando, FL: Academic Press.

Schonbach, P. (1972). Likeableness ratings of 100 German personality-trait words corresponding to a subset of Anderson's 555 trait words. *European Journal of Social Psychology, 2(3)*, 327–334.

Shrauger, J. S., & Sorman, P. B. (1977). Self-evaluations, initial success and failure, and improvement as determinants of persistence. *Journal of Consulting and Clinical Psychology, 45*, 784–795.

Steele, C. M. (1988). The psychology of self-affirmation: Sustaining the integrity of the self. In L. Berkowitz (Ed.), *Advances in experimental social psychology* (Vol. 21, pp. 261–302). New York: Academic Press.

CHAPTER 3

MANAGING YOUR PERSONAL LIFE

In this chapter, you will learn about:

- The negative experience of stress

- Where stress comes from in general

- General techniques to deal with stress

- The effects of the stress of relationships

- How to deal with romantic breakups and with loneliness

LEARNING OBJECTIVES

The Case of Pietro

▶ Pietro is a busy first-year college student who is trying to adjust to a new educational facility at a higher level than he has ever experienced before. His girlfriend just broke up with him and he's very lonely without her. He hasn't made many new friends at college because of his basic shyness and because much of his spare time is spent working at a part-time job. His parents expect great things from him, and he often worries that he will disappoint them, especially since his performance on his first tests was not outstanding. His younger brother used to be a good friend of his, but lately all they seem to do is fight. Pietro is having difficulty concentrating right now, which worries him further, especially since he has to make some critical decisions about what courses to take next semester and about his job. And now Pietro is sick with the flu. He feels physically and emotionally rotten; he worries that he's losing everyone and everything he cares about. Pietro is burdened with stress.

STRESS IN GENERAL

WHAT IS STRESS?

stress
any circumstances that threaten or are perceived to threaten one's well-being and thereby tax one's coping abilities (Weiten & Lloyd, 2003)

Stress may be defined as "any circumstances that threaten or are perceived to threaten one's well-being and thereby tax one's coping abilities" (Weiten & Lloyd, 2003, p. 63). So, for example, you may get a dry mouth and a pounding heart (typical stress reactions) when your instructor tells you that today there will be a surprise test worth 30 percent of your final mark. Or when your boyfriend/girlfriend looks grim and says, "We have to talk about something." Or when the doctor looks at the results of your blood test and frowns. Or when the person you love most in the world asks you to spend your life with him/her. Or when you discover that you have the winning lottery ticket. Stress, then, can be the result of negative events that we want to avoid or of positive events that we welcome. In either case, a demand is placed upon us to deal with a new situation and this forces us to come up with a method to cope. The more we believe we can deal with this stress, the better we will feel (Lazarus & Folkman, 1984), which is probably why it's a lot easier on us and a lot more fun to deal with the positive events. Life is a series of stressful events that constantly make demands upon us, and there is always something to cope with. But life would be pretty boring if we never had any stress; in fact, a lack of any stress is stressful in itself.

A notable point about stress is that it's like beauty—it's in the eye of the beholder. What one person finds stressful is not necessarily what another person finds stressful. While many of us find the prospect of going to a party to be a pleasant way to reduce the stress of a working day, Pietro, a shy, quiet person, finds the idea of going to a party to be very unpleasant. He would rather walk over burning coals than socialize with a large group of people. There is no right or wrong in the appraisal of whether going to a party is stressful or not: there are simply reactions according to different personalities and experiences, which have influenced how we interpret what going to a party means. Another point to note is that going to a party is not always pleasurable for any of us. For example, when our work piles up and deadlines are approaching, we may feel that we really can't afford to take the time to go to a party. If we go, we may not enjoy ourselves because the thought of all the work facing us gets in the way of pleasure. The party would provide more negative stress for us at this time because of the situation we are in with our workload. The message, then, is that an event is felt as stressful depending upon the individual and depending on the other factors in his/her life at the time the event is experienced. A situation is stressful if you interpret it as stressful (Monroe & Kelley, 1995).

Pietro's stress is coming from both his professional life as a student and his personal life, including his social life as a son, boyfriend, and friend. We will examine Pietro's personal stress in this chapter and his professional stress in the next chapter.

WHAT EFFECTS DOES STRESS HAVE ON US?

The physical effects of stress may be very severe. In the short term, when stress hits us, we may feel our muscles tense, our mouths go dry, our stomachs churn, and a cold sweat bead our foreheads. In the long term, more and more evidence indicates that prolonged stress (which is what most of us undergo) is a factor in coronary artery disease, arthritis, stroke, tuberculosis, multiple sclerosis, diabetes, high blood pressure, headaches, cancer, and even the common cold (see, for example, Critelli & Ee, 1996; Hubbard & Workman, 1998; Selye, 1956). One of the ways that stress is so harmful is in the way it weakens the immune system: when we have undergone stress over a long period of time, our immune systems become less able to fight off viruses, bacteria, and other foreign substances (Kiecolt-Glaser & Glaser, 1995). This is not to say that everyone who experiences stress will get sick, but it does shed some light on why more students seem to have a cold or the flu at exam time than at any other time of the semester.

Emotionally, too, stress can affect us profoundly. In a nutshell, negative stress tends to make us feel miserable (Lazarus, 1991, 1993). How miserable and what kind of misery depends on us and the situation we are in. In some cases, we may feel angry and resentful when confronting stress. In other cases, we may feel grief or sadness. Sometimes fear and anxiety are the predominant emotions. In some situations we may even feel guilt, shame, jealousy, envy, or disgust. Just to make the picture even more complicated, sometimes we may feel a mixture of several of these emotions, and it's pretty plain that these emotions can and do get in the way of thinking clearly. On the other hand, if the stress is positive, we may have many of the same physical symptoms, but our emotions may be ecstatic. The state of falling in love is a prime example of how a positive stress can produce the same fluttering in the stomach, but the emotions of joy, wonderment, and utter bliss (although sometimes mixed with a little fear and apprehension). Thinking rationally, though, is often very difficult.

When we are under positive or negative stress, it becomes very difficult to think as clearly and effectively as we do in more relaxed times. It's intuitively obvious and scientifically demonstrated that after we have experienced a severe stress, such as being in a car accident, we may feel disoriented, numb, confused, and unable to think at all (Weisaeth, 1993). But even in less dramatic situations, stress may disrupt our performance and thinking (Baumeister, 1984; Keinan, 1987). Imagine that you have been asked to do a task that requires concentration (e.g., add several columns of numbers in your head, write a poem, make suggestions for alleviating world hunger). Do you think you will do better when you are left alone in a room with unlimited time to do the task, or when you are in a room with a ticking clock reminding you of a time limit, and a severe-looking instructor standing over your shoulder, examining everything you do? In this case, the time limit and the severe-looking instructor provide stress for you, and, chances are, will make concentrating more difficult for you. You may be providing stress for yourself too. Under these conditions, you may be saying to yourself, "I can't do this. This assignment is too hard. I don't understand the question. I wish that person would go away and leave me alone. How much time do I have left?" and so on. (Have you found yourself thinking these things when you first receive a test paper? We'll talk more about that later.) What you are actually doing is cluttering up your mind with thoughts that can only stress you further and that get in the way of concentration so that your problem becomes even worse.

The bottom line is that stress is always with us and it can make our lives very difficult. How prone to stress are you? Take the test in Exercise 3.1 and get an idea of your own vulnerability. For fun, you might also wish to try the stress tests at http://www.2h.com/personality-tests.html and http://www.lessons4living.com/stress_test.htm.

EXERCISE 3.1

▶ **Stress Vulnerability Scale**

Rate each item from 1 (almost always) to 5 (never), according to how much of the time each statement applies to you.

I eat at least one hot, balanced meal a day.   _____

I get 7 to 8 hours sleep at least 4 nights a week.   _____

I give and receive affection regularly.   _____

I have at least one relative within 50 miles on whom I can rely.   _____

I exercise to the point of perspiration at least twice a week.   _____

I smoke less than half a pack of cigarettes a day.   _____

I take fewer than 5 alcoholic drinks a week.   _____

I am the appropriate weight for my height.   _____

I have an income adequate to meet basic expenses.   _____

I get strength from my religious beliefs.   _____

I regularly attend club or social activities.   _____

I have a network of friends to confide in about personal matters.   _____

I have hope and faith in my future.   _____

I am in good health (including eyesight, hearing, teeth).   _____

I am able to speak openly about my feelings when angry or worried.   _____

I have regular conversations with the people I live with about
domestic problems, e.g., chores, money and daily living issues.   _____

I do something for fun at least once a week.   _____

I am able to organize my time effectively.   _____

I drink fewer than 3 cups of coffee (or tea or cola drinks) a day.   _____

I take quiet time for myself during the day.   _____

Subtotal   _____

Total (subtotal minus 20)   _____

Total your score and subtract 20. Any number over 30 indicates a vulnerability to stress. A total score between 50 and 75 suggests serious vulnerability, and over 75 means extreme vulnerability.

Source: Susceptibility to Stress scale from the Stress audit, version 5.0-OS, developed by Lyle H. Miller and Alma Dell Smith. Copyright © 1987, 1994 Biobehavioral Institute of Boston, Brookline, MA 02146. Reprinted with permission.

WHAT ARE THE GENERAL SOURCES OF STRESS?

Stress comes from just a few recognizable situations. No matter what the specific cause of the stress you are feeling, there are shared elements in all stress. It's important to know this because it's difficult to cope with something we don't understand or can't identify.

1. Frustration

frustration
the feeling experienced when we are kept from meeting some goal because of an obstacle in our way

One general source of stress is **frustration**, which we feel when we are kept from meeting some goal because of an obstacle in our way. Pietro feels stress from frustration when he wants to spend time with his girlfriend, but she doesn't want to spend time with him anymore. He feels stress from frustration when he can't get his computer to behave properly: his goal is to work on the computer, but the malfunction or his lack of expertise prevents this. He feels stress from frustration when he can't seem to get along with his brother: his goal is to have a good relationship with his brother, but this is being thwarted by the way the two young men argue with each other. It could be that you are feeling stress from frustration right now because you have to read this chapter, which gets in the way of your goal of meeting your friends or watching TV or sleeping. Sometimes this frustration is experienced as anger, but in general the real difference is that frustration occurs when we don't get something we want, whereas anger occurs when we don't get something we need. It can be difficult to tell the difference however, perhaps because we often confuse what we want with what we need.

2. Conflict

conflict
the uncertainty we may feel when we have to make a decision or choose between two options

Another general source of stress is **conflict**. What we mean by conflict is not the usual definition of an argument or disagreement, but rather the uncertainty we may feel when we have to make a decision or choose between two options.

approach-avoidance conflict
there are pluses and minuses to the option—elements that one would like to approach, and elements that one would like to avoid

For example, Pietro has been offered extra hours at his part-time job. If he takes the extra hours, he will earn needed extra money and perhaps make his employer feel more favourably toward him, but the work is at night, so he won't get much sleep on school nights and the job will take up more of his valuable time. Pietro has an **approach-avoidance conflict**, meaning that there are pluses and minuses to the offer of extra working hours—elements that he would like to approach, and elements that he would like to avoid. He may find it difficult to make a choice about whether to take the extra hours or not, and until he makes his decision, Pietro will experience stress from an approach-avoidance conflict.

Pietro is facing another conflict as well: he is enrolled in one course that he doesn't like, and he must choose whether to study for the test in this course or begin to write the essay for this course. No matter which choice he makes, he is not going to enjoy himself. Both options are ones he would like to avoid, so this is called an **avoidance-avoidance conflict**.

Pietro also has another, more pleasant, source of stress: he has to choose between two courses for next semester, both of which he is sure he would enjoy as they are very popular with students. He is experiencing **approach-approach conflict** because both options are positive, or ones that he would like to approach. His stress lies in the fact that he can't have both options, but since both options are ones that Pietro would enjoy, it is likely that he will not feel too much negative stress.

In the preceding examples, the approach-approach conflict causes the least stress and is the easiest one to deal with. An approach-avoidance conflict is much more difficult to handle and causes more stress. In some ways, the avoidance-avoidance conflict is the most difficult because no matter how it is resolved, the individual has to face something unpleasant. In these cases, people often feel so much stress that they put off making the decision as long as they can. Sometimes, when people have avoidance-avoidance conflicts, they put off making the decision for so long that the choice is taken out of their hands. For example, if Pietro puts off deciding whether to study or write his essay, he may find that the day of the test is upon him and he isn't prepared, *and* the deadline for the essay has arrived and he hasn't begun to write it.

3. Change

A further general source of stress is **change**. While variety may be the spice of life, making changes takes a toll on us. Sometimes the changes are good and the stress is less, but note that the stress is still present. For example, even though falling in love is very pleasant for you (we hope!), it does cause a large change in your psychological state and your socializing. In 1967, Holmes and Rahe devised a scale to determine how much stress people were under by assigning points to life-change items, and this was later modified to make it pertinent to students in post-secondary institutions (Anderson, as cited by Brehm, 1998). Take the test yourself in Exercise 3.2 to see how much stress you have been under because of change. While the results may be interesting, don't take the numbers too seriously. One of the major flaws in any of the life-change scales is that the numbers assigned to any event are derived by measures of the whole population (not just first-year students, for example), and may not apply to any one individual. Stress, as we have said, is in the eye of the beholder. So moving away from home may be highly stressful for one person who has a warm, loving family and lots of friends and activities at home, and who doesn't know what he/she really wants from a post-secondary education. The stress may be less, but still large, for the shy person who has been dependent on his/her parents to take care of everyday needs and to provide support and companionship. But for other people, whose family is dysfunctional and abusive, moving away from home is a relief and a break from stress. For still others, whose family is wonderful but who have always dreamed of living in a large city and meeting a wide variety of new people, the stress may be moderated by excitement.

What is more important in looking at the life-changes you have made is to see how many changes have occurred in the past year. One of the most critical discoveries was that stress is additive: the stress of each change builds up in an individual, until a small change may be exceedingly difficult to deal with (Holmes & Rahe, 1967). This is the proverbial straw that breaks the camel's back. Perhaps you have had the experience yourself. When you have been feeling a great amount of stress in your life, you may find that some small thing—which wouldn't normally trouble you to a great extent—seems like too much to bear. No, you haven't suddenly "lost it": you are simply experiencing the additive effect of stress.

avoidance-avoidance conflict
both options have elements that one would like to avoid

approach-approach conflict
both options are positive, or ones that one would like to approach

change
alterations in one's life requiring one to make adjustments and adaptations

EXERCISE 3.2   ▶ *Life Events Scale: College Students*

Check each event that has occurred in your life during the last year. If the event has happened more than once, multiply the value given by the number of occurrences. Add the values of the items you have checked. Don't take the numbers too seriously, though: remember that stress is determined by *your* interpretation of events. So even though the Life Events Scale allots more stress points to getting married than to experiencing the death of a close friend, for example, the death of your friend may have been more stressful for you than getting married. Use this scale only to get an idea of how much change has really occurred in your life in the past year. In general, the higher your score is, the more stress you may feel from life event changes.

Value	Life Event	Score
50	Entered college	_____
77	Married	_____
38	Had either a lot more or a lot less trouble with your boss	_____
43	Held a job while attending school	_____
87	Experienced the death of a spouse	_____
34	Experienced a major change in sleeping habits (sleeping a lot more or a lot less, or a change in part of the day when asleep)	_____
77	Experienced the death of a close family member	_____
30	Experienced a major change in eating habits (a lot more or a lot less food intake, or very different meal hours or surroundings)	_____
41	Made a change in or choice of a major field of study	_____
45	Had a revision of your personal habits (friends, dress, manners, associations, etc.)	_____
68	Experienced the death of a close friend	_____
22	Have been found guilty of minor violations of the law (traffic tickets, jaywalking, etc.)	_____
40	Have had an outstanding personal achievement	_____
68	Experienced pregnancy or fathered a child	_____
56	Had a major change in the health or behaviour of a family member	_____
58	Had sexual difficulties	_____
42	Had trouble with in-laws	_____
26	Had a major change in the number of family get-togethers (a lot more or a lot less)	_____
53	Had a major change in financial state (a lot worse off or a lot better off than usual)	_____
50	Gained a new family member (through birth, adoption, older person moving in, etc.)	_____
42	Changed your residence or living conditions	_____
50	Had a major conflict in or change in values	_____
36	Had a major change in church activities (a lot more or a lot less than usual)	_____
58	Had a marital reconciliation with your mate	_____
62	Were fired from work	_____
76	Were divorced	_____
50	Changed to a different line of work	_____
50	Had a major change in the number of arguments with spouse (either a lot more or a lot less than usual)	_____

47	Had a major change in responsibilities at work (promotion, demotion, lateral transfer)	_____
41	Had your spouse begin or cease work outside the home	_____
74	Had a marital separation from your mate	_____
57	Had a major change in usual type and/or amount of recreation	_____
52	Took a mortgage or loan *less* than $10,000 (such as purchase of a car, TV, school loan, etc.)	_____
65	Had a major personal injury or illness	_____
46	Had a major change in the use of alcohol (a lot more or a lot less)	_____
48	Had a major change in social activities	_____
38	Had a major change in the amount of participation in school activities	_____
49	Had a major change in the amount of independence and responsibility (for example, budgeting time)	_____
33	Took a trip or a vacation	_____
54	Were engaged to be married	_____
50	Changed to a new school	_____
41	Changed dating habits	_____
44	Had trouble with school administration (instructors, advisors, class scheduling, etc.)	_____
60	Broke or had broken a marital engagement or a steady relationship	_____
57	Had a major change in self-concept or self-awareness	_____
	Total	_____

Scoring:

under 150: You are not experiencing a great deal of change, but remember to monitor yourself for stress reactions if more change comes into your life.

150–199: You have been experiencing some life changes in the last year and need to be careful to pace yourself. In general, about 1 in 3 people in this range become ill during the following year as their immune systems diminish, making it less likely that they can fight off illness.

200–299: You have been experiencing several life changes in the last year, and this may be providing a large amount of stress for you. In general, about half the people who score in this range become ill during the following year as their immune systems diminish, making it less likely that they can fight off illness.

over 300: You may be under severe stress with a high number of life changes over the last year. It is very important for you to recognize the number of changes that you have had to adapt to, and to cut yourself some slack. Practising some stress management techniques is highly advised for you. In general, about three-quarters of the people who score in this range get ill during the following year as their immune systems diminish, making it less likely that they can fight off illness.

Sources: Adapted from Brehm, 1998; Anderson, 1972.

4. Pressure

pressure
what we feel when there are many expectations placed upon us

A further general source of stress, common to everyone but perhaps especially to students, is **pressure**. Pressure is what we feel when many expectations are placed upon us. These expectations can come from a number of sources. For Pietro, the sources are:

■ his parents—who have great expectations of him, telling him continually that they are proud of his ability as reflected by his grades.

■ his teachers—Pietro was in a small school with a very demanding program in which each student was personally known to the teachers. He felt their expectations of him all the time: he liked them, they liked him, and he didn't want to disappoint them by doing poorly in his work or missing deadlines. He still feels that he must make them proud of him by excelling in post-secondary school.

■ himself—Pietro is also experiencing stress from the pressure he puts on himself. He is a perfectionist and is having a difficult time recognizing that perfection is impossible in most cases, and that his workload means that while he can (and should) strive for excellence and his personal best, all he can really do is the best he can with the time and resources that he has. Pietro's expectations of himself are unrealistic and are causing him trouble.

In many cases, people experience pressure from more than one source. The stress from expectations placed upon us, even if they are our own, can be crushing.

5. Daily Hassles

daily hassles
the problems that come up in day-to-day life that the individual must cope with

The final general source of stress that we need to examine is that of **daily hassles**. We may actually cope with the big stresses of life better than with some small stresses because these big events come infrequently and we typically have support from our friends and family at these times (Kanner, Coyne, Schaefer, & Lazarus, 1981). For example, how often do we really have to make life-changing decisions? And when we do, the people around us usually try to help or at least sympathize with what we're going through. This is also the case when major life-change events occur, such as a death in the family. But what about this all-too-common scenario for Pietro?

He slept in. His alarm clock didn't go off and now he was going to be late for a test. He jumped out of bed, stepping into something that the cat coughed up. Racing to the shower, he found that there was no hot water. He pulled on the same clothes he'd worn yesterday since nothing else was clean. Come to think of it, yesterday's clothes weren't too clean either. He grabbed a container of milk out of the refrigerator and raced out the door, only to see the bus leaving before he could get to it. The next bus was not due for 10 minutes, so he sat on a bench (he'd find out later that it had just been painted and was not dry yet) and opened his milk. One mighty gulp told him in no uncertain terms that the milk was sour. Now feeling sick, he got on the bus and found that he had left his wallet containing his bus fare at home. He got off the bus, went back, and was highly tempted just to go back to bed. The rest of Pietro's day didn't get any better.

Does this type of scenario feel familiar? We all have those kinds of days sometimes. Nothing earthshakingly horrible happens, but every conceivable hassle seems to come our way. Pietro's example is an extreme one, but it's important to point out that the daily hassles are stressful too, and they, like all other stress, add up until the amount of stress in our day has become choking. In examining the daily hassles more closely, note that they can be grouped as you can see in Table 3.1 (Lazarus, DeLongis, Folkman, & Gruen, 1985). Take the test in Exercise 3.3 to see how much daily hassles affect your life.

TABLE 3.1 Daily Hassles

Household hassles	Planning, shopping for, and preparing meals; home maintenance, etc.
Health hassles	Minor physical illness, concern about medication/medical treatment, etc.
Time-pressure hassles	Really having too much to do in too little time, too many responsibilities, etc.
Inner-concern hassles	Being lonely, unassertive, etc.
Environmental hassles	Crime, neighbourhood deterioration, excess traffic noise, dormitory noise, etc.
Financial/responsibility hassles	Concern about owing money, tuition payments, cost of books, etc.
Work hassles	Job dissatisfaction, problems with co-workers or boss, hours conflicting with school, etc.
Future security hassles	Concern about job security, concern about a future career, etc.

Source: Adapted from Lazarus, DeLongis, Folkman, & Gruen, 1985.

EXERCISE 3.3

▶ *Hassles Scale for Students in College*

Instructions

The items below describe circumstances you may sometimes find unpleasant if they make you frustrated, irritated, or anxious. Think of them as events—they happen and end. For your experiences in the past month or so, circle the ratings next to each event to describe its frequency, the degree of unpleasantness it usually produced for you, and the extent to which you dwelled on or were bothered by it when the actual event was not present (before or after). Use all three rating scales, which are defined below.

Frequency: rate how often in the past month or so the event occurred, using a scale that ranges from 0 = "never" to 5 = "extremely often."

Unpleasantness: rate how unpleasant the event usually was when it actually happened, using a scale that ranges from 0 = "Not at all" to 4 = "Extremely unpleasant." Mark 0 if the event didn't occur.

Dwelling: rate the extent to which you usually were bothered by each event when it was not actually present, before or after it occurred. Use a scale from 1 to 5, where 1 means you dwelled on it either not at all or very little (thinking about it briefly for less than an hour) and 5 means you dwelled on it very often and for more than a week. Mark 1 if the event didn't occur.

	Never/not at all				Extremely

1. Annoying social behaviour of others (e.g., rude, inconsiderate, sexist/racist)

Frequency:	0	1	2	3	4	5
Unpleasantness:	0	1	2	3	4	
Dwelling:		1	2	3	4	5

2. Appearance of self (e.g., noticing unattractive features, grooming, weight)

Frequency:	0	1	2	3	4	5
Unpleasantness:	0	1	2	3	4	
Dwelling:		1	2	3	4	5

3. Accidents/clumsiness/mistakes of self (e.g., spilling beverage, tripping)

Frequency:	0	1	2	3	4	5
Unpleasantness:	0	1	2	3	4	
Dwelling:		1	2	3	4	5

4. Boredom (e.g., nothing to do, current activity uninteresting)

Frequency:	0	1	2	3	4	5
Unpleasantness:	0	1	2	3	4	
Dwelling:		1	2	3	4	5

5. Dating (e.g., noticing lack of, uninteresting partner)

Frequency:	0	1	2	3	4	5
Unpleasantness:	0	1	2	3	4	
Dwelling:		1	2	3	4	5

6. Extracurricular groups (e.g., activities, responsibilities)

Frequency:	0	1	2	3	4	5
Unpleasantness:	0	1	2	3	4	
Dwelling:		1	2	3	4	5

7. Family: obligations or activities, relationship issues

Frequency:	0	1	2	3	4	5
Unpleasantness:	0	1	2	3	4	
Dwelling:		1	2	3	4	5

8. Food (e.g., unappealing or unhealthful meals)

Frequency:	0	1	2	3	4	5
Unpleasantness:	0	1	2	3	4	
Dwelling:		1	2	3	4	5

9. Forgetting to do things (e.g., to tape TV show, send cards, do homework)

Frequency:	0	1	2	3	4	5
Unpleasantness:	0	1	2	3	4	
Dwelling:		1	2	3	4	5

10. Friends/girl/boyfriend: relationship issues, annoyances

Frequency:	0	1	2	3	4	5
Unpleasantness:	0	1	2	3	4	
Dwelling:		1	2	3	4	5

11. Getting up early (e.g., for class or work)

Frequency:	0	1	2	3	4	5
Unpleasantness:	0	1	2	3	4	
Dwelling:		1	2	3	4	5

12. Exams and grades (e.g., preparing for exams, getting a low grade)

Frequency:	0	1	2	3	4	5
Unpleasantness:	0	1	2	3	4	
Dwelling:		1	2	3	4	5

13. Health/physical symptoms of self (e.g., flu, PMS, allergies, headaches)

Frequency:	0	1	2	3	4	5
Unpleasantness:	0	1	2	3	4	
Dwelling:		1	2	3	4	5

14. Schoolwork (e.g., working on term papers, reading tedious/hard material, low motivation)

Frequency:	0	1	2	3	4	5
Unpleasantness:	0	1	2	3	4	
Dwelling:		1	2	3	4	5

15. Job/work issues (e.g., searching for or interviews, demands or annoying aspects)

Frequency:	0	1	2	3	4	5
Unpleasantness:	0	1	2	3	4	
Dwelling:		1	2	3	4	5

16. Lateness of self (e.g., for appointment or class)

Frequency:	0	1	2	3	4	5
Unpleasantness:	0	1	2	3	4	
Dwelling:		1	2	3	4	5

17. Money: noticing lack of

Frequency:	0	1	2	3	4	5
Unpleasantness:	0	1	2	3	4	
Dwelling:		1	2	3	4	5

18.   Oral presentations/public speaking

Frequency:	0	1	2	3	4	5
Unpleasantness:	0	1	2	3	4	
Dwelling:		1	2	3	4	5

19.   Privacy: noticing lack of

Frequency:	0	1	2	3	4	5
Unpleasantness:	0	1	2	3	4	
Dwelling:		1	2	3	4	5

20.   Instructors/coaches (e.g., unfairness, demands of, unavailability)

Frequency:	0	1	2	3	4	5
Unpleasantness:	0	1	2	3	4	
Dwelling:		1	2	3	4	5

21.   Tedious everyday chores (e.g., shopping, cleaning apartment)

Frequency:	0	1	2	3	4	5
Unpleasantness:	0	1	2	3	4	
Dwelling:		1	2	3	4	5

22.   Time demands/deadlines

Frequency:	0	1	2	3	4	5
Unpleasantness:	0	1	2	3	4	
Dwelling:		1	2	3	4	5

Scoring:

Add your scores for each of frequency, unpleasantness, and dwelling. Most post-secondary students score around 50 for frequency, 40 for unpleasantness, and 55 for dwelling.

If your score is below 50 for frequency, you probably have the same number of daily hassles as your classmates. Lucky you if your score is below, and poor you if your score is higher! If your score is substantially higher than 50, did you realize you had so many daily hassles? Can you reduce the number in any way? For example, if you have a number of hassles with relationships (family, peers, girl/boyfriend), perhaps you can find ways of resolving conflicts or you can spend more time with other people.

On the scale measuring unpleasantness, women often score higher than men do, but both sexes find most daily hassles they experience to be aversive. If your score is higher than 40, take note of which hassles are the most unpleasant for you. Is there something you can do to make some of your daily hassles less unpleasant? For example, if cleaning your room or apartment is a hassle for you, consider sharing the task with someone else (e.g., on Mondays your space is cleaned by the two of you, on Tuesdays his or hers is tackled). Playing music while you clean is helpful too.

The scale measuring dwelling is an important one: a score over 55 suggests that you spend a lot of time worrying about the hassle. Is this true for you? If so, is it because you aren't confident of your ability to handle the hassle? Or do you expect further negative events to occur? Examine your thoughts about this. Box 3.2 may help you in changing your thinking about the hassles.

Source: Adapted from Sarafino & Ewing, 1999.

WHAT ARE THE STRESSES THAT STUDENTS FEEL THE MOST?

In a survey, 100 male and female students at a university in the American Midwest were asked about the areas in which they felt the most stress. Box 3.1 shows their top results (Ross, Niebling, & Heckert, 1999). How do these results compare to the stresses you feel in your life? Note that these areas of stress are really what we would call daily hassles, and some of them seem quite specific and perhaps a little puzzling (e.g., how is a vacation break so stressful for students?).

Stresses on Students

BOX 3.1

Ross and her colleagues (1999) found the following numbers of students (out of 100) reporting these stresses. Almost all students reported several areas of stress.

Source of Stress	Number of Students Reporting This Source
Change in sleeping habits	89
Vacation/breaks	82
Change in eating habits	74
Increased class workload	73
New responsibilities	73
Change in social activities	71
Financial difficulties	71
Waiting in long lines	69
Computer problems	69
Lower grade than anticipated	68
Held a job	65
Roommate conflict	61
Spoke in public	60

Source: Reprinted by permission of Project Innovation, Inc.

Additional surveys examining the stresses on students found that other areas were implicated as well (Ross et al., 1999). In no particular order, these include:

■ Being away from home for the first time

■ Finding a job

■ Finding a potential life partner

■ Unclear assignments

■ Uncomfortable classrooms

■ Relations with faculty members

■ Time pressures

■ Relationships with family and friends

■ Loneliness

These stresses have powerful effects on students. For example, the more students felt stresses, the more they saw themselves as not as bright or competent at school or work, not as socially integrated into the environment, and not even as physically attractive (Goldman & Wong, 1997). In short, their self-esteem was low. Also, students with high stress typically do not have healthy lifestyles; for example, they are more likely to eat junk food, smoke, etc. (Hudd et al., 2000). Whether stress lowers self-esteem or whether students with low self-esteem to begin with feel more stress, we don't know.

Students who have been out of school and then return have pretty much the same amount of stress that other students have, but their stress tends to lie in other areas. The returning student usually has developed a life away from school that may include a job and family. One of the large stresses of the returning student, then, lies in juggling role demands and at-home responsibilities with the demands of being a student. The returning student does have certain advantages, though: he or she usually enjoys classes and homework more, and has less concern about meeting family expectations about grades or making friends (Dill & Henley, 1998).

DON'T OUR INSTRUCTORS SEE HOW STRESSED WE ARE?

Yes, they do. In the first place, your instructors have been in the situation you're in now. Also, think about when they see you: for the most part, in class, often as one of a sea of faces. Often the only time they see you individually is when you approach them with a problem. When asked about how much stress they think students are under, faculty members believed that students were under more stress than the students themselves thought they were under (Misra, McKean, West, & Russo, 2000)! Many of you are now muttering to yourself, "Then why do they put so much stress on us?" In some cases, of course, they do put undue stress on you, perhaps because they are unaware of how heavy the workload they impose is or how high their expectations are. But in most cases, the simple and painful truth is that the problem is not with the instructors, but with the way you approach your work and deal with your stress. This is not meant as a criticism of you. This is all part of learning the skills involved in being a student at the post-secondary level, and that's what this book is about. And by the way, your instructors are under a good deal of stress themselves: it isn't always easy to stand up in front of perhaps 200 students (who are often the toughest audience in the world), and to lecture and be ready for any questions that might be thrown your way. The student has to get 50 or 60 percent to pass a course (depending on the subject and the school), but the instructor has to know 100 percent to teach the course. Then there is the issue of marking, performing research, writing, doing administration, and so on. No one is having a stress-free life!

HOW CAN WE STOP STRESSING OURSELVES OUT?

Before we look at dealing with the stresses the world puts on us, we need to examine ourselves. In most cases, we judge something to be stressful because of the way we interpret the situation and the things we say to ourselves. Have you ever noticed yourself saying very negative things to yourself, things that are much meaner than anything you would say to someone else? When Pietro does poorly on a test, he thinks, "Idiot! You're not smart, you'll fail this course, and you'll probably get thrown out of school." It's easy for us to see that Pietro is thinking some pretty nasty and illogical thoughts, putting a great deal of pressure on himself as well as feeding his frustration. He's putting more pressure on himself when he thinks about losing his girlfriend: "You're such a loser. Why would anyone want to be in a relationship with you?" he thinks. If someone else kept saying such things to us, we would avoid that individual completely. But if someone we couldn't avoid and who knew us well kept saying those things, we would probably start to believe it and to feel worse and worse about ourselves. We would start to fear that we would fail in everything we did. Eventually, we would probably stop trying.

Psychologists such as Albert Ellis (1994) think that this is exactly what many of us do, increasing our stress and our potential to be depressed. Pietro is thinking and forming expectations in absolute terms: if you fail one test, you'll fail every course; if one girl breaks up with you, no one will ever love you. If someone other than yourself (such as a friend of yours) made such a statement, you would probably be very quick to point out its unreasonableness. Ellis suggests that we do this for ourselves, be a good friend to ourselves and not let ourselves get away with such irrational thinking. He has devised what he calls the **ABCD technique** to change irrational thinking in ourselves. In this technique, you learn to replace negative self-statements with more realistic positive self-statements. Your negative self-statements (based on illogic) have led you to believe something that is bad about yourself, and in the same way, positive self-statements (based on logical thinking) can lead you to believe something much better about yourself. This technique isn't difficult to learn, and with practice it can become automatic. Best of all, many, many people report that it really helps to cut down on self-imposed stress. Try the technique in Box 3.2, and

ABCD technique
a self-help method to change irrational thinking in ourselves by learning to replace negative self-statements with more realistic positive self-statements

---

Albert Ellis's ABCD Method for Eliminating Irrational Thinking   **BOX 3.2**

1. Identify the **A**ntecedent event(s). For example, if you are feeling down because you have just done poorly on a test, a presentation, or an interview, the antecedent event is your poor performance.

2. Identify the **B**elief. That is, determine what faulty thought process(es) you are using. For example, you may be thinking "I seem to fail no matter what I do. I really should always perform in a stellar fashion. I'm just not as good as everybody else. Either you perform perfectly or you're a failure."

3. Identify the **C**onsequence. That is, the feeling. In this example, the consequence of these irrational beliefs is feeling down. Notice how the faulty beliefs will only lead to feeling badly, but will not solve the problem.

4. **D**ispute the irrational beliefs and **D**evelop alternatives to the faulty processing styles. Thus, you might think, "Just because I did poorly this one time doesn't mean that I'll do poorly in the future, or that I'm a failure. Instead of feeling sorry for myself, I'll try to determine why I didn't do well so I can do better next time." Notice that these rational beliefs will not only help you to feel better, but will also help you take control to perform better in the future.

To stop irrational thoughts, you need to say or think "Stop!" to yourself, or even snap a rubber band on your wrist. (Yes, it's supposed to hurt a little! That's what will stop you!)

Sources: Ellis, 1994; McGinn, 1997.

---

be persistent. Over time, what you are telling yourself intellectually will filter down to the emotional level, thereby reducing the pressure you put on yourself and getting rid of some self-imposed obstacles that cause you frustration.

Closely related to this is a strategy called **situational reconstruction**. In this strategy, we rely upon the idea that stress is in the eye of the beholder, that whether you find a situation stressful or not really depends on how you perceive the situation.

One example we have used before is the social situation of a party: if Pietro could perceive a party as a chance to relax and enjoy being with friends, possibly even to meet new friends, he would most likely see the party as a means of reducing stress. But since he regards this social situation as one in which he has to perform to keep people entertained and where his worth will be judged based on his social skills (which a shy person has little confidence in), a party will be stress-inducing. With situational reconstruction, Pietro recognizes that how he perceives and interprets a situation is up to him: he has a choice. He can choose to see the situation as stress-inducing, or he can change his thoughts by questioning his perception and interpretation of it (the ABCD technique is one means of doing this), leading him to see it from a different perspective. For example, he may view the party as a chance to listen to other people and make himself known as an attentive listener who is a joy to have around.

As another example, when you don't get the job you want, instead of telling yourself what a tragedy this is and how you will never be happy and must be a failure, etc., you can choose to tell yourself, "It just wasn't for me. A better job is out there for me, and now I know what more I need to be qualified for a job like this one," etc. Likewise, when your instructor switches to a new software right after you have learned the old one, you can see this change as a source of stress, or, more adaptively, you can see it as a challenge. Situational reconstruction is what your family and instructors are talking about when we tell you, "Take this as a learning experience." Instead of feeling so personally threatened and diminished by a disappointment, try to be more objective and discover what the experience can teach you. The more you learn from the experience, the more you can take control of your life and avoid such an experience in the future. Techniques such as these are called **appraisal-focused coping** because we modify our appraisal or evaluation of the situation and our own abilities in order to recognize that the stress is manageable for us.

situational reconstruction
changing one's thoughts about a situation by questioning one's interpretation of the situation, leading one to see it from a different perspective

appraisal-focused coping
modifying our appraisal or evaluation of the situation and our own abilities in order to recognize that the stress is manageable

SPECIFIC PERSONAL STRESSES

HOW CAN I HANDLE THE STRESS OF LONELINESS?

It was clear in looking at the reports of students that other people provide both comfort and stress for them. Many students entering a post-secondary institution are away from their family and friends for the first time in their lives. In some cases, they may be international students, away from their families, their countries, and their cultures. They may not know anyone else on campus. They feel isolated and lonely. If they are shy to begin with, the feeling may be worse. This is, of course, completely natural, but what can we do about it? The answer is to make friends. But this is not always so easy. Box 3.3 gives some suggestions for making friends and overcoming loneliness.

Dealing with Loneliness   BOX 3.3

- Don't mistake aloneness for loneliness. Sometimes solitude is a refreshing and renewing experience. If you are busy, optimistic, and able to look within yourself for interesting things to do and think about, you probably don't need to have people around you all the time. If you are not accustomed to having solitude (e.g., you are one of many children), you may assume that you need other people's presence to keep from feeling lonely. This isn't the case.

- Don't assume that you have to get rid of loneliness quickly. If you really do feel lonely, try just experiencing it for a little while. You may learn things about yourself that the presence of other people masked. Western society assumes that any negative feeling is "abnormal" and must be banished immediately. But negative feelings are part of life, and loneliness is an experience for everyone. Embracing it (not actively pursuing it!) may result in a growth period for you.

- Take an interest in your environment, especially if the environment is new to you. Look around, see what the surroundings are. What's going on in different parts of the campus, for example? What areas look particularly pleasant? Let your face reflect your interest: other people are very attracted to people who look pleasant and interested.

- Talk to people, especially around campus and in your classes. Start slow, with a smile and pleasantries and questions ("That's a really beautiful fountain." "Do you know what's in that building?") to open a conversation. Look for other people who also seem to be alone to start conversations with.

- Learn the art of chatting. In your initial conversations with people, keep the conversation pleasant (e.g., this is *not* the time to list your complaints!) and relatively superficial (e.g., this is *not* the time to discuss the surgery you had last year either!). If you have problems with light social encounters, consider taking a class in social skills. The counselling centre at your school either has these classes or can point you to classes in your area.

- Join clubs or activity groups. Students who do this feel more integrated into their post-secondary environment and have a much more enjoyable experience. What are you interested in? Whatever your hobbies or interests are, from sports to stamp collecting, there is a good chance that your school has a club devoted to that area. Find out what is available and join. There are probably also groups based on ethnic or religious affiliations too. By all means check this out. But remember not to devote yourself entirely to groups of people who have similar backgrounds and interests as you: an important part of post-secondary education is to broaden your experience of others' viewpoints and interests.

- Make the acquaintance of several people, but don't rush into being close friends with the first person who says hello. You may find yourself swept into a group of people that you are not comfortable with or who would not be of your choosing. Be aware that befriending a lonely and sad-looking newcomer is sometimes a technique used by cults and manipulative and exploitative groups, so be selective in your choice of friends. By the same token, you may be tempted to rely on chat rooms on the Internet for your social activity. These can be fun, but they must never take the place of connecting with people in person.

- Keep in touch with old friends, especially as you are making the transition to your new environment. E-mail is wonderful for this, but again, don't rely on it to the exclusion of making contact with people you come face-to-face with.

- Be careful of new online relationships and romances. Remember that although it can be very comfortable to talk to other people without the pressure of seeing them face-to-face, it is also possible to hide much more from others in this way. When we talk to people face-to-face, we can see their expressions, hear the inflections in their voices, read their body language. We get a great deal of information about them in this way, and this is lacking when our only information comes from the written word online. Use caution: keep yourself safe, both physically and emotionally.

HOW CAN I HANDLE THE STRESS OF ROMANTIC RELATIONSHIPS?

Students also indicate that one of their major concerns has to do with romantic relationships: finding one, maintaining one, and dealing with a breakup. These stresses are not unique to students! The best way to find a romantic relationship is to make friends. This is the place for a special note, however: try very hard not to make friends *only* with those who are like you. Part of the education you should receive is in getting to know and value people from different backgrounds, countries, and belief systems. And if you find a romantic relationship here, that's wonderful. Falling in love involves stress, and people rarely think clearly (especially at the beginning of a new relationship), so be aware of this.

There may be another problem: romantic relationships are more likely to last if the partners share a basic value structure (e.g., Lauer & Lauer, 1985). This means that both of you need to agree on such things as a philosophy of life (e.g., is it a dog-eat-dog world, or is universal kindness the preferred route?). You do not need to share all the same viewpoints and interests, and it makes absolutely no difference if one of you likes to eat popcorn at the movies while the other likes peanuts. But it does matter if one of you finds adherence to a religious system to be important in life while the other feels negatively toward religions. It matters if one of you believes that involvement with the extended family is the obligation of every person, while the other believes that once you leave home, your only obligation to family is to visit occasionally. That is, the little things don't matter, but the big things do. If you start a romantic relationship with someone who does not share your core values, you may run into extra difficulties in the relationship.

Maintaining a good relationship once you have found it is tricky as well. Couples who have been together for many years have been asked how they do it (Lauer & Lauer, 1985), and their answers are revealing. They emphasize the importance of *liking* their spouses as individuals. They stress the need to be committed to the idea of the relationship, hanging in when times get tough and working out issues as they arise. In addition, the communication patterns of married couples can predict whether they will stay together or not (Gottman, 1994). It seems that couples who eventually break up are more likely to criticize each other more, become defensive in the face of problems rather than work them out, refuse to listen to each other, and use a tone that indicates contempt for each other. In other words, these couples really don't seem to treat each other very well. Learning to communicate in a constructive fashion is obviously important in maintaining a relationship, and in all areas of our lives. Sometimes when we quarrel with a person we care about, we find ourselves saying and doing things that we really don't mean. That makes the situation worse, and whatever it was that we were quarrelling about doesn't get resolved. Box 3.4 lists some suggestions for how to quarrel without being destructive to the relationship.

Often, however, romantic relationships just don't work out. It may be that neither person in the relationship has done anything wrong, nor are there insurmountable problems. It may be that two perfectly wonderful people just don't belong together. That may be sad, but it happens all the time. The painful reality is that it takes two people to make a relationship, but only one to break it, and a relationship breakup is one of the very difficult events that most of us have to deal with.

Let's take the case of Stacy and Irwin. They met in the first semester of college and have been going together for a year. In the beginning, they were extremely happy, but they had very unrealistic expectations about their relationship. Stacy, for example, was often heard to say, "Irwin always knows how I feel without my having to say a word." Stacy was apparently mistaking Irwin for a clairvoyant! No matter how sensitive Irwin has been to her, he isn't a mind reader, and now, a year later, Stacy is finding that perhaps Irwin doesn't read her as well as she thought. Irwin was equally unrealistic. When the relationship was in its early stages, Irwin thought, "I'll never be lonely again." But everyone is lonely sometimes, and to expect Stacy to be able to fulfill all of his needs all the time was really unfair of Irwin. Even so, he now feels a little cheated. So this couple is about to break up. In an ideal world, they could talk about this and part with mutual accord and amicability, but such

How to Quarrel Constructively

BOX 3.4

1. Quarrel about only one thing at a time. We have a tendency to drag every "wrong" the other person has committed into the argument. This diverts the discussion away from the real issue of the quarrel, and nothing is resolved. Old issues should have been handled when they came up, not stored for future quarrels.

2. Sometimes we say or do very hurtful things and then walk away, slam a door, or hang up the phone. That isn't fair. We have wounded the other person terribly and then abandoned him or her to the pain. If you find yourself doing this, come back or phone back.

3. Don't shout. People who shout sometimes "win" an argument, but the reality is that they have only proven that they can shout louder than the other person. Shouting louder is often a bullying action, or at least it is perceived that way. Shouting doesn't make a point or resolve an issue: it just makes people resentful. Besides, keeping your voice level and pitched down commands attention.

4. Have you ever found yourself exaggerating when you quarrel? For example, "You always ignore me!" Always? In every single encounter? Really? "You never want to do what I want to do." Never? Not even once? This kind of exaggeration only hurts your credibility and complicates the argument needlessly.

5. Use "I" statements rather than "you" statements. Accusations such as "You never think about anybody else" are bound to provoke resentment and defensiveness, whereas statements such as "I feel hurt when I think you don't care about my feelings" are much more likely to elicit concern and a desire to resolve the issue.

6. Does this interaction sound familiar? "What's wrong?" "Nothing." "Come on, I know something's wrong. What is it?" "Nothing, I told you." "Are you sure? It seems to me like there's something wrong." "You know very well what's wrong!" Forcing the other person to be a mind reader or giving him or her the silent treatment doesn't work in most cases, and it really isn't fair. Tell the other person what's wrong as clearly as possible. This is no time for miscommunication!

7. If the argument is getting too heated and you find yourself about to say or do something extreme, call for a time-out. Both of you need to walk away at this point and agree to meet later to discuss the issue calmly.

8. Once you have heard what the other person is saying, try to repeat it in your own words: "So what you're saying is. . . ." This will ensure that you are getting the right message, without distortion caused by the anger of the moment, and it will reassure the other person that he/she is really being heard.

9. Don't ever do anything physical—no hitting, pushing, grabbing, or poking with a pointing finger. Do not throw things. If you do somehow break something or spill something, it is up to you to clean up and replace the broken item, no matter who is wrong or right in the argument. Physical responses only demonstrate that a person has lost control or is trying to intimidate someone else.

10. Don't retaliate: "You did it to me, so I'm going to do it to you so you'll see how it feels." This rarely works. It only shows that you can do something as wrong as the other person. Two wrongs never make a right. Take the high road instead.

11. Don't bring other people into the argument. This means that you shouldn't ask another person to join with you in berating someone else, and it means that you shouldn't use someone else's name and opinion in your quarrel ("My sister said you were wrong.") The quarrel is between two people and should remain that way.

12. If you threaten something, be prepared to follow through. So never say, "I'm leaving" or "I'll never speak to you again," for example, unless you are in fact ready to do just that. Otherwise you will lower your credibility for the future.

13. Recognize that blaming will never resolve an issue. And that's your goal, isn't it? So, as soon as an issue arises, attack it as "our problem" rather than "your problem" and join together to look for workable solutions.

mutuality is rare in life. Typically what happens is that one member of the couple makes the break, that is, one member is the "dumper" and one is the "dumpee." In this case, Stacy is making the break and telling Irwin that she wants to end the relationship. Irwin is very troubled by this and wants to try again. Stacy says, "No, but we'll still be friends."

That line is so popular: "We'll still be friends." But is it possible? And if so, how can it come about? Stacy feels guilty, especially since Irwin hasn't done anything "wrong." This guilt may lead Stacy to hold out hope for Irwin to assuage her guilt, or perhaps because she feels that she may be making a mistake and at some future time she will feel differently, or because Stacy has been close to Irwin for so long that she can't really imagine life without him. What this actually means is that Stacy may want to have her cake and eat it too. So she may soften the blow by saying to Irwin, "I need some time to myself," and Irwin is given the faint hope that if he hangs in there waiting for Stacy to make up her mind, they may become a couple again. This may be OK if Stacy truly does want some space to re-evaluate her commitment to Irwin, but in that case, a time limit should be put on the separation and Stacy should be seen to be doing some real work, whether it involves meditating on a mountaintop or seeing a counsellor. But often, a dumper like Stacy does nothing with the "space" offered her because she really did want her freedom from Irwin. Stacy certainly doesn't mean to be cruel, but she is: she is keeping Irwin's emotional wound from healing because the wound is forced to stay open with the faint hope that she will finally decide to come back.

Stacy, in trying to assuage her guilt and perhaps because she does want Irwin waiting in the wings in case she finds she made a mistake, calls Irwin several times after the breakup, "just to see if he is doing all right" and to "stay friends." Again, this is cruelty because it keeps hope alive in Irwin, who desperately wants Stacy to keep calling, just to maintain any contact with his loved one. The wound can't heal when someone keeps picking at the scab. Logically speaking, Irwin's response to Stacy's offer to stay friends should be "not yet," but he's bleeding; Irwin may be so upset that he is willing to take whatever crumbs of comfort are offered. He doesn't want the relationship to be over and is urgently looking for ways to hang on to it, even if he doesn't realize he's doing this. He may say, "I know it's over," but he's still asking his friends, "Do you think she will ever come back?" and having fantasies about the relationship being healed. We can see more clearly than he can that Irwin has not, in fact, accepted the breakup.

The question "Can a couple remain friends after a breakup?" is answered in this way: Stacy and Irwin would both rejoice if a close friend told them that he/she had met the person of his/her dreams and they were going to marry. Until Stacy and Irwin can feel this way about each other, that is, until each is able with a glad heart to dance at the other's wedding, they can't be friends. When they really do accept the end of the relationship and move on with their own lives, they may feel a slight pang on hearing of the other's romantic success with someone else, but mainly they will be glad, just as they would for any other friend.

The effects of being dumped are, to a large extent, grief reactions, just as one feels when a death has occurred. In this case, the relationship—with all its hopes and dreams and plans—has died. In addition, there are feelings of inadequacy, diminished self-worth, diminished confidence, and often a lack of trust in people/relationships/the world, especially for the person who has been dumped. Box 3.5 lists some suggestions for getting over a breakup, but we must all remember that it takes time, a lot of time.

HOW CAN WE REDUCE STRESS MORE GENERALLY?

Some people live in a perpetual state of anxiety and tension. In the very complicated and very busy world we live in, most of us have at least periods of time when we feel a state of chronic, unremitting stress. How do we deal with this? Often we take approaches that aren't very adaptive, such as drinking, taking drugs, overeating, sleeping too much, procrastinating, getting into arguments with people around us, and so on. This indicates that stress is controlling us; we are not controlling our stress.

In order to manage stress, we need to work on techniques before the difficult times are upon us; we need to practise when we are relatively unstressed. If you were going to run a marathon, you wouldn't start training the day before the race, would you? By the same token, in order to deal with stressful times, you need to start training in advance. There are strategies that people who deal well with stress can vouch for and that research has indicated are very beneficial. People who use some of these strategies actually feel less stress when times get rough and they deal with stress more effectively. What are these wonderful techniques?

The first is to take good care of yourself. Eat properly, get enough sleep, don't overindulge in alcohol, and don't smoke—all the things that you probably already know

How to Get Over a Breakup   BOX 3.5

1. Call a moratorium on contact with the ex. Unless the breakup has truly been a matter of the two you laughing together and saying, "Hey, we're better at being friends than at being lovers!" (which is the case perhaps one time in ten thousand), you need time for the wound to heal, whether you are the one who initiated the breakup or not. It will not heal if you stay in contact with each other right after the breakup. Give yourself a few months apart, at least. Remember the guideline: You can't be friends until you can dance at each other's wedding.

2. Don't try to run away from the grief you feel over the loss of the relationship. The grief is a part of life and a valuable growth experience for you. Trying to avoid pain by excessive drinking, drug-taking, jumping into another relationship, or (fill in the blank with your favourite distraction)—these techniques never work in the long run, and just make more trouble in the short run. That doesn't mean you should never use distraction: no one can spend all the time grieving without doing harm. But don't deny your pain either—it's part of you.

3. Social support helps us cope with all kinds of stress, so surround yourself with supportive friends. Let them know that you don't need them to tell you how horrible your ex was (the relationship wasn't completely horrible or you wouldn't be in pain now!) or to tell you to cheer up (obviously you would if you could!). Let them know that the support you need from them comes from their unfailing belief in your worth and strength, their desire to allow you to mend at your own pace, and their help both in listening to you express your emotions and in distracting you. Be aware that when you ask them for advice of any kind ("What should I do to get him/her back?" for example), you are putting the responsibility for your choice of action on them, not shouldering it yourself. Don't blame them if their suggestions fail. Similarly, if you are asked for advice, be aware that you are taking on someone else's responsibility and, if your advice doesn't work out, you may be blamed for it. Ask your friends to help you come up with a variety of

options for what you *can* do instead of advice on what you *should* do. Then make the decisions yourself.

4. It may be that you feel diminished as a result of the breakup. This is more likely if you were not the one who initiated it. Understand that the *relationship* failed, not *you*, as a person, and that there is a welcoming future for you, even if you are not part of a couple. Ellis's ABCD technique can be very useful in the face of negative and illogical self-talk, such as unreasonable self-blaming.

5. This is the time to be very good to yourself physically and emotionally. Eat, sleep, and exercise regularly. Pamper yourself. Sometimes chocolate really does help, and so might a day at a spa, or checking out new cars, or spending hours watching football games. Do whatever makes you feel good.

6. While social support from established friends is very helpful, take the opportunity to join new clubs or activity groups and meet new people. But don't get into a romance on the rebound. Doing this is a temptation since it may soothe a shaky sense of self-esteem, but you first need a chance to mourn your lost relationship and to re-establish your sense of yourself on your own, apart from the old relationship. Besides, a rebound romance rarely works out and isn't fair to the new person, even if he/she understands and is willing to take the chance.

7. This is a perfect time for you to indulge yourself in interests and activities on which you haven't spent much time in the past. Try a new sport or hobby, or take a course in something you've always been interested in. This will not only distract you and allow you to meet new people, but it will also increase your feeling of self-efficacy, and so, your self-esteem.

8. Give yourself a couple of months to feel badly, but if after that time you find yourself unable to think about much besides your ex or how horrible the situation is or how you have no future without your ex, consider getting some professional help. Your school counselling centre can help you in this.

about. There's a reason why you have been told over and over to do these things: they really do work to reduce stress and to keep you functioning at your best (Weiten & Lloyd, 2003)!

Physical exercise is also important. People who exercise regularly cope with stress better, in terms of both their physical reactions to stress and their psychological reactions (Hays, 1999; Plante, Capoto, & Chizmar, 2000). Some exercises are better than others: if you want to reduce stress, competitive sports wouldn't be a good choice! People who do aerobic exercises that increase the heart rate are helped to deal with the adrenalin surge that comes with stress (Lee, Rexrode, Cook, Manson, & Buring, 2001). People who do exercises such as yoga or t'ai chi are helped in maintaining concentration when stress is upon them because these exercises also function as a form of meditation (Schafer, 1996). We'll discuss meditation more later.

deep muscle relaxation
a method of inducing a heightened state of relaxation in the body

Relaxation is important for everyone in coping with stress. We all think that we know how to relax, and that's fine on a very casual basis. But this kind of normal relaxing doesn't go far enough in preparing ourselves to meet stress. **Deep muscle relaxation** is a technique used by doctors and psychologists for people who feel anxiety, for pain relief, for insomnia, and for a host of other problems. It seems that people who practise deep muscle relaxation cope with stress better too. The technique is outlined in Exercise 3.4. It takes daily practice to learn this technique, but once you do, you will be able to trigger relaxation in your body at a mere thought. And while it's impossible to be stressed out while you're physically relaxed, it's not impossible to think and plan!

EXERCISE 3.4

▶ *Deep Muscle Relaxation*

The object of this exercise is to become aware of the sensation of relaxation that arises when you release the tension from a muscle group. To do this, find a quiet place to lie down comfortably on your back with your hands at your sides and your eyes closed. Take two or three slow, deep breaths and relax your body as much as you can between one step and the next.

1. Clench the fist of one hand and tense your arm as much as you can; hold this position for five seconds. Concentrate on how this tension feels. Now relax your arm and let your fingers straighten out. Concentrate on how this relaxation feels. Now do the same for the other hand and arm.

2. Raise your shoulders in a shrug until you feel the tension in your shoulders and your neck. Hold this position for five seconds. Concentrate on how this tension feels. Now relax your shoulders. Concentrate on how this relaxation feels.

3. Tighten the muscles in your stomach. Hold them in this position for five seconds, concentrating on how the tension feels. Now relax your stomach muscles and concentrate on the feeling of relaxation in these muscles.

4. Tighten the muscles in your legs and concentrate on the tension for five seconds. Now relax your legs. Concentrate on how this relaxation feels.

5. Frown and close your eyes as tightly as you can for five seconds, concentrating on the feeling of tension in your face. Now relax your face and eyes. Concentrate on how this relaxation feels.

6. Clench your teeth as hard as you can for five seconds and concentrate on the tension in your jaws. Now relax and concentrate on how this relaxation feels.

7. Check your whole body: concentrate on relaxing each part of your body and imagine that all tension is flowing out of you. Stay like this for two or three minutes, then open your eyes and start to gradually look around you. Stretch lightly, and then, when you feel like it, stand up and stretch lightly. It's a good idea not to jump up since the procedure will have decreased your heart rate and blood pressure and getting up too quickly might make you dizzy.

The greatest benefits of deep muscle relaxation are achieved when you practise the procedure twice a day for about four weeks. Then, you will probably find that, in the course of your normal day when the stress gets high, you can simply *think* about a relaxation session and your body will begin to relax.

meditation
a method of using focused attention to calm the mind

mindfulness meditation
a form of meditation that concentrates on being fully aware of the body's sensations

emotion-focused coping
coping techniques that target calming a general emotional state

Another technique that has been known to the East for millennia and is only recently being used by the West is **meditation**. Once thought to be the province of only those who practise Eastern religions, meditation today is known to be a highly effective means of calming the individual and clearing the mind (e.g., see Kabat-Zinn, 1990). Like deep muscle relaxation, meditation also takes practice, but the long-term gains are large. There are many different methods of meditation, one of which is explained in Exercise 3.5. But, as all meditators know, the technique is not as important as the stilling of the chattering mind, so explore other methods as well. Several excellent books are available on these methods. One that describes several techniques and is highly entertaining is *Meditation for Dummies* (Bodian, 1999). Another is *Full Catastrophe Living* (Kabat-Zinn, 1990), which outlines a whole stress management plan based on what is called **mindfulness meditation**, a form of meditation that concentrates on being fully aware of the body's sensations. Deep muscle relaxation and meditation are called **emotion-focused coping** because they target calming our general emotional state.

EXERCISE 3.5

▶ *How to Meditate*

Meditation is a very easy practice that should be done in a quiet comfortable place, with no interruptions for the duration of meditation. So turn off the telephone, TV, radio, or anything else that might distract you. It's best to sit in a comfortable chair in which your neck and spine are supported and aligned and in which you will not fall asleep. Let your hands rest in your lap or on the arms of the chair. Relax your muscles as much as you can, and then forget about relaxation. Meditation is *not* "work," so don't spend energy trying to stay relaxed. Just observe what happens and how you feel.

Close your eyes and concentrate on your breathing without trying to control it. Silently say the word "one" or "in" every time you inhale and the word "two" or "out" every time you exhale. That's it. That's all you have to do. When (not "if") you find your mind straying away from your breathing, don't worry, just gently bring your attention back to your breathing.

Meditation is best done for about 20 minutes twice a day, but in the beginning, you may want to start with 10- or even 5-minute sessions. You can check your watch or a clock once or twice, but very soon, you will begin to estimate the time accurately. Don't use an alarm clock—it's too alarming! Most people find the times before a meal to be most conducive to meditation since the body is not busy with digestion. Similarly, it's best not to have any caffeine (coffee, tea, cola, chocolate) or nicotine (cigarettes) before meditating since these substances are stimulants that will rev you up instead of slowing you down.

End the meditation session just as you would a deep muscle relaxation session: gradually open your eyes and focus on your surroundings, get up slowly and stretch lightly to avoid dizziness from your lowered heart rate and blood pressure.

One other important technique for managing stress is finding the humour in a situation if at all possible (sometimes laughter really is the best medicine). Over the last 20 years, more and more evidence has accumulated indicating that humour can reduce stress greatly (Lefcourt, 2001). Using humour often means not taking oneself too seriously. This, in turn, may require some situational reconstruction and some modifying of self-statements for some people, but it seems to be more than worth it. For example, a colleague of ours tripped getting on the bus one day, falling right into the bus driver's lap. As she got up, she said to him, "I bet you have people falling for you all day." The bus driver and the other passengers laughed, as did she, appreciating her handling of the potentially stressful and embarrassing event with style and grace.

Have you ever kept a diary? Diaries or journals can be highly beneficial in dealing with stress. If you write down how you feel, you clarify your thinking, you have an outlet for expressing your feelings, and you have a chance to learn more about yourself (Francis & Pennebaker, 1992). You can keep a journal for specific purposes, such as monitoring a self-control procedure that you are implementing, but don't overlook the pleasures and benefits of keeping a more general journal. In this journal, you can write whatever you like; add cut-out cartoons, pictures, articles, and poetry from any source; draw pictures; do anything that resonates with you. The important point is not to censor yourself; just put in whatever comes to your mind. Try not to let your journal become simply a place to record your complaints and negative feelings; record the joys and satisfactions of your life as well. Don't feel that you have to make an entry into the journal every day. If you do that, journal keeping may become another stress in your life! Use a format that works for you. Some people prefer attractive formal journals and coloured ink, others prefer to use a computer, still others are more comfortable talking into tape recorder. Use what you wish—this is all for you! If this idea appeals to you but you aren't certain how to get started, see the online study guide that accompanies this book for journalling questions.

By practising general stress management techniques such as deep muscle relaxation and/or meditation, and by using specific techniques that have been outlined in this chapter, you will find yourself more able to deal with the stress of being a student and, we hope, get more enjoyment out of your post-secondary experience.

w(w)w

http://www
.postsecondarylearning
.nelson.com

Advice for Pietro

▶ **P**ietro clearly needs help in dealing with his stress. The table below outlines some of the things he can do to decrease his stress and function better in his personal life and in general.

PIETRO'S STRESS	WHAT HE CAN DO	THE EFFECTS
His girlfriend broke up with him.	Use the tips for getting over a breakup and give himself time to grieve.	Pietro will recover faster and with fewer long-lasting effects of the breakup.
He and his brother are fighting.	Discuss the tips for constructive quarrelling with his brother and agree to implement them the next time a quarrel erupts.	The issues between Pietro and his brother are more likely to be solved with no hurt feelings or anger on either side.
He hasn't made new friends.	Pietro needs to allot a certain proportion of his time to his social life and to use the tips for overcoming loneliness.	He will make new friends, increase his social activity, and develop a stronger social support group.
He uses negative self-statements in worrying about whether he will disappoint his parents.	Pietro can use Ellis's ABCD technique to change his negative self-statements to positive ones and use situational reconstruction to make negative experiences into learning experiences.	He will emotionally feel better and cognitively function better when he views his situation more positively and realistically.
He is getting sick.	Pietro must make sure that he is eating properly and getting enough rest and exercise.	Since stress reduces the efficiency of the immune system, developing healthy habits helps to keep the immune system at a good operating level.
He is chronically stressed.	Pietro needs to begin to use a long-term stress management technique, such as meditation, physical relaxation, yoga, or journal keeping.	When the next critical stress comes upon him, Pietro will be "trained" to deal with it much more effectively.

CHAPTER SUMMARY

■ Stress is defined as a situation that taxes our abilities to cope. What is stressful for one person may not be stressful for another, but even positive events may provide stress.

■ The experience of stress weakens our immune system and impairs our ability to think clearly. It makes us feel anxious, fearful, and even depressed. It lowers our self-confidence and decreases our enjoyment of life in general.

■ Stress comes from situations in which a goal is blocked (frustration), we have a difficult decision to make (conflict), a change occurs in our lives requiring us to adapt, or when expectations placed upon us by ourselves or others become burdensome (pressure). Stress also arises from the daily hassles that we commonly experience.

■ Many of our stresses arise from the negative self-statements we make: we tell ourselves that we are not worth much, that we will fail, and that any failure will be a total catastrophe.

Learning to make more positive and realistic statements to ourselves and learning to see stressful situations as learning experiences and challenges decrease stress substantially. In these ways we may modify our appraisal or evaluation of the situation and our own abilities in order to recognize that the stress is manageable for us.

■ Common student stressors are in the realm of social networks: lack of social support provides loneliness, while romantic relationships provide positive stress when they begin and negative stress when they end.

■ Besides learning to cope with specific stresses, we can also decrease our stress levels by practising general stress management techniques, such as proper nutrition, enough sleep, exercise, muscle relaxation, and meditation.

KEY TERMS

ABCD technique
appraisal-focused coping
approach-approach conflict
approach-avoidance conflict
avoidance-avoidance conflict
change

conflict
daily hassles
deep muscle relaxation
emotion-focused coping
frustration

meditation
mindfulness meditation
pressure
situational reconstruction
stress

INDIVIDUAL ACTIVITIES

1. What is the biggest stress in your life? Describe it fully and analyze what the sources of the stress are: frustration, pressure, change, conflict, daily hassles. Does this analysis help you to see ways of handling the stress?

2. Try some journal keeping. Get out a piece of paper and write anything that comes to your mind for a few minutes. Don't censor yourself—no one will see this but you, so write whatever you like. Tomorrow, try it again. Do this for a week, then look back on what you have written. Are there common themes coming out? For example, do your writings indicate a worry that keeps coming into your mind, or some other preoccupation? What can you do to handle this?

3. Take 10 minutes each morning or evening for a week to practise meditation. After one week, how do you feel? Is this a technique you would like to continue? Have you had particular problems with this technique? Are there other meditation techniques you might like to try?

GROUP ACTIVITIES

1. As a group, discuss experiences you have had with breakups of romantic relationships. What did you find were the most helpful and least helpful techniques for coping with a breakup?

2. In a group of four or five students, make a list of the most common negative things that people say to themselves. What positive statements could be used to take the place of these negative statements? How could you help someone to replace negative self-statements with positive self-statements?

3. Find a tape or CD designed to induce physical relaxation. With a partner, or in a group of three or four students, play the tapes and/or CDs in order to experience different relaxation techniques. Which one is best for you?

REFERENCES

Anderson, G. E. (1972). *Stress management: Increasing your stress resistance*. Unpublished master's thesis. North Dakota State University, Fargo.

Baumeister, R. F. (1984). Choking under pressure: Self-consciousness and paradoxical effects of incentives on skillful performance. *Journal of Personality and Social Psychology, 46*, 610–620.

Bodian, S. (1999). *Meditation for dummies: A reference for the rest of us*. New York: Wiley.

Brehm, B. A. (1998). *Stress management: Increasing your stress resistance*. New York: Longman.

Critelli, J. W., & Ee, J. S. (1996). Stress and physical illness: Development of an integrative model. In T. W. Miller (Ed.), *Theory and assessment of stressful life events*. Madison, CT: International Universities Press.

Dill, P. L., & Henley, T. B. (1998). Stressors of college: A comparison of traditional and nontraditional students. *Journal of Psychology, 132*, 25–32.

Ellis, A. (1994). *Reason and emotion in psychotherapy*. Secaucus, NJ: Birch Lane Press.

Francis, M. E., & Pennebaker, J. W. (1992). Putting stress into words: The impact of writing on physiological, absentee, and self-reported emotional well-being measures. *American Journal of Health Promotion, 6*, 280–287.

Goldman, C. S., & Wong, E. H. (1997). Stress and the college student. *Education, 117*, 604–611.

Gottman, J. M. (with Silver, N.). (1994). *Why marriages succeed or fail . . . And how you can make yours last*. New York: Simon & Schuster.

Hays, K. F. (1999). *Working it out: Using exercise in psychotherapy*. Washington, DC: American Psychological Association.

Holmes, T. H., & Rahe, R. H. (1967). The Social Readjustment Rating Scale. *Journal of Psychosomatic Research, 11*, 213–218.

Hubbard, J. R., & Workman, E. A. (1998). *Handbook of stress medicine: An organ system approach*. New York: CRC Press.

Hudd, S. S., Dumlao, J., Erdmann-Sager, D., Murray, D., Phan, E., Soukas, N., & Yokozuka, N. (2000). Stress at college: Effects on health habits, health status and self-esteem. *College Student Journal, 34*, 217–227.

Kabat-Zinn, J. (1990). *Full catastrophe living: Using the wisdom of your body and mind to face stress, pain, and illness*. New York: Dell.

Kanner, A. D., Coyne, J. C., Schaefer, C., & Lazarus, R. S. (1981). Comparison of two modes of stress measurement: Daily hassles and uplifts versus major life events. *Journal of Behavioral Medicine, 4*, 1–39.

Keinan, G. (1987). Decision making under stress: Scanning of alternatives under controllable and uncontrollable threats. *Journal of Personality and Social Psychology, 52*, 639–644.

Kiecolt-Glaser, J. K., & Glaser, R. (1995). Measurement of immune response. In S. Cohen, R. C. Kessler, & L. U. Gordon (Eds.), *Measuring stress: A guide for health and social scientists*. New York: Oxford University Press.

Lauer, R., & Lauer, R. (1985). Marriages made to last. *Psychology Today, 19(6)*, 22–26.

Lazarus, R. S. (1991). *Emotion and adaptation*. New York: Oxford University Press.

Lazarus, R. S. (1993). Why we should think of stress as a subset of emotion. In L. Goldberger & S. Breznitz (Eds.), *Handbook of stress: Theoretical and clinical aspects* (2nd ed.). New York: Free Press.

Lazarus, R. S., DeLongis, A., Folkman, S., & Gruen, R. (1985). Stress and adaptational outcomes: The problem of confounded measures. *American Psychologist, 40*, 77–779.

Lazarus, R. S., & Folkman, S. (1984). *Stress, appraisal and coping*. New York: Springer.

Lee, I. M., Rexrode, K. M., Cook, N. R., Manson, J. E., & Buring, J. E. (2001). Physical activity and coronary heart disease in women: Is "no pain, no gain" passé? *Journal of the American Medical Association, 285*, 1447–1454.

Lefcourt, H. M. (2001). The humor solution. In C. R. Snyder (Ed.), *Coping with stress: Effective people and processes*. New York: Oxford University Press.

McGinn, L. K. (1997). Interview: Albert Ellis on rational emotive behavior therapy. *American Journal of Psychotherapy, 51(3)*, 309–316.

Misra, R., McKean, M., West, S., & Russo, T. (2000). Academic stress of college students: Comparison of student and faculty perceptions. *College Student Journal, 34*, 236–245.

Monroe, S. M., & Kelley, J. M. (1995). Measurement of stress appraisal. In S. Cohen, R. C. Kessler, & L. U. Gordon (Eds.), *Measuring stress: A guide for health and social scientists*. New York: Oxford University Press.

Plante, T. G., Caputo, D., & Chizmar, L. (2000). Perceived fitness and responses to laboratory induced stress. *International Journal of Stress Management, 7*, 61–73.

Ross, S. E., Niebling, B.C., & Heckert, T. M. (1999). Sources of stress among college students. *College Student Journal, 33*, 312–317.

Sarafino, E. P., & Ewing, M. (1999). The Hassles Assessment Scale for Students in College: Measuring the frequency and unpleasantness of and dwelling on stressful events. *Journal of American College Health, 48(2)*, 75–92.

Schafer, W. (1996). *Stress management for wellness* (3rd ed.). Orlando, FL: Harcourt Brace.

Selye, H. (1956). *The stress of life*. New York: McGraw-Hill.

Weisaeth, L. (1993). Disasters: Psychological and psychiatric aspects. L. Goldberger & S. Breznitz (Eds.), *Handbook of stress: Theoretical and clinical aspects* (2nd ed.). New York: Free Press.

Weiten, W., & Lloyd, M. A. (2003). *Psychology applied to modern life: Adjustment in the 21st century.* (7th ed.). Belmont, CA: Wadsworth.

Managing Your Professional Life

In this chapter, we will discuss the common student stress areas of:

- Test anxiety
- Time management
- Procrastination
- Managing money
- Making decisions

The Case of Pietro

► Next month, Pietro is scheduled to write five exams within a week. But before he gets to this point, he has to finish three essays, a presentation, and a group project. He knows what he has to do, but sometimes he finds himself watching extra TV instead of studying, or cleaning off his desk for an hour instead of getting down to the job of writing an essay. He has always had a bit of a problem with procrastination, but it's getting worse. Pietro did not do well on his first set of tests, and this worries him very much. He has always had test anxiety, but now it has become severe: the very thought of the exams makes his stomach churn and his mouth become dry. In addition, Pietro has a part-time job that takes 20 hours a week (not counting the time he spends commuting to his job). Pietro thinks he needs the money to stay in school, but he's not very happy with his job, and he wonders whether he should quit or not. If Pietro quits this job, he isn't sure where he will get another, and he is having difficulty deciding what he should do about this situation. Pietro has very little time to spend with his family, and this is a concern to him as well.

stress
any circumstances that threaten or are perceived to threaten one's well-being and thereby tax one's coping abilities (Weiten & Lloyd, 2003)

We met Pietro in the last chapter, and helped him to cope with some of his personal stresses. But he still has problems dealing with the stress of his professional life as a student and as an employee. **Stress** occurs when we are confronted with a situation that we perceive to threaten our well-being, and requires us to work at coping with it. This is an unpleasant state of affairs, usually, and Pietro needs help in dealing with the difficulties he is encountering in his professional life.

ANXIETY

HOW DO WE HANDLE TEST ANXIETY?

problem-focused coping
solving the specific problem that is causing stress

Now we enter the area of **problem-focused coping** as we tackle the problem itself head-on. One of the most common stressors of the post-secondary experience is the area of formal evaluation. It would truly be wonderful if classes could be conducted on a one-to-one discussion basis with an instructor who could clearly tell from the discussion that the student had learned a subject. But the days of holding a lecture in an olive grove seem to be over, and rather than having one-to-one discussions with an instructor, classes are often too large for the instructor to even know students' names. Sadly, the only way to gauge whether a student has learned material—enough to be awarded a diploma, certificate, or degree—is to engage in a formal evaluation. This tends to strike dread into the heart of even the most intrepid student, and the words "Surprise quiz!" from an instructor are the deadliest of all! Marks matter if you want to attain that diploma or certificate or degree; marks matter more to some students than to others, for a variety of reasons. Whatever the reason, some students (and not necessarily those for whom marks matter the most) panic when it's time for a test.

Pietro is a typical student with test anxiety. The closer in time the test is, the less appetite Pietro has, and the more disturbed his sleep is. The night before the test he usually doesn't sleep at all. Sometimes, in the morning, he vomits. Certainly he can never eat a bite of breakfast. He checks his backpack repeatedly for pens and pencils (but he still often forgets something), and with all the checking, he is often either late for the test or much too early. When the test is finally in front of him, he looks at the paper and the questions make no sense to him. "I have no idea what this test is about! I don't remember this in the book! I'm sure the instructor never taught this! I must have missed something! I can't remember anything that I studied anyway! I'm going to fail! I should never have taken this course in the first place. As a matter of fact, what am I doing in this school? I thought I was smart, but I'm not. I'm too stupid to be here . . ." and on and on. Pietro is so busy thinking these negative thoughts that there isn't room in his mind to read the questions on the test properly. This is a more common experience than many people realize. It's so common that in some schools, like Pietro's, students are not permitted to leave the test room for the first 30 minutes of the test. This is to prevent people like Pietro from panicking too readily and walking out before they have tried to answer any questions. So Pietro sits at his desk looking at the clock. "I'm leaving in 30 minutes. No one can make me stay. I'm really going." Having made the decision to leave, Pietro starts to calm down. His mind, which has been chattering a mile a minute about how inadequate he is, now begins to quiet. As his mind quiets, and because he has nothing else to do, Pietro takes another casual look at the test paper. Much to his amazement, he finds that maybe he does know what the questions are asking, and maybe he does know some correct answers. He starts to write, and before you know it, he has finished the test. But he wasted valuable time, and he probably did not do as well as he could have. His performance will probably not reflect his knowledge of the subject matter.

An experience like Pietro's is a common one for students with test anxiety—if they can calm themselves a little, they may find that they know and understand more than they thought they did. But look at the misery they have been through up to that point!

And what of the students who aren't in schools that force them to stay in the test situation for a prescribed period of time? They might have left the test without writing a word. There are ways of reducing this stress, however. Most of us may never enjoy being tested (although there are some people who use situational reconstruction to see a test as a challenge instead of a threat—there's your first tip), but we can learn to deal with evaluations more adaptively.

First of all, the situation of test anxiety may be related to time management. If you have managed your time adequately, you should have been able to do the studying you needed for the test. If Pietro's test anxiety always came from a feeling that he was not prepared for the test, his time management skills would need to be sharpened. In this case, adequate time management might be enough to calm the anxiety. We will discuss time management shortly.

It may be, though, that Pietro never feels adequately prepared no matter how much time he has spent studying. If this is his feeling, although he has done a great deal of studying, it is likely that he is engaging in some illogical thinking. He may believe that post-secondary courses are like many high school courses in which the student can memorize all the material and achieve perfection on a test. As we discussed in the first chapter of this book, that is rarely the case in courses at the post-secondary level. The reality at this level is that Pietro has to do the best he can with the time and resources available to him. This probably will mean that he will never feel completely prepared for a test, just as he will never feel that an essay or an assignment is perfect. Once Pietro recognizes that his expectations are not reasonable, he may begin to give himself a break and not feel so terrible with his state of preparation. That could calm his anxiety too.

Then again, maybe Pietro learned somewhere in his life that tests are threatening, that failure is catastrophic, and that every test (even a small one) is a matter of life and death. This might be a good time for Pietro to use the ABCD technique to tame his runaway illogical negative thoughts and replace them with more positive logical thoughts (see Box 3.2 in Chapter 3). For example, he could think, "I'm a little nervous right now, but I've done well on tests in the past and I've worked as much as I could for this test. The world will not come to an end if I don't do well on this test, so I think I'll just pretend this is a question paper that no one will read but me, and I'll see what I can come up with for answers." Then he could take a few deep breaths (inhale to the count of five and exhale to the count of seven, a quick muscle relaxer). We will discuss study techniques and give you tips for writing different sorts of tests in Chapter 5. Knowing these will help calm Pietro's anxiety as well. If Pietro is still having so much trouble with anxiety that his academic performance is diminished, it's time for him to seek help at his school's counselling centre, where counsellors deal with this problem daily.

TIME MANAGEMENT

HOW DO YOU HANDLE TIME?

You don't have to be a student to know that time pressure is a major source of stress because there are so many expectations and demands upon us (some from ourselves) and only so many hours in the day in which to meet these expectations. This is obviously one of the stresses that is affecting Pietro. Since we are all given the same amount of time in a day, why is it that so many of us can't seem to get everything done, while other people manage to accomplish so much? For most of us, the problem is that we waste time and don't prioritize tasks properly. Pietro was very offended when it was suggested to him that he wastes time, so he kept a journal of exactly what he did for a week. Use the table in Exercise 4.1 to try this for yourself. Remember that you can't manage a problem until you see exactly what the problem is, so be honest and try not to change your usual behaviour while you are keeping this journal.

EXERCISE 4.1   ▶ *Time Management Table*

Use this table to keep track of how you are spending your time, and how you would like to spend your time.

	MONDAY	TUESDAY	WEDNESDAY	THURSDAY	FRIDAY	SATURDAY	SUNDAY
7:00–7:30							
7:30–8:00							
8:00–8:30							
8:30–9:00							
9:00–9:30							
9:30–10:00							
10:00–10:30							
10:30–11:00							
11:00–11:30							
11:30–12:00							
12:00–12:30							
12:30–1:00							
1:00–1:30							
1:30–2:00							
2:00–2:30							
2:30–3:00							
3:00–3:30							
3:30–4:00							
4:00–4:30							
4:30–5:00							
5:00–5:30							
5:30–6:00							
6:00–6:30							
6:30–7:00							
7:00–7:30							
7:30–8:00							
8:00–8:30							
8:30–9:00							
9:00–9:30							
9:30–10:00							
10:00–10:30							
10:30–11:00							
11:00–11:30							
11:30–12:00							
12:00–12:30							
12:30–1:00							

HOW DO WE WASTE TIME?

What Pietro found was that he had some real time wasters on his hands. See if any of these sound familiar to you:

- *He always said yes to his friends' requests.* He had planned on studying in the library between his classes, but a friend asked him to join her for a coffee, and Pietro said yes. There went two hours. Pietro thought that he would make up the studying he'd missed by putting in a couple of extra hours at home that evening. But another friend called him on the telephone and Pietro didn't say that he was busy; he just talked with his friend for another hour. Then Pietro's brother reminded him that a favourite TV program was about to come on, so of course Pietro had to watch it. When it was over, Pietro noticed that another program that didn't look too bad was about to come on, so he watched that as well. By the time he was finished watching TV, he tried to cram in some studying, but he was really too tired to absorb anything he was reading, so he went to bed. He told himself that he would study more on the weekend. When the weekend came, however, he had to work at his part-time job, and after work, his brother asked him for help on his high school project. Pietro didn't feel he could say no to that. It seems that other people manage Pietro's time more than he does.

- *He overscheduled.* Pietro also found that he had the tendency to believe that he could do more than was really possible in a short period of time. For example, he planned on reading a chapter of his economics textbook on the bus ride to school, which typically takes 40 minutes. Not surprisingly, Pietro did not finish the chapter in that length of time under those conditions. Now he found himself behind in his reading, so he planned on reading the rest of the chapter and an assigned chapter for his sociology class that evening. That meant he wouldn't have time to start his history essay, but, he reasoned, the history essay wasn't due until next week, so he could do it on Sunday, after work. Unfortunately, Pietro found that on Sunday, he was not really clear on what was expected for his essay, and he had not done all the reading he needed to do for his other courses. And there were exams coming up.

- *He lacked organization.* Pietro found that just getting ready for school in the morning was taking him more time than he realized. Perhaps that's one reason why he was so often late for his classes and some of his instructors were giving him a cold glance when he habitually walked in late. But why was Pietro taking so long to get out of the house in the morning? Because he couldn't find his wallet and had to spend 15 minutes looking for it. Because the books he needed for school that day were somehow lodged under his bed and he couldn't find them either. Because the class notes he needed for today's work were on small bits of paper strewn on his desk under one of his piles of paper (he wasn't quite sure which one) and it took another 15 minutes to find them and put them all together. By then, Pietro barely had time to shower and throw on some clothes (he'd thought his white shirt was clean, but it wasn't, so he had to rummage for something else to put on).

- *He lacked priorities.* On one day, Pietro decided to get to work on his philosophy assignment. The assignment was due in two weeks and it was his favourite course, taught by his favourite instructor. In preparation for this hard work, he made himself a sandwich and a cup of coffee. Then he sharpened all his pencils. Then he selected what he thought would be appropriate "mood music" for this enterprise. By this time, 30 minutes had gone by and Pietro still had not done any work. But he got to it: he started reading the material required and found it so interesting that he read more, much more than he needed to. In fact, he read for so long that he didn't have time to start on his assignment that evening. "That's OK," he thought, "the assignment isn't due for two weeks and besides, it's only worth 5 percent of my final mark." While Pietro is to be respected for his interest in the philosophy reading material, the sad fact is that he could have used his time better if he had worked on his economics reading (since the economics essay worth 30 percent of his final grade was due next week) or if he had tackled his history presentation, which is due a week earlier than his philosophy assignment and is worth 25 percent of his final mark. Pietro has to learn to use the time available to him in the most efficient manner possible. To do this, he has to recognize how to prioritize all the work that he has: what's due earliest and is worth the most in terms of grades probably needs to be done first.

■ *He gave in to perfectionism.* Pietro prides himself on the quality of his work, but without realizing it, goes overboard in this area. On Tuesday, for example, he spent two hours re-doing a chart for his economics assignment rather than handing in the one on which he'd used white-out on one letter at the bottom corner. His classmates, looking over his shoulder, shook their heads in amazement because if Pietro had not pointed out the white-out, no one would have noticed it, it was that tiny. Pietro adamantly insisted, however, that he would never hand in something that had an erasure or any indication of any kind of error in it. He also spent another two hours going to different stationery stores to find what he considered to be the "perfect" blue cover for his assignment. He never did find it, so now he is planning an excursion to more stores in more distant locations. Are you a perfectionist? Take the test in Exercise 4.2 to find out.

■ *He procrastinated.* Pietro noticed that he spends a great deal of his time and energy in avoiding his work. Going with his friends to have coffee, watching TV, sharpening his pencils, cleaning his desk before he begins work, etc., may all be necessary and potentially enjoyable parts of his day, but Pietro is doing these things without getting much enjoyment out of any of them. Even while he is watching TV or socializing with his friends, he's got a nagging guilt at the back of his mind, a little demon saying, "You should be working." He knows that if he keeps on procrastinating about his work, he will not have a very successful or pleasant time in school. He may even fail. If he keeps procrastinating when he is out of school and in a full-time job, he will get fired. Pietro has an all-too-common habit that many people are prone to. Why is this so? This is such a common problem for so many people that a longer discussion is worthwhile.

EXERCISE 4.2   ▶ *Perfectionism Scale*

Indicate how much you agree with each statement according to the following scale:

+2 = I agree very much

+1 = I agree somewhat

0 = I feel neutral about this

−1 = I disagree slightly

−2 = I disagree strongly

There are no "right" or "wrong" answers, so try to respond according to the way you usually feel or behave.

1.   If one is to attempt anything, one should do it perfectly or not at all.

2.   I am oversensitive to criticism.

3.   I have a clear idea of the kind of person I would like to be, or ought to be, but I feel that I always fall short of this.

4.   As soon as I succeed in reaching a goal, I have to set myself an even more difficult target to work toward.

5.   I constantly compare myself with people I consider to be better than me.

6.   I try to avoid the disapproval of others at all costs.

7.   I am harshly critical of myself.

8.   I set very high standards for myself.

9.   No matter how successful my performance, I still feel that I could/should have done better.

10.   If I do badly in something, I feel like a total failure.

Total your score:

A score over +10 indicates that you have very high and probably unrealistic expectations of yourself. If your score is close to 20, you may have a serious case of perfectionism! You may be demanding the impossible of yourself. At best, you may be dooming yourself to a life of disappointment and dissatisfaction, and at worst, you are opening yourself to an impaired immune system and a host of stress-related disorders.

Remember that there is a difference between striving for excellence and striving for perfection: perfection is unattainable, but excellence and "personal best" are goals that make us grow and improve throughout life.

Source: "Preliminary development of a questionnaire designed to measure neurotic perfectionism in the eating disorders," by S. F. Mitzman, P. Slade, and M. E. Dewey, from *Journal of Clinical Psychology*, Vol 50, Issue 4, pp. 516–522. Copyright © 1994. Reprinted with permission of John Wiley & Sons, Inc.

WHY DO WE PROCRASTINATE?

There are many reasons why people may procrastinate, and in many cases, people procrastinate for more than one reason.

One common reason that people procrastinate over doing a task is that they find the task to be overwhelming or unpleasant. There is often a tendency to want to do the more enjoyable work first, but people who spend all their time on the "fun" assignment that's worth 10 percent of their final mark instead of on the less "fun" assignment that's worth 35 percent find that they've run out of time and are in trouble.

self-efficacy
Albert Bandura's term for our judgment regarding how well we can do a certain action or task

fear of failure
the fear of catastrophic consequences if one should not be successful at some task

Another reason for procrastination may have to do with **self-efficacy**, our belief that we are capable of doing a task. Sometimes we fear that we will not be able to do the task, or that we are not smart enough or talented enough or good enough to do what is expected of us. This is termed **fear of failure**. No one likes to fail, but some people find it more unpleasant than others. Pietro, for example, feels that if he should fail at some school task, it will mean that he is truly too unintelligent to do post-secondary work. It's so much easier just to avoid the work. Then, if he fails or gets a low mark, he can justify this to himself by saying, "Hey, what can you expect? I only wrote the essay the night before it was due. I didn't read all the chapters assigned, etc." This is so much more comforting to the ego than to believe that his low mark was not because he chose to procrastinate, but because he really couldn't do any better. Pietro will never know how smart he is or how much he could do, however, because his fear is getting in the way. He may even start to believe that he does better under pressure, but he's kidding himself.

Another reason that some people procrastinate is because they don't know how to take advantage of small segments of time, thinking instead that a task needs a large block of time. For example, Pietro believes that he has to wait until the weekend to work on an essay because he will need many hours of concentrated work to get it done. But large blocks of time are hard to come by! When Sunday comes, Pietro may have other things to do, he may be sick, or his family may have a crisis . . . anything might happen! Pietro found, when he kept a log of his week, that if he had only an hour between classes, he typically spent that hour looking for someone (anyone!) to socialize with: he might just as well, he thought, since one hour isn't enough time to really do anything profitable. Depending on his school timetable, in the course of a day Pietro might lose four hours or more this way.

A further reason that people procrastinate is because they truly do not know how to start a task. For example, one of Pietro's chores is a history presentation. The instructor has assumed that the students understand how to plan and deliver a presentation before the class, but Pietro has never done this before. He has never done library research in history and he doesn't know whether he should simply write an essay to read to the class, or present his material in some different fashion. He has a true fear of failure but also is procrastinating because he does not know how to begin or where to get help. If this situation seems familiar, take a look at Chapter 12 to help you get started.

While there are probably as many reasons for procrastination as there are people who procrastinate, there is another reason that bears examination. We live in a society that *says* that it is bad to be stressed, but actually looks with a certain admiration on the person who is so terribly busy that he or she feels constant stress. We equate busyness with importance in many cases. Sometimes we find that people procrastinate just so that they will be rushed to accomplish some task. Then they tell us about how busy they are and how little time they have, and they expect—and get—our sympathy and respect. The person who is always rushing and always seems to be so very busy often makes the rest of us feel that we must be slackers and we feel guilty that we aren't moving at the same breakneck speed to accomplish more. But we must remember that many of these "busy" people are only busy because they have not managed their time well, and they have procrastinated doing the important things while they concentrated on "micromanaging" insignificant details or things that could best be designated to other people.

HOW CAN WE STOP PROCRASTINATING AND USE TIME BETTER?

There are two questions here. The first applies only to those who procrastinate, and the second applies to everyone. But since we can't manage time better until we stop procrastinating, let's deal with that issue first.

Many techniques can be used to stop procrastinating. Which one or ones you use will depend on why you procrastinate and simply what works best for you.

First, whether you procrastinate or not, determine what tasks must have priority. In general, the task that has a deadline because of a due date or because of an upcoming test needs to be done first. If two or more tasks have the same deadline, it is usually best to give priority to the task that is worth more of your final grade or, if it is a group project, to the need to have your part completed so that others can do their parts.

Again, whether you procrastinate or not, break large tasks down into small components. If you need to read a chapter for the next class, look at the chapter first to see if it has sections under headings (as this book does, and most textbooks do). If it does, don't think about reading the whole chapter; think about reading one section. When that's done, look around, stretch, yawn, and then think about reading the next section. And so on. Before you know it, the whole chapter will have been covered. It's hard to climb a mountain (read a chapter), but it's easy to climb a series of small molehills (read a section). You can stop anytime you want without the feeling of "I didn't read the chapter." Instead, you will have the satisfied feeling of "I read three sections." Similarly, you can break an assignment or an essay into small components as well, and concentrate on just doing one component, not on finishing the whole assignment or writing the whole essay.

When it is difficult to break a piece of work into smaller blocks, say to yourself, "I will work for five minutes." It's not so difficult to make yourself work for five minutes, and when that period of time is over, it is more likely that you will continue. If not, you can simply say to yourself, "I'll work for another five minutes" and do so. This is similar to the writer's trick of taking a blank piece of paper and writing the word "The" at the top left-hand corner. Once the first word is written, it is more likely that we will go on.

Make a time budget. If we don't control our time, time has a way of controlling us so that we are more rushed than we would like and we wind up not having enough time to do the things we want to do. The first step is to examine everything we have to do in a large period of time. For students like Pietro, looking at the whole semester's work is usually a good idea. Most students know within the first couple of weeks of school when their tests will be and what the due dates of their essays and presentations are, so they can plan their semester. Many students find that getting a large calendar and writing down all due dates and test dates (as well as special occasions and appointments) keeps them on track. Several school councils hand out "daybooks" to students to help with this. If your school council does, make sure to get one right at the beginning of the semester and start filling in due dates and essay/assignment/presentation dates as soon as you get them. This technique allows you to see at a glance what's coming up so that you are not left at the last minute saying, "Oh no! There's a test today!" See Tables 4.1 and 4.2 for examples of Pietro's long-term commitments.

Pietro can see at a glance what's coming up in his semester, in both his personal and his professional life, and what's coming up each week. The next step is to plan how to manage time on a day-to-day basis so that all the work can be accomplished without too much rush or strain.

TABLE 4.1 Pietro's Semester

WEEK	SEPTEMBER	OCTOBER	NOVEMBER	DECEMBER
1	Brother's birthday	Economics test, English essay 1	History presentation	English essay 2
2	Parents' 25th wedding anniversary	History test, Philosophy test	Philosophy essay, History essay (based on presentation)	Exams: Economics, History, Philosophy
3	Biology lab report	Biology lab report	Biology lab report	Biology exam, holidays!
4		Economics assignment 1	Economics assignment 2	Holidays!
5		Biology test	Biology test	

TABLE 4.2 Pietro's Schedule for October

SATURDAY	SUNDAY	MONDAY	TUESDAY	WEDNESDAY	THURSDAY	FRIDAY
1	2	3	4 Economics test	5 English essay 1 due	6	7
8	9	10 History test	11 Philosophy test	12	13	14
15	16	17	18	19	20 Biology lab report due	21
22	23	24	25 Economics assignment 1 due	26	27	28
29	30	31 Biology test				

On a day-to-day basis, some people find a "to-do" list to be sufficient. To-do lists should be realistic. The tasks listed can be rated in terms of priorities: the items that *must* be done today can be designated with an asterisk, an *A*, in red ink, or in whatever other manner you may choose so that you can see clearly that the item is vital. These are the items that you must concentrate on first. Three top-priority items in one day is enough, or even more than enough, depending on their nature. Other items—the *B* items or the blue-ink items—are those that you can do if there is time, but they are not of such pressing need. These may become "red-letter" items as time passes and deadlines approach, or they may be items that can be on hold indefinitely. You can keep this list going all week or even all month, writing the items on a calendar such as Pietro's in Table 4.2, and scratching off items as you accomplish them (that feels so good!), changing blue-ink items to red-ink items, and adding new items as the need arises. By the way, you will accomplish more and feel better if you do your least-preferred task first; getting it out of the way makes the rest of the day look easier!

A special note needs to be made about the student who is returning to school and may also have responsibilities outside of school (e.g., children to raise, a job to do, community service obligations to fulfill). A time budget is even more important for this student, but given the many demands put upon him or her, more flexibility is required. For example, Judson has a six-year-old son whom he is raising alone. Judson's to-do list may be irrelevant if his son gets sick—essays, lectures, and reading don't mean much when your child has a high fever. The priorities of the returning student may be different, then. The same principles apply though: what has highest priority must be handled first, and the individual must make that judgment call with the understanding that all one can do is one's best with the time and resources available. Since pressure is often such an issue for the returning student who must satisfy so many demands, the student's expectations must reflect this. By the same token, some students may shoulder extra family responsibilities through cultural expectations and/or through special circumstances within the family. Other students may have special needs and physical and/or cognitive challenges. The same principles of time and stress management apply here: the individual cases all require individual solutions. Your school's counselling centre may be able to provide valuable assistance, both practical and emotional, in handling the conflicting expectations and demands placed on the individual.

Some of us need to take more control of our time than a simple to-do list would allow. Time management for a returning student like Judson must include plenty of planning ahead since he can never count on being free the night before a due date or a test to put the finishing touches on his preparation. Pietro, who was shocked to find how much time he wasted, is also someone who needs plenty of planning. He took the table in Exercise 4.1 as his model and used it to organize and budget his time. As you can see, the table is broken into 30-minute segments, beginning at 7:00 A.M. and ending at 1:00 A.M. This was convenient for Pietro, but if you wish to use something like this and you typically get up at noon and go to bed at 4:00 A.M., feel free to change the table to suit your own life.

To use a table like this for yourself, you might consider enlarging Exercise 4.1 so that you have plenty of room to write. Another idea is to make up your own table, perhaps putting the daytime hours on one side of the page and the evening hours on the reverse side. First fill in blocks of time that are definitely accounted for. This would include classes, job hours, childcare, etc., and time for personal needs such as bathing, dressing, and eating. Don't forget to include time for commuting to and from school or work. A note on this: for some strange reason, when asked how long it takes them to get to work or school, people often give what is, in fact, the "best" time. If, on a day when every stoplight is green and every bus is waiting for you to board and no traffic ever gets in your way, you can make it to school or work in 20 minutes, you must remember that this is a "best" time and that traffic and life rarely cooperate with you so much on a regular basis. What is the *usual* time that it takes you to commute to school or work? Take this time and add a few minutes on to it so that you can make it to your destination without being late. (Consistent lateness in class is rude and disrespectful to your instructor and your fellow students because, no matter how quiet and unobtrusive they try to be, latecomers disrupt the class, breaking both the instructor's and the class's concentration and flow. Consistent lateness on a job will get you fired.) In filling up blocks of time, include those times when your favourite TV shows come on (you need *some* relaxation!), and keep at least one block per day free for just you. You may use this to catch up on tasks, watch TV for an extra half-hour, talk to friends, or simply contemplate your own state of being—it doesn't matter—this is *your* sacred time to do whatever you want. Then schedule items that you do regularly, including grocery shopping, doing laundry, or exercising. Next, fill in study/schoolwork time. You can specify exactly what schoolwork is to be done during these times on a week-to-week basis. Overestimate how much time you will need for schoolwork; your work probably will take you more time than you realize, but if you have time left over, you can spend it as you want. Bear in mind, if you are a full-time student, that a full-time job is one that takes over 30 hours a week. If you are spending less time than this doing schoolwork-related activities (in class and doing homework), you may not be doing enough work. The rule of thumb in post-secondary education is that you should be spending approximately 2.5 to 3 hours in studying for every 1 hour in class. In budgeting your study time, don't forget to pay attention to your own personal style: if you are a morning person, don't attempt to have late-night study sessions. It's better for you to get up earlier to study. By the same token, night owls should recognize that early morning study sessions are not the best for them. Take advantage of what are your "peak" hours, when you feel most alert and awake, to tackle your most demanding work.

What you are doing in your time budget is managing your time as you would manage your money, allocating your resources to the areas of greatest need and greatest return. Try to balance your day so that you get something accomplished each day, but you still have time for leisure. In doing this, you can see how beneficial it is to break your work into small components. Pietro will find that small components fit small blocks of time very well, so his argument that there is no time to do anything in the hour between classes no longer holds up; he will accomplish more, but feel much less time pressure. Pietro, and you, need to realize that, if you are new to making a time budget for yourself, your first efforts may not work out very well. You need to make your budget, try it out, and modify it in the places where it doesn't work (e.g., you didn't leave enough time for commuting; reading the sociology text takes more time than you thought; you forgot to include your yoga classes, etc.). Your time budget is an ongoing work that may change often, just as your life changes or just as you need it to change. The important point is that you are taking control of your time.

Table 4.3 gives an example of how Pietro can plan his weekday schedule. He is an early riser, so he has planned his week in terms of getting up early and going to bed early. Note that he has scheduled his classes and his job, one-hour mealtimes, his favourite TV shows, and he has given himself study time with breaks and free time to catch up on his work or do as he wishes. On the weekends, Pietro works for eight hours on Saturday and four hours on Sunday. He feels that he can take off Saturday night after his job to be with his friends and/or family and on Sunday, he only needs to put in five or six hours of schoolwork to make sure all his work gets done. Our suggestion to Pietro is to try out this schedule for a couple of weeks; he may find that he needs less free time and more study time at certain points in his schedule. Or he may find that he needs less study time for some subjects. At some points, he may find that he has unexpected time free, because a class has been cancelled, for example. He may also find that if he gets sick or some other unforeseen occurrence arises, he can't utilize his time the way he planned. He will need to be flexible and ready to tinker with his plan so that he uses his time optimally.

TABLE 4.3 Pietro's Weekday Schedule

	MONDAY	TUESDAY	WEDNESDAY	THURSDAY	FRIDAY
7:00–7:30	Shower, dress, breakfast	Shower, dress, breakfast	Shower, dress, breakfast	Shower, dress, breakfast	Shower, dress, breakfast
7:30–8:00					
8:00–8:30					
8:30–9:00	Commuting time	Schoolwork: read, write, study, library research, etc.	Commuting time	Commuting time	Commuting time
9:00–9:30	History class		History class	Biology class	Biology class
9:30–10:00					
10:00–10:30	Schoolwork: read, write, study, library research, etc.			Schoolwork: read, write, study, library research, etc.	Philosophy class
10:30–11:00		Commuting time			
11:00–11:30	Biology class	Economics class	Schoolwork: read, write, study, library research, etc.	Economics class	English class
11:30–12:00					
12:00–12:30	Lunch		Lunch	Philosophy class	Lunch
12:30–1:00					
1:00–1:30	Schoolwork: read, write, study, library research, etc.	Lunch	Schoolwork: read, write, study, library research, etc.	Lunch	Schoolwork: read, write, study, library research, etc.
1:30–2:00					
2:00–2:30		Philosophy class		Schoolwork: read, write, study, library research, etc.	
2:30–3:00	Break				Break
3:00–3:30	Schoolwork: read, write, study, library research, etc.	Schoolwork: read, write, study, library research, etc.	English class		Schoolwork: read, write, study, library research, etc.
3:30–4:00				Break	
4:00–4:30					
4:30–5:00	Free time—go home	Free time—go home		Free time—go home	Free time—go home
5:00–5:30			Free time—go home		
5:30–6:00					

Time					
6:00–6:30	Dinner	Dinner	Dinner	Dinner	Dinner
6:30–7:00					
7:00–7:30	Schoolwork: read, write, study, library research, etc.	Schoolwork: read, write, study, library research, etc.	Schoolwork: read, write, study, library research, etc.	Job	Job
7:30–8:00					
8:00–8:30	TV				
8:30–9:00	Schoolwork: read, write, study, library research, etc.				
9:00–9:30		TV	Break		
9:30–10:00			Schoolwork: read, write, study, library research, etc.		
10:00–10:30	TV				
10:30–11:00					

You might wish to check out the following websites for more information on procrastination and how to overcome it: http://www.sas.calpoly.edu/asc/ssl/procrastination.html; http://mentalhelp.net/psyhelp/chap4/chap4r.htm.

HOW CAN WE MAKE SURE THAT WE KEEP TO THE TIME BUDGET?

positive reinforcement
in its simplest form, in general, any behaviour that is rewarded is likely to occur again in the future

In order to make sure that you can keep to your time budget, you will need to exercise some self-control. There are several ways of doing this. One way is to use some of the principles of learning that you will discover in the next chapter. Let's concentrate on the most important principle for our purpose of managing time: the principle of **positive reinforcement**. In its simplest form, the principle says that in general, any behaviour that is rewarded is likely to occur again in the future. That means that when you have done something that you would like to repeat (such as stayed with your schedule, studied, exercised, etc.), you need to reward yourself for having done so. The reward can be anything that you find pleasant: a snack, the opportunity to listen to music or watch TV or talk to a friend or play with a pet, or whatever is good for you. The crucial condition is that you may not have the reward unless you have done the behaviour you want to increase. So Pietro may choose to reward himself for reading three sections of his textbook by taking a break to listen to some of his favourite music. He may further stipulate that if he stays with his schedule for five days out of seven in the week, he will go to a movie with friends on the weekend, for example. Box 4.1 outlines details of using principles of learning to manage your behaviour, and so, to take control of your time.

It is also important for most of us to learn to say no to others who tempt us away from our schedules. This isn't always easy to do since we may really want to be tempted away from work, and because other people can be very persuasive, if not insistent. Being able to state our own needs and wants firmly, but without infringing on the rights of others, is called **assertiveness.** Assertiveness is a major means of handling stress that is related to the actions of others and is best used whenever there is a reasonable chance of success. This can include saying no when someone asks you to do something you don't want to do or haven't the time to do; it can include returning an improperly cooked meal

assertiveness
the ability to state our own needs and wants firmly, but without infringing on the rights of others

Self-Control: Managing Your Own Behaviour

BOX 4.1

STEP ONE: IDENTIFY A PROBLEM BEHAVIOUR

Decide on the *one most important* problem behaviour that you would like to change. Be specific. Instead of saying "I want to stop procrastinating," rephrase it as "I put off studying for a test until the day before."

STEP TWO: SELECT SPECIFIC TARGET BEHAVIOURS

Now decide what your goal is. This too should be specific. What specifically do you need to do to attain your goal? For example, if your goal is to lose weight, you probably need to eat less and/or different foods and exercise more regularly. Be realistic! It's not realistic to say, "I'll eat only 500 calories' worth of food a day and I'll start working out for three hours each day. Then I'll have 10 pounds off by the weekend!" That could kill you! If you are not being realistic, break your goal into smaller steps (e.g., start by exercising for half an hour a day, reduce your calories by 500) and consider a longer time-frame (e.g., losing one pound per week). The steps can never be too small, but they can be too big.

STEP THREE: COLLECTING BASELINE DATA

Sometimes, we aren't really aware of how often we do a problem behaviour or if it is more likely to occur at some times rather than at others. This information is called *baseline data*. For example, if you want to quit smoking, you need to know how many cigarettes you smoke each day or if you smoke more at certain times or places or with certain people. For at least a week before you begin a self-control plan, keep track of the occurrence of the behaviour, what precedes it, and what its consequences are. For example, "Monday afternoon, felt anxious about a test, smoked two cigarettes, felt more relaxed. Monday evening, had a beer with Ken, smoked three cigarettes, felt relaxed," etc. In this example, you can see that feeling tense and being with Ken seem to cue smoking. We call these cues *discriminative stimuli*. Smoking is positively reinforced by a feeling of relaxation.

STEP FOUR: PLAN YOUR PROGRAM

When you have collected baseline data, you should be able to identify the discriminative stimuli (the cues) for your behaviour and what reinforces it. The next step is to plan your program. First, you need to control discriminative stimuli or cues for the behaviour. You might do this by eliminating, avoiding, or reducing these cues. For example, if you bite your nails every time you watch television, you might want to avoid watching television for a while. Next, make sure that the steps you developed in Step Two really are small and realistic. Now give yourself a schedule of reinforcement, making sure that you are reinforced frequently. Don't punish yourself! Make up a contract for yourself in which you state what reinforcer you will receive for what behaviour. So, for example, if you are going to increase your studying, your contract may say, "For every hour I study, I will allow myself 15 minutes of listening to music. If I study for more than seven hours in a week, I will allow myself to watch TV for two hours." Note that the contract specifies both short-term and long-term rewards.

STEP FIVE: CARRYING OUT THE PROGRAM

Now that the planning is done, it's time to begin. Be prepared to make some adjustments to your program. You may realize that the steps you planned are too big, you may have come across new cues for your behaviour, you may find that what you thought would be very reinforcing really isn't, and you may find that you aren't getting reinforced frequently enough. Give your program a week or two, but if changes are needed, then make them and go on with the plan. Give the plan some time to work. The behaviour you wish to change has probably been around for some time; don't expect it to disappear overnight.

STEP SIX: TERMINATING YOUR PROGRAM

When you have reached your goal, don't just end your program abruptly. Instead, gradually phase the program out by making reinforcement less and less frequent over time. (This also decreases the probability of extinction of your new behaviour.) Make these changes slowly—again, the steps cannot be too small, but they can be too big. You're done! Good for you!

Sources: Watson & Tharp, 2002; Masters, Burish, Hollon, & Rimm, 1987.

in a restaurant or a defective product to a store, or anything else in which you feel that you are being taken advantage of or led away from what you have determined is good for you. The counselling centre at your school probably has assertiveness training classes in which you, along with other people, learn to state your position clearly and politely through role-playing and practice. When we are assertive, we stand our ground and we don't get drawn into arguments, we don't get defensive, and we don't insult anyone else. So, for example, when your friend wants you to do something that you don't want to do, you could say,

"No, I'm sorry, that's not something I want to do," or "No, I'm sorry, I've got something else booked for that time."

Sometimes people persist in the face of our turning them down: "Why can't you come?" "Do your studying some other time." "But I want to talk to you." Note that when people do this, they are being rude: you have politely responded to them, but they aren't showing concern or respect for what you want, they are much more concerned with getting you to do what *they* want. Refuse to be manipulated or drawn into a conversation in which you try to justify your actions. You have no need to explain to these people why you cannot do what they want, and they have no right to ask you to do so. Don't get defensive—you have the right to manage your time! One technique that is useful in situations like this is to act like a broken record. Keep repeating the same sentence over and over again: "I'm sorry but those are the rules. I'm sorry but those are the rules. I'm sorry . . .," "I'm afraid I can't fit this in. I'm afraid I can't fit this in. I'm afraid . . ." When the other people finally realize that you are using the same line over and over again, they understand that you are an immovable object and they give up. The key is to keep your voice calm and modulated and don't let yourself be drawn into an argument.

When you are asked to do something in the future that you don't want to do, but you find it difficult to say no, try to buy time for yourself. Say "I'll have to check my calendar and get back to you," or "Let me sleep on that." In this way, you can't be accused of responding with an unthinking 'no' that the other person will be able to challenge; you will give the impression that you are not dismissing the person out of hand but are considering the situation, which you may choose to do. Often the other person will not get back to you, but will find someone else to ask, or you will find it easier to say "Sorry, I checked my schedule and I find that I just can't possibly fit this in." Once more, though, don't get drawn into a conversation in which you feel you have to defend yourself and your use of your time.

FINANCES

HOW CAN WE DEAL WITH FINANCIAL STRESS?

There is no question about it: it takes more and more money every day to attend a post-secondary institution. Unfortunately, not everyone has adequate financial resources, nor does everyone win a scholarship that will cover all expenses. For most people, post-secondary education involves a major financial burden for themselves and their families. While money may not be the most important factor in your life, it may play a large part in the stress you feel over the course of your education.

Pietro found a job during the school year to help him finance his education. He has to be careful, though: he's a full-time student, and if he takes on more than about 20 hours a week of outside work, his marks in school will drop (Santrock & Halonen, 2002). Callie's family is financing her education for her, but her parents aren't wealthy and they have to be careful with money if they are to have anything left over for their own retirement. It's vital for both Pietro and Callie to manage their money wisely.

First, they have to know what their financial resources are. This involves not only knowing how much money they can expect to have, but planning for the unexpected as well: they need to know what to do if suddenly they need more money. Students often don't realize what potential sources of financial aid exist for them. Many students indicate that they have never checked with the financial aid office in their schools to discover what scholarships, fellowships, bursaries, and loans are available for them. Also, many schools have emergency funding for students who are suddenly in financial trouble. Having this information will potentially get Pietro and Callie more money, and it will decrease the stress they may feel about money.

Next, Pietro and Callie have to make a financial budget. They have to itemize their unavoidable monthly expenses—such as tuition, books, housing, food, transportation, etc.

They also have to estimate their other expenses, such as entertainment, telephone charges, clothing, etc. It may be difficult to do this without being completely aware of where money is going in the first place. Keeping a strict account of expenses for one week is an enlightening experience. Most of us spend more than we realize in a week, and sometimes we discover that our money does seem to fly away! Callie kept an account for a week and found that she was drinking far more expensive coffeehouse coffee than she had realized! She had no idea that it was so easy to go through $30 a week in mocha lattés! When she multiplied $30 by 4 to account for about one month's worth of expenses, she was even more stunned to see $120 a month slip out of her hands. And when she considered her yearly expenditure ($3600), she found her taste for mocha lattés drying up somewhat. This points up how crucial it is for Pietro and Callie to be able to know the difference between what they *need* and what they *want*. Callie is now ready to find a cheaper alternative to her mocha lattés.

Pietro and Callie also need to budget for emergency money. One of the few things about life that we can count on is that the unexpected will occur! Pietro may get sick and not be able to work part-time for a few weeks. Callie's car may break down. Planning for the unexpected is a way of alleviating many anxieties and worries.

Now, the test: is the money available per month adequate for the expenses that must go out? If not, then Pietro and Callie will need to tap other sources. They have already explored these options, so they need to act on them quickly.

WHY NOT USE CREDIT CARDS?

At this point, Pietro and Callie may be very tempted to overuse credit cards, which are usually readily available to students in post-secondary school. Credit cards are so easy and convenient to use that it's easy to forget that they have to be paid off in the long run, and

| EXERCISE 4.3 | ▶ ***Budgeting Your Money*** |

You will have large fixed expenses such as tuition and rent that are paid in lump sums or by the month. These payments require long-term planning using savings, a scholarship, or a loan. Most people are very much aware of these expenses, but their budgets may get tripped up by the smaller expenses that they are not as aware of. The following table will help you recognize these expenses.

Income		Expenses	
Scholarship or bursary: total amount/number of months in school	_____	Tuition: total amount/ number of months in school	_____
Parents (e.g., monthly allowance): amount/month	_____	Books, computer, supplies: total amount/number of months in school	_____
Part-time job: amount/month	_____	Food	_____
Total income	_____	Entertainment	_____
		Clothes	_____
		Phone, utilities	_____
		Personal (toothpaste, shampoo, etc.)	_____
		Transportation	_____
		Laundry or dry cleaning	_____
		Unplanned expenses	_____
		Total expenses	_____

 The aim is to have lower total expenses than total income. Whatever is left over can be used for the "extras": plane tickets home or to visit a friend, special occasion gifts for friends and family, etc. Here's a website that contains tips and worksheets for managing money: http://www.managingmymoney.com/.

their interest rates are high. Many people, not only students, have found themselves in serious financial trouble because of this. Using credit cards in moderation, for convenience, is usually not a problem, especially if you pay off the balance each month. This helps you to establish a good credit rating for your future as well. But allowing debt to mount can ultimately ruin your credit rating and leave you with a crippling financial burden. Exercise 4.3 contains a chart to help you budget your money. Your expenses and income may be different from the contents of this table, so be sure to amend it to fit your own needs.

By now, the suggestions for dealing with financial stress no doubt sound familiar to you. The key is control: making good decisions that give you as much control as possible (both in terms of managing your money and in knowing where to go to look for more money) will reduce the pressure, frustration, and change that you feel in dealing with the typical financial problems of a student.

DECISION-MAKING

HOW CAN WE MAKE GOOD DECISIONS ABOUT MONEY, TIME, AND OTHER ASPECTS OF OUR LIVES?

We have seen that much of the work that we must do in coping with stress involves making decisions. In fact, as we said in the previous chapter, making decisions involves conflict of various types, and conflict is one of the main sources of stress. We make decisions all the time, from the simple and probably trivial (e.g., what clothing should I put on in the morning?) to the more important decisions that will impact on our lives (e.g., what program will I enter in school? what major will I take? what career path will I follow?). Irving Janis and his colleagues have conducted major studies of the decision-making process to see what we do right and wrong (e.g., Janis & Mann, 1977), and they suggest that we ask ourselves certain questions when we make our decisions:

- Have you really considered all the possible options? Very often, we come up with one or two options and stop looking for alternatives. Brainstorming with a friend for other possibilities is a good idea.

- When you look at the options you have arrived at, are you really sure that they will accomplish what you want? For example, Marty wanted his instructor to raise the mark on his essay from *B* to *A*. One of his options, he believed, was to tell his instructor that he is an *A*-student, so obviously a *B* on the essay must be incorrect. Will this get Marty what he wants? No. The instructor is not influenced by what a student's other marks are; if he/she were, then it would be impossible for *C*- or *D*-students ever to raise their marks! So Marty needs to recognize that this option will not achieve his goal.

- Every choice has pros and cons, or points for and against it. Have you recognized what these pros and cons are for each option? Remember that the pros and cons often apply not only to you, but to others as well. For example, whether you go away for the weekend will not only affect your time management budget, but it may also affect the people who are working on a group project with you if you are delaying them. You also need to consider how you will feel about yourself if you choose a particular option; will you feel good about your decision or a little guilty? Will you approve or disapprove of yourself? Will other people approve or disapprove of your choice? Others' approval may or may not be important to you for the choice that you are making, but since we don't live in a vacuum, it usually needs to be considered. Many people draw up a pro and con list. This is a good idea, but make sure you look at the pros and cons for *each* option before making your choice. Petra is trying to decide whether to go to her hometown school or to an equally good school out of town. One thing she needs to ask herself is whether her parents will undergo financial hardship if she chooses to live away from their home. Box 4.2 gives you an example of a balance sheet that Petra might use. You can adapt the balance sheet for decisions that you need to make.

■ Especially for major decisions, we may stop looking for new information too soon. The next question, then, is: is there any new information that you haven't taken into account yet? If there is new information, it may not fit with an option that we prefer, and it is thus very tempting to ignore it. This is a big mistake. For example, Callie needs to buy a new car, and she's finding the car choice decision to be difficult. One car she examines is inexpensive to run and very safe, but rather drab. The other is flashy and cool, and is the one Callie would really like. But now Callie learns that consumer reports say that the cool car is unsafe. Which car will Callie buy? If she's wise, she'll pass up "cool" for "safe and inexpensive."

■ If the decision is important, it is a good idea to review the options—along with their pros and cons—one more time, asking yourself if you have missed anything. Do you really know what the best- and worst-case scenarios might be if you choose each option?

Decision-Making Balance Sheet   BOX 4.2

Petra is trying to decide whether to go to her hometown school or to an equally good school out of town. First, she thinks of all the possible gains and losses she may incur to herself and to others for each option. Then she anticipates the approval or disapproval she will feel from herself and from others for each option. Next, she determines whether each element is a pro (+) or a con (−) for her.

Anticipated Consequences	Alternative 1: Hometown School		Alternative 2: Out-of-Town School	
	+	−	+	−
Gains & Losses for Self				
1. Independence		−	+	
2. Expense	+			−
3. Loneliness?		−		−
4. New friends		−	+	
Gains & Losses for Others				
1. Financial loss for parents	+			−
2. Friends and family will miss me	+			−
3. Sister will have bedroom all to herself		−	+	
Self-Approval/Disapproval				
1. It's time to be independent		−	+	
2. I don't want to cause my parents financial hardship	+			−
Social Approval/Disapproval				
1. My parents don't want me to go	+			−
2. My sister does want me to go		−	+	
3. My friends don't want me to go	+			−
	6+	6−	5+	7−

From her chart, Petra can see that there are more pros for going to her hometown school than for going to an out-of-town school, and more cons for going to an out-of-town school. If this were a matter of simply counting pros and cons, it would be clear that going to her hometown school would be the best decision. But decisions are rarely that simple. This kind of simplicity presupposes that all pros and cons are valued equally, and that may not be the case. For example, the pro of gaining independence may be much more important to Petra than the fact that her friends don't want her to leave town. Petra may want to consider weighting the factors, then. She could give each factor a value from 1 to 5 based on how important that factor is to her. Then her chart might look like the one below:

Anticipated Consequences	Alternative 1: Hometown School		Alternative 2: Out-of-Town School	
	+	−	+	−
Gains & Losses for Self				
1. Independence (5)		− − − − −	+ + + + +	
2. Expense (2)	+ +			− −
3. Loneliness? (1)		−		−
4. New friends (2)		− −	+ +	
Gains & Losses for Others				
1. Financial loss for parents (2)	+ +			− −
2. Friends and family will miss me (2)	+ +			− −
3. Sister will have bedroom all to herself (1)		−	+	
Self-Approval/Disapproval				
1. It's time to be independent (5)		− − − − −	+ + + + +	
2. I don't want to cause my parents financial hardship (2)	+ +			− −
Social Approval/Disapproval				
1. My parents don't want me to go (2)	+ +			− −
2. My sister does want me to go (1)		−	+	
3. My friends don't want me to go (1)	+			−
	11+	15−	14+	12−

Now the situation seems to be that going to an out-of-town school will be the better decision for Petra, based on the factors that she values most.

Sources: Adapted from Jewell, 1989; Janis & Mann, 1977.

■ Once you make a choice, have you figured out how to put the plan into action or how to deal with a worst-case scenario, if it arises? Pietro, for example, chose to go to a football game on Sunday afternoon rather than attend his girlfriend's party. He planned on telling her he was sick so that she wouldn't get angry about his choice. Can you guess what happened? His girlfriend found out he lied and broke up with him. As she said, "All you had to do was to be honest with me." Pietro is devastated. He can't imagine life without his girlfriend, and he desperately wants to win back her trust. He had convinced himself that she would never find out about his lie, so he never thought about how to handle the situation if she did find out. This is the point at which one can say, "If you can't do the time, don't do the crime," meaning, if you can't deal with the worst-case scenario of an option, you probably shouldn't choose that option!

Janis and Mann (1977) found that people who take the time to ask themselves these questions do make better decisions, and they feel more confident and less stressed by the decision-making process.

WHAT'S THE BOTTOM LINE ON STRESS?

The bottom line is that stress is always with us, in our personal lives and in our professional lives. We will never escape it, but we can handle it. Either we control it, or it controls us. The more we know about stress, the more we practise handling stress, the better we are in dealing with it. How successful your post-secondary career is, how much you enjoy these years, depends to a great extent on how well you handle the stress that is involved in being a student at this level. We hope that we have provided you with some help.

Advice for Pietro

▶ Pietro clearly needs help in dealing with his professional stress. The table below outlines some of the things he can do to decrease his stress and function better in his professional life as a student.

PIETRO'S STRESS	WHAT HE CAN DO	THE EFFECTS
He wastes too much time!	Find out how he spends his time, by keeping a journal using the table in Exercise 4.1 for a week.	Pietro will discover what his time wasters are, how much he really does procrastinate, and where he can find extra time to do what he needs to do.
He procrastinates.	Implement the tips for reducing procrastination, start a self-modification project in which Pietro reinforces himself for doing schoolwork.	Pietro will gain control over his procrastination so that he will be able to keep to his time schedule and get his work done.
He is trying to do all his work.	Make a time schedule using the table in Table 4.3. Make a to-do list of priority tasks for each day.	Pietro will see where he has blocks of time to do his schoolwork and he will be able to organize his time to accomplish his goals.
How much does he need his job?	Use the table in Exercise 4.3 to find out what his expenses and income are.	This will help Pietro to determine whether he really does need a part-time job, and how many hours he needs to work.
Should he quit his job?	Pietro can use the table in Box 4.2 to help him decide whether quitting his job is a good decision.	He will be more likely to make a good decision and will feel more satisfied with his choice by using this technique.
He suffers from test anxiety.	Develop good study habits, monitor negative self-statements, use Ellis's ABCD technique to change negative self-statements, use some general stress-reducing techniques from Chapter 3.	When Pietro has had enough time to study, has studied appropriately, has learned how to relax, and has modified his expectations so that he is realistically striving for his best, his anxiety will diminish.

CHAPTER SUMMARY

■ One of the most common problems students have is dealing with test anxiety. The anxiety that many students feel has the effect of producing negative and catastrophic self-statements, which then interfere with the ability to focus on the test and answer the questions. Recognizing that students rarely feel completely prepared for a test on the post-secondary level will help to eliminate unrealistic expectations about performance, and time management techniques will help you use the time available for preparation as efficiently as possible. It is also important to learn to relax in the face of stress and to control negative-self-statements.

■ In order to cope with the often heavy demands of post-secondary school, it is necessary to budget your time by first finding out what your particular time wasters are and eliminating them.

■ Procrastination is a common problem, often caused by the unpleasantness of the task, fear of failure, inability to take advantage of small blocks of time, and lack of knowledge regarding how to do a task. Procrastination can be managed by techniques such as breaking large tasks into smaller ones or working for set, small blocks of time.

■ Time budgets may be detailed and complex or simple to-do lists, depending on what works for you. The important part is to make sure that you have enough time allotted to do the things that are necessary, including a little time for rest and relaxation. Reward yourself for sticking to your schedule.

■ Learn to be able to say no to unreasonable demands on your time. Assertiveness may be difficult at first, but relieves a great deal of stress in the long run.

■ Money can be the source of a great deal of student stress. Learning to balance a budget and use credit cards appropriately will decrease the anxiety that many students have when money gets tight.

■ All the issues we have discussed come down to the common factor of making good decisions. When making decisions, we need to make sure we have all the information and have weighed the pros and cons of all the options that are available to us.

KEY TERMS

assertiveness	positive reinforcement	self-efficacy
fear of failure	problem-focused coping	stress

INDIVIDUAL ACTIVITIES

1. Do you procrastinate? Keep track of your time for a few days and try to identify any time wasters that are cluttering up your life.

2. Make up a large calendar and mark in the due dates of all your assignments and the dates of any tests and exams that you know of. Now make a schedule of when, where, and how you are going to work on these.

3. Make up a budget for yourself. How much are you spending without realizing it? Can you find a way to save a little money to buy something you really want?

GROUP ACTIVITIES

1. In a group of four or five students, take one of the following problems and form a plan of action to solve the problem, outlining options and pros and cons of each.

   a. Barry is a full-time student whose boss is asking him to work extra hours at his part-time job, with the threat of dismissal if he doesn't. But Barry is already feeling overloaded with his schoolwork.

   b. Morgan's professor believes that Morgan cheated on her last essay. Morgan knows she is innocent and doesn't want to be given a zero on the assignment.

2. In a group of four or five students, make up a financial plan for someone who is entering university. Create categories of expenses. How much money should be allocated to each category? How much money will the student need for the year? Where can the student get this money? To do this, go to your school's financial centre and ask for information.

3. In a group of four or five students, take the following situations and role-play assertiveness. As a group, decide on the best way to respond to these situations:

   a. At a restaurant, Helen's meal is served cold.

   b. Harold's roommate doesn't bathe or brush his teeth often enough.

   c. Keshia's best friend is depressed about a recent breakup with her boyfriend and phones Keshia every night to talk about it for hours. Keshia's schoolwork is not getting done.

REFERENCES

Janis, I. L., & Mann, L. (1977). *Decision-making.* New York: Free Press.

Jewell, L. N. (1989). *Psychology and effective behavior.* St. Paul, MN: West Publishing Co.

Masters, J. C., Burish, T. G., Hollon, S. D., & Rimm, D. (1987). *Behavior therapy: Techniques and empirical findings.* New York: Harcourt Brace Jovanovich.

Santrock, J. W., & Halonen, J. S. (2002). *Your guide to college success: Strategies for achieving your goals* (2nd ed.). Belmont, CA: Wadsworth.

Watson, D. L., & Tharp, R. G. (2002). *Self-directed behavior: Self-modification for personal adjustment.* Belmont, CA: Wadsworth.

CHAPTER 5

LEARNING

The Case of Ravi

▶ **R**avi is feeling frustrated. He has been in his Introduction to Philosophy class for five weeks now. He has attended every lecture and studied every reading, yet he received a grade of 52 percent on his first test. He knows that he was lucky to have passed the test at all because he just can't seem to learn philosophy. When the instructor talks, Ravi feels like he is in a fog, never quite understanding what is being said. When he studies his textbook, he finds that he constantly has to re-read pages and still does not really understand the main points.

To make matters worse, Omar, who sits beside Ravi in class, seems to understand everything without even trying and is always volunteering answers to questions. Ravi asked Omar how he "gets" this class so easily and Omar seemed confused by the question. "I just listen and I understand," Omar replied.

Ravi wishes he could drop philosophy, but it is required for his degree program so that is not an option. Ravi knows that he has to score above 60 percent in philosophy to remain in his program. Ravi is worried and that is not helping his situation. He wonders if there are better ways to learn philosophy.

Ravi is in good company, wondering how to learn philosophy. Early Greek philosophers wondered how man could know anything, since the world is constantly changing. Over time, they became less interested in what man could learn, but rather *how* man could learn. These philosophers argued that man learns through individual experience (Hergenhahn, 2005). Today, most researchers agree that life experience has an important role in learning. Thus, because individuals have unique experiences, they learn in many different ways. That is, while there are many ways to learn, we each have our own unique preferences or learning styles. This does not mean that you cannot learn in ways that are not part of your own style. There are many aspects of learning that are common to most learners.

When studying learning, there are several important facts to remember.

- First, you have your own personal learning style. That is, you have ways of learning that seem to work best for you.

- Second, you don't always have to put in a lot of effort to learn. You often learn by just observing events and other individuals. For example, Omar seems to learn philosophy just by listening to his instructor.

- Third, learning can be due to trial and error. When solving a problem, sometimes we come to the solution by trying the problem over and over again. In this approach, you try the problem and if you get the wrong answer, you learn from your mistake and try again until you solve the problem. Learning from your mistakes can sometimes lead to insight. Ravi could be helped in learning philosophy by looking at the mistakes he made on his first test and correcting them. When similar problems are presented in the future, Ravi may be able to solve them with little thought.

- Fourth, when people learn, it is not always obvious. It is important to distinguish between learned knowledge and performance. Have you ever heard anyone say, "I don't understand why I didn't do well on the test. I knew the material."? This happens often. There are a variety of reasons why people fail to perform, including anxiety, fatigue, poor motivation, inadequate study methods, poor memory triggers, and confusion about what is being asked. Thus, it is possible that you may have knowledge but due to these factors you do not perform. For example, occasionally a great golfer does very poorly in a tournament. This does not mean that the golfer has lost the knowledge of golf, but rather, the golfer just did not perform. The good news about factors that affect performance is that you can control them. Once you learn to control these factors, your performance will benefit and your knowledge will show.

LEARNING STYLES

All students have ways in which they learn best. For example, Omar seems to be able to just listen to a lecture and know the material. On the other hand, Ravi feels like he is in a fog in lecture; never quite understanding what is being said. Learning from lecture does not seem to be Ravi's preferred style. Understanding your own learning style can help you to organize both lecture and reading materials in ways that will increase your understanding of the course content. In addition, you can use your preferences to reinforce what you are learning in class and devise/learn new study methods that fit well with your personal learning style.

Learning styles are usually broken down into preferences based on cognition (information processing), personality, and perception.

WHAT ARE COGNITIVE LEARNING STYLES?

cognitive learning styles
preferences for the way in which one best understands and learns information; based on thought processes

concrete experiencer
someone who understands by actively experiencing information, by working on examples

abstract conceptualizer
someone who prefers to understand by hearing theories and creating theories to explain experiences

active experimenter
someone who prefers to learn by doing or experimenting

reflective observer
someone who prefers to learn by watching others and reflecting on experience

One popular theory of **cognitive learning styles** is that of Kolb. Usually cognitive preferences focus on how we take in or understand information and then how we process or learn it. Preferences vary in two ways within each individual (Kolb, 1976).

First, individuals have preferences for the ways in which they best *understand* information. That is, some people prefer to actively experience information, that is, they understand by working on examples (a person like this is called a **concrete experiencer**). For example, if you were a concrete experiencer, you might better understand the optics of light by working on problems that involve the properties of light rather than listening to your physics instructor talk about light. Others understand by hearing theories and creating theories to explain their experiences (such a person is called an **abstract conceptualizer**). For example, if you were an abstract conceptualizer, you might better understand memory by theorizing on how memory works, rather than trying memory games that your instructor provides to you.

Second, individuals have preferences for the way in which they *learn* information. Some people learn by doing or experimenting (such a person is called an **active experimenter**). For example, if you were an active experimenter, you might best learn the properties of chemicals in your chemistry class by experimenting with the actual chemicals. Others learn by watching others and reflecting on experience (a person like this is called a **reflective observer**). For example, if you were a reflective observer, you might prefer to learn about child development by watching movies on the topic and thinking about the meaning of the scenes that were presented. Many tests have been designed to tell students how they best understand and learn information. Knowing how you best understand and learn might help you to better organize your lecture and text materials.

What cognitive learning styles best describe me?

Trying a cognitive learning styles test might help you to determine your cognitive preference. You can try one online test at http://adulted.about.com/cs/learningstyles/a/lrng_style.htm. Take "A Learning Style Survey for College," by clicking on the hyperlink in the third paragraph of "What Is Your Learning Style." This online test combines both cognitive preferences and personality preferences.

Exercise 5.1 is a self-reflection exercise that examines your preferences in the area of understanding and learning. Note that you will not likely fall perfectly into any category. You fit into more than one category because your learning experiences are unique to you and thus, your learning and understanding profile will also be unique. In Exercise 5.1, decide what features best describe you in each category.

Can I use my personal cognitive learning styles to my advantage?

No instructor will teach to your personal learning style. This is because each student has a unique style. For example, you likely found that none of the categories in Exercise 5.1 perfectly fit you because you are unique. However, knowledge of these learning styles can help in two ways. First, knowing how you best understand and learn can help you to focus your studies. For example, if you understand material better when examples are used, you might want to focus on lecture examples and text examples. If you learn best during class discussions, you might want to become actively involved in them or initiate them (when appropriate) by asking questions. Second, knowing areas that are not your preferences can help you to increase ability in a weaker performance area. For example, if you find you do not prefer learning by reading your text, you can reflect on why. Perhaps the material feels overwhelming, the text is too large, or the vocabulary in the text is difficult.

In order to begin to understand his own learning, Ravi takes a cognitive learning styles test and reflects on how he learns best. He finds that he understands best when lots of examples and exercises are given, especially if he can relate these examples and exercises to himself. This makes Ravi a concrete experiencer in the way he understands. He also finds

EXERCISE 5.1

▶ *Cognitive Learning Styles*

How do you best *understand* material?

Concrete Experiencer

I understand best when using:

- Examples
- Exercises
- Simulations/acting out
- Information relating personally to me
- Guessing for problem solving

Abstract Conceptualizer

I understand best when using:

- Reason and logic
- Information that is impersonal
- Theoretical readings
- Case studies

How do you best *learn* material?

Active Experimenter

I learn best when:

- Having class discussions
- Doing homework
- Working on projects
- Running experiments

Reflective Observer

I learn best when:

- Listening to lectures
- Observing others
- Thinking about course materials
- Reading the textbook
- Keeping a journal of my learning

Source: Based on Kolb, 1984.

that he learns best when he is working on projects and having class discussions. This makes Ravi an active experimenter in learning. He realizes that he does not seem to learn much from theoretical readings in philosophy or from sitting in lectures. Yet, he knows that this is the method from which the instructor expects him to learn.

Ravi decides to use his cognitive strengths to make material more understandable. For example, to understand the lectures, Ravi decides to try the exercises at the end of each chapter and in his study guide. He also tries to think of how each topic in philosophy relates to him. He finds that if he can make up a personal example, he recalls the material better.

Ravi also begins to work on his weaknesses. He does not like reading his textbook. It seems too impersonal. To remedy this, at the end of each section in the chapter, Ravi thinks of personal examples to help him understand the information. In lectures, Ravi uses a highlighter to highlight important points and difficult vocabulary. He plans to review these points and vocabulary at home, and then perhaps discuss these important concepts with Omar.

Ravi is learning that difficult material can be made easier by understanding his cognitive learning style. Reflect on your own style from Exercise 5.1 and think of ways you could use your personal style to enhance your learning and improve on your weaknesses.

WHAT IS A PERSONALITY-BASED LEARNING STYLE?

introvert
someone who is quiet, shy, and prefers to be alone

extrovert
someone who is very outgoing and sociable

sensor
someone who is very logical and detailed in his/her approach to life

A second way of viewing learning style preference is based on personality. Many theorists use the work of psychotherapist Carl Jung as the basis of their theory. Based on Jung, Gardner and Jewler (2003) argued that learning styles depend upon personality, and that personality can be categorized into different areas or dimensions. People can be **introverts** (quiet, shy, prefer to be alone) or **extroverts** (very social). People can be **sensors** (logical in approach) or **intuitors** (creative). They can be **thinkers** (analytical) or **feelers** (emotional). Or people can be **perceivers** (gather much information) or **judgers** (quick to decisions). Every person has each of these traits in differing levels. For example, you may most often be shy or quiet (introverted) but around your family you are very outgoing (extroverted). The important point here is that different personality profiles result in different learning styles.

intuitor
someone who is very creative and imaginative in his/her approach to life

thinker
someone who is very analytical and objective in his/her approach to life

feeler
someone who is very emotional and empathic in his/her approach to life

perceiver
someone who gathers a great deal of information before making a decision

judger
someone who makes decisions quickly and is task-oriented

personality-based learning styles
preferences for learning that are unique to your personality type

What personality-based styles best describe me?

You can try a learning styles inventory at www.e-radiography.net/articles/learningstyles/learningstyles1.htm. You will notice that you have many traits from all these categories, but some categories represent you better than others.

Exercise 5.2 lists some learning preferences under each personality category. Use it to reflect on your **personality-based learning styles**.

Can my personality-based learning style be used to my advantage?

Like with cognitive learning styles, you can use what you know about your personality to both focus your studying and increase study-related abilities.

First, if you are aware of your personality tendencies, you can use them to your advantage. For example, if you know that you are introverted, you may realize that you work best alone. You can then arrange your studying in an area that allows you a quiet working environment (e.g., the library). On the other hand, as an introvert you might know that you like to be very careful in your work and in fact you are so careful that you re-do your assignments over and over again. Your tendency to be so careful might be a disadvantage in some assignments, as reworking assignments requires considerable time and the workload at post-secondary school does not always suit this level of care. Some assignments will carry little weight over your semester, and you may need to hand in work that is good but not letter-perfect in order to finish your many assignments. You will need to select your level of performance based on the type of assignment you receive.

Second, if you are aware of your personality-based learning styles you might be able to work on improving some academic areas. For example, if you are a judger, quick to come to decisions about your work, you might find that those decisions do not always result in quality work. Knowing you generally come to quick decisions might help you to slow down and remind yourself that course instructors want you to think about issues from many perspectives and consider available information before making decisions.

Using a learning styles test, Ravi has discovered that he is an extrovert and also both an intuitor and a feeler. Ravi likes to work quickly and in groups. He does not like working on details of problems and likes to relate issues to himself. From this, he realizes that part of his problem with philosophy is that it is not a group activity, it requires attention to detail, and the instructor does not make the material personal. Ravi needs to reorganize the material so that it fits his personality style. He can make the material personal by relating concepts to himself. Knowing that he does not attend to detail is a warning for Ravi—he needs to force himself to watch for detail in this course. He decides to highlight important concepts and create study notes that emphasize detail. He also decides to read through the study guide that came with his textbook. Study guides offer students new ways to look at material presented in the book and in class. The additional examples, demonstrations, and ideas found in the study guide often help students to memorize course details. In addition, study guides often include practice test questions that aid in studying for examinations. Finally, Ravi decides to form a study group to discuss philosophy. In this way, Ravi is using his strong extroverted personality to his advantage. Not only will he have group interaction, but also meeting with other students will help him focus on important concepts and details.

WHAT ARE PERCEPTION-BASED LEARNING STYLES?

auditory learning style
preference for learning and understanding by listening

tactile learning style
preference for using touch when learning; learning best by doing or manipulating objects

visual learning style
preference for using visual imagery when reading, studying, or listening to lectures

A third way of viewing learning styles is to categorize styles based on perception. Most often these styles are categorized as visual-based styles, auditory-based styles, and tactile-based styles. Those with a **visual learning style** prefer to use visual imagery when reading, studying, or listening to lectures. Those with an **auditory learning style** learn from listening. Finally, those with a **tactile learning style** prefer to use touch when learning. These individuals learn best by doing, for example, moving the pen to make lecture notes when listening to lectures.

What perception-based styles best describe me?

You might want to try some online learning styles inventories based on perception. You can find these at http://www.berghuis.co.nz/abiator/lsi/lsiframe.html and http://lookingahead .heinle.com/filing/l-styles.htm.

Exercise 5.3 will also allow you to think about how you learn best from a perceptual viewpoint.

EXERCISE 5.2

▶ *Personality-Based Learning Styles*

Introvert

- Works alone
- Thinks independently
- Is very careful in work

Extrovert

- Works in groups
- Works quickly
- Avoids routine or repetitive work

Senser

- Recalls detail well
- Has detailed projects
- Does work in a logical manner

Intuitor

- Has many creative ideas
- Does not like working on details
- Can work out complicated problems

Thinker

- Thinks in a critical/logical way
- Is very objective about issues
- Has strong opinions that do not easily change

Feeler

- Is considerate of others' opinions
- Relates issues to self
- Will compromise in group work

Perceiver

- Looks at more than one side of an issue
- Examines data before making decisions
- Easy to work with, not judgmental

Judger

- Quick to make decisions
- Likes to plan out projects
- Will stay on task

Source: From *Your College Experience: Strategies for Success, Media Edition* (Non-Info Trac Version) 5th edition by GARDNER/JEWLER. © 2003. Reprinted with permission of Wadsworth, a division of Thomson Learning: www.thomsonrights.com. Fax 800 730-2215.

EXERCISE 5.3

▶ *Perceptual Learning Styles*

Visual Learners

- Learn best if provided with visual slides of the lecture
- Recall information better if they write it out
- Often see their notes and book in their mind when taking a test
- Are helped by drawing diagrams of difficult problems
- Are helped by mapping out concepts to see how they are related

Auditory Learners

- Learn best by hearing information in the lecture
- Talk out loud when studying
- Like to rehearse to-be-remembered items
- Sometimes misread words that sound similar (e.g., chair and care)
- Are helped by teaching concepts to others

Tactile Learners

- Like to learn by doing practical examples
- Are helped by hands-on experience
- Often use a trial-and-error approach to problem-solving
- Are helped by re-writing notes
- Are helped in reading by using a highlighter to highlight important points

Source: Adapted from Berghuis, 2004.

Can my perception-based learning styles be used to my advantage?

You likely found in Exercise 5.3 that many but not all of your perception-based preferences are in one category. Understanding your perception-based preferences can help you focus your studies and also improve your abilities.

First, knowing the perception-based ways in which you learn best allows you to modify lecture notes, concepts, and readings into a form that is easier for you to understand. For example, if you find that you learn best through vision, you can create diagrams of lecture concepts that will help you to reinforce those concepts (see mind maps in Chapter 7 for an example).

Second, if you find that you do not seem to take in much information from lectures because of your visual learning style, you might modify the way in which you take lecture notes by using a highlighter on important words that you can look for in your text. You might also decide to record lectures on audiotape (with permission) for later review (in case you have missed important points), or to view resource materials available in video/computer format.

Ravi is not learning by listening to lectures. His personal style is visual, and he does not learn well through auditory presentations. Ravi needs to pay particular attention to slides presented in class and to tables and diagrams in his textbook—these are particularly valuable to Ravi as they suit his learning style. Ravi also needs to re-write his lecture notes in a format that will help him. He might consider using mind-mapping diagrams (presented in Chapter 7) to organize his material visually.

WHAT ARE THE BENEFITS OF KNOWING MY LEARNING STYLE?

personal learning plan
a summary of personal learning objectives, self-assessments, and suggestions to meet objectives

In summary, there are two main benefits of knowing your learning styles: (1) you can better organize course material into ways that maximize your learning; (2) you can identify weaknesses in learning and compensate for them. Overall, this means that it is not enough to *know* your style, but rather you must *use* your personal learning style to improve your learning. When we reflect on ways to maximize learning through our learning styles we create a personal learning plan. A **personal learning plan** usually contains a summary of your learning objectives, a self-assessment of your current learning style, a list of your general strengths and weaknesses, and methods you plan to use to improve upon learning. An example of a personal learning plan that might help Ravi can be found in Box 5.1. The exercises provided at the end of this chapter give you an additional opportunity to reflect on styles and create a personal learning plan to maximize your learning.

While understanding your personal learning style is an important first step in understanding learning, it is also important to recognize that people have commonalities in the way they learn. The methods that people use to learn depend very much on the lessons that they are trying to learn.

WHAT IF MY LEARNING STYLE IS DIFFERENT FROM THE INSTRUCTOR'S TEACHING STYLE?

Instructors teach in many different ways. Some prefer to lecture, some prefer to have class discussions, some show films and slides, some prefer that students give presentations to other students, etc. The instructor's style may not be consistent with your personal learning

Personal Learning Plan and an Example Plan for Ravi   BOX 5.1

In general, personal learning plans involve:

- General objectives
- Specific objectives
- An evaluation of learning styles
- An examination of strengths and weaknesses based on learning styles assessment
- Methods to meet your objectives that consider your learning style

EXAMPLE
Ravi's Plan

General objective: To increase my grade in Introduction to Philosophy

Specific objectives: 1. To better understand lectures

2. To better understand the textbook

3. To improve study methods for philosophy

My self-assessment, after completing both learning styles tests and Exercises 5.1, 5.2, and 5.3:

LEARNING STYLE	MY LEARNING STYLE	MY STRENGTHS	MY WEAKNESSES
Cognitive-based, from Exercise 5.1	Concrete experiencer	Using examples, using exercises, recalling personal information	Understanding impersonal information, reading theory
	Active experiencer	Class discussion, experimenting, projects	Listening to lectures, reading my book
Personality-based, from Exercise 5.2	Extrovert	Working in groups, working quickly	Working alone, attending to detail
	Intuitor	Creative, can work out problems	Using logic
Perception-based, from Exercise 5.3	Visual	Understanding diagrams, seeing notes in my mind, mapping concepts	Listening to lectures, making detailed notes

Meeting Objectives

Ravi's objective 1: Better understanding of lectures

OBJECTIVE	METHOD	WHY
Understand lecture	Tape lecture if permitted	Allows for later review
	Complete chapter exercises	Fits my cognitive style
	Focus on the examples of concepts the instructor uses	Fits my cognitive style
	Think about how lecture material applies to me	Fits my cognitive style
	Create a study group	Fits my personality style
	Slow down my work to ensure I attend to detail	Fits my personality style
	Ask self what details I am missing	Fits my personality style
	Create maps of concepts and how they join together	Fits my perceptual style
	Write out study notes so I can see them	Fits my perceptual style
	Make diagrams of important concepts	Fits my perceptual style
	Highlight important concepts (using a highlighter pen)	Fits my perceptual style

Ravi would continue this plan for each of objectives 2 and 3.

preferences. However, knowing your personal learning style could help you to re-organize material that the instructor presents into a format that is better suited to your learning needs. For example, if your instructor prefers to lecture but you prefer visual presentations, you could concentrate on the instructor's slides and on visual examples in your book and on the class web page, which might help you to better understand the lecture material. It is always a good idea to prepare for these lectures by looking over the text material and slides (if available) prior to class. In this way, you can better concentrate on what the instructor is saying in class because you have entered class with some knowledge of the day's topic. You can later re-write your lecture notes into a format that better meets your needs (e.g., tables, or mind maps).

LEARNING

HOW DO PEOPLE GENERALLY LEARN?

There are a variety of ways that people learn, and these different methods of learning are used for different purposes. Further, all people use all methods. In general, these methods include learning by association, learning by consequences, self-control procedures, observational learning, insight, and information processing methods. Let's examine each.

LEARNING BY ASSOCIATION

When two things occur close in time to one another, they often become associated. In other words, we learn to expect the second thing to occur after the first. For example, a baby might associate the sight of her mother with food and thus be content when she sees her mother. The baby expects food when seeing mother. A student might associate the sight of an exam with failure and thus be anxious when she sees the exam. The student expects to fail when seeing the exam. This **associative learning** is sometimes referred to as classical conditioning. How does this association happen?

associative learning
learning that takes place when two events are linked; creates expectations

Learning by association has long been known and it received much attention due to the work of a Russian physiologist named Ivan Pavlov in the early 1900s. Pavlov began to study these associations when he found that the animals he worked with came to expect food every time they saw his research assistant (he knew they expected food because they began to salivate whenever they saw the assistant).

Pavlov determined that some associations occur naturally (without learning). For example, animals and humans will salivate when food enters their mouth. They do not need to be taught to do this. A baby will make sucking motions when something is placed in her mouth. She is not taught to do this.

Pavlov also determined that some associations are not natural, but rather, they are learned after two events are paired together. For example, Pavlov's dogs often saw the research assistant give them food. After many days of seeing the research assistant give them food, they began to expect food whenever they saw the assistant. You can probably think of many examples of associations that you have learned. For example you have learned that thunder follows lightning and when you see lightning you listen for the thunder, perhaps counting the seconds to determine how far away from you the lightning was. You have learned that a red light means stop and when you see a red light you expect that cars will stop. These expectations occurred after experiencing the two events happening close in time many times. The first time you saw a red light you had no expectations, but you noticed that cars stopped. After experiencing this over many days, you grew to expect cars to stop when the light was red. In general, learning by association builds up our expectations.

Because associations build up our expectations, they also affect our emotions about events. For example, if your aunt always brings you gifts, you begin to expect a gift when you see your aunt. You may feel excitement when you know she is going to visit. If on the other hand she arrives with no gift, you will feel disappointment. These emotions are a result of pairings that built up expectations and when an event leads to an emotional response, we call this a **conditioned emotional response (CER)**.

Many pairings occur at post-secondary schools, leading to a variety of emotions. You might have found in high school that when you studied for a test you received a good grade. You began to pair tests and good grades and expect good grades when taking tests. However, you might have studied for a test at your post-secondary school and received a lower grade. You feel both anxiety and disappointment when receiving your test back. You might then start to pair tests with poor grades and this expectation leads to considerable anxiety. Later when you know you are to be tested, you feel anxiety. Uncontrolled anxiety can affect your performance.

conditioned emotional response (CER)
an emotional response that is largely involuntary but is learned originally through classical conditioning

WHAT DOES ASSOCIATIVE LEARNING TEACH ME?

In general, as indicated above, we learn expectations and emotions through associative learning. One important factor to remember is that if some emotions are learned, they can be unlearned or changed. In other words, to some extent, emotions can be controlled.

HOW DO THESE ASSOCIATIONS APPLY TO ME AT SCHOOL?

Many aspects of the post-secondary environment result in conditioned emotional responses. For example, Ravi feels anxiety and frustration when sitting in his philosophy class. He now associates his philosophy class with failure. Omar feels confident in his philosophy class because he associates his class with good grades. Both Ravi and Omar have emotional responses due to pairings of their philosophy class with bad or good outcomes. These emotional responses will affect the way in which these students perform in class. If Ravi continues to associate this class with poor outcomes, his anxiety could lead him to focus poorly in class or worse, he could stop trying to achieve better grades in this class.

CAN I CONTROL MY EMOTIONAL RESPONSES TO CLASSES, TESTS, ASSIGNMENTS, AND PRESENTATIONS?

The general answer to this question is yes and many techniques will be presented in other chapters of this book to help you control emotional responses in these situations. However, in general, the methods you will be taught will involve extinction and discrimination techniques.

Extinction involves ending the associated pairings, and **discrimination** involves limiting associations to very particular situations. Let's take an all-too-common example. Suppose that every time you approach your instructors you feel knots in your stomach. Perhaps in the past you had an instructor with a rude and impatient attitude who made you feel upset. After some pairings, just the sight of the instructor made you upset because you paired the instructor with rude attitudes. With **generalization**, this response spread to other instructors, and you are now anxious when approaching any and all of your instructors even though only one instructor was rude to you. One way to deal with this is to get to know your other instructors. Say hello to your instructors outside of class, discuss class material, or just ask the instructor questions. Most instructors are happy to speak to students. By doing this, you are extinguishing your anxiety response by breaking the pairings you had between instructor and rude behaviour. In some cases you may find that discrimination training is necessary. This means that you teach yourself to feel anxious only in front of the rude instructor. Consider, however, that the rude instructor might have not meant to be rude; perhaps the instructor was having a bad day and is generally a nice person, one whom you do not need to fear. However, try to talk to your other instructors. Most will want to talk to you. In this way, you may still feel anxious in front of one rude instructor but comfortable in front of others.

extinction
in associative learning, the removal or reduction of the response when the two events are no longer paired or associated

discrimination
in associative learning, showing a response to an original stimulus, but not to a stimulus similar to the original stimulus

generalization
in associative learning, showing a response to a stimulus similar, but not identical, to the original stimulus

Ravi feels anxious and frustrated in his philosophy class. The anxiety is likely distracting him from achieving in this class. He needs to end the pairing of philosophy with failure. To do this, he needs to achieve some success in this course, after which he will feel less anxious and will begin to expect some successes in class. However, achieving success will involve many changes for Ravi. He will need to change his study methods, improve his critical thinking, improve his note taking and reading, and deal with his test anxiety (all these topics are covered in chapters of this book).

Exercise 5.4 lists some things that cause considerable anxiety in students. Think about each item and suggest what the original pairing might have been. Consider ways to break the pairing and improve school performance. The first item is completed, however you could probably think of alternative pairings that lead to the anxiety, and alternative ways to break the pairings. You might want to team up with another student for this activity and compare your lists. Does your fellow student have any different suggestions to break these pairings?

EXERCISE 5.4

▶ *Dealing with Anxiety-Producing Associations*

Below is a list of items that often make post-secondary students feel anxious. Speculate on the original pairings and methods to break down the pairings.

Item

- Tests
- Seminar presentations
- Answering questions in class
- Assignment due dates
- Having papers returned
- The first day of class
- Talking to the instructor
- Receiving grades

Example

Tests

Original Pairing: Pairs the test with a low grade

Methods to break the pairing:

- Try practice tests
- Work out study methods that improve performance
- Be well prepared for the test by avoiding cramming
- Think of times when test performance has been good

LEARNING FROM CONSEQUENCES

When consequences are provided for our performance, we are motivated to perform. If the consequence is positive (e.g., receiving a good grade), we are motivated to continue to study in the same way. If the consequence is negative (e.g., receiving a poor grade), we may be motivated to change our study methods. For example, when Jasmine performs well at school, her parents call her relatives to talk about their brilliant daughter. This motivates Jasmine to continue to perform well. Sometimes **consequential learning** is called operant or instrumental conditioning.

consequential learning learning that takes place because voluntary behaviour is attached to a consequence

Interest in instrumental conditioning stemmed from the study of animal intelligence. In the late 1800s, some researchers, such as Thorndike, wondered whether animals could think (Hergenhahn, 2005). Overall, researchers agreed that the animals seemed to be motivated by the rewards and punishments (consequences) they received. Behaviours that resulted in reward seemed to be repeated and behaviours that did not result in reward or that resulted in punishment were dropped. In other words, animals learned from their mistakes by not making them again.

Since that time, researchers have speculated that much human behaviour is motivated by consequences. At times, humans are motivated to increase a behaviour to receive something. For example, Omar increases his class participation because he receives a positive response from his instructor. At other times, humans increase behaviour to avoid something. Ravi is planning to increase his time spent reading philosophy to avoid another poor grade. Finally, at times humans decrease behaviour to avoid something. For example, Ravi might decrease looking at his philosophy instructor to avoid being called upon to answer questions.

Like with learning by association, **generalization** often occurs as we learn from consequences. For example, if Ravi changes his study methods and receives a higher grade on a philosophy test, he will be motivated to continue using these study methods for philosophy. In addition, Ravi may also decide to use these new study techniques in his other classes. In other words, Ravi will generalize his study techniques to all his classes in order to receive rewards (higher grades) in each.

Sometimes an inappropriate behaviour must be extinguished or brought to **extinction**. That is, some behaviours at the post-secondary level will not lead to a positive outcome. It is often difficult to identify which behaviours caused the positive or negative outcome at school. Sometimes students study but do not receive good grades. Ravi has this problem: he did study for his philosophy test but that did not help his performance. Ravi needs to examine his study methods, decide which study behaviours are not working for him, and discard or extinguish them. One simple way to examine your own study behaviours is through self-control procedures. These procedures will be discussed in the next section of this chapter.

At times **discrimination** training is required at school. Sometimes it is appropriate to show behaviour in one situation and not in others. For example, you may have a fun friend who is loud and boisterous at parties. This behaviour is appropriate at parties but not in class. To control your friend's behaviour, you might reward his behaviour by laughing with him at parties but ignore this behaviour when it occurs in class. In this way, your friend learns that his behaviour is only acceptable in some circumstances.

Finally, a few words need to be said about **learned helplessness**, which occurs when people are rarely or never rewarded and nothing they do seems to lead to a positive outcome. Under these circumstances, individuals usually stop responding at all and often become depressed. For example, Ravi has tried a number of things to improve his philosophy grades, such as reading more and spending more hours studying, but to no avail. Ravi may feel that nothing he can do will result in higher grades and he may be tempted to stop trying, as people often do when they expect to fail. However, you can inoculate yourself against learned helplessness by recalling previous successes. This reminds you that you can achieve success (Seligman & Maier, 1967). Learned helplessness can happen at post-secondary school: 70 percent of post-secondary students need some help with academic skills (Seon & King, 1997). Many students arrive at their school with study skills that are not well suited to higher education and thus their grades suffer. In addition, instructors tend to give you only corrective feedback (i.e., they only discuss what you did wrong), which you might perceive as punishment. Less often will instructors tell you that what you are doing is right: they assume that you will interpret the absence of criticism as encouragement. In this environment, you might sometimes feel that no matter what you do, you cannot win. You might be tempted to give up and leave school. The highest loss of students (attrition) from post-secondary schools is in first year (Matusky, 2001). However, remember that helplessness is learned and it can be unlearned. In addition, you can learn to reward your own efforts and change your study style to improve your success at school.

generalization
in consequential learning, responding to a situation similar, but not identical, to one in which reward has been given

extinction
in consequential learning, the removal or reduction of behaviour because the behaviour is no longer followed by a reward

discrimination
in consequential learning, not responding to a situation that is similar, but not identical, to one in which reward has been given

learned helplessness
occurs when people are rarely or never reinforced, when nothing they do can affect whether they are rewarded

WHAT DOES LEARNING THROUGH CONSEQUENCES TEACH ME?

Consequential learning focuses on changes to voluntary behaviour. We say this because when someone is rewarded, he or she can choose to repeat the behaviour to be rewarded again. Thus, consequential learning is often used as a motivator to increase studying, improve presentation techniques, reduce conflict in group work, etc. While consequential learning is involved in motivating students to learn course material, these are generally not the procedures that help you to understand the content of your course. However, do not underestimate the value of this motivation. Students who learn to reward themselves for their own efforts are often more successful at post-secondary studies (Kennett, 1994). Further, when you rely on others to reward your efforts, you are more likely to feel negatively about your post-secondary experience (Heiby, 1982).

HOW DOES CONSEQUENTIAL LEARNING APPLY TO ME AT SCHOOL?

Learning from consequences is seen in almost all aspects of the post-secondary setting. You are rewarded and punished by the grades you receive, the attitudes of your instructors, the peer interactions you have, the administration you deal with, etc. Setting up consequences can help to motivate you and help you to control outcomes inside and outside of school. In many work environments, workers are motivated to work through external rewards. However, of more interest to students is how consequences can be used to improve the post-secondary setting.

Students can use consequences to control the post-secondary environment and to provide motivation to study. This is done though reciprocal interactions and self-control procedures. **Reciprocal interaction** means that the environment affects your behaviour and your behaviour also affects the environment. For example, when you smile at someone, they often smile back. Thus, while you are rewarding someone else, they are rewarding you to smile more. Using reciprocal interactions in dealing with peers and instructors is usually very effective. For example, when working in groups, giving verbal rewards for appropriate behaviours while ignoring inappropriate behaviours can have the effect of improving the entire group experience by promoting reciprocal respect.

reciprocal interaction
the environment affects your behaviour and your behaviour also affects the environment

SELF-CONTROL PROCEDURES

self-control procedure
the application of learning principles to change one's behaviour

A **self-control procedure** is a method you use to change your own behaviour. These are often used to improve study skills and improve motivation to study.

HOW ARE SELF-CONTROL PROCEDURES CONDUCTED?

Setting up a self-control procedure requires three steps. First, you need to understand the antecedents (when and why your behaviour occurs). To do this, you need to observe your own behaviour by keeping a journal. Let's take the example of Ravi. Perhaps after a week of journalling, he realizes that he has only studied for two hours. Other study time was spent talking to roommates, cleaning his room, making snacks, daydreaming, etc. Based on the journal, Ravi realizes that he needs to increase studying. To increase studying Ravi will need to figure out the best ways to learn at the post-secondary level, since studying at the post-secondary level is different from studying at high school. He will need to learn new study techniques through his study skills centre, through reading books about these techniques, by watching others, by seeing demonstrations of these techniques, and by practising the techniques (Mahoney & Thoresen, 1974). Throughout this book you will find instruction on study techniques that, if practised properly, could help to improve your post-secondary experience.

The second step in a self-control procedure is to set goals. You need to set long-term goals (e.g., improve my philosophy grade) and short-term goals (e.g., read Chapter 2 in my philosophy book).

Third, you will need to control consequences. This is not simply rewarding yourself for studying, but rather controlling the study environment to maximize the chance that you will study. For example, if roommates keep Ravi from studying, he needs to change his study location. He may decide to move to the library for most of his studying. After studying, he needs to find a suitable reward for meeting a short-term goal. A walk and a coffee with a friend following his studying may be what Ravi finds most appealing. Self-control procedures can be applied to many aspects of student life, such as increasing study time, time management, and completing assignments. You might find it helpful to complete the self-control exercise suggested at the end of this chapter as a way of reinforcing your understanding of these concepts (Individual Activity 4).

OBSERVATIONAL LEARNING

observational learning
an indirect method of learning in which the learner learns by watching a model perform a behaviour

In **observational learning** methods, the learner learns by watching rather than doing. In observational learning, a skill is demonstrated by a model. Watching a model perform a skill can help you to acquire and improve your own skills. Modelling has been used to reduce fear of dentistry, improve presentation techniques, teach job-related skills, and improve writing/academic skills. Modelling is an effective way to increase self-efficacy (what we think we are competent at) (Hergenhahn, 2005). For example, you could watch a model effectively give a presentation. By watching the model, you could both pick up presentation skills and view consequences of the presentation (the audience response). This knowledge could help to improve your own presentation skills and could lead to changes in self-efficacy (I saw the model do that and I think I can too).

WHAT DO I LEARN WITH OBSERVATIONAL METHODS?

procedural learning
learning how to perform an action

Observational learning offers the individual an opportunity to learn two important things. First, you can understand how to perform an action. This type of learning is sometimes referred to as **procedural learning**. Second, you can see the consequences of an action. In this way, you can compare your current skills with modelled skills and evaluate your own progress, as well as learn to anticipate what the results of your actions will be.

WHEN IS OBSERVATIONAL LEARNING USED AT SCHOOL?

Observational learning is important in the post-secondary environment. Instructors and teaching assistants use observational modelling techniques to demonstrate difficult concepts and job-related skills. For example, instructors frequently will model an *A* essay for students. Part of the essay is read to the class. The instructor expects the students to compare what they have written with the *A* paper and gain a better understanding of expectations in writing.

HOW DOES OBSERVATIONAL LEARNING HELP ME AT SCHOOL?

To some extent, using your instructors, teaching assistants, and other students as models can help you to gauge and evaluate your performance in terms of the quality of your work, your ability to meet deadlines, and your capabilities. These models should also help you to know when you need extra help. Modelling is a technique that we will use a great deal in this book. In addition, observational learning highlights the need for lecture attendance. Since some information can be gained through models, the student who attends a lecture has an advantage over those who do not.

INSIGHT

insight
occurs when one discovers the solution to a problem without having made an effort to solve the problem

Most students experience insight at some point. **Insight** occurs when the solution to a problem comes, but no effort to solve the problem was made. You might have had the experience that you were listening to music or relaxing when suddenly you knew the answer to a problem you had previously been working on. This is insight. Many researchers have tried to understand insight. They acknowledge that while humans do have insight, they may not suddenly come upon a solution, but rather unconsciously replay the problem in their minds until it is solved (for an interesting discussion see Best, 1999). However, to have insight requires considerable knowledge of a topic area.

WHEN DO I HAVE INSIGHTS?

Insight is a process that is used in finding solutions to problems. Whether people have insight or not depends very much on their current knowledge base. For example, you are very unlikely to solve a complex physics problem if you have no knowledge of science. With insight, you apply your current knowledge to come to a solution, however, during instances of insight, you do this without effort or being aware that you are doing it. It seems to you that the answer just appears in your mind.

HOW DOES INSIGHT HELP ME AT SCHOOL?

divergent thinking
thinking of a problem from more than one angle

Instructors ask students to work alone or within groups to solve problems or theorize on solutions to questions. Frequently, these questions do not have one clear solution and the instructor expects you to show creativity. Creative problem-solving requires **divergent thinking**, meaning that you should think of the problem from more than one angle. When you use creative problem-solving, you often have insights into new ways of doing things. Another advantage of insight is that it speeds up the time to solve problems. However, for this to happen, you need knowledge of your topic area.

HOW CAN I ENSURE THAT I HAVE INSIGHT WHEN WORKING ON PROBLEMS IN CLASSES?

You can maximize the possibility that you will have insights. First, to have insights you need a strong knowledge base. This means that, when given an assignment in which insight could occur, you will more likely have insights if you have great knowledge in the topic area. For example, you are not likely to have insights on a statistical problem if you do not have basic mathematics skills. You are not likely to have insights to theorize on literature if you do not know the context in which it was written. Ravi is not likely to have insights in philosophy because he does not understand it. One of the first steps is to increase your knowledge of a topic area through reading. What have others said about similar problems? What other topic areas are related to your topic area? This means that when choosing assignment topics (if given a choice) you should pick a topic that interests you and a topic about which you have some preliminary knowledge (or at least have read what your course textbook says about the topic). This does not mean you should only take topics in which you already have strong knowledge, but it will help you to have a preliminary under-standing through your textbook and library research. Starting a research paper or a problem solution with some ideas about a topic usually results in more creativity, better paper organization, and a more concise discussion of the topic. In addition, if after beginning to research a potential topic you find it dull or uninteresting, you can change it (if allowed). In general, you will be more successful in your assignment if you like the topic you choose to write on.

INFORMATION PROCESSING PROCEDURES

information processing
the study of how information moves through the human mind

encoding
entering information into the mind

storage
holding information in the mind

retrieval
pulling into awareness information that has been previously stored

Information processing theorists study how information moves through the human mind. Their interest is in how information enters into your mind, how it is retained in your mind, and how you later recall it. Three stages in processing are generally studied: encoding, storage and retrieval.

Encoding means getting information into the mind. While this seems simple, it is sometimes difficult for students to decide what information from their text and lecture is relevant. This is, in part, Ravi's problem: because of the large amount of information that is presented in philosophy, Ravi will not likely be able to encode it all. Instead, he needs to focus on information that is most important. Information, once chosen as important, is then stored in his mind.

The method of information **storage** determines what can be later recalled. Ideally, information should be stored in a highly organized, meaningful fashion. Information that is meaningful will most likely be later recalled. This again is a problem for Ravi. Because he understands very little of the material in the course, he is having trouble determining how to make it meaningful to himself. Ravi needs to organize material into meaningful categories. To get a better understanding of relevant categories, he can look at the instructor's presentation slides, where topics are categorized. In addition, Ravi's textbook will be organized by titles and subtitles, which can help Ravi to begin to organize material. Then, at the **retrieval** stage, when remembering information during a test, he can recall the categories, which will help him recall more detailed points. The stages of information processing are shown in Figure 5.1. Information processing theorists have developed numerous techniques to increase encoding, storage, and retrieval of information. Information processing will be discussed in detail in Chapter 6.

FIGURE 5.1 Information Processing Theory

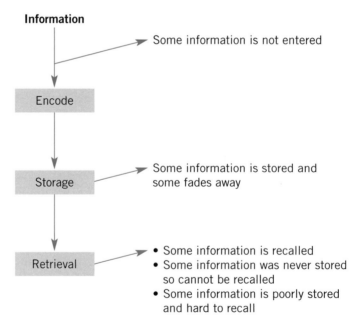

WHAT DO I LEARN WITH INFORMATION PROCESSING METHODS?

Successful information processing allows you to store and retrieve course content. Information processing itself is not a learning procedure but rather a study of how information is organized. However, knowing information processing theory allows you to remember more information by organizing it to maximize recall.

HOW DO I APPLY INFORMATION PROCESSING METHODS AT SCHOOL?

Information processing theory has led to numerous techniques to aid in the recall and understanding of course materials. These techniques will be presented in Chapter 6. All techniques focus on choosing relevant information to study, re-organizing course material to better fit the organization of your mind, using relevant categories when studying, and making course materials meaningful. In Box 5.2 we present a suggested method for making study notes in meaningful ways. As you can see, this lecture summary is organized by categories (Definitions, Evidence, and Relationships). Recalling these categories can help you to recall the content within them.

Lecture Note Summary	BOX 5.2

TOPIC: LEARNING WITH ASSOCIATION

Definitions

Associative learning:
- The association of two things in the environment (example: sight of instructor and rude behaviour)
- After many pairings, leads to expectations of rude behaviour from instructor

Learning from associations:
- Learn expectations and emotions

Evidence

Supportive:
- Pavlov's dogs salivated to lab assistants after they associated the assistant with food (expect food when see assistant).
- Students fear exams after they pair exams with failing. They expect to fail when they see the exam.

Contrary:
- Emotional responses could also be innate or due to consequences rather than expectations.

Relationships

Relates to:
- Generalization, Extinction, Discrimination

Relates to me:
- Whenever I see my mother, I feel hungry. I expect food when I see mother.

HOW CAN I USE MY KNOWLEDGE OF INFORMATION PROCESSING TO IMPROVE MY PERFORMANCE?

At the post-secondary level, instructors largely determine the information content for their courses. However, the ways in which information is presented can vary. Information is often conveyed in text format and through lectures and seminars. You may feel overloaded when information is presented and this may be because the information does not always appear to be organized. Thus, you do not see the relationship between lecture, seminar, and text materials within a single course. Students like Ravi can reduce their study load by integrating text, lecture, and seminar material in an organized fashion.

For example, you might rework notes taken at lectures and from the textbook. (This method is shown in Box 5.2.) This example is a study note created from text and lecture material in the area of learning by association. In this method, you take lecture and text material and organize it in such a way that it may be applied to particular exam questions. As shown, the method uses meaningful categories to make efficient study notes. The categories include Topic (title), Definition (general definitions needed), Evidence (which supports and refutes this concept), Relates To (other topics that relate to this one), Relates To Me (an example of the use of the concept in your life).

Notes that emphasize both definitional and relational information allow you to formulate insightful answers in examination situations. Frequently, students find that these types of notes directly answer exam questions. For example, instructors often ask students to define, contrast, and give evidence for particular issues.

Advice for Ravi

▶ Ravi is having difficulty understanding his philosophy lectures and textbook and has recently received a low grade on a philosophy test. Becoming aware of his own learning styles and understanding and applying general learning methods will help Ravi. Below is a summary of the steps that Ravi may choose to take to help him grasp the content of his philosophy class and successfully complete his course.

STEPS	PROPOSED OUTCOME
Discover personal cognitive, personality, and perceptual learning styles	Helps to uncover strengths in learning
	Helps to uncover weaknesses in learning
Use learning style strengths	Helps to focus and organize studies around strengths (i.e., a visual learner may concentrate on diagrams in the text)
Know learning style weaknesses	Helps to know what does not work well in learning and to refocus these learning activities (i.e., if listening to the lecture is difficult, view topic slides, focus on lecture examples, etc.)
Develop a personal learning plan	Sets out goals, objectives, and methods to achieve these goals
	Forces students to reflect on their learning needs
Understand learning by association	First step in understanding anxiety in learning situations
	Highlights pairings that lead to expectations and emotions
	Allows students to reflect on anxiety-producing pairings that result in test and presentation anxiety
Understand learning by consequences	Helps to discover motivations that keep students learning
	Helps to discover factors that distract from learning
Keep a learning journal	Helps to understand personal study behaviours, distractions, and motivations
Develop study-related self-control procedures	Helps students to focus and organize studying
Understand observational learning	Models help to show correct performance
	Models allow students to compare their own performance with that of the model, thus evaluating themselves
	Models can demonstrate work-related skills not easily acquired at school
Understand insight	Encourages students to gain topic-related knowledge
	Emphasizes the need to review returned assignments and tests to correct errors
Understand information processing	Encourages students to think about how information is best entered and stored
	Encourages students to create meaningful and organized study notes

CHAPTER SUMMARY

- A number of methods to understand personal learning styles based on cognition, personality, and perception have been developed. These learning styles help to point out personal learning strengths and weaknesses so that the learner can better modify learning tasks to maximize learning potential. A personal learning plan can be developed to help guide personal learning.

- Learning through association of events helps to create expectations in the learner. Emotions or feelings towards people or events are often learned through association.

- Learning through consequences can help motivate the learner. Consequential learning is used in developing self-control procedures, which help the learner set up and attain learning goals by controlling the learning environment.

- Learning by observation often involves learning models. Models show the learner how to complete a procedure (e.g., how to write an essay) and then can help the learner to understand how the learning will be evaluated.

- Having insight in learning requires the learner to have considerable knowledge of the insight topic.

- Learning is often described by information processing theory. This theory emphasizes that learners need to understand the meaning of information in order to better retain and recall it.

KEY TERMS

abstract conceptualizer
active experimenter
associative learning
auditory learning style
cognitive learning styles
concrete experiencer
conditioned emotional response (CER)
consequential learning
discrimination (in associative learning)
discrimination (in consequential learning)
divergent thinking
encoding
extinction (in associative learning)
extinction (in consequential learning)

extrovert
feeler
generalization (in associative learning)
generalization (in consequential learning)
information processing
insight
introvert
intuitor
judger
learned helplessness
observational learning
perceiver

personal learning plan
personality-based learning styles
procedural learning
reciprocal interaction
reflective observer
retrieval
self-control procedure
sensor
storage
tactile learning style
thinker
visual learning style

INDIVIDUAL ACTIVITIES

1. Review Exercises 5.1 to 5.3 and list your learning preferences and strengths. List ways in which these preferences and strengths can be used to improve learning in lectures, reading your textbook, and preparing assignments.

2. Create an individual learning plan for a course that you are taking. Follow the style in Box 5.1, by listing your learning goals, self-assessment, and methods to meet your goals.

3. For one week, keep a study journal. Your journal should describe each study session that you had during the week. Be sure to note the time that you studied, the distractions,

your accomplishments, and study interruptions. Once you have completed your journal, review it to see if you need to change your study environment or your study methods, or reduce distractions.

4. Pick one academic behaviour to change. For example, you might want to increase your reading, improve your writing, increase your studying, or improve your understanding of lectures. Create a self-control procedure, which includes knowing the antecedents for your current behaviour (e.g., difficulties studying because of loud roommates), methods proposed to improve the behaviour (e.g., a new study environment), and consequences you give yourself for properly performing the behaviour (e.g., after an hour of studying, I can watch a TV show). Try your self-control procedure to see if it works.

5. Imagine you were asked to evaluate your friends' learning. Using divergent thinking (looking at the issue from many angles) and considering what you know from this chapter, list ways in which you might do this.

6. Create some study notes for this chapter using meaningful categories after reviewing Box 5.2.

GROUP ACTIVITIES

1. Brainstorm with group members to create an individual learning plan for a student who has difficulties reading. Be sure to specify goals (e.g., improve reading speed), current assessment (choose some learning style preferences for this student from Exercises 5.1 to 5.3), and ways to meet these goals.

2. As a group, create a self-control procedure for a student who is failing a course due to inefficient use of time (assignments are late, chapters are not read, studying is minimal).

3. As a group, choose Exercise 5.1, 5.2, or 5.3. Suggest activities that would help students within each learning style to better understand lecture material.

REFERENCES

Berghuis, A. J. (2004) http://www.berghuis.co.nz/abiator/lsi/lsiframe.html, retrieved September 27, 2004.

Best, J. B. (1999). *Cognitive psychology* (5th ed.). New York: West Publishing Company.

Gardner, J. N., & Jewler A. J.(1993). *http//www.e-radiography.net/articles/learningstyles/questionnaire.htm*. Retrieved September, 19, 2004.

Gardner, J. N., & Jewler A. J. (2003). *Your college experience: Strategies for success* (5th ed.). Belmont, CA: Wadsworth.

Heiby, E. M. (1982). A self-reinforcement questionnaire. *Behaviour Research and Therapy, 20*, 397–401.

Hergenhahn, B. R. (2005). *An introduction to the history of psychology* (5th ed.). Belmont, CA: Thomson Wadsworth.

Kennett, D. J. (1994). Academic self-management counseling: Preliminary evidence for the importance of learned resourcefulness on program success. *Studies in Higher Education, 19*, 295–307.

Kolb, D. A. (1976). *Learning style inventory: Technical manual*. Boston: McBer.

Kolb, D. A. (1984). *Experiential learning: Experience as the source of learning and development*. Englewood Cliffs, NJ: Prentice Hall.

Mahoney, M. J., & Thoresen, C. E. (1974). *Self-control: Power to the person*. Monterey, CA: Brooks/Cole Publishing Company.

Matusky, J. G. (2001). Retention efforts take hold. *University Affairs, 42(8)*, 19–22.

Seligman, M. E. P., & Maier, S. F. (1967). Failure to escape traumatic shock. *Journal of Experimental Psychology, 74*, 1–9.

Seon, Y., & King, R. (1997). *Study skills can make a major difference*. Paper presented to the Annual Conference of the American Mathematical Association of Two-Year Colleges, Atlanta, GA. (ERIC Document Reproduction Service No. ED417791)

MEMORY

In this chapter, we will:

- Examine how to select important information for study

- Apply this selection process to lecture note taking

- Examine memory and apply memory theory to studying

- Examine why people forget, and use this information to organize study sessions

- Examine the use of visual imagery and mnemonics to improve recall of information

- Apply information selection, memory, and forgetting theory to multiple-choice and short-answer tests

The Case of Jacinta

▶ Jacinta just received several mid-term examinations back and her grades were much lower than she had expected. Her biology exam in particular was poor: she did not even pass. Jacinta had studied for this exam, but it did not seem to help. It looked like she had studied many of the wrong items, things that were not on the test. During the test, she'd forgotten several key theories and confused others. When she looked them up in her book after the exam, she remembered studying them. Jacinta wonders why she is having so much difficulty in remembering biology. She hopes that there are some ways of memorizing biology that will help improve her grade on the final exam.

Jacinta realizes that she must critically evaluate theories in biology, however, to do this she must first recall and understand these theories. Remembering lecture and textbook material is not the only goal at school but, as Jacinta has found out, it is an important one. Recalling material itself is not generally difficult, however, at the post-secondary level the enormous amount of material makes remembering it difficult. Thus, it is important to learn and recall in an efficient manner, since it is unlikely that you could recall every word of your textbook and lectures. You will need to select important information to study. You will also need to memorize selected materials, show an understanding of that material, analyze it, apply it to new situations, and critically evaluate it.

ATTENTION

HOW DO I SELECT IMPORTANT INFORMATION?

In Exercise 6.1, there is a short story in which some words are in boldface and others are in regular type. Read only the words in bold, and then answer the questions below the box without looking back at the story.

EXERCISE 6.1

▶ *Attention Demonstration*

Read only the words in bold, and then answer the questions below the box without looking back at the story.

> The **The** children **students** ran **were** all **busy** over **working** the **on** garden **their** and **presentation** caused **for** considerable **their** damage **class**. Their **They** parents **had** were **been** quite **told** annoyed **that** with **the** them **instructor** and **was** sent **usually** them **a** to **very** bed **difficult** without **marker** supper.

1. What did the message in boldface say?
2. What did the message in regular print say?

selective attention
the process of attending to some information while ignoring other information

If you are like most students, you will recall the boldfaced message and know very little about the regular-type message. The process in which you select important information and ignore other information is called **selective attention**. Selective attention allows you to enter a limited amount of information into your mind so that you do not become overloaded. Some researchers have suggested that your mind is rather like a funnel: a lot of information is poured in but only a small amount gets through (Broadbent, 1958; Solso, Maclin, & Maclin, 2004; Treisman, 1964). Information that does not get through is lost. However, under some circumstances you do recall information that you did not attend to. For example, at a party you might be listening to some conversations and not others, but you can hear your name in a conversation that you are not attending to. This shows you that information that is highly important or meaningful can be recalled with little attention. Yet, it is clear that we do recall best when we pay attention to an event.

HOW DOES SELECTIVE ATTENTION APPLY TO STUDYING AT SCHOOL?

While learning for the joy of learning is an honourable goal, you most likely wish to commit to memory facts that will later be tested. Thus, you must first select information that is important to learn. This might seem like an easy task, but many students have difficulty in choosing relevant versus irrelevant information when studying. For example, Jacinta studied many hours for an exam only to realize, during the exam, that the material she had studied was irrelevant. Finding out too late that the wrong information was studied is an all too common experience.

HOW CAN I PICK OUT IMPORTANT INFORMATION FROM THE LECTURE?

You likely attend lecture classes in which the instructor talks for two to three hours. Usually in these lectures the instructor is attempting to teach a few concepts, which are embedded around examples, stories, class discussions, and demonstrations. Your job is to pick out the concepts through the examples, stories, discussions, and demonstrations. Because of the many different lecturing styles, however, a concept cannot always be clearly distinguished from the examples and stories. That is, what Instructor Jones is trying to get across isn't always obvious to anyone except Instructor Jones.

encoding
entering information into the mind

You also need to write lecture notes so that the lecture is available to you for studying. Writing lecture notes will help you with **encoding**, or entering information into your mind. When information is presented in more than one format—through listening to the lecture (auditory format) and writing down the lecture (visual format)—it is entered through two senses. Information entered in more than one way is more likely to be recalled. However, you still need to be able to distinguish important information from other information.

Taking lecture notes that emphasize important concepts requires practice. Most students try to write down everything the instructor says in the way the instructor says it. However, notes like this do not clearly distinguish the concept being taught from the examples, stories, discussions, and demonstrations.

To distinguish important concepts within lecture notes, many students use the Cornell system in note taking. To use the Cornell system, you first must distinguish important information or concepts from other less important information. There are a number of ways that students can pick important information out of the other entertaining material.

1. *Attend to overheads or slides the instructor presents.* Often, the slides are grouped by concept, and the important concept being taught is either a title or a bulleted point.

2. *Listen for repetition.* Many lecturers repeat important information, and they tell examples or stories that lead back to the important concept. In addition, important concepts are often repeated in the required reading.

3. *Use different areas of your page for certain information.* In the Cornell note taking system (see Table 6.1), highly important concepts/information/titles are presented in the left margin of the page. This helps to highlight the information for later study or when creating study notes. Definitions, evidence, and information details about the concept are presented on the right.

Another highly popular method of note taking is Guided Inquiry. In this method, during the lecture, you compose a question and answer the question through the lecture. Table 6.1 presents three examples of notes taken by three different students during the same lecture about a phenomenon called classical conditioning. Notice that in all of the examples, the students try to use short forms for words in order to keep pace with the instructor.

Notice, in Table 6.1, that in typical note taking, the student is trying to write down everything the instructor is saying. The main problem here is that when it is time to study, the important concepts are embedded with other information. This will make these notes difficult to use.

There are advantages of using Cornell and Guided Inquiry over typical note taking. First, these systems emphasize important material. The Cornell system allows for quick identification of important information by viewing the titles/concepts on the left. The Guided Inquiry system groups important information under a question. Thus, the Guided Inquiry adds meaning to material, since materials provide answers to student-developed questions. In contrast to the Cornell and Guided Inquiry systems, typical note taking requires you to later read through your notes to find the important information. This re-reading may occur many days after the lecture and you can miss important concepts while reading. Second, both the Cornell and Guided Inquiry systems add organization to lecture notes and organized materials are generally easier to memorize.

TABLE 6.1 **Three Lecture Note Taking Styles**

TYPICAL NOTE TAKING	CORNELL SYSTEM		GUIDED INQUIRY
Classical conditioning is the association between two stimuli in the environment. CI con was demonstrated by a Russian physiologist named Pavlov. He was interested in the dog's digestive system. He gave dogs meat powder so that they would salivate. After doing this for a few days he noticed that when his lab assistant entered the room the dogs began to salivate without the meat powder. The dogs salivated at the sight of the lab assist. They likely were anticipating food when seeing the lab assistant. Pavlov called the meat powder an unconditioned stimulus and the salivation to meat powder an unconditioned response because you do not have to learn to salivate to food, it is a natural response . . .	**Classical conditioning** **Pavlov** **Unconditioned stimulus** **Unconditioned response**	• association between two things in the environment • studied Cl. Con. • something that causes a natural reaction • meat powder if put in the mouth causes salivation, mp is the US • natural response (unlearned) • salivation occurs naturally to mp, sal is UR . . .	**What is classical conditioning?** • association between two things in the env. **How does it work?** • Pavlov showed that you can pair something unnatural with a natural response. Meat powder (unconditioned stimulus) causes salivation (unconditioned response). Later, animals salivate to the lab assistant because he is paired with the meat powder. So many pairings of lab assistant and meat powder are followed by sal. Later the lab assistant (now the cond stimulus) causes sal (now a cond. response). **Does this work in humans?** . . .

Many successful students re-write their lecture notes following the lecture. Re-writing notes has two important functions. First, it forces you to rehearse important information and, as will be discussed in the following sections, rehearsal is a key to remembering. Second, it allows you to organize lecture notes. These study notes can include text and lecture material.

Some students use both the Cornell and Guided Inquiry systems together. In class they use the Cornell system so that important concepts are highlighted, and at home they re-write their notes using the Guided Inquiry system. In this way they have the advantages of both systems and re-writing their notes gives them extra rehearsal of information (more on this later).

Successful use of either the Cornell system or the Guided Inquiry note taking system requires practice. One good way to practise these systems is to try the exercise (Individual Activity 1) at the end of this chapter, where you will be given a short lecture piece in written format. Read the information and take notes. Afterward, see the list of points that the instructor felt were important at the very end of the chapter and compare these points to your notes.

HOW CAN I PICK OUT IMPORTANT INFORMATION FROM THE TEXT?

Reading the text and picking out the important concepts is crucial. To identify important concepts or information, you can:

■ read the chapter summary first

■ find concepts that were also in lecture

- attend to section titles and definitional words (often bolded in textbooks)
- read through the questions presented at the end of the chapter (when available)

You should be aware that while many instructors include some text materials within their lectures, they also test readings that were not discussed in class, on the reasonable and practical assumption that students have learned this material on their own.

WHAT FACTORS AFFECT MY ABILITY TO PICK OUT RELEVANT INFORMATION?

Lack of time, stress, and lack of organization are most frequently associated with poor test results. You will also find that these issues can affect attention. At times, you will feel overloaded and may divide your attention among too many tasks, causing you to miss important information. Students in this situation often report, as did Jacinta, that they studied all the wrong materials for their test.

MEMORY

HOW DO WE RECALL INFORMATION?

Researchers have proposed that we have three memory systems that interact and work together. These systems streamline information coming into the mind and also remove or delete irrelevant information (Atkinson & Schiffren, 1968; Solso et al., 2004). The three systems are called the sensory memory, short-term memory (STM), and long-term memory (LTM). How these three systems work and interact give us hints about how best to recall information and how information is forgotten.

SENSORY MEMORY

sensory memory
a memory system that gathers vast amounts of information from the senses (vision, hearing, touch, smell, taste) and holds it only briefly

short-term memory
a memory system that analyzes current information and selects it for further processing

long-term memory
a memory system that can store information indefinitely

All information coming to you through your vision, hearing, touch, smell, and taste systems is recorded in **sensory memory**. Given that so much information is constantly aimed at your senses, much more information is available to you than your brain could possibly process. For one minute, just try to become aware of the stimuli around you: listen to all the sounds, look at all the sights, smell the air, be aware of the taste in your mouth, feel each part of your body as it sits or reclines in comfort or with tension. When you start to become aware of it, there's an immense amount of information bombarding you, isn't there? Clearly, then, only a very select amount of information is retained by the sensory memory and sent on to the **short-term memory** (STM).

The information retained is selected through attention. Sensory experiences that you attend to are sent on and those that you do not attend to are lost. For example, Jacinta may be sitting in a lecture listening to the instructor. She attends to the voice of the lecturer, and that information is passed on. Someone in the third row is coughing, but Jacinta does not notice because she did not attend to that cough. Diane, on the other hand, is sitting in the third row beside the cougher. Diane is feeling annoyed because she is trying to listen to the instructor but the person beside her keeps coughing. Diane will likely recall the cough later because she is attending to it. Information about the coughing is passed on from the sensory memory to the STM (and perhaps even to the **long-term memory** (LTM)).

HOW DOES THE SENSORY MEMORY AFFECT ME AT SCHOOL?

Sensory memory is the first step in the memory process. The sensory experiences that you attend to will be passed on to the short-term memory, where some information will be selected and passed on to the LTM. As described above, selection of relevant information is important in sifting through the many materials you encounter at your school. Not everything is important to remember, so focusing your attention on certain items will maximize performance.

CAN I CONTROL SENSORY MEMORY?

You can control sensory input through selective attention and focusing on your environment. At the sensory level, you are recognizing information that could be important later and sending it for further analysis. This is difficult in some situations. For example, in lecture environments there are many distractions that can cause you to lose important lecture material: students around you chat, eat, cough, and crinkle paper; cellphones ring; instructors may at times be less interesting; etc. To maximize the chance that you will catch the most important information, it is important to examine your environment when entering a lecture. Try to sit in a location where there are fewer distractions (usually closer to the instructor) and where important material is easy to see and hear.

Environmental analysis is generally important in any situation when learning is involved. Locating and avoiding the distractions when studying is part of developing strong post-secondary skills. One means of determining where distractions occur is through journalling. Keeping a journal of your study behaviour, lecture distractions, etc., is the first step in modifying your learning environment.

Examine your own learning environment. Next time you go to lecture, look around you. Why did you choose your seat? What are the benefits of sitting in this location? What distractions do you notice? What is the effect of these distractions on your learning?

SHORT-TERM MEMORY

The short-term memory (STM) is sometimes referred to as working memory. Its purpose is to analyze current information. It represents the first stage of true information analysis in that it receives input from the sensory memory but compares it to information stored in LTM (Solso et al., 2004). For example, right now, the words describing STM are coming into your STM. Your STM notes that there is nothing in your LTM that relates to this, so it's information you don't already know but had better learn. Thus, the relevance and importance of information are judged in the STM.

Since the STM deals with current information, it has only a limited amount of space and time to analyze information. To demonstrate this, Exercise 6.2 below shows a series of letters; read them one at a time without going back to rehearse, then cover them and try to recall the letters.

EXERCISE 6.2 ▶ *Short-Term Memory Demonstration*

Read the following series of letters one at a time without going back to rehearse. Then cover them and try to recall the letters.

A P R T U K H M V B Z Q S O L

If you are like most students you probably can recall between five and nine letters (Miller, 1956). In general, no matter what you are viewing (letters, numbers, words) you recall between five and nine items when you do not rehearse. However, what constitutes an item depends on how the items are organized. To demonstrate this, look at Exercise 6.3 and read each letter as before but do not rehearse, then try to recall.

EXERCISE 6.3   ▶ *Non-Chunked Letters*

Read the following series of letters without going back to rehearse. Then cover them and try to recall the letters.

AV—EP—CET—CC—DF—MBB—C

You likely once again recalled between five and nine letters. However, if we reorganize these letters as in Exercise 6.4 and try again, you may notice an increase in the amount you can recall.

EXERCISE 6.4   ▶ *The Effect of Chunking*

AVE—PC—ETC—CD—FM—BBC

chunking
grouping material into meaningful units

Now you may perfectly recall all of the letters. The difference is that the letters were reorganized into meaningful groups (e.g., AVE is short for avenue). Thus, in the first attempt you needed to recall 15 single letters, but in the second attempt you needed to recall six meaningful items. The process of reorganizing material into meaningful groups is called **chunking**; it allows you to hold more information in the STM (Solso et al., 2004). To take another example, as you read this section, you don't store each letter of letter (e.g., L-E-T-T-E-R), you store the whole word as one unit (LETTER).

A second important aspect of the STM is that it analyzes only current information and holds it for less than one minute. If information is not rehearsed in that minute, it will be lost. Try the example in Exercise 6.5. Read the letters once, cover them, and work out the following mathematical problem. When you complete the math problem, try to recall the letters.

EXERCISE 6.5   ▶ *The Effect of Time on STM*

Read the letters once, cover them, and work out the following mathematical problem. When you complete the math problem, try to recall the letters.

R S Y G F K N D W V Z S L

Mathematical problem: $((5 + 67 - 3)/32) + 20 =$

You likely found that when you shifted your attention to the math problem, you recalled even fewer letters later. The information in STM seemed to fade from memory. But all information does not always fade from STM: some of the information that enters the STM is rehearsed and passed on to the LTM.

HOW CAN I APPLY WHAT I KNOW ABOUT STM TO THE POST-SECONDARY ENVIRONMENT?

While most testing focuses on LTM, STM is a very important factor in entering information into LTM. Three facts about the STM affect outcomes in the LTM and thus affect whether students will recall course materials:

1. The STM has limited capacity; only a limited number of items can be dealt with at a single time. However, chunking can expand this capacity.

2. Items stay only for a limited time, after which they are lost. However, rehearsal can hold these items longer or send them on to LTM.

3. Lack of rehearsal due to distraction from the information can reduce the amount entered into the LTM.

These three facts suggest three important strategies in study organization. First, since capacity can be increased through chunking by meaning, and meaning can aid in recall in the

LTM, it is a good idea for you to create study notes. A study note is different from a lecture note. Lecture notes are essentially reviews of what was said in class. A study note emphasizes important concepts and allows you to integrate text and lecture material in a meaningful way. Thus, study notes need to be organized within meaningful categories. Table 6.2 shows a study note made from a lecture note. Notice that the meaningful categories make material easier to recall (more on this will be presented in the section on LTM below). Recall that, in Chapter 5, we showed you another way to make a categorical study note.

The categorical method of making study notes enhances both the short-term memory and the long-term memory. The categories for the chunked material cause rehearsal in STM and become cues to recall in LTM.

Second, since items only stay for a limited time without rehearsal, rehearsal of items is a key to recall. As we will see, rehearsal is also a technique of importance in the LTM. Once information is attended to and rehearsed in STM, it is passed on to LTM. However, rehearsal must continue for the information to be maintained in LTM (more on this below). One difficulty students often have is in rehearsal. For example, Jacinta had not recalled several biology theories during her test, but after her test she re-read them in her book and realized that she had studied them earlier. Clearly, the theories had not been properly rehearsed and other information in the book had distracted Jacinta from them.

One method to ensure rehearsal of important concepts and theories in STM (first to place them in LTM and second to maintain them in LTM) is to use flash cards. Many post-secondary students use flash cards as a means of maintaining definitions and concepts. In this method, while reading or at lecture, important concepts/theories are placed on one side of a card and the definition or explanation on the other (for lectures this is usually done immediately following the lecture, and the words that will go on flash cards are highlighted in lecture notes). You then take these cards with you during the day and whenever you have a few moments (like on the bus or while waiting for the lecture to begin), you flash some cards to see if you can correctly identify the definition or explanation. An example of a flash card is shown in Figure 6.1.

Third, distractions reduce rehearsal. This suggests that multi-tasking during studying can reduce the likelihood that studied information will be rehearsed and passed on to LTM. For example, if you watch TV while studying for mid-terms, you may recall the entire television

TABLE 6.2 Organizing Study Notes (Categorical Method)

LECTURE NOTE	ORGANIZED STUDY NOTE		
The short-term memory system has limited ability to store information. Usually this is between five and nine items. However, chunking or putting things into meaningful units helps. Also, the system stores information for less than one minute. Distractions result in a loss of information and rehearsal passes on the information. The LTM also uses rehearsal and other techniques to store information. An infinite number of items can be stored in the LTM. The items can stay in the LTM indefinitely (Solso, Maclin, & Maclin, 2004).	*Category*	*STM*	*LTM*
	Capacity	• 5 to 9 items	• Infinite
	Duration	• Less than a minute	• Indefinitely
	Maintained	• By rehearsal	• By rehearsal, organization, imagery
	Information lost	• Distraction preventing rehearsal (interference), time	• Interference from other items, time

FIGURE 6.1 **Study Flash Cards**

Card Front	Card Back
Duration of memory in STM	**Less than one minute**

show but very few of the concepts being tested. Minimizing distractions that will reduce study effectiveness can be beneficial. Students need to identify these distractions in their environment, and distractions are not always obvious. For example, George noted that he was able to recall very few concepts so he kept a journal of his own behaviour while studying. From his journal he noted that the study room was quiet, his roommates did not bother him, and the lighting was good. Yet, he found that he had only studied for 15 minutes. What was the distraction? By looking at his journal, George realized that he had spent the rest of his study time daydreaming about a recent date he'd had. Internal distractions can be as disastrous as external ones to rehearsal of information. When internal distractions happen, it is important to realize they are happening and refocus. Using self-statements such as "I will think about my date later" often help you to refocus. Setting an actual time to daydream (or to worry!) can be useful: "I will daydream from 4:00 to 4:30," or "I will worry for one-half hour after dinner." Often people find that they don't need this much time to daydream or to worry, but the technique has helped them to pull their attention back to the task at hand.

LONG-TERM MEMORY

Information that is rehearsed in the STM is passed on to the LTM where it *can* be stored indefinitely, however, not everything *is* stored indefinitely. We often lose information due to poor organization of information and interference from other memories. There are several important factors about the LTM. First, you are more likely to recall information if it is organized the same way it will be stored. Below in Exercise 6.6 is a list of random words. Study the list (you can read the words over and over in this demonstration); after studying the list for about two minutes, cover the words and recall them in any order.

EXERCISE 6.6

▶ *Long-Term Memory Demonstration*

Study the list (you can read the words over and over in this demonstration); after studying the list for about two minutes, cover the words and recall them in any order.

Jane	spider	apple	Joe	banana
fly	cockroach	Billy	pear	Tom
Amanda	Phil	grapes	Beatle	grapefruit

Examine your list; if you are like most people, you probably recalled all the fruits together, the names together, and the insects together. It appears that, when you study, your mind organizes or categorizes the information. Thus, when these words need to be recalled you simply have to recall the category and attempt to recall the items in the category.

If your LTM prefers categorical information, it is a good idea to categorize information prior to studying. Below are two further memory tasks in which the words in one task are pre-categorized and the words in the other are not. Study each word one at a time, reading down each column of words in Exercise 6.7. Go through the list twice; cover the words, then recall them in any order.

▶ *Memory Organization Demonstration*

Study each word one at a time, reading down each column of words. Go through the list twice; cover the words, then recall them in any order.

classical conditioning	learned helplessness	reinforcement
reciprocal interactions	encoding	self-control procedures
conditioned emotional response	expectation	retrieval
storage	meaningful categories	Pavlov

Try the task again using the organization imposed in Exercise 6.8; the difference is that the words in Exercise 6.8 are now categorized for you.

▶ *The Benefits of Categorization*

Study each word one at a time, reading down each column of words. Go through the list twice; cover the words, then recall them in any order.

Learning by Association	Learning by Consequences	Information Processing
classical conditioning	reinforcement	encoding
Pavlov	learned helplessness	storage
conditioned emotional response	reciprocal interactions	retrieval
expectation	self-control procedures	meaningful categories

This task shows you that recall of categorized information is much easier than recall of random information. Another advantage of categorization is that many of the categories become associated with one another. For example, when you recall "Learning by Association," you will often recall "Learning by Consequences" as well. The one category leads you to recall other categories. Thus information becomes related or associated in your mind.

Another important feature of the LTM is that meaning "drives" it. Not only is your memory affected by the amount you rehearse, but it is affected by the way in which you rehearse (Craik & Lockhart, 1972). The idea is that the way in which you study will determine how long information will be maintained in memory. If a person studies only **surface characteristics** of material (like skimming it or just looking at the words), material will be quickly forgotten. If people study through **elaboration** (that is, by understanding meaning and expanding on concepts), they will recall the material longer (Craik & Lockhart, 1972). To demonstrate this, try Exercise 6.9. You will be asked to examine a list of words. Do not attempt to memorize them; rather, first count the number of words in all capital letters, and then count the number of five-letter words. Once this is done, cover the list and attempt to recall the words.

surface characteristics studying print such as looking at words rather than understanding the words

elaboration or deep processing studying by understanding meaning or providing examples for the to-be-remembered item

▶ *Shallow Study*

Use the following words to answer the questions. Do not try to memorize the words.

1.   Count the number of words in all capitals.

2.   Count the number of five-letter words.

3.   Cover the words and try to recall them.

CHAIN	jump	GLASSES
BERRY	STRAW	Silly
Story	time	TREAT
RUN	TALE	Find

In Exercise 6.10 are more words. Once again, do not try to study the words; rather, find the words that fit into the following sentences, then recall them.

EXERCISE 6.10

▶ *Deep or Elaborate Study*

Use the following list of words to fill in the blanks (choose all that apply). Afterwards, cover the list and try to recall the words.

1. The boy brought the _____ to school.
2. I _____ animals.
3. She made a _____.
4. I like to _____ cookies.

eat	pet	pen
house	chicken	star
child	pony	love
paper	dress	decorate

You likely remember many words from the second set. This is because during the review of the words, you were required to know their meaning and to expand on that meaning to put them into the sentences. In addition, elaboration can make material stand out in your mind. For example, Anna was trying to learn the meaning of *conditioned emotional response* (an emotional response due to learning by association), so she put it into a sentence: "When I saw my mother's locket I had a conditioned emotional response and began to cry because I could imagine watching the locket as my mother danced with me in her arms." This is a good elaboration because it is distinct in that the story is personal and holds the idea that a conditioned response, the crying, is a response to an object that is associated with the real focus of Anna's love, her mother. Jenny also tried to elaborate on this topic. The sentence she used was "A conditioned emotional response is an emotional response to a once neutral stimulus." While this is also an elaboration, it is not so distinctive and requires a clear understanding of other conditioning terms such as *neutral stimulus*. Jenny will likely have more difficulty in recalling this term than will Anna.

HOW CAN I APPLY WHAT I KNOW ABOUT LTM TO SCHOOL?

Methods presented in the STM section focused not only on getting materials to LTM but on maintaining them in LTM. These methods were both organizational and rehearsal based. Further, study of LTM suggests a number of methods that could help you in studying.

First, rehearsal alone is not enough to ensure that you will recall information. While the flash card techniques work very well for definitional and concept information, the flash cards will not easily show you how information is categorized and associated with other concepts or how information is applied to real life. This suggests that in your notes you should categorize information and think about how that information relates to other topics. The study note example in Table 6.2 not only gives categories and elaborations, it asks students to think of how this concept relates to others.

Second, it is necessary to elaborate on topics and make them distinctive in your mind. You should ask yourself questions and answer the questions during study sessions. Box 6.1 summarizes how you might study, following the information presented thus far.

BOX 6.1

Summary of Study Based on Memory Theory

Technique	Effect
1. During lecture, use the Cornell or Guided Inquiry note taking system	Notes are organized, giving attention to important concepts; dual codes concepts
2. Try to sit in a location in lecture and while studying where distractions are minimal	Increases attention to important concepts
3. Listen for cues from the lecturer about what is most important (i.e., repeating concepts, stories on concepts, etc.)	Increases attention
4. After lecture, re-write notes into study notes	Increases attention and rehearsal, helps to show relationships between concepts
5. When reading and going over lecture notes, put important definitions and concepts on flash cards	Increases rehearsal and causes maintenance rehearsal
6. Put information from the text into study notes	Increases rehearsal and elaborates on concepts
7. Categorize material in study notes to see how they relate	Causes elaboration of material
8. When studying, ask yourself questions	Increases elaboration
9. When studying, use concepts in unique and personal sentences	Makes material distinctive

WHY DO I FORGET?

decay theory
memory fades over time

interference theory
old or new memories interfere with current memory

failure of organization
a memory is stored but not accessed because it has not been properly categorized

There are likely many reasons why you forget. The factors that may be involved in forgetting are (1) memory decay, (2) interference from other events, and (3) failure of organization (Solso et al., 2004).

Your memories may be lost because over time your memories fade away. This is known as **decay theory**. Decay can be demonstrated on many memory tasks. If individuals are asked to recall information immediately, they usually recall more than if they were to recall the same information at a later time. While it is likely that memory decay does occur (do you remember what you had for dinner a week ago last Tuesday?), it is likely that other factors are also involved in memory losses.

A second factor that may be involved in forgetting is that you forget because some memories are pushed out of your mind by competing memories (**interference theory**). Old memories can interfere with the recall of new memories. For example, Jacinta took her chemistry exam last week and is now in her biology exam. She studied for biology, but she is staring at her exam with a look of confusion on her face as she tries to recall a biological theory. However, all Jacinta can recall is a theory from her chemistry class. Information that was previously in Jacinta's mind is affecting her memory for biology. Interference can also come from new information. In other words, new memories interfere with the recall of old memories. For example, Jerry was just taught a formula for computing a statistic in his statistics class and now he can't recall the formula for computing a different statistic that was taught last week. New information is interfering with old information.

A third factor that may be involved in forgetting is **failure of organization**: memories that are not properly organized will not be available when needed. That is, the information is "in there" somewhere, but you can't find it. Recall that you most often store information categorically. If a memory is entered into the wrong category, it might not be recalled because the question being asked on an examination does not cue you to search the category where the memory is stored. This most often happens when you do not completely understand the material that you are studying. Thus, categorizing the material properly is important.

HOW CAN I STOP FORGETTING AT SCHOOL?

It is likely that the reasons people forget are varied. Considerable information is presented in lectures and in the text. Without rehearsal, that information may be lost over time. Minimizing the loss of information can be achieved by rehearsal through flash cards, creating study notes, and continued review.

Because of the volume of information presented at school, considerable interference from other classes is likely to occur. Interference in memory from other classes and lectures can be minimized. Interference is less likely to occur if subjects that are quite different are studied closer in time than subjects that are similar. For example, if you are studying English, French, Spanish, and Sociology, studying Spanish immediately following French could lead to much confusion. However, studying Sociology after French will likely lead to better recall. You are more likely to remember things you study when they are quite different. Often students have interference even within the same class. Earlier lectures interfere with the one you need to know for a quiz. It is important that you make information distinct in your study notes. As an example, the chapter on learning in this textbook could interfere with the chapter on memory. When asked to talk about different types of memory, you might only recall different types of learning. To reduce the risk of this interference, students need to make these topics distinct. This can be done by categorizing topics.

Sometimes information is misclassified in the student's mind. When students don't understand materials, they may enter material into general categories. For example, Tina needed to know philosophies of early Greek philosophers and early Humanist philosophers, but studied them under the general heading of philosophers. Thus, when she was asked about these two philosophies she confused them. On the other hand, Jordan categorized her study notes around the two different philosophies, Early Greek as one category and Humanist as another. Then, the specific philosophers were sub-categories under each type of philosophy. See Table 6.3.

Jordan's notes clearly categorize information and this reduces interference and allows for better retrieval. The exam question—"Contrast and compare Early Greek and Humanistic philosophies. Include within your discussion the ideas of at least two philosophers from each era"—has cues in it. That is, the words "Early Greek" and "Humanist" were meant to cue the student to search those categories of information. Clearly the professor wishes the students to distinguish both philosophies and philosophers. Jordan's organization contains categories that distinguish Early Greeks and Humanists and thus Jordan will more likely be successful in her answer.

Table 6.3 **Student Philosophy Notes**

TINA'S NOTES	JORDAN'S NOTES	
Philosophers	*Philosophies*	
There are a number of ways to view philosophy. . . . The following are the views of some philosophers	Early Greek In general early Greeks believed . . .	Humanistic Humanistic philosophies during the Renaissance . . .
• Thales: Thales believed . . .	Greek Philosophers	Humanist Philosophers
• Erasmus: Argued . . .	• Thales: No idea is . . .	• Pico: Humans have a . . .
• Hippocrates: In general . . .	• Hippocrates: Illness has . . .	• Erasmus: Fanatical belief . . .
• Pico: Argued that . . .		

MNEMONICS

CAN I IMPROVE MY MEMORY?

mnemonic
method to improve memory

A **mnemonic** is any method that is intended to improve memory. There is no single mnemonic technique that will help with all aspects of learning, and most mnemonic techniques take time to learn. Thus far in this chapter, mnemonic techniques that involve rehearsal and organization of materials have been discussed. Below is a discussion of other mnemonic techniques that involve visual imagery and verbal/auditory associations.

VISUAL IMAGERY

Most people have the ability to imagine a visual scene in their heads. For example, imagine that you are eating at a restaurant. You likely imagine yourself sitting in a chair at a table, with a meal in front of you, etc. You did not need us to describe the table and chair and food. You filled that in yourself from your knowledge of restaurants. Thus, you interpreted what we were saying and added the details yourself. Your ability to add to stories helps you to interpret information quickly. These images can help our memory. Creating an image of a to-be-remembered item allows you to both hear about the item (in lecture) and see the item (through visual imagery) and, as suggested above, you can recall information better when it comes to you in two ways. In addition, creating the image forces you to elaborate on the material, which will in turn aid memory.

VISUAL IMAGE-BASED MNEMONICS

Many techniques have been developed to help students learn information through the use of visual imagery. Two popular techniques are the method of loci and the keyword method. In these techniques, visual images are associated with to-be-remembered items. When recall is needed, the image is recalled, which helps with the item recall.

THE METHOD OF LOCI

method of loci
a mnemonic method in which to-be-remembered items are attached to locations

The **method of loci** is among the oldest known imagery-based recall methods and dates back to early Greek orators. In early Greek times, one form of entertainment was listening to orators give speeches. However, paper was a rare commodity and individuals needed to recall speeches without the aid of paper. Thus, techniques were developed to help in this recall. In the method of loci, the speaker imagines a location such as her home. She attaches topics for the speech to different rooms in that location. Then when the speaker needs to recall these topics, the speaker takes an imaginary walk through the house (Solso et al., 2004). Box 6.2 gives you an idea of how this works.

The method of loci can be quite helpful in recalling categories that you are studying or in recalling topics for presentations.

THE KEYWORD METHOD

keyword method
a mnemonic method for learning foreign-language words

The **keyword method** is typically used to learn vocabulary in second-language learning. In this method, the foreign-language word and the translation are paired through a keyword. A keyword is a familiar word that sounds like the foreign word and is associated with the translation

Method of Loci

Imagine that you need to recall a list of supplies for a school project. You need to buy coloured paper, glue, markers, a notebook, pencils, a stapler, and a calculator. To recall these items, you might attach each item to a location in your home and then, while at the store, imagine walking through your home. For example:

I drove into my driveway and could not park because a car made out of <u>coloured paper</u> blocked the driveway. I went to open the garage but it was stuck because someone had <u>glued</u> it shut. I decided to go inside and took my front door key out and noticed it looked like a <u>marker</u>. Once inside I went to hang up my coat in the closet but <u>notebooks</u> were hanging from all of the hangers. I heard a noise in the kitchen and went in. My mother was chopping up <u>pencils</u> for dinner. I decided to go to the family room to watch TV but someone had used a <u>stapler</u> to put staples all over the screen. I went to my bedroom and was about to lie down when I noticed that a giant <u>calculator</u> had replaced my mattress.

When part of the home is named, see if you can recall the school supply from memory: driveway, garage, front door, closet, kitchen, family room, and bedroom.

Source: From Robert L. Solso, *Cognitive Psychology,* 2nd edition. Published by Allyn and Bacon, Boston, MA. Copyright © 1988 by Pearson Education. Reprinted by permission of the publisher.

(Solso et al., 2004). For example, suppose you were trying to learn the French word *garçon*, which means *boy*. *Garçon* sounds like the English word *garden*. Thus, you use the keyword *garden* and pair that with *boy*. You imagine a boy playing in the flower garden. Later when you hear *garçon*, you recall the garden and that makes you think of the boy (see Table 6.4).

Table 6.4 The Keyword Method

French Word	Keyword (sounds like French word)	Translation
Garçon	Garden	Boy

Test yourself to see if this method works. Below in Exercise 6.11 are some French words, keywords, and their translations. We have provided the associations for you in the last column.

▶ The Keyword Method Demonstration

Read through the table and imagine the items described. Then cover the table, except for the French words, and see if you can remember their meanings.

French Word	Keyword	Translation	Association
Chien	Chain	Dog	Imagine a dog on a chain attached to a tree on a summer afternoon
Batteur	Bat	Drummer	Imagine a drummer playing the drums with a baseball bat
Visage	Visor	Face	Imagine looking at someone's face but it is blocked by the brim of a visor
Feu	Foe	Fire	Imagine fighting your worst foe, who is made out of fire
Drapeau	Drape	Flag	Imagine your mother replaced her living room drape with a flag
Chaton	Hat-on	Kitten	Imagine going to put your hat on and you accidentally place a kitten on your head

There has been considerable study of the keyword method. Students who learned Russian vocabulary by the keyword method were able to recall more vocabulary and for longer periods than did those who studied the same vocabulary by rehearsal (Atkinson & Raugh, 1975).

Many other visual imagery memory techniques have been developed. All imagery methods commonly pair the to-be-remembered item with an image that aids in recall.

WHY DOES IMAGERY HELP RECALL?

You recall best if you explore the meaning of the to-be-remembered item and expand on it. Visual imagery techniques require that the user think about each item deeply. He/She needs to understand the meaning of the item and afterward to expand on it to relate the image to the item.

HOW CAN I USE VISUAL IMAGERY TECHNIQUES AT SCHOOL?

Any technique that helps students more deeply process content is helpful in the post-secondary environment. The imagery techniques presented above could help in making class presentations and learning a second-language vocabulary. But imagery can help in many other ways, too. Drawing diagrams or making images of content through stories, drawings, or poems will help you to process information more deeply. Using imagery usually takes more time than simply rehearsing information, however, because you need to create the image to interact with the to-be-learned material. This time allows for deep processing.

VERBAL/AUDITORY ASSOCIATION MNEMONICS

Another type of mnemonic device is word association, such as rhymes and phrases. These verbal association methods often also employ visual imagery through story-like features (Solso et al., 2004). However, these methods are generally meant to recall topic highlights or words rather than detailed content. Thus these methods often use less elaborate study strategies, which can lead to errors in recall.

RHYMES/POEMS

One popular way to recall information is through lyrics or rhymes. For example, "In fourteen hundred and ninety-two, Columbus sailed the ocean blue." This rhyme could successfully help recall specific dates. However, it could also easily be confused. For example, if someone were to use 1692 rather than 1492, the rhyme would still work, but the information would be wrong. In another example, "*I* before *E* except after *C* or when it says 'ay' as in neighbour and weigh" is a grammatically correct guideline, however, without an understanding of the rules of grammar, the letters *D* and *B* would seem to work just as well in the rhyme as *C* (but would be incorrect). Since the studying for the date in the Columbus rhyme did not involve more elaborate strategies, such as thinking of other world occurrences during the era, and studying for grammar with a rhyme did not involve a deeper understanding of grammar, it would be easy to make errors in recall.

CODING

coding
a mnemonic method in which phrases represent to-be-remembered items

Coding involves creating a code to recall specific material. Often codes are created in which the first letter of in each word in a phrase represents to-be-remembered material. For example, "*Every Good Boy Deserves Fudge*" allows an individual to recall the names of the lines on the musical staff (*EGBDF*). If you wanted to recall the types of learning presented in Chapter 5, you might say "*All Cats SCat Over Inclines In Paris*' to recall *Association,*

Consequence, Self-Control, Observational, Insight, and Information Processing. Each word's first letter relates to a type of learning. While this system might help in the learning of topics, it does not help you to understand the content of these topics. This is because, like rhyming, this method of study does not allow you to elaborate on what you are learning.

LINKING

In the linking method, topics or to-be-remembered items are linked together in a sentence or story. For example, if you wanted to recall the names of the mnemonics presented in this chapter—Rehearsal, Loci, Keyword, Rhyming, Coding, and Linking, you might devise the following story.

> The boys and I needed to enter the *rehearsal* hall, Club *Loci,* but the man at the door said we needed to know the *keyword* to enter. Jimmy tried *rhyming* words and Billy tried a *coding* system and none was correct. We finally pushed our way in by *linking* our arms and running.

The method works well to recall specific topics, but once again the system does not necessarily help with the content of those topics. However, this system could be modified to describe some content within a topic area. For example, the story below was created to describe the short-term memory.

> Sally decided that she would try out for the lead role in the play. Once she was handed her lines she thought that it would be best to try to memorize each before giving them. She read the first line to herself and looked up at the director. Just as she was about to give the line, the director started speaking. Drat, more than a minute went by and the line was no longer in her short-term memory. Since she had not rehearsed it, she knew that she would have to review it again. The director instructed her to read and recall seven lines of information. "Thank goodness," Sally thought, "that is within the five to nine items that I can recall in my short-term memory."

HOW CAN I APPLY VERBAL ASSOCIATION TECHNIQUES AT SCHOOL?

Verbal association mnemonics are usually applied to recall topic/list or categorical type information. In post-secondary schools, you frequently need to recall this type of information; however, it is important that you realize that recalling the name of the topic is not the same as understanding a topic. You need to use further elaboration techniques, such as rehearsal, flash cards, and self-testing to ensure that you understand the depth of the topic.

TEST-TAKING STUDY STRATEGIES: APPLYING MEMORY THEORY

STUDYING FOR AND TAKING MULTIPLE-CHOICE TESTS

Multiple-choice tests are sometimes called tests of recognition. This means that rather than having to produce the answer from your mind, you are given the correct answer but must recognize it as correct. Studying for multiple-choice tests requires that you be able to recognize material from your lecture and text and distinguish it from incorrect or incomplete material. Most multiple-choice tests require that you choose the MOST correct answer. Therefore, on some questions there will be answers that are partially correct, but you are not to choose them.

A variety of types of multiple-choice questions are given on post-secondary tests. These include items that are definitional, items that examine relationships, and items that require you to apply concepts. Thus, in studying for multiple-choice tests, you need to do much more than define concepts.

Definitional multiple-choice items

Example:

The keyword mnemonic method is often used to

   a.   learn categorical information

   b.   learn translations

   c.   learn topics for a speech

   d.   chunk information in STM

Correct answer: B

   Studying for definitional material is helped through the use of highlighting important concepts and terms, flash cards, and organizing and creating study notes that include definitions.

Relationship multiple-choice items

Example:

Consequential learning affects _____ behaviours while learning by association affects _____ behaviours.

   a.   positive, negative

   b.   higher, lower

   c.   voluntary, involuntary

   d.   short-term, long-term

Correct answer: C

   Studying for relationship items requires that you use the techniques for definitional items to understand basic concepts and also elaborate on these to understand relationships between items. Inquiry study notes or asking yourself questions often helps with relationship information. In addition, categorizing material as shown in Jordan's study notes in the 'forgetting' section of this chapter (Table 6.3) can help to draw out relationships.

Application multiple-choice items

Example:

Jenny has been trying to get her lazy lab partner to do his work. Jenny calls her lab partner each day to see if he has completed his work and now it seems that her lab partner has completely stopped working. Jenny's behaviour can be viewed as:

   a.   reward

   b.   negative reinforcement

   c.   learned helplessness

   d.   punishment

Correct answer: D

   In this question, you are applying concepts to real-life situations. The ability to recognize applied knowledge requires that you understand and elaborate on material. Studying for this type of question usually requires methods for definitional and relationship questions plus further elaboration. You might use imagery or stories to elaborate on your study topics. You might write a small lecture and teach it to your family or yourself.

TAKING MULTIPLE-CHOICE TESTS

Some students find multiple-choice tests to be very challenging. One of the most common errors in multiple-choice tests is poor reading. You need to read the item carefully and underline the important parts of the question. In general, when writing a multiple-choice test, it is best to try to answer each question in your head before picking the correct answer. Once you have the answer in your mind, look over all of the answer options even if you are sure of the answer. This is because sometimes two answers are very close. Next, eliminate the answers you are sure are not correct. This should leave you with one or two possible choices. If you are left with two choices, ask yourself why one choice is better than the other. If you do not lose marks for guessing, you should guess on items that you are unsure of. Once you have completed the test, go back and review items. Only change answers if you are sure that the new answer is correct. Finally, many item answers will contain words like *never* and *always*. Usually these are wrong item answers because they are too absolute.

ESSAY AND SHORT-ANSWER TESTS

Creating organized and clear study notes is the key to doing well on essay and short-answer questions. Study notes that are organized around definitions, examples, supporting and contradictory evidence, and relationships (Chapter 5, Box 5.2), will allow for success in essay and short-answer questions. It is a good idea when studying to make up exam questions and answer them. Often you will make up the same questions that your instructor does on the exam.

During the examination, you should first read through the question and underline key words. Words like *contrast* (compare two or more concepts, showing their differences), *define*, *explain/discuss* (expand beyond a definition), *evaluate* (provide pros and cons usually with evidence), *critique* (explain the positive and negative aspects), *analyze* (break down the concept), *provide evidence*, etc. should be underlined.

Often students answer part of a question but seem not to read the entire question. It is usually a good idea to make a quick outline of your answer in the margin (if allowed) prior to writing the answer. Students often lose marks on essay and short-answer questions because their answers are not well organized and the marker has to hunt to find the answer. Students often believe that the best technique is to write down everything they know about the topic, certain that the correct answer is contained in this and the marker will find it. Be aware that on a post-secondary level, this may lose marks instead of gaining them! This technique often suggests to the instructor that the student has not understood the material well enough to be able to pick out the pertinent information. Once the outline is complete, go back to the question to be sure you have included all parts of the question in your outline. Once you have written your answer (try to double-space if possible), go back and read the answer to ensure that it makes sense and clearly and concisely answers the question. If you need to insert some statements, clearly mark where they should be inserted and then add them at the end of your answer or within the double-spaced lines (for word or short additions).

If you do not know the answer to the question, think of what you do know and apply that to the question in an attempt to receive part marks. Unless the instruction indicates that you are to choose a certain number of questions to answer, it is usually a good idea to answer all questions. Leaving questions blank nets no marks. Thus, if you are not penalized for attempting, answer all questions even if you are unsure of the answer. Remember, though, that if you are instructed to answer, say, five of the following six questions, and you answer all six, you will probably be marked on the first five, not on your best five. Finally, try to avoid going off on tangents in your answer; you are likely to lose marks for straying off topic.

Advice for Jacinta

▶ Jacinta has been having difficulties recalling information that is on her examinations. She wonders if there are some ways to study that will help her recall theories needed in class. The table below outlines steps that Jacinta might follow that will help her to increase attention to relevant material, store material effectively, recall material from cues, expand on material, and make material meaningful. These steps should aid Jacinta in her performance.

TECHNIQUE	EFFECT
1. During lecture use the Cornell note taking system	Notes are organized giving attention to important concepts, dual codes
2. Try to sit in a location in lecture and while studying where distractions are minimal	Increases attention
3. Listen for cues from the lecturer for what is most important (i.e., repeating concepts, stories on concepts, etc.)	Increases attention to important concepts
4. After lecture re-write notes into study notes	Increases attention and rehearsal, helps to show relationships between concepts
5. When reading and going over lecture notes, put important definitions and concepts on flash cards	Increases rehearsal and causes maintenance rehearsal
6. Put information from the text into your study notes	Increases rehearsal and elaborates on concepts
7. Categorize material in study notes to see how concepts relate	Causes elaboration of material
8. When studying, ask yourself questions	Increases elaboration
9. When studying, use concepts in unique and personal sentences	Makes material distinctive
10. Rehearse lecture and text information right after the lecture	Reduces decay of information
11. When studying many topics, study those that are most different closest in time	Reduces interference
12. Make study notes distinctive by categorizing information	Reduces interference, increases the likelihood that information stored will be cued in the question
13. Use visual images such as diagrams, keyword method, and loci method	Helps to elaborate on the topic
14. Use mnemonics when trying to recall topic and list information	Provides a hook for memory
15. Use a variety of methods when studying for multiple-choice questions (flash cards, categorization, study note creation)	Not all multiple-choice questions are definitional and thus techniques that elaborate on information are needed
16. When writing exams, read questions carefully, underline important words, create an outline (for essay questions), and review your answers	Reduces errors in the interpretation of questions

CHAPTER SUMMARY

■ Selecting important information is the first step in learning. There are many distractions to this selection process, so it is important that distractions are minimized. Ways students can minimize distractions are to (1) evaluate distractions in their learning environment, (2) notice important titles and concepts presented through titles on presentation slides and in the textbook, and (3) re-write lecture notes.

■ Attention is needed to transfer information from the sensory memory to the short-term memory, and rehearsal of information will transfer it to long-term memory. Re-writing lecture notes, creating flash cards, creating study notes from lecture and text material, and categorizing information provided in texts and lectures are good ways to rehearse information.

- When we elaborate on and categorize information, it is more likely to be retained in long-term memory. Asking yourself questions about the material you study and using concepts in unique and personal sentences further elaborates on the material.

- Making topics from different classes distinctive can help to increase the recall of these topics. To do this, you should study topics that are most different from one another closer in time.

- Visual and auditory mnemonics can help to increase recall of information. Mnemonics often involve associations, imagery, rhymes, poems, and stories. Most mnemonic techniques take time to learn.

- Use a variety of study techniques when studying for tests. Even multiple-choice questions often require more elaborate knowledge of a topic than just the definition.

KEY TERMS

chunking	failure of organization	mnemonic
coding	interference theory	selective attention
decay theory	keyword method	sensory memory
elaboration or deep processing	long-term memory	short-term memory
encoding	method of loci	surface characteristics

INDIVIDUAL ACTIVITIES

1. Read the selection in Box 6.3 and pick out the most relevant points. Treat the information as though you were listening to a lecture and write notes in either the Cornell or Guided Inquiry method. Afterward check to see if you chose the main points by viewing a list of main points at the end of the individual activities section.

2. Create some flash cards of the glossary terms in this chapter. Take these flash cards with you this week. Flash the cards when travelling on the bus to and from school, while waiting for lectures to begin, when waiting between classes, etc. After one week, test yourself to see if you have learned this information by studying in these short study periods.

3. Elaboration of material increases recall. In this chapter we have often elaborated on material to improve recall of the material. List ways material was elaborated. See the end of this section for a list of elaborative techniques used.

Example Lecture   **BOX 6.3**

In observational and incidental learning methods, the learner learns by watching rather than doing. In observational learning, a skill is demonstrated by a model. Watching a model perform a skill can help you to acquire and improve your own skills. Modelling has been used to reduce fear of dentistry, improve presentation techniques, teach job-related skills, and improve writing/academic skills. Modelling is an effective way to increase self-efficacy (what we think we are competent at, Hergenhahn, 1986). For example, you could watch a model effectively give a presentation. By watching the model, you could both pick up presentation skills and view consequences of the presentation (the audience response). This knowledge could help to improve your own presentation skills and could lead to changes in self-efficacy (I saw the model do that and I think I can too).

A second type of indirect learning (learning by watching) is called incidental learning. In this method, elements of a situation (such as where the event occurred) are recalled even though the individual made no particular effort to commit them to memory. These elements can be used as cues or hooks to help you remember specific content of to-be-learned materials (i.e., recalling the location of the event helps to recall the event). There are many elements in class that can help you to recall specific lecture materials (Underwood, 1983).

ANSWERS TO INDIVIDUAL ACTIVITIES

List of points for Question 1

- Observational and incidental methods: learn by watching
- Observational: watch someone model/perform task
- Modelling allows for skill acquisition and viewing the consequences of behaviour
- Modelling increases self-efficacy (learn what you can do)
- Incidental learning: learn without effort to learn
- Elements learned (e.g., location of an event) can be used as cues to help learn content

List of elaborative techniques used for Question 3

- Descriptive examples (instances when modelling is used successfully)
- Demonstration exercises (e.g., Exercise 6.6)
- Case studies
- Bracketed identifiers (e.g., surface characteristics of material like skimming it or just looking at the words)
- Boldfaced words that are further defined in the glossary
- Re-organization of materials onto step-by-step charts (e.g., Advice for Jacinta)

GROUP ACTIVITIES

1. As a group, discuss the differences and similarities of studying for multiple-choice tests and essay answer tests. What methods would be most helpful in studying for each type of test? Is the level of knowledge needed really different between the two types?

2. Tables 6.5 and 6.6 give you some practice with the keyword technique. Divide into groups of at least five members. Two members will be the keyword learners and two members will be the rehearsal learners. The remaining member is the tester. The keyword learners should learn the translations to the words by looking at the Imagine column of the keyword list. The rehearsal learners should learn the rehearsal list by simply rehearsing the words and their translations. The tester should allow all learners four minutes to learn their words and then ask the learners to turn over their lists. While the learners are learning, the tester should write out the foreign words in random order on a piece of paper. Once the learners have finished their learning period, they should wait one minute before being tested. The tester should put the random list of foreign words on the table for the learners to see. Their job will be to provide (individually, written down on their own paper) the translation of each word. Once complete, mark the number of correct translations each member provided. Did the keyword group outperform the rehearsal group? Why or why not?

3. As a group, discuss the following case. Sue has just received a failing grade on her first physics test. She does not know where she went wrong. She always had As in high school. As a group, outline how Sue can learn from this experience, figure out where she went wrong and improve her study techniques/memory. How is post-secondary learning different from learning in high school?

Table 6.5 Group Exercise: Keyword Table

FOREIGN WORD	KEYWORD	TRANSLATION	IMAGINE
CLONOK	CLOCK	DESK	Imagine sitting at your desk looking at your clock
ZORAK	ZORRO	LAUGHING	Imagine Zorro laughing as he wins a battle
PRINISH	PRINT	ANNOYED	Imagine feeling annoyed as the work you sent to the printer does not print
MYLEN	MIGHTY	CHAIR	Imagine a mighty baby lifting up a chair
SHOLFEER	SHOPPER	CHEESE	Imagine a store full of shoppers grabbing cheese from the shelf
NORVEN	NORTH WIND	CAT	Imagine a cat battling to walk against the cold and strong north wind
BLECKEN	BLACKEN	TEETH	Imagine someone smiling but his/her front teeth have been blacked out
SENZAT	SENSE IT	AUTUMN	Imagine sensing cold air, and knowing it's the beginning of autumn
FRIZO	FRYING	CUP	Imagine pouring oil from a cup into a frying pan
PLORINT	PLOWING	FLOWER	Imagine plowing a field where a single red flower stands in the middle
RELTIVE	RELATIVE	HOUSE	Imagine a relative coming to stay at your house
CHENVY	CHEVY	CRY	Imagine a man who is about to cry because his Chevy car has hit a post
CRAWVER	CRAWFISH	HOTEL	Imagine going into a hotel room where you find 10 crawfish walking around
MARTLIV	MARKET	MOUSE	Imagine looking through the produce at the market only to find a mouse in the tomatoes
PECKISH	PECKING	WATER	Imagine watching a chicken pecking at some water

Table 6.6 Group Exercise: Rehearsal Table

FOREIGN WORD	TRANSLATION
CLONOK	DESK
ZORAK	LAUGHING
PRINISH	ANNOYED
MYLEN	CHAIR
SHOLFEER	CHEESE
NORVEN	CAT
BLECKEN	TEETH
SENZAT	AUTUMN
FRIZO	CUP
PLORINT	FLOWER
RELTIVE	HOUSE
CHENVY	CRY
CRAWVER	HOTEL
MARTLIV	MOUSE
PECKISH	WATER

REFERENCES

Atkinson R. C., & Raugh, M. R (1975). An application of mnemonic keyword method to the acquisition of a Russian vocabulary. *Journal of Experimental Psychology: Human Learning and Memory, 104,* 126–133.

Atkinson, R. C., & Shiffrin, R. M. (1968). Human Memory: A proposed system and its control processes. In W. K. Spence and J. T. Spence (Eds.), *The psychology of learning and motivation. Advances in research and theory, 1,* (pp. 89–195). New York: Academic Press.

Broadbent, D. E. (1958). *Perception and Communication.* London: Pergamon Press.

Craik, F. I. M., & Lockhart, R. S. (1972). Levels of Processing: A framework for memory research. *Journal of Verbal Learning and Verbal Behavior, 11,* 671–684.

Miller, G. A. (1956). The magic number seven plus or minus two: Some limits on our capacity for processing information. *Psychological Review, 63,* 81–97.

Solso, R. L., Maclin, M. K., & Maclin, O. (2004) *Cognitive psychology* (7th ed.). Toronto: Allyn and Bacon Inc.

Treisman, A. M. (1964). Selective attention in man. *British Medical Bulletin, 20,* 12–16.

CRITICAL THINKING AND SOLVING PROBLEMS

LEARNING OBJECTIVES

The Case of Josh

▶ Josh has just received an assignment in his urban politics class. He must write a 10-page essay on the cause(s) of poverty and homelessness in urban centres. He is relieved that this is the topic because he feels he knows a lot about poverty and homelessness. You see, his uncle is a lawyer who has had to represent many landlords who deal with people on welfare. Also, his mom works in the clerk's department of his town and often discusses eviction cases. Josh's uncle and mother believe that people who are poor need a better work ethic. They claim that if these people would just get up and get a job, then their problems would be solved. Josh plans to take this view in his essay. He plans to argue that the cause of poverty and homelessness is laziness on the part of the poor. He feels that he could write this essay without any research but his professor has insisted that he read at least five peer-reviewed articles.

All post-secondary schools want their students to learn to think critically: to have the skills to recognize assumptions made in theories and beliefs, evaluate the truthfulness of theories and beliefs, become aware of limitations in theories and beliefs, think of alternative plausible theories, use theoretical knowledge to solve problems and make decisions about their post-secondary work (Petress, 2004; Walker & Diaz, 2003). Critical thinking is important for all areas of study. Theories are put forward in all study areas (e.g., engineering, science, social science, and humanities courses) and it is important that you know how to evaluate them.

BELIEFS AND THEORIES

HOW DO PEOPLE COME TO THEIR BELIEFS AND THEORIES?

belief
a statement that is deemed true by the individual who holds it

premise
a statement that is deemed true

theory
a set of statements that may be true, usually a theory will be argued or tested

A **belief** is a statement that is deemed true by the individual who holds it. We sometimes call a statement that is deemed to be true a **premise**. We all hold beliefs of many kinds. Some of our beliefs are factual in nature. For example, Maureen believes that Valerie is her mother. John believes that a cat is an animal. Some beliefs may or may not be factual. Pierre believes that animals have communication systems that are equivalent to those of humans. Claude believes that some people can read the minds of others. Some beliefs have been demonstrated to be wrong. For instance, people used to believe that the sun revolved around the earth and that the atom could not be split. Other beliefs are about the causes of things. In the introductory example, Josh believes that the cause of poverty is laziness. Susan believes that her friends reject her because her friends are mean. Scientists believe that there are chemicals in the brain that affect mood. A **theory** is also a belief, but usually the author of the theory *recognizes* that it *may* be true rather than deeming it to actually *be* true. In addition, authors of theories often test their theories to see if they are valid. In academics, authors of theories are usually willing to modify their theories if evidence does not support the theory. In contrast, with beliefs, people often do not examine the truth of their belief. For example, a scientist may theorize that ozone depletion causes global warming, and then seek evidence to support or refute this theory. On the other hand, an individual might believe that youth today are violent but not seek appropriate evidence to support or refute this claim.

There are many ways that individuals can come to a belief. Some common ways are through authority and through personal experience.

People believe because an authority told them to. For example, Josh believes that people who are poor are lazy because his uncle and mother, whom he believes to be experts in the area, have told him so. People believe that the earth is round because scientists have told them so. Some people believe that the world is a dangerous place because there are many stories involving violence in the newspaper: these people take for granted that the authority is correct without personal examination of the belief or the source of the belief.

A second common way that people come to a belief is through personal experience. Some people believe that Canadian children are obese because they have seen many obese children. Tiffany believes that ghosts exist because when she came home one day several of the pictures on her mantle had been moved.

IS IT WRONG TO BASE BELIEFS ON AUTHORITY AND PERSONAL EXPERIENCE?

The general answer to this is no, sometimes authority and personal experiences do reflect reality. However, students are asked at the post-secondary level to evaluate these sources before adopting a belief or theory. For example, Josh believes that people who are poor are lazy because an authority (his mother and uncle) says so.

The first question Josh needs to ask when basing a belief on an authority is, "What are the qualifications of this authority?" In Josh's case, the qualifications of his uncle are a law degree with expertise in landlord–tenant disputes, and the qualifications of his mother are her job as a county clerk. In both cases, these authorities have little background in sociology, political policy, economics, or psychology, all of which are academic areas that have expertise in the study of poverty and homelessness.

The second question Josh needs to ask when using an authority in adopting a belief is, "What evidence does the authority provide when presenting his/her belief or theory?" In Josh's case, the evidence provided by his uncle is that many of his landlord–tenant cases involve people on welfare, and the evidence provided by his mother is hearsay around the clerk's office in eviction cases. Josh needs to reflect upon this evidence, decide if the evidence is relevant to the belief and if so, evaluate the evidence. We will discuss evaluation of evidence later in this chapter.

The second method of adopting a belief or theory is through personal experience. Personal experience can be accurate, but you should also question this source. The fact that you may have met many obese children may not mean that children in Canada are generally obese. In using personal experience to adopt a belief, you need to carefully examine whether your experiences are similar to others' or unique to yourself. For example, you might have met many obese children while hanging around a fast-food restaurant. That experience might not adequately represent all Canadian children. You are asked to evaluate your experiences by comparing them to other sources of information (such as Canadian statistics, journal articles, etc.). In addition, you need to reflect on your experiences and think of many plausible explanations for your experience. Tiffany thinks that ghosts moved pictures on the mantle—is it possible that her mother moved them?

WHAT ASSUMPTIONS DO PEOPLE MAKE WHEN ADOPTING BELIEFS AND THEORIES?

motivational biases
assumptions that help the individual hold to a belief that meets individual needs

cognitive biases
assumptions that result from inappropriate analysis of the information provided

When people adopt beliefs and create theories, they use many assumptions. For example, Jessica believes that there is human life on other planets. To hold this belief, she assumes that there are some planets that have a similar atmosphere to Earth. She also assumes that humans could survive on these planets.

There are many possible sources of error in the assumptions people make that can affect the validity of the belief and theory. These errors are usually categorized into two types: motivational biases or cognitive biases (Kruglanski & Ajzen, 1983). A **motivational bias** is one that helps the individual hold to a belief that meets his/her own individual needs. A **cognitive bias** is one that results from inappropriate analysis of the information provided. For a detailed discussion of motivational and cognitive biases evident in beliefs, see Kruglanski and Ajzen (1983).

MOTIVATIONAL BIASES

At times, people hold beliefs that help them to cope. For example, Instructor Jim Frenicki believes that eventually hard work will be rewarded. This belief helps him to deal with the ever-mounting responsibilities he has at work. Instructor Frenicki's belief is based on a number of assumptions that increase his confidence in his own belief. For example, Instructor Frenicki assumes that people see his hard work in a positive light and that the world is a just place where people eventually get what they deserve. However, while the assumptions he makes help him to cope with his workload, the assumptions of the positive light and just world may be errors or biases. Perhaps others do not view his extra work positively. Perhaps no one even notices his extra effort. Possibly no reward will follow his great efforts.

WHAT KINDS OF MOTIVATIONAL BIASES AND ASSUMPTIONS ARE THERE?

self-serving bias
people see themselves in a more positive light than other people see them

The following are some typical motivational biases or assumptions that people make.

Self-serving bias: People see themselves in a more positive light than other people see them. This bias can affect theories and beliefs because if you feel that others view you positively, you are less likely to question your beliefs. For example, Susan's belief that her friends reject her because they are mean guards her from having to contemplate that perhaps she is the one who is doing something wrong in relationships. She is free to maintain her self-view as a warm and wonderful friend.

False consensus bias: People assume that their own theories and beliefs are common and generally accepted by others and the inconsistent beliefs of others are uncommon and inappropriate (Kruglanski & Ajzen, 1983). The result of false consensus is that individuals will hold on to inappropriate beliefs because they think that others support them. It is not uncommon, for example, for volunteers in political parties to be shocked when their candidate loses the election: the volunteer believed in the candidate so strongly that it seemed unthinkable that other voters would not believe in the candidate as well.

Belief in a just world: People assume that the world is a just place and we get what we deserve (Kruglanski & Ajzen, 1983). For example, if Josh believes that the world is just, then those who are poor must be so because they deserve to be poor. The problem with holding this bias is that it causes people to ignore other equally plausible theories or beliefs (e.g., people are poor due to faulty economic policies).

Avoidability of physical harm: People believe that undesirable outcomes are avoidable. That is, when bad things happen to people, there must have been a clear cause that could have been avoided. For example, Josh believes that people can avoid being poor by getting a job. Some people believe that when accidents occur, someone is always at fault. The problem with holding this bias is that it results in poor examination of the information available. Does getting a job always reduce poverty? Are there no poor people with jobs?

Fundamental attribution error: People overemphasize internal causes of others' behaviour. In this bias, the person looks for internal (e.g., personality) rather than external causes of behaviour. Josh wonders why people are poor and suggests that it is because they are lazy, an internal cause, rather than looking at possible external causes (e.g., environmental), such as lack of opportunity to get an education, poor working wages, low employment rates, etc.

false consensus bias
people believe that their own theories and beliefs are common

belief in a just world
people believe that the world is a just place and we get what we deserve

avoidability of physical harm
people believe that undesirable outcomes are avoidable

fundamental attribution error
overemphasizing internal causes of others' behaviour

COGNITIVE BIASES

When people accept beliefs without examining all the information or data available, we say their belief is based on a cognitive bias. In other words, they make assumptions because they have misinterpreted the evidence provided for the belief. Some typical cognitive biases are listed below.

WHAT ARE THE TYPICAL COGNITIVE BIASES PEOPLE MAKE?

availability bias
people adopt beliefs based on how easily they can recall instances of something

Availability bias: People adopt beliefs based on how easily they can recall instances of something. For example, someone might believe that divorce is a typical outcome in marriage because she knows many divorced couples. The problem with holding this bias is that other potentially useful information sources, such as governmental statistics reports, are ignored.

sample bias
people adopt beliefs based on their own experience or experiences of a few others

Sample bias: People adopt beliefs based on their own experience. Thus, the sample or group they use as the basis of their belief may not well represent the whole population. For example, Tina believes that course instructors are rude because the instructors of her courses have been rude to her. However, it is likely that these instructors do not represent all instructors. Similarly, a brand new instructor who encounters a few students who talk during his/her lectures may believe that all students are rude.

selective attention biases
people pay attention to information that is most prominently presented

Selective attention biases: People pay attention to information that is most prominently presented. For example, television newscasts often focus on crime in urban centres. This leads people to believe that there are high crime rates in the city. These people ignore other important statistical information.

covariation bias
people assume that certain things exist together

Covariation bias: People assume that certain things exist together; if you see one thing, then the other must also be present. Josh believes that being poor and being lazy exist together; thus if one is poor, he/she must also be lazy. The problem with this assumption is that many lazy people are not poor, and many poor people are not lazy.

representativeness bias
people judge based on how many features one thing has in common with a prototype

Representativeness bias: People judge based on a prototype; that is, an 'ideal' of what belongs in this group (Kruglanski & Ajzen, 1983). For example, Josh's prototype of a lazy person is that he doesn't work, he collects welfare, and he scams the social service system. His mother tells him about a man who doesn't work, collects welfare, and scams the social service system. Josh assumes, then, that this man must be lazy because the man's behaviours fit Josh's prototype. But the man Josh has heard about is actually spending his days caring for his five motherless children. Certainly this man is not lazy. The problem with Josh's assumption is that he is trying to make someone fit his prototype without having all the information needed.

causal theories
in this bias, the individual inappropriately believes that things that happen together cause one another

Causal theories: In this bias, the individual inappropriately believes that things that happen together *cause* one another. For example, Beatrice had a headache that would not go away. While walking to school she found an unusual looking stone and picked it up. Soon she noticed that her headache was gone. She now believes that the stone caused her headache to go away because picking up the stone and headache relief happened at the same time. The problem with believing that things that happen together are causing one another is that you fail to consider other possible causes. Beatrice did not consider that her headache might have gone away because of the fresh air, the medication she took, the exercise of walking, etc.

failure to discount
in this bias, people fail to consider alternatives to their belief or theory

Failure to discount: In this bias, people fail to consider alternatives to their belief or theory. In other words, equally plausible alternative theories exist but they are not considered. For example, Stacey theorizes that nursing shortages in Canada have resulted in poor health for people in poorer neighbourhoods. She does not consider other equally plausible reasons for their poor health, such as poorer nutrition, poorer access to health information, etc.

DO THESE BIASES ALWAYS MEAN THAT MY BELIEF OR THEORY IS WRONG?

The answer to the above question is no. It is possible to adopt a theory based on poor assumptions, but the theory is still acceptable. For example, Hippocrates (460–377 B.C.E.) argued that mental illness was due to physical cause. He believed this because he agreed with earlier philosophers that the body was made up of four elements that needed to remain in balance, and when the elements became unbalanced, the person experienced some disease (Hergenhahn, 1992). As it turns out, we now know that Hippocrates' belief that mental illness has a physical cause is at least partially correct. Numerous medical studies have shown that chemical imbalances in the brain can lead to mental illness. However, Hippocrates' reliance on an authority and his assumption of the four elements were incorrect. We could argue that Hippocrates had a selective attention bias. He believed the predominant theory of body elements that must remain in balance. However, using this bias did not result in an incorrect first theory; mental illness can have a physical cause.

Even though one can come to proper conclusions with a biased approach, students are more likely to be limited in their thinking by holding onto biases. Josh has used several biases in his belief that poor people are lazy. These biases have led to inadequate examination of alternative theories and his instructor is likely to state that he has not critically evaluated his belief.

To better understand these biases, you might want to try the exercises (Individual Exercise 2 and Group Exercise 1) provided at the end of this chapter.

EVALUATING BELIEFS AND THEORIES

HOW DO I EVALUATE THE LOGIC OF BELIEFS OR THEORIES?

In general, when evaluating a theory or belief, you need to evaluate the logic of the theory or belief, the source of the theory or belief, and the evidence presented to support the theory or belief.

Upon hearing a theory or belief, the first step in evaluation is to decide if the theory or belief makes sense. Some beliefs do not need evidence to show that they are true: they are *self-evident*. These are called **a priori beliefs**. A priori beliefs are usually statements that link facts together. For example, one such a priori belief is that people cannot steal their own property (Govier, 2001). Thus, in a court case in which someone is accused of stealing a car but the car is registered to the accused thief, we cannot say that the accused stole the car. Another example of an a priori belief is that over time you cannot grow younger. You do not need evidence to show that this statement is true.

a priori beliefs
beliefs do not need evidence to show that they are true

Another instance where evidence to support a belief is not needed is when the belief is common knowledge. For example, Canada is a country. This statement is taken as true and does not need evidence to support it. However, at times what people take as common knowledge is actually a myth. For example, some people state that babies are nearly blind at birth. This was taken as common knowledge until the 1960s when researchers such as Fantz, Ordy, and Udelf (1962) developed procedures that showed that babies can indeed see reasonably well in some circumstances. When common knowledge is used as the basis of an argument it should be carefully examined (Govier, 2001). You might hear the following arguments based on common knowledge (adapted from Govier, 2001).

1. Instructors at post-secondary schools are educated.

2. If you counted all the degrees of all the instructors in Canada, it would take a long time.

3. By the time you finished counting, some new instructors would have started working and others would have retired.

4. Having a number of people counting in each province would not avoid the problem.

While the first three statements are common knowledge and probably do not need supporting evidence, the fourth statement is not common knowledge and would need testing or at least clarification. How many people would count? Would the count be limited to a specific time period, etc.?

Sometimes in academic research it is difficult for students to determine whether a statement is common knowledge. For example, Morgan wrote in his paper that Canada has a chronic doctor shortage. He thinks that this is common knowledge but is not sure. It is possible that some parts of Canada do not have a doctor shortage. In instances in which you are not sure if a statement is common knowledge, it is best to cite a reference to support that statement (see Chapter 10).

Finally, when evaluating the logic of a belief or statement, you need to recall possible biases presented above to decide if the theory or belief is reasonable or if one or more of these biases are evident.

SHOULD I EVALUATE THE SOURCE OF THE THEORY OR BELIEF?

Another important aspect in evaluating a theory or belief is evaluating the source of the information. This is especially true when adopting a theory or belief from an authority.

reliable
the source provides information that is generally accepted or has consensus and can be replicated

First, is the source **reliable**? Does this person simply generalize from his/her own experience or is he/she using other sources of information as evidence in formulating the theory or belief? Usually we hold a source as more reliable if the theory or belief is based on evidence rather than personal experience.

Second, when using an authority as the basis of belief, we also need to know the expertise of the individual promoting the belief. Does the individual truly have an expertise in the area in which he or she is theorizing? Josh has to examine the experts he cites in his belief that poor people are lazy. Neither his uncle nor his mother has an expertise in the area of poverty. Thus, when reading articles for essays, you need to examine the credentials of the author of the article to see if the author has credibility in the area in which he or she is offering an opinion. (This is especially true if Internet sources are used; see Chapter 9.)

Third, when using an authority, we need to examine the motivations of the authority. Often companies use celebrities to market their products. When the celebrity tells us that brand X is a superior brand, we have to wonder if the celebrity really thinks this or is saying so in order to be paid by the company. For this reason, when researchers publish articles, they usually note conflicts of interest within the acknowledgments. For example, if a researcher is promoting a new drug, it is important that the reader know whether or not the researcher is being funded by the drug company producing the drug.

HOW CAN I EVALUATE THE EVIDENCE USED TO SUPPORT A THEORY OR BELIEF?

Most beliefs and theories are based on some sort of supporting evidence. Evaluation of this evidence is critical when adopting the theory or belief. Evidence supporting or refuting a theory or belief should be viewed in several ways (Petress, 2004).

First, the evidence should be *sufficient*. That is, the theory is supported by many sources of information. For example, if a scientist claimed that a particular eye exercise would improve vision and cited the finding that a group of patients did the exercise and had improved vision, we would suggest that this one source is not sufficient. Is there enough evidence to support this result?

Second, evidence to support a theory should be *relevant*. That is, does the evidence actually relate to the theory or belief? For example, Josh's uncle evicts people on welfare; Josh concludes that people on welfare are lazy. However, does the fact that people are evicted mean they are lazy? No. Thus, we would argue that this evidence is not relevant to the theory or belief.

Third, evidence should be from *reliable sources* as described in the section above. Evidence should be *consistent* (Petress, 2004). In other words, we check to see if the evidence is collected by acceptable methods, and other sources have come to similar conclusions.

Fourth, evidence should be *recent* (Petress, 2004). Is the data presented to support an argument still accepted today? Some older theories are still accepted today, but others are not. For example, in the late 1800s, Galton argued that the size of a man's head related to his intelligence and took hat size measures to support this theory. Today, this would not be acceptable evidence since many studies have since shown that physical characteristics do not relate to intellect. In another example, the high numbers of physicians who smoked cigarettes could be used to support the idea that cigarette smoking is harmless to health. But these data were gathered in the 1930s, before anyone knew of the dangers of smoking. At that time, physicians were smoking because they didn't know any better! Today, the situation is very different and these data on physicians would not be acceptable. When using older sources, it is a good idea to check more recent sources to see if they are still acceptable.

Finally, evidence should be *objective* (Petress, 2004). That is, arguments made in support of theories and beliefs are balanced. This relates to the bias of selective attention. If only supporting evidence is cited, and inconsistent evidence is not explained or examined, then the theory or belief should be questioned.

PROBLEM-SOLVING

HOW CAN I MAKE PROBLEMS EASIER TO HANDLE?

Josh may not realize it, but the assignment his instructor has given him requires him to solve a problem: what accounts for poverty in society? In almost all cases, essays and assignments given to students by their instructors in most subject areas (e.g., math, physics, English) can be thought of as special cases of problem-solving.

sub-goals
small components of a problem created by dividing the problem

For example, when giving essay assignments, we often ask students to rephrase their topic as a question and seek to find the answer to the question. Once the question is developed, students are asked to break their essays into a series of smaller tasks called **sub-goals**. These sub-goals include making a research plan (see Chapter 9), an essay plan, formulating arguments for their essay, then following previously established rules of writing to create the introduction, body, and conclusions (see Chapter 10).

Other assignments at school should also be thought of as problem sets and solved in similar ways. For example, when given a statistics assignment, students first examine the question or goal state they wish to answer (e.g., is there a relationship between good health and income?). They then break the task into smaller components or sub-goals including problems involving what statistics to use, calculation of these statistics by following prescribed rules, and interpreting the outcome.

Problem-solving is an important component of work at the post-secondary level. You will find that there are many individual differences in problem-solving. For example, you may find that some students can easily solve problems in math and science, while other students struggle. This is because how well you solve these problems depends on your prior knowledge, your knowledge of similar problems, your previous training in the topic at hand, and the resources you have in solving problems (i.e., access to a computer or knowledgeable teacher). However, understanding how problems are generally solved will enable you to quickly recognize goal paths within many assignments.

ARE THERE DIFFERENT PROBLEM-SOLVING APPROACHES I CAN CONSIDER?

When approaching many problems there are two general methods that need to be considered prior to working on the problem. That is, will your approach be inductive or will it be deductive? Both approaches have advantages and disadvantages.

inductive methods
information (studies, experience, surveys, interviews) is first gathered, then a solution or theory is determined

In **inductive methods**, information (studies, experience, surveys, interviews) is first gathered, then a solution or theory is created. For example, if you were asked to determine why some women suffer from depression after childbirth, you would first gather many studies of the issue, read them, and create a theory. The advantage of the inductive method is that prior to solving the problem, you have an open mind. The research or data will guide you to a conclusion. The main disadvantage of inductive methods is that the information you collect must be extensive and very critically reviewed. If you limit your information gathering to three or four articles, you may find very diverse conclusions in these articles or limited conclusions when the few articles you chose only address a single issue. You may miss other important alternative theories. In addition, the information that you gather must be viewed to ensure that no cognitive biases (as described above) have been committed, that the evidence is sound, reliable, consistent, recent, and objective. At times, this is difficult for students to achieve in an assignment.

deductive methods
a theory is proposed, then evidence is gathered to support or refute that theory

In **deductive methods**, a theory is proposed, then evidence is gathered to support or refute that theory. Under deductive methods, if you were asked why some women suffer from depression after childbirth, you would begin with a theory. You might believe or theorize that a biochemical imbalance following childbirth results in depression. You would then focus on that theory when gathering your research. You would then find evidence to support or refute your theory. The advantage of this method is that the research you conduct is focused on one issue. However, the main disadvantage of this method is that you are so focused on one theory that other potentially important theories are ignored. You may selectively choose articles and evidence that supports your view while ignoring inconsistent evidence, which might have pointed you to more accurate conclusions and led you to write a more interesting paper.

Exercise 7.1 shows an example of inductive and deductive methods to answer a simple question. Follow this example to answer the question, "Why are extra-curricular activities helpful to post-secondary students?" Be sure to think of possible research sources and the possible problems you might have due to the inductive or deductive methods.

EXERCISE 7.1 ▶ *Using Inductive and Deductive Methods*

Question: Why do students seek higher education?

Inductive Methods

Step 1: Conduct research

Possible research sources

- Conduct a survey of students

- Library research on students in higher education

- Look at government data on students in higher education

Step 2: Based on research, formulate a theory

Theory: Students seek higher education because they are influenced by their parents.

Step 3: Know cautions with the inductive methods

- The survey must not show bias

- The research must be extensive

- The type of government data used could bias the theory (i.e., if the data only looked at parental education compared to child education, then a bias might exist)

Deductive Methods

Step 1: Formulate a theory

Theory: Students seek higher education because they are influenced by their parents.

Step 2: Conduct research that is relevant to the theory

Possible research sources:

- Conduct a survey of students about parental influence

- Library research on influence of parents on students' higher education

- Look at government data education of parents vs. children

Step 3: Know cautions with deductive methods

- You will likely only use questions on the survey that are relevant to your theory, thus not allowing for knowledge of other issues

- You might only look for literature on parental influence, when there may be many other influences

- You may focus only on government data about parental influence, thus ignoring other factors that influence students

WHEN DO I NEED TO USE THESE INDUCTIVE AND DEDUCTIVE METHODS?

In general, you will decide on inductive or deductive methods when faced with essays or examination questions. Some examination questions will be phrased such that deductive methods will be favoured. For example, "Discuss Bandura's theory that children imitate what they observe and provide evidence to support this theory. What are the limitations of this theory?" This question is asking you to go from a theory to evidence (deduction). Some questions suggest that inductive methods are appropriate. For example, "Do children imitate what they observe?" Here you are to examine evidence and theorize on the evidence; that is, derive a theory based on the evidence (induction).

WHAT ARE THE PROBLEM-SOLVING STAGES?

Regardless of the way in which you approach a problem (inductive or deductive), researchers have found that people use several stages in solving problems. From this research, we have learned that humans often solve problems in stages and use short cuts to get to their conclusions (Newell & Simon, 1972). In general when faced with a problem, individuals first define the problem, often breaking it down into smaller parts. Second, they form a **hypothesis** (a possible suggested solution) about the problem and third, they test their hypothesis and evaluate the solution. If their solution appears inadequate, they may give up on the problem or start over.

hypothesis
a possible suggested solution

Defining the problem

One of the difficulties in solving problems is defining the problem. That is, in knowing what you are being asked to do. Take the case of Alex, who was asked to view a demonstration in his chemistry class and write a discussion paper about it. In his paper he clearly described the demonstration, however, he received a grade of 50 percent. He failed to understand the task's instructions, which included reflecting on the demonstration and theorizing on outcomes, not simply describing it. Many instructors clearly outline problems for students; however, some problems are not well defined. Often, the point and the challenge of the assignment lie in your ability to recognize the problem and how to solve it. Ingrid is an engineering student who has been asked to evaluate the plans for a bridge. What she does not know is that there are several structural flaws in the plan that will compromise the safety of the bridge. Her instructor wants her to recognize that a problem exists in the plan and to suggest solutions. In recognizing a problem, you must rely on previous experience—personal experiences, previous assignments, lecture material, text material, and library research.

Past experience can help to guide problem-solving but it can also limit one's ability to solve the problem. Read the problem in Exercise 7.2 to see how past experience can negatively affect outcome.

EXERCISE 7.2

▶ **The Picture Problem**

A man has been asked to hang a picture in an attic room that has many crossbeams on the ceiling. The picture has to be hung so it does not hit the crossbeams. The picture has a wire attached to it on the back. The man has been instructed that he may not tie the string to a crossbeam. To hang the picture, the man has only been given string, paper, and scissors. How will he do it?

While there are many possible solutions to this problem, one that would be successful is to tie the string to the picture wire, throw the string over the crossbeam, and tie the scissors to the other end of the string as a counterweight. You would ignore the paper as in this case it is not relevant. The problem people have in coming to this solution is their past experience. Scissors are used to cut things and we are unable to see them as being used for something else. Having trouble using old objects and ideas in new ways is called **functional fixedness**. This fixedness limits you to only produce old solutions, rather than to create new ones. Some argue that to be a creative problem-solver you need to have multi-contextual thought (Swede, 1993). This means that you need to approach a problem by considering many viewpoints.

functional fixedness
having difficulty seeing new uses for old objects and ideas

Forming and testing a hypothesis

Usually, when faced with a problem, the individual will form a hypothesis. That is, he or she will think of one possible solution and test it. One way to ensure that you properly solve a problem is to test every possible solution and figure out which ones work. This rule is called an **algorithm**. You will always be successful, but thinking of and testing every solution could take great amounts of time. We rarely use algorithms to solve problems. Exercise 7.3 contains a scrambled word. Look at the letters and decide what the word is. One way to solve this problem is to consider every possible letter combination and choose the one that spells a word. However, there are 40,320 different letter combinations and thus arranging each would take considerable time. The fact that you could solve this problem so quickly indicates that you did not consider all 40,320 solutions. In fact, you likely took a shortcut by not considering any combination where the letters were not in a permissible order in English. For example, you know from your reading experience that in English no words begin with the letters *NL*, thus you did not consider those in forming a solution. When we take shortcuts in finding solutions to problems, we are using a **heuristic**. In both everyday and academic problem-solving there are many types of shortcut solutions or heuristics. Some common heuristics are sub-goals, uphill patterns, analogies, and diagrams.

algorithm
testing all possible solutions

heuristic
a shortcut solution

EXERCISE 7.3

▶ *Scrambled Word*

Look at the letters and decide what the word is.

TOLOUSNI

WHAT ARE SOME COMMON HEURISTICS?

When forming a hypothesis about a problem, we need to consider the current state of the problem and the goal state. For example, Brian has to write a paper for his philosophy class that discusses the question "Does man have free will?" He knows that the answer to the question is the goal of his paper (yes, no, or sometimes). He also is aware that his instructor will expect him to argue the point, and to do this he will have to consider many ways in which he could answer this question: through personal experience, through current events, through expert opinion of philosophers, etc. Brian decides to break his work into smaller tasks to answer this question. Breaking work into smaller tasks is called creating a sub-goal. It will not lead to a solution but will move you towards one. He will first list personal experiences that suggest he has free will and those that suggest he does not. Next he will read newspapers to find events that show free will does or does not exist. Third, he will go to the library and find writings of philosophers who have contemplated this question. Once each sub-goal is completed, Brian will formulate his paper, starting with an essay plan (another sub-goal). The plan will include general arguments, evaluation of the arguments, and the answer to the question. Once the plan is complete, he will begin his essay following practices suggested in Chapter 10, including learning MLA format, essay structure, etc. (another sub-goal). Each of these tasks moves Brian closer to his goal of answering the original question. Moving in the direction of a goal is known as an **uphill practice**.

uphill practice
moving in the direction of a goal

Not all post-secondary problems are academic but sub-goals and uphill practices are often involved in finding solutions to these non-academic problems. Suppose you realized that you have only $25 in your bank account and seven weeks left at school. Luckily, you live in residence, which includes meals, and both your residence and tuition have been paid in full. However, with no spending money, you believe that life at school will not be much fun. You have some choices. You could phone your mother and ask for $500. You could borrow money from friends. You could go only to free parties. You could find some part-time work on campus. You decide on the latter. Now your goal is to have a part-time job (you hope for about five hours a week). To achieve this, you must move from your current state (no job) to your goal state (a job). You break down finding a job into sub-goals: visiting the career centre on campus, writing a résumé, choosing possible jobs, getting the résumé to the potential employers, and following up with each potential employer. Each step is a sub-goal that will not lead to a guaranteed job but could move you towards a job, an uphill practice.

DO I NEED TO USE SUB-GOALS?

Most assignments at the post-secondary level are complex, and working towards completion requires many steps or sub-goals. It is beneficial for you to begin the assignment by writing out the many steps involved for the assignment. This allows you to see that your assignments are a series of tasks, rather than one large task, and you can work on each of these sub-goal tasks. Having sub-goals helps to alleviate the stress in large projects, since you can better see your progress towards completion. Setting up sub-goals will also allow you to better manage your time, since you will now be aware of all steps involved in your project.

ANALOGY HEURISTICS

analogy heuristic
occurs when someone uses a previously learned solution to help solve a new problem

An **analogy heuristic** occurs when someone uses a previously learned solution to help solve a new problem. When receiving a problem, especially at post-secondary school, you must decide if this problem is similar to others that have been encountered. If so, then using methods in a solution that previously worked is an effective way of tackling the problem.

There are several important points that you need to know when using analogies. First, sometimes old solutions are not appropriate, because you have misidentified the problem. Take the case of Alley. Several problems on her physics examination looked like ones that she had solved on her previous examination, but she used the wrong formula. Alley did not properly identify the problem. Part of studying in any class is to learn the different types of problems that regularly occur and categorize these problems. Learn to distinguish these problems. Your instructor will likely spend considerable time on problem identification. Second, sometimes analogies are simply a case of functional fixedness. You are having trouble seeing a new solution because you can only recall the old one.

Do I need to use analogies?

Analogies and problem identification are an important part of all post-secondary programs. For example, in the practice of law, social work, nursing, medicine, and engineering, many problems are constantly repeated and need to be quickly identified and solved. Analogies allow for quicker solutions. However, in post-secondary school you also need to use your past failures as feedback to solve a problem. Often students receive poor grades on assignments and exams. It is tempting for students to toss these papers in the recycling bin, however, this is a poor approach: negative outcomes can provide extremely important feedback. You need to review and correct your errors (this may require visiting the instructor during office hours). This will allow you to build proper problem-solving skills and solutions.

DIAGRAM HEURISTICS

One very popular heuristic is converting the problem and possible solution into a diagram. Diagrams can help students to better visualize the problem. Take the case of Phil. In statistics he must identify a problem to determine what statistic to use in an analysis. After reading about a study that was conducted, Phil must suggest an appropriate statistical procedure. Phil is confused so he decides to draw the study. See Box 7.1 for Phil's problem and his drawing of the study. Phil was better able to see the comparisons needed by making his drawing.

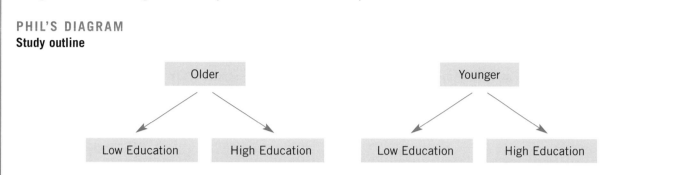

Diagram Heuristic: Statistics Problem for Phil   BOX 7.1

A researcher wonders about the effect of age and education on memory. Older and younger subjects of high and low education are brought into the lab and given a memory test. Their results are compared.

PHIL'S DIAGRAM
Study outline

```
        Older                              Younger
        /    \                             /    \
Low Education  High Education    Low Education  High Education
```

Phil: Based on this design I need an analysis that compares older and younger people but also compares low and high education within each group.

---

mind map
a diagram of how concepts are linked together

Some people draw a problem-solving diagram known as a **mind map**. The purpose of a mind map is to identify the sub-goals and see how they are related to each other and to the solution to the problem. Recall your imagined financial problem. You decided to find a job. You could create a mind map so you could better see the actions you need to take. Your mind map can be found in Figure 7.1.

FIGURE 7.1 Mind Map for a Job Search

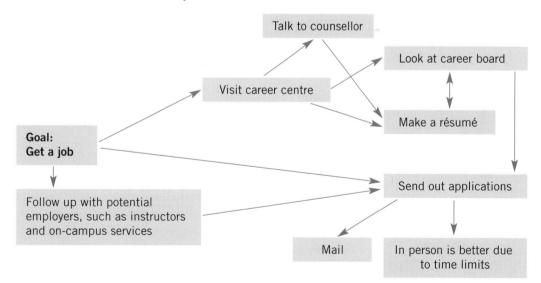

DO I NEED TO USE DIAGRAMS?

Not all students find diagrams the most useful way to understand material. Diagrams do offer a new view of the problem and can often suggest a solution or at least the steps to the solution. To show yourself the possible use of mind maps or diagrams, try to make a mind map for some other problems that may occur during your time at post-secondary school. For example, you could map the steps that you might need to write a term paper, or how you might come up with enough money to pay your tuition, or how you might find good off-campus housing. If possible, compare your maps with those of other students in your class.

WHAT IF THERE IS MORE THAN ONE POSSIBLE SOLUTION?

Many problems have more than one solution; often there are multiple solutions to problems. For example, students in computer science will learn that there are many ways to program the same outcome. A student may be asked to create a program that can track crime statistics. Many different programming languages could be used and many different programming steps could be taken. Computer students are often asked to evaluate their solutions in terms of efficiency. That is, the good solution required fewer steps than other potential solutions. In general, for all problems, efficiency is important. Because students have limited time, they need to evaluate and choose solutions that are efficient (require the fewest steps). Students need to make arguments in papers that are succinct or to the point. Most instructors want students to clearly address the problem at hand without adding tangential information that clouds the outcome.

ARE THESE PROBLEM-SOLVING METHODS HELPFUL IN SOLVING EVERYDAY PROBLEMS OR PROBLEMS AT WORK?

In general the answer to this question is yes. For example, many reports that you will create in your place of employment will require the skills you learn here. That is, you will need to define the scope of the report (problem), use sub-goals in creating your report, work on uphill practices, look for analogies when considering recommendations, and use diagrams for a better understanding of the report solutions.

DECISION-MAKING

HOW DO I MAKE DECISIONS?

Making decisions can be considered a special case of problem-solving applied to everyday situations. In making a decision you need to define a problem, hypothesize on alternative solutions, choose one alternative and, if that alternative is not successful, you may try another.

When individuals make decisions, most research suggests that they do so by taking into account the expected utility of the outcome and the probability that the outcome of the decision will be realized (Reisberg, 1997; Solso, Maclin, & Maclin, 2004). By **expected utility**, we mean that you take into account the value you place on the decision. For example, you imagined that you had to decide whether you should take a part-time job or ask your parents for money. In coming to the decision, you had to decide first how much value you placed on each choice. For example, taking a job would mean more independence from your parents and your parents would not lecture you about wasting money. Thus, the choice to take a job might have high expected utility; it was highly valued. Second, you had to decide if the decision could be realized. Could you get a job? You went to the campus career centre to discover whether there were jobs available and how to properly apply. This visit would help you decide whether your choice to get a job would be realized.

expected utility
taking into account the value you place on the decision

WHAT FACTORS AFFECT HOW I MAKE A DECISION?

Early theorists in decision-making argued that decisions made by people followed rational choices. This rational choice theory implied that when people made decisions they did so rationally by weighing the choice based on their experience and based on logic (Mellers,

Schwartz, & Cooke, 1998). In other words, it was believed that people use critical thinking in making decisions. However, we know today that the way people come to decisions is affected by many factors that are not rational. Risk perceptions and attitudes, emotions, task instructions, and the decision-making environment affect decisions that people make (Mellers et al., 1998).

Risk perceptions and attitudes

Decisions are affected by the risk the individual perceives in making that choice. For example, Sonia perceives that walking at night is dangerous so she avoids that choice; Sam perceives that walking at night is safe and often walks at night. These perceptions of risk are affected by many factors, such as education, age, and gender. Some individuals value risky decisions, while others value less risky decisions. This value may well be related to previous experience with risk. For example, Sandra decided not to hand in her term paper in geography, making a risky decision that it would be accepted late. She decided this because in a previous class she had handed in a paper late and was not penalized. One's attitude towards risk is guided by utility value; that is, expected gains and losses (Mellers et al., 1998).

Emotions

People's emotions, both before and after decisions, affect decision-making. Positive emotions increase creative problem-solving and thus lead to more decision alternatives (Mellers et al., 1998). For example, Patricia needs to get her group working on their term project, but they seem unwilling to meet. Patricia feels positively about her team members and truly likes them. She decides to hold a team party as an alternative to the usual meeting. She believes that her team will show up to a party and this will allow them to talk in a fun environment.

Negative emotions tend to cause poor attention to information provided during the decision-making process. Lack of attention to relevant information can lead to poor decision choices. For example, Miranda has received a failing grade in her physics mid-term and feels negatively towards the subject and her instructor. She can't stop thinking about the mid-term and feels that it was unfair, the instructor is poor, and her failure is a reflection of a poorly organized class rather than a reflection of her studying (note that she only studied the day before the exam). She is now faced with a physics assignment that is quite difficult. Given that she feels the instructor is unfair, she decides not to bother with her assignment. Now, not only will Miranda fail her mid-term, but she will fail an assignment that could have helped her to better understand the topic.

Emotions felt after a decision is made also affect future decision-making. People more often regret decisions that they did not make than actions that they did take (Mellers et al., 1998). Not making a decision about where to go to school, for example, will lead to not going to any school, a regrettable situation. In addition, memories of emotions following a decision often guide current decisions. For example, Vivian recalls the joy she felt when she decided to spend her money on a slot machine that resulted in a win. She often plays slots now, and is sure the next button push will lead to joy. Over time, she has lost much more money than she ever won.

Task instructions

Decisions are often affected by the wording of a problem or task. This is very evident in advertising. Mellers et al. (1998) reviewed a study of decisions made in two states by people buying identical insurance policies. In one state, the individuals were offered extra insurance coverage for extra cost; only 20 percent chose this option. In the second state, the individuals were told that their extra coverage was part of their insurance package but they could reduce the cost of their insurance by removing the extra coverage; 75 percent chose to keep the coverage and pay the higher costs. Thus, the wording of offers is critical in affecting decisions made. Emphasis on positive features of a decision option increases it as a preference, and emphasis on negative features reduces it as a choice. In other examples that we see every day on television and in magazines, advertisers tell us that if we buy their product, our lives will be improved. They don't threaten us that our lives will be terrible if we don't buy their product!

THE DECISION ENVIRONMENT

Decisions made by individuals are often different from decisions made by the same individuals in a group. In general, individuals make less extreme decisions (less risky or less conservative) than do groups. Social decisions often involve communal sharing and authority ranking (Fisk, 1992; as cited by Mellers et al., 1998). These factors may explain risk taking in groups. **Communal sharing** means that the group shares the stress of the decision outcome and the responsibility for the decision. Thus, an individual in the group does not feel responsible for poor decisions and will take more extreme choices. **Authority ranking** means that in groups, people often silently rank group members as those of high status and those of low status. Because stories of people who are successful after a risky decision (e.g., invested all their money and became millionaires) are often valued, members with riskier attitudes often rank higher than the middle of the road members (members who make decisions that have only moderate risk). In addition, group decisions often involve social pressure. Members fear rejection of the group if they do not comply with group decisions, even if they do not agree with them (Mellers et al., 1998, p. 460).

communal sharing
the group shares the stress of the decision outcome and the responsibility for the decision

authority ranking
people often silently rank group members as those of high status and those of low status

WHAT DOES DECISION-MAKING THEORY HAVE TO DO WITH MY STUDIES?

You are constantly faced with decisions relating to school and recognizing factors that might adversely affect decision making is important. We previously saw in Chapter 4 that decisions can lead to considerable stress. Here we will discuss decision-making in relation to expected utility and the probability that these decisions will be realized (cost–benefit analysis). Some decisions you make involve two positive choices (an approach-approach conflict). Should I take psychology or sociology as my elective? Should I go to Janet's party or to the pub? Both choices lead to rather pleasant outcomes and thus do not cause much stress in students. However, even some positive choices options require a careful cost–benefit analysis. Should I sleep in (cost: miss class material, benefit: sleeping is fun) or should I go to class (cost: can't hang out with my friends, benefit: I will do better on the exam).

Some decisions are easy to make because one alternative is negative and the other is positive (an approach-avoidance conflict). Should I hand in my assignment or should I fail the assignment by not handing it in? Should I cheat on my exam and risk expulsion or should I study? Just because the correct course of action is clear, however, does not mean that people always choose this course. Factors discussed above—such as risk perceptions, emotions, and environment—affect these decisions.

Finally, sometimes decisions are both negative (avoidance-avoidance conflict). Given that I procrastinated and do not have time for both, should I do my history essay or my English assignment? As discussed in Chapter 4, these decisions cause much stress and require much thought about costs and benefits. For example how much is each assignment worth? Which is more likely to be completed in the time left, etc.? Sometimes these negative alternatives cause students to freeze. They don't know what to do or how to start making a decision. Freezing during the decision process can have disastrous effects at school, and getting started again is important. Usually getting started again involves a trip to your academic skills centre, making a plan for your work, itemizing your tasks, and visiting your instructor or teaching assistant.

Advice for Josh

▶ Josh believes that people who are poor become this way due to a poor work ethic. In essence, Josh has decided to use deduction as a method to examine the cause of poverty and homelessness. Josh is starting with a theory and plans to use "expert" opinion, personal experience, and some articles to support his theory (deductive methods). However, if Josh is to satisfy his instructor, he will need to critically evaluate his theory. He needs to examine the assumptions he has made when coming upon his original belief. This examination might lead Josh to reject his current theory. Below are questions that Josh will need to ask himself when critically reviewing his theory. If Josh asks himself these questions, he will probably realize that his theory has little supporting evidence, relies on inappropriate authority, uses evidence that is not relevant, and does not have consensus among expert researchers. He may then start to consider alternative theories for the cause of poverty, such as inequities in the social system, education, and access to resources.

CRITICAL QUESTION	OUTCOME AND FURTHER THOUGHTS
Where did the current theory come from?	Allows you to think of the assumptions you made in believing a particular theory.
If the theory came from authority, is the authority appropriate?	Allows for evaluation of the expert—Is the expert really an expert, what motivations guide the expert, does the expert supply relevant evidence for theory?
What motivational biases do you hold in believing this theory?	Is the theory self-serving or does it have false consensus? Does it make you feel safe? If so, there may be biases causing poor evaluation of the theory.
What cognitive biases do you hold in believing this theory?	Allows you to better evaluate assumptions you hold by believing a theory. Are you selectively attending to information, are you making inappropriate causal and covariation biases, did you discount other potential theories, do you believe this theory because you can think of some cases where it applies? If these biases are apparent, further examination of the theory is needed.
What was your evaluation of the sources used as evidence for the theory?	Were sources reliable, relevant, sufficient, consistent, and objective? If not, then further examination of this theory is needed.
When working on the paper, were heuristics used?	Were sub-goals, such as an essay plan, and research plan, developed? Were different arguments considered? Was the essay problem clearly defined? Were the sources of information used appropriate for a post-secondary paper? Did you think of past feedback on papers you have written as a model for the current paper? All these are needed to ensure the paper is written to post-secondary standards.
Did your decision to adopt this theory result from a real analysis of the issue?	Were your decisions in choosing this theory based on evidence or based on other factors (e.g., it will require little research)?

CHAPTER SUMMARY

- There are many ways that people come to certain beliefs. Sometimes beliefs are based on what authorities tell us, and other times beliefs are based on personal experience. However, beliefs that are created through these methods are often based on faulty assumptions.

- There are many biases that can be evident in people's beliefs. Motivational biases help people to hold onto beliefs that help them cope. Cognitive biases in beliefs result from poor analysis of available information. Both these bias types can limit your thinking about particular topics.

- It is best to evaluate theories to see if they are supported by appropriate evidence. Evidence should be sufficient, relevant, reliable, consistent, and recent.

- Most post-secondary assignments and essays can be thought of as problems to solve. Assignments should be broken down into tasks or sub-goals that need to be completed.

- When problem-solving, it is a good idea to consider possible problem-solving methods. If inductive methods are used, research must be completed before considering a theory or belief. If deductive methods are used, a theory is first created and research to support or refute the theory is collected. Both inductive and deductive methods need to be used with caution because both can lead to biases.

- When solving problems, it is best to define the problem, understand task instructions, formulate a solution, and test this solution to see if it is correct. A number of heuristics, or techniques, can help you to better solve problems in school assignments; these include using analogies and making diagrams or mind maps.

- Another special type of problem-solving is decision-making. When we make decisions, we evaluate the value of our decision and the possibility that the decision will work out. Decisions are very much affected by the value we place on risk, our emotions, task instructions, and whether we make our decisions alone or in groups.

KEY TERMS

a priori beliefs
algorithm
analogy heuristic
authority ranking
availability bias
avoidability of physical harm
belief
belief in a just world
causal theories
cognitive biases
communal sharing

covariation bias
deductive methods
expected utility
failure to discount
false consensus bias
functional fixedness
fundamental attribution error
heuristic
hypothesis
inductive methods
mind map

motivational biases
premise
reliable
representativeness bias
sample bias
selective attention biases
self-serving bias
sub-goals
theory
uphill practice

INDIVIDUAL ACTIVITIES

1. Think of two beliefs that you have. Using the information in this chapter, evaluate those beliefs. Where did your beliefs come from? What motivational and cognitive biases may be present in your beliefs?

2. List the cognitive biases discussed in this chapter, then think of two examples where you see these biases in everyday life.

3. Take an assignment from one of your classes and break it down into sub-goals. Keep a journal of your work on each sub-goal to see how each fits into an uphill practice.

GROUP ACTIVITIES

1. As a group, discuss the biases in the assumptions for the following advertisements.

   * Two out of three dentists say that Cleano toothpaste is superior to Dulex toothpaste.
   * 50 percent of the people of Smithville say they will try Blue Laundry Detergent again.
   * Golfer Bogey James uses clubs made by Athetico.
   * Dr. John says that eating Saunders Cheese will increase your intelligence.

2. A friend tells you that he is having a serious problem and asks for advice. It seems that your friend is required to build a catapult in his engineering class that can launch a potato a minimum of 100 yards. Your friend understands what he is to do but does not seem to know how to get started. Using heuristics mentioned in this chapter, as a group, give your friend advice.

3. Kogan and Wallach (1967) suggested using stories to study the way people take risks. Based on their work, try the following exercise. Read the following story. You will be asked to advise Mr. C, based on what you believe to be acceptable risk.

   Mr. C is a travelling salesman. He is driving in Northern Alberta, along a country road. He has not seen a house in the last hour. A very bad snowstorm hits. Mr. C's car gets stuck and he is soon going to run out of gas to run the car heater. He can stay in the car or he can walk along the road in the storm. If he stays in the car, he may survive or he may die if help does not come along soon. If he walks, he may find help but he does not know how far he must go.

   a) Pick the following option that best represents your opinion of how much risk Mr. C should take. Mr. C. should risk walking only if:

      * there is a 9 out of 10 chance that he will make it to help
      * there is a 7 out of 10 chance that he will make it to help
      * there is a 5 out of 10 chance he will make it to help
      * there is a 3 out of 10 chance he will make it to help
      * there is a 1 out of 10 chance he will make it to help

   b) Once you have chosen the option that you feel is most acceptable, move into a group of five individuals. Discuss the problem with your group for 15 minutes and, as a group, unanimously choose a single option of what level of risk is acceptable (using the same options above as you did as an individual). Once this discussion is over, examine individual choices and compare them to your group choice. What seemed to influence group members?

REFERENCES

Fantz, R. L., Ordy, J. M., & Udelf, M. S. (1962). Maturation of pattern vision in infants during the first six months. *Journal of Comparative and Physiological Psychology, 55*, 907–917.

Govier, T. (2001). *A practical study of argument* (5th ed.). Belmont, CA: Wadsworth Thomson Learning.

Hergenhahn, B. R. (1992). *An introduction to the history of psychology* (2nd ed.). Belmont, CA: Wadsworth Publishing Company.

Kogan, N., & Wallach, M. A. (1967). Risk taking as a function of the situation, the person and the group. In G. Mandler, P. Mussen, N. Kogan, & M. A. Wallach (Eds.), *New directions in psychology* (Vol. 3). New York: Holt, Rinehart & Winston.

Kruglanski, A. W., & Ajzen, I. (1983). Bias and error in human judgment. *European Journal of Social Psychology, 13*, 1–44.

Mellers, B. A., Schwartz, A., & Cooke, A. D. J. (1998). Judgment and decision making. *Annual Review of Psychology, 49*, 447–477.

Newell, A., & Simon, H. (1972). *Human problem solving*. Englewood Cliffs, NJ: Prentice Hall.

Petress, K. (2004). Critical thinking: An extended definition. *Education, 124*, 461–466.

Reisberg, D. (1997). *Cognition: Exploring the science of the mind*. New York: Norton.

Solso, R., Maclin, M. K., & Maclin, O. (2004). *Cognitive psychology* (7th ed.). Toronto: Allyn and Bacon, Inc.

Swede, G. (1993). *Creativity: A new psychology*. Toronto: Wall & Emmerson Inc.

Walker, S. E., & Diaz, L. G. (2003). Promoting critical thinking in the classroom. *Athletic Therapy Today, 8(5)*, 64–65.

MOTIVATION

The Case of Bethany

▶ Bethany is from a small rural community and is now at a city college where she knows no one. She saw entering college as a fresh start and a new life. She had looked forward to studying in a program that included courses she was highly interested in and that she hoped would be relevant to the career she would later develop. She promised herself that she would drop all her bad habits of high school: she would get all her reading done ahead of time, never procrastinate doing assignments, attend all classes, and truly demonstrate her interest and ability by paying more attention to the academic factors of school and less to the social factors.

For the first four weeks of the first semester, she remained faithful to her resolutions. But gradually, around the end of the fourth week, she found herself slipping a little. Now, in the eighth week of classes, she's behind in her reading, she has three essays due in a few weeks that she hasn't started, and she didn't do as well as she had hoped (and knew she could do) on some of her mid-term tests. Now she finds herself spending more and more time either talking with her new friends or watching television. She knows she has to get it together if she is to finish the semester successfully, but somehow the days slip away from her and she can't seem to muster the energy to do her schoolwork. She finds she doesn't care about her work as much as she did at the beginning of the term. "I just can't get motivated," she says, and she wonders what happened.

If this is about the middle of your semester, you may be feeling much like Bethany right now, and this lack of motivation may be making you feel uncomfortable and anxious. An experience such as this is unfortunately not uncommon for students. When you were in elementary school, your teachers probably tried all sorts of tricks to keep you motivated, from giving you stickers to finding ways of teaching through games. Your books had lots of pictures and bright colours to keep you interested and motivated. But now, the books have fewer pictures and more writing, and there are rarely games or stickers. While most instructors are concerned with students' motivation and try very hard to make the information they present interesting and engaging, the bottom line is that you are responsible for your own motivation.

WHAT IS MOTIVATION?

motivation
what makes us behave the way we do and keeps us performing a certain behaviour; the "why" of behaviour

It's hard to find a good definition of motivation, but generally speaking, **motivation** is what makes us behave the way we do and keeps us performing. It's the "why" of behaviour. When you ask yourself why you did something ("What was I thinking? What was in my head?"), you are asking what motivated you to do what you did. This is obviously the most complex question for us to ask because there are so many possible explanations for behaviour. To illustrate this, let's take the simple example of one of Bethany's daily behaviours. Each day at 3:00 P.M. she goes to the doughnut shop to get a coffee and a cruller. Why does she do this? Because she's hungry? Yes, but how hungry can she be? She had lunch, and dinner is only a few hours away. Because she has a habit? Yes, but how did this habit form and what makes it keep going? Because crullers and coffee taste good? Yes, but so do tea and muffins. Why did she choose a cruller and coffee? To boost her blood sugar? Yes, but again, a muffin or an apple would have done the trick. Bethany's behaviour looks very simple, but in fact there are probably many reasons why she does what she does. Her motivation is complex.

Think about how complex the question becomes when we look at what motivates us to start post-secondary school. What you are doing is expensive, labour-intensive, and sometimes frustrating and stressful. Why are you doing it? There may be times when you ask yourself this very question! It's a good idea, then, to understand what motivation is all about.

THEORIES OF MOTIVATION

WHAT MOTIVATES US?

Bethany had good reasons to start a post-secondary education: she wanted to learn and to prepare for a career that would stimulate her and satisfy her. Of course, she also wanted that career to pay her a decent, living salary as well. If it made her rich, that wouldn't hurt, even though she felt that her satisfaction in her work was more important than getting enormously wealthy. Are these the reasons why you decided to continue your education after high school? Did you have other reasons? Do you have much in common with Bethany? Many researchers have asked whether we all have much in common when it comes to why we do what we do, what motivates our behaviour. There have been many theories of motivation over the years, and most have given us some good ideas about the factors involved in why we behave as we do. Let's look at some of the more recent theories that have been proposed and see if they can shed some light on why we, and Bethany, behave as we do.

Arousal theory

It's unpleasant to be hungry. It's also unpleasant to be too full. It's unpleasant to have too much to do and not enough time to do it all. But it's also unpleasant not to have anything to do. When we are hungry, we say that our need for food is aroused. When we have eaten too much, our need for food is so thoroughly satisfied that we feel like we may never have our need for food aroused again. When we have too much to do, our feeling that we want to be occupied and interested is overwhelmed, and we often wish that some of the things that are occupying us would go away. On the other hand, when we are bored, we look for something to interest and occupy us, even if it's just changing TV channels with the remote control. These examples demonstrate that we all have an optimum level of arousal. That is, there is a point at which we are most comfortable. Whether it's food or drink or sleep or activity, we want the level that's not too much and not too little, but is just right for us as individuals.

Arousal theory recognizes that sometimes we need extra stimulation to feel good. For example, monkeys will play with a latch and figure out how to work it even though the latch opens nothing (Butler, 1954). It seems as if the monkeys are just curious. We are also motivated by curiosity. For example, when Bethany was little, she took apart her toys, just to see how they worked. When she got a little older, she took apart more complicated "toys," learning how to fix her car and small appliances. Love of travel can be seen as another example of the need for extra arousal. Going to new places satisfies some curiosity. Arousal theory provides a simple explanation for why you decided to enter post-secondary school. You want to know things because you are curious about many topics. This seems like a promising explanation, but it's a fair bet that many of you didn't think in terms of your curiosity when you decided to enter post-secondary school. But this theory can account for why, when you have options outside your main program of study, you take certain courses simply because they look interesting to you. Nevertheless, this theory seems a little too simple to account for the complex reasons why we do what we do sometimes. There must be more.

Incentive theory

When we think about Bethany's reasons for entering post-secondary school, it's clear that some of the reasons concern her desire to form a happy and productive future for herself. She wants to be able to support herself well and to enjoy her work, and avoid having to worry about money or dread going to work.

Like Bethany, we are not only *pushed* by a need or desire to obtain something, we are also *pulled* by the idea of what we might obtain or avoid in the future. The things and the situations that we might obtain or avoid in the future are called **incentives**. **Incentive theory** suggests that we do what we do because we think about the rewards or punishments that we will receive (incentives). So Bethany goes to a doughnut shop because the coffee and cruller will taste good and make her feel better (an incentive). She is pulled to the doughnut shop by this thought. She is thinking that her education will result in a career (an incentive) that she might not be able to have without the education. At the same time, she views her education as a way to avoid a dead-end job (another incentive). Deep down, Bethany has another incentive: she has heard, correctly, that higher education is a way to enhance the quality of her thinking.

What are the anticipated rewards that you hope to gain from an education? What do you hope to avoid? We can see your behaviour as being pulled by what you want to gain and what you want to avoid in the future. This theory seems promising, but a little vague. It wouldn't be surprising if many people did things (like go to school) not really knowing why they are doing them. What are the incentives for them? Is there a theory that can give them, and us, some clues?

Abraham Maslow's hierarchy of needs

Incentive theory seems to be coming closer to explaining the complex behaviours that we show because we know that we are at times motivated to gain or avoid something. A more complex theory of motivation that includes some the incentive components that we have discussed is that of Abraham Maslow (1970). Maslow had great faith in the human being. He believed that each and every one of us wants ultimately to be the very best, most fulfilled

arousal theory
a theory of motivation that says we perform actions in order to maintain a sufficiently high level of arousal in ourselves

incentive
reward that is anticipated and/or received that causes our behaviour

incentive theory
a theory of motivation that says we perform actions in order to achieve certain outcomes as a result of our behaviour, to gain favourable outcomes and avoid unfavourable outcomes

hierarchy of needs
Maslow's formulation of levels of needs, the satisfaction of which drives our behaviour

physical needs
in Maslow's hierarchy of needs, the most basic level at which we have needs to keep our bodies alive

safety needs
in Maslow's hierarchy of needs, our need to live in a stable, secure environment in which we have some degree of ability to predict what will happen

person that we can be. But in order to get to that place, we must satisfy many requirements for ourselves. Maslow suggested that we have a **hierarchy of needs**. That is, we have needs at different levels that we must discharge in order to finally reach fulfillment in ourselves. The way he diagrammed this can be seen in Figure 8.1.

The first level is **physical needs**. We have need for food, water, air, etc. This is the level at which we have needs to keep our bodies alive. These are certainly the most fundamental needs in most cases. Starving people, for example, don't have much else on their minds except getting food; their motivation is to find food somewhere, somehow. If we can't satisfy this level of needs, we can't move up the hierarchy to the next level. Sometimes students have financial problems and these problems can become a focus of the student's life. If you are hungry and have no money for food, you might not be able to think of much else, including your studies. It's important for you to have the finances to buy food, shelter, etc., in order to be able to concentrate on education.

The second level of Maslow's hierarchy is **safety needs**. The need for safety is also very much at a physical level, but it includes a psychological dimension as well. Here, we are concerned with our need to feel safe. That is, we need to live in a stable, secure environment where we can predict what will happen. We are generally safe in our day-to-day lives. However, sometimes students experience difficulties in their living situations. For example, there is one person on the same floor as Bethany in the dormitory whose idea of fun is to play rather cruel practical jokes on people. Bethany had the disagreeable experiences of finding sand in her bed and having the brownies her mother sent her stolen. Now, when Bethany goes to her dorm after school, she feels anxious and uncertain about what will be waiting for her. This is relatively minor compared to the lack of safety that some of Bethany's classmates feel: because of lack of funds, they are forced to live in dangerous neighbourhoods. But for all of these people, the sense of not being entirely safe or secure in their living arrangements makes it difficult for them to concentrate on getting an education.

You, like Bethany, also need the safety of feeling free from harassment at school. You need to know that it is not acceptable for anyone to give you a hard time because of your age, race, gender, sexual preference, religion, nationality, or even your physical appearance, and that your school has very serious sanctions against people who harass you in any way.

FIGURE 8.1   Maslow's Hierarchy of Needs

Maslow's Hierarchy of Needs

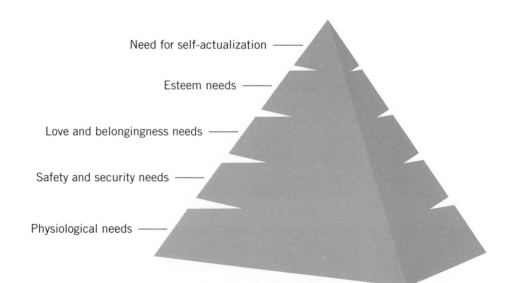

Need for self-actualization

Esteem needs

Love and belongingness needs

Safety and security needs

Physiological needs

If you have ever been harassed, or know someone who has, you know at first hand how terrible it is not to feel safe from this kind of psychological warfare in your living and studying/working situation. Your school recognizes that you have the right to an environment in which you do not have to expend your valuable energy worrying about this kind of behaviour from others, and unless you are free from harassment, you may not be able to think of much else. In this case, of course, schoolwork suffers.

If we satisfy the first two levels of Maslow's hierarchy, having our physical needs met and feeling safe and secure in our environments, we can move to the next level. The next level of Maslow's hierarchy of needs is psychological. At this level, called **the need for love and belongingness**, we have a need to feel a closeness with others. We need to love and be loved. We need to feel that we are part of a group of other individuals. Other students and instructors can make us feel that we belong, or not. This is a need that many people become aware of when they first enter a post-secondary school. Bethany, who is from a small rural community and is now at a city college where she knows no one, feels the need most keenly. No doubt Bethany will spend a great deal of time and energy using the telephone and e-mail to connect with her family and friends in her home community. As she could testify, when love and belongingness needs are not satisfied, we feel lonely and isolated. It's worth noting that even when we have a wide circle of friends, we may still not have this need satisfied. The number of people we connect with is not as important as the quality of the relationships we have. So Bethany doesn't need to make many new friends as long as the relationships she develops are of high quality. We need people whom we trust and feel we can confide in. Just as importantly, we need to feel that there are people around us who trust us and want to open up to us as well. It's wonderful to have a wide circle of acquaintances, but nothing compares to having a few people that we can truly be close to.

On the next level are **esteem needs**. What we mean by this is that we need to feel respect from others and from ourselves. We get this respect by our competence and our achievements. That is, we *earn* satisfaction at this level. Even though we often have great achievements—such as producing quality work at school, thereby earning the respect and admiration of everyone who knows us—we often do not recognize our own achievements and do not give ourselves the recognition that we deserve. This need may be a difficult one to fulfill for many people. Take the case of Barbara. She is an *A*-student who works at a part-time job 15 hours a week, volunteers at a community centre for developmentally delayed children every Sunday, and is a warm and loving friend and family member. She seems like a Superwoman to us, but to herself, she feels that she should do more. Barbara, then, has not completely fulfilled her esteem needs: the respect that we give her is not enough. She has to respect herself or she will be stuck at this level, unable to move forward to the next level. Connie has a different problem: she does as much as Barbara does, and has as many accomplishments, but her father treats her like a child who is not capable of making her own decisions. While he undoubtedly loves her and wants the best for her, it is not clear to her that he respects her. Connie's esteem needs are not fulfilled either, so she too is stuck.

When we get stuck at a particular level, we concentrate our efforts on achieving satisfaction of our needs at that level. This makes perfect sense and seems very reasonable at the first two levels: obviously, a starving person should look for food, and a person whose life may be in danger should try to find safety. But what about the need for love and belongingness? Or the need for esteem? Will we die if we aren't loved or respected? Perhaps not, but we may be very unhappy. Maslow said that we will try desperately to fulfill the needs that we lack, and sometimes we even use techniques that are not very adaptive for us. For instance, maybe this is part of the reason why someone who has never felt loved becomes clingy and has to have a romantic partner even if the partner is abusive. Maybe trying to gain respect is part of the reason why some of us brag about our accomplishments or become so driven to become or achieve more than other people.

The highest level of needs is very different from the ones proposed on the lower levels. This level is reached by few of us. Most of us spend our lives trying to fulfill our love and

love and belongingness needs
in Maslow's hierarchy of needs, the need to love and be loved; the need to feel that we are part of a group of other individuals

esteem needs
in Maslow's hierarchy of needs, the need to feel respect from others and from ourselves

self-actualization need
in Maslow's hierarchy of
needs, the highest level
of needs, encompassing
the need to maximize our
potentials, becoming the
best that we can be

belongingness needs and our esteem needs. But for those of us who achieve this, we find that we are still not complete as people. We are still not the person we want to be and know that we could be. We want to become the very best 'us' that we can: we have a **self-actualization need**. At this level, we become different from the way we have been. Exactly what self-actualization means is different for each individual. As a student, this may mean, in part, being the best student that you can be. Take a moment to reflect on this for yourself by looking at Box 8.1.

Self-actualized people have been described in various ways. In general, though, they seem to be people who get more out of their daily life than the rest of us do. They have a greater ability to appreciate the moment and not worry about the future. They have more success in whatever they try to do, but they don't measure themselves by their accomplishments. Instead, they feel a connectedness to the rest of the universe and recognize their own basic worth, and that of others, as part of the fabric of the cosmos.

One of the issues that we need to note in this motivation theory is that while we may all have the motivation to self-actualize if we have (pretty much) fulfilled the other needs, we don't all do so. Why not? One reason is that the culture and environment we live in may have the effect of limiting us. For example, some people will have an extra challenge in their quest for self-actualization because their environment is one of a repressive political regime in which there is a curtailment of freedom, such as the freedom of speech and the freedom of assembly. Other people may live in cultures where they are denied the chance to become all they can be because of their sex or their religion or their ethnic background. There are great barriers to self-actualization here, although it can still be done. One shining model of this is the case of Nelson Mandela, a black African, living in South Africa at a time when there was prejudice and discrimination against the colour of his skin. Apartheid meant that he could not have opportunities that most of us take for granted. Yet his courage, sensitivity, and insight made him a hero who was probably the foremost figure in ending such a repressive situation and in insisting on forgiveness rather than vengeance for the wrongs of the past. Most people would agree that Mandela represents a modern example of a self-actualized person.

Jonah Complex
Maslow's name for the fear of
being one's best, leading to
non-actualization

Another situation blocking growth toward self-actualization is called the **Jonah Complex**, the fear of being one's best. In understanding this fear, we turn to the biblical account of Jonah, who was swallowed by a fish. According to the story, God called upon Jonah to be a prophet and lead his people. But Jonah thought that this task was too great for him, so he tried to escape God's command by taking flight on a ship. But God cannot

---

Self-Actualization	**BOX 8.1**

What do you see as being "the best you can be"? Try to go beyond superficial matters, such as losing or gaining weight, being physically fit, having a high-paying job, getting married to the perfect person, etc. These goals are important, but they may not be related to self-actualization. Instead, consider what you want to be inside. What kind of person do you want to be? What are the talents and potentials you have that you would like to fully maximize? Here are some examples that students have stated in their desires to self-actualize. See if any of these fits you.

- I want to live in the present, without worrying about tomorrow or replaying what happened yesterday.

- I want to have a chance to try writing/music/painting, etc. I think I have talent, but I've never had the opportunity to really explore this side of myself.

- I want to appreciate the world as it is, to see the beauty and the wonder without always finding fault.

- I want to be able to open myself to others and to be responsive and sensitive when other people open to me.

- I want to get over my "it's all about me" attitude.

- I want to create a purpose in my life, to live and work for something that is bigger than just me.

- I want to have the wisdom to know when it is appropriate to behave spontaneously and the courage to do so.

be escaped, and the ship encountered a terrible storm in which everyone was in danger. The sailors realized that Jonah was the object of God's wrath, so they threw him overboard and he was swallowed by a big fish. When Jonah realized that he could not escape God and that he must follow God's instructions and heed the call to greatness, the fish regurgitated him on land. Maslow used Jonah as the model of a man who had the potential for magnificent accomplishments inside him, but who was so afraid of it that he ran away and almost died. Most of us have a degree of the Jonah Complex, representing a fear of success, a fear of being our best, and a feeling of awe in the presence of greatness.

Why do we run away from greatness and self-fulfillment? One reason may be that we aren't physically strong enough to endure the joy of fulfillment for any length of time. At some point we think, "This is too much" or "I can't stand it anymore." Another explanation revolves around the idea that we are either naturally, or we have been trained to be, humble. We may have a secret desire to become a rock star or prime minister or a billionaire, or write a great novel, or become world renowned in some way, but when we compare ourselves to people who have actually done these things, we feel inadequate and stupid. We berate ourselves for our arrogance, and we lower our hopes, in part by running away from even trying to do any of the things that would bring us greatness and fulfill our potentials. It's easier and less burdensome to just be ordinary. But we still harbour a secret desire to achieve greatness and a secret belief in our ability. Unfortunately, we push this away and often resent those who have achieved some degree of greatness. This may be why we love reading about the troubles of the rich and famous: their troubles make them more like us and demonstrate that wealth and fame don't assure one of happiness.

Maslow's theory rings a responsive chord in many of us, but it still runs into problems, such as the problem of circular reasoning. How do we know we have a need for love and belongingness? Because we strive for affection. Why do we strive for affection? Because we have a need for love and belongingness. There are other technical problems, such as the precise meaning of self-actualization. But all in all, Maslow's theory has been useful for most of us in understanding ourselves. We can understand better why those who are homeless focus on simply getting enough money to live through the day; we can comprehend why people who live in high crime areas and in tenements may place their whole concentration on finding some way to be safe, for themselves and their families. We start to understand why we feel lonely when we don't have someone to talk to, we understand what it means to say, as did the poet and philosopher, John Donne, that no man is an island. We see why we feel diminished and inadequate when people around us don't respect us, and why we need self-respect so badly. At all levels, we can see why we may get stuck trying to satisfy a need and not move on to what would be more profitable endeavours in the long run. And we see the heights to which we can aspire, the possibilities that are within us.

Attribution theory

attribution theory
a theory of motivation that looks specifically at how we account for our successes and our failures

The theories that we have covered so far seem to be bringing us nearer to answers we can use, but questions still remain. Despite Maslow's discussion of the Jonah Complex, we may still wonder why we fear the possibility of our own success. The idea of fear of success, and the more intuitively obvious fear of failure, played a large part in **attribution theory** (Heider, 1958). This theory looks specifically at how we account for our successes and our failures, or, to what we *attribute* the cause of our successes and failures. Bethany received a low mark on a test. She said, "This test wasn't fair. The instructor never told us to study these concepts. And besides, I didn't have time to study with all the other work the instructor gave us." Bethany is attributing the cause of her low marks to factors outside herself, that is, to the instructor, instructions, and time constraints. It isn't surprising to find that Bethany also blamed her mother when her library book was overdue and claimed that the interviewer was biased when she didn't get a job she wanted. On another occasion, Bethany blamed her low mark on the test on luck: "Just my luck," she said. "I got a phone call last night so I couldn't study any more and the instructor chose questions from material

locus of control
refers to whether we attribute the causes of our behaviour to factors outside of us or factors inside of us

external locus of control
the belief that our lives are regulated by factors external to ourselves

internal locus of control
the belief that we regulate our own lives

that I hadn't covered. What lousy luck! It's just like the way I didn't get into the course I wanted—because the bus came late, making me a little late for registration."

The way Bethany is justifying the unfortunate things that have happened to her is part of what is known as locus of control. **Locus of control** refers to whether we attribute the causes of our behaviour to factors outside of us or factors inside of us. Bethany has what is called an **external locus of control**. That is, she believes that things outside of herself are controlling her outcomes.

Contrast Bethany's responses to those of Elizabeth, who also got a poor mark on the same test. Elizabeth said, "It's all my fault. I'm not as smart as I thought I was. I deserve to fail." Elizabeth also contends that the reason her boyfriend cheated on her was because she wasn't a good girlfriend. Then there's Wayne, who says his low mark is because he didn't study enough and his study technique was wrong. He also says that he didn't get into the college he really wanted because he forgot to mail his application in by the school's deadline. "I really blew it," he said. "But never again!" Elizabeth and Wayne have an **internal locus of control**: they blame outcomes on things within themselves.

Before we discuss this any further, take the test in Exercise 8.1 to determine where your locus of control is.

EXERCISE 8.1

▶ *Locus of Control Scale*

For each of the pairs of statements given, choose the one that best describes your feelings.

1. a. Grades are a function of the amount of work students do.

    b. Grades depend on the kindness of the instructor.

2. a. Promotions are earned by hard work.

    b. Promotions are a result of being in the right place at the right time.

3. a. Meeting someone to love is a matter of luck.

    b. Meeting someone to love depends on going out often so as to meet many people.

4. a. Living a long life is a function of heredity.

    b. Living a long life is a function of adopting healthy habits.

5. a. Being overweight is determined by the number of fat cells you were born with or developed early in life.

    b. Being overweight depends on what and how much food you eat.

6. a. People who exercise regularly set up their schedules to do so.

    b. Some people just don't have the time for regular exercise.

7. a. Winning at poker depends on betting correctly.

    b. Winning at poker is a matter of being lucky.

8. a. Staying married depends on working at the marriage.

    b. Marital breakup is a matter of being unlucky in choosing the wrong marriage partner.

9. a. Citizens can have some influence on their governments.

    b. There is nothing an individual can do to affect governmental function.

10. a. Being skilled at sports depends on being born well-coordinated.

    b. Those skilled at sports work hard at learning those skills.

11. a. People with close friends are lucky to have met someone to be intimate with.

    b. Developing close friendships takes hard work.

12. a. Your future depends on whom you meet and on chance.

    b. Your future is up to you.

13. a. Most people are so sure of their opinions that their minds cannot be changed.

    b. A logical argument can convince most people.

14. a. People decide the direction of their lives.

    b. For the most part, we have little control of our futures.

15. a. People who don't like you just don't understand you.

    b. You can be liked by anyone you choose to like you.

16. a. You can make your life a happy one.

    b. Happiness is a matter of fate.

17. a. You evaluate feedback and make decisions based upon it.

    b. You tend to be easily influenced by others.

18. a. If voters studied nominees' records, they could elect honest politicians.

    b. Politics and politicians are corrupt by nature.

19. a. Parents, teachers, and bosses have a great deal to say about one's happiness and self-satisfaction.

    b. Whether you are happy depends on you.

20. a. Air pollution can be controlled if citizens would get angry about it.

    b. Air pollution is an inevitable result of technological progress.

Scoring:

Give yourself one point for each of the following answers:

1. a	6. a	11. b	16. a
2. a	7. a	12. b	17. a
3. b	8. a	13. b	18. a
4. b	9. a	14. a	19. b
5. b	10. b	15. b	20. a

Most people score near 10 on this scale; that is, right in the middle. That suggests that sometimes they feel that the cause of their behaviour is within themselves and sometimes they feel that the causes and the control are contained in factors in the environment, other people or situations.

If you scored above 10, this indicates that you have an internal locus of control and tend to believe that the control of your behaviour is within yourself. The higher the score, the more you feel this way. That means that you usually take responsibility for whatever happens to you and whatever you do. If you score near 20, be careful! Sometimes what happens to you is not within your control, and you can make yourself very miserable by trying to take responsibility for what is not, in fact, within your control.

If you scored below 10, this indicates that you have an external locus of control and tend to believe that what happens to you is outside of your control and what you do is determined by other people and the situation you are in, not your own free choice. The lower the score, the more you feel this way. If your score is close to 0, you need to be careful: it may be that you are not taking enough responsibility for your life and that you actually have more power and influence over what happens to you than you realize. You can stop feeling like a victim and make your life more pleasant by taking more control in those situations where control is possible.

Source: From *Comprehensive Stress Management*, 7th edition, by J.S. Greenberg, © 2002. Reproduced with permission of The McGraw-Hill Companies.

In the examples on page 160, who do you think is more likely to keep plugging away at schoolwork—Bethany, Elizabeth, or Wayne? You probably picked Wayne, and you're right. Someone with a strong external locus of control like Bethany doesn't have much reason to keep working because, according to her way of thinking, it doesn't matter what she does: factors external to herself get in the way and mess up her efforts. In some cases, she may have a point. Sometimes factors external to ourselves do get in the way: sometimes instructions are unclear and sometimes interviewers are biased. But not that often. If Bethany doesn't start taking some responsibility for what happens to her, she is going to wind up accomplishing very little. Some people with a strong internal locus of control, like Elizabeth, have a different problem: Elizabeth takes responsibility for her low mark, but she thinks that she can't control what happens to her in school either. If she is right in believing that she isn't smart enough for post-secondary education (and the fact that she even made it this far suggests that she is certainly smart enough!), then there's no point in her working harder or finding other strategies. Why bother? The problem, she says, is her lack of ability, which she can't control. It's no surprise to find that Elizabeth also believes that when she succeeds, she thinks that she just got lucky. For her, failure comes from within, but success comes from without. Wayne is the motivated student because he believes (probably rightly) that a low mark on one test doesn't mean that he has low ability or that he will score low on other tests. Rather, he believes that it is within his power to correct the situation, to find other strategies that will lead to success, for which he will take justifiable credit. With a realistic internal locus of control, people can determine what is within their control and what is not. Then they can take responsibility and act in ways to maximize the good things about themselves and in their lives and minimize the bad things. Still, they need to realize that no one can control everything.

Attribution theory tells us quite a bit about why some people can come back from failure and disappointment more easily than other people can. But does attribution theory go far enough? For example, does it really tell you why you have chosen to continue your education or why you chose that particular path of study? We seem to need more explanation for some behaviours.

The expectancy–value model

Today, one predominant theory to understand student behaviour is the **expectancy–value model** (Pintrich & DeGroot, 1990). This theory incorporates much of what previous theories said, and extends our understanding by bringing in other relevant factors. This model suggests that there are several components that affect motivation. The first, as the name of the model implies, are the **expectancies** we have of a situation. Do we expect that we have what it takes to be able to accomplish a task? If we think that we are not up to the task, why would we even attempt it? Clearly, our motivation to work would be very low. On the other hand, if we expect that we can do the work, there is ample reason to try, and so our motivation to work is much higher.

The second component suggested by the expectancy–value model is **values**. In this case, the model refers to your belief about how important the work is, and how interested you are in it. This component gets to the heart of the question, "Why am I doing this?" The values component suggests that you may be motivated by goals outside yourself or goals inside yourself. Vernon is in university to get a degree in science as a preparation for entry into medical school. He works hard to get high marks because that's the biggest criterion for admission to medical school. He has external or **extrinsic motivation**: his goal, a **performance goal**, is outside himself. Bethany also has an extrinsic motivation, but in her case, she works hard to get high marks because she doesn't want her family or her friends to think that she's dumb or lazy. She is said to have a **performance avoidant goal** because she wants to avoid a negative consequence more than she wants to achieve a positive end. Harry, on the other hand, is taking only courses that have a particular interest for him. His motivation is simply to learn for the sake of learning, a **mastery goal**. Harry's is **intrinsic motivation**, internal to himself. Find out a little about your motivational values by taking the test in Exercise 8.2.

expectancy–value model
a model suggesting that several components affect motivation; they are the expectancies we have of a situation and our values, or our beliefs about how important the situation is, and how interested we are in it

expectancies
in the expectancy–value model of motivation, this refers to our sense of self-efficacy or how much we believe that we are able to do a particular task

values
in the expectancy–value model of motivation, this refers to your goal in attempting the task, your belief about how important the work is, and how interested you are in it

extrinsic motivation
motivation that is derived from factors outside oneself

performance goal
the object of behaviour is in external validation, such as grades, awards, etc.

performance avoidant goal
the object of behaviour is to avoid some undesirable external outcome

mastery goal
the object of behaviour is in the inherent worth of the behaviour

intrinsic motivation
motivation that is derived from factors inside oneself

EXERCISE 8.2   ▶ *Motivational Values*

Check each statement that you agree with in each category.

Mastery Goals (Intrinsic Motivation)

1. I like schoolwork that I'll learn from, even if I make a lot of mistakes.
2. An important reason why I do my schoolwork is because I like to learn new things.
3. I like schoolwork best when it really makes me think.
4. An important reason why I do my work in school is because I want to get better at it.
5. I do my schoolwork because I'm interested in it.
6. An important reason why I do my schoolwork is because I enjoy it.
7. Curiosity is the driving force behind much of what I do.
8. I want to find out how good I really can be at my work.
9. I enjoy doing work that is so absorbing that I forget about everything else.
10. What matters most to me is enjoying what I do.

Performance Goals (Extrinsic Motivation)

1. I would feel really good if I were the only one who could answer the instructor's questions in class.
2. It is important to me that the other students in my classes think that I am good at my work.
3. I want to do better than other students in my classes.
4. I want high grades to get accepted to post-graduate work.
5. I want high grades to obtain or keep a scholarship.
6. I want high grades so that my parents will be proud of me.
7. To me, success means doing better then other people.
8. I believe there is no point in doing a good job if nobody else knows about it.
9. I'm less concerned with what work I do than what I get for it.
10. I'm concerned about how other people are going to react to my ideas.

Performance Avoidant Goals (Extrinsic Motivation)

1. It's very important to me that I don't look stupid to my instructors.
2. The reason I do my schoolwork is so that others won't think that I'm dumb.
3. One reason I don't participate in class much is that I don't want to look stupid.
4. I do my schoolwork so that I won't have to experience the humiliation of flunking out.
5. I do my schoolwork because my parents will kill me if I get low marks.
6. I work hard in school because I don't want to wind up in a dead-end job someday.
7. I work hard so that people will not think that I'm lazy.
8. I work hard in school because I'm afraid that I won't get a job if I don't have high marks.
9. I study hard to get good marks so that I won't lose my scholarship.
10. I try to keep my marks up so that I won't be left behind when all my friends graduate.

Did you check more statements in one category than in another? If so, that category indicates your prime motivational values at the present time.

Sources: Adapted from Midgley, Kaplan, Middleton, & Maehr, 1998; Amabile, Hill, Hennessey, & Tighe, 1994.

A great deal of research has indicated that both intrinsic and extrinsic sources of motivation keep people working hard (Elton, 1996; Jordan, 2001; Fazey & Fazey, 2001; Thompson & Thornton, 2002). This suggests that both Vernon and Harry will be motivated to work hard. Many instructors feel that Harry is the one on the right track in his intrinsic motivation, but the reality seems to be that most people need both external (extrinsic) motivation in the form of grades, salary, praise, etc., as well as internal (intrinsic) motivation in the form of interest and love of learning to maximize the amount that is accomplished in post-secondary education (Brownlow & Reasinger, 2001; Elton, 1996; Hwang, Echols, & Vrongistinos, 2002). It's also important to note that motivation is not all-or-none. That is, it isn't fair to make the blanket statement that someone "isn't motivated." It's not only possible, it's actually likely that your motivation is specific to each particular piece of work that you confront. So Bethany, who hates writing essays but loves anthropology, is highly motivated to do the reading required for the course, but is much less motivated to start writing the paper that is required. Similarly, she finds that her motivation to do her anthropology homework is greater than her motivation to do her geophysics homework. Why? Because she really doesn't like geophysics, she's only taking the course because she has to. Bethany can be said to value anthropology more than she values geophysics.

It's important to note that we may have extrinsic and intrinsic motivation at the same time. Vernon, for example, may be motivated by the aim of getting into medical school, but that doesn't mean that he isn't also interested in the subjects he is studying and valuing learning for itself. In general, though, the transition from high school to post-secondary education usually involves a transition from extrinsic to intrinsic goals (Fazey & Fazey, 2001). In high school, there was typically plenty of praise for good work and reproof for bad work: that is, there were ample external rewards and punishments, and students may have become accustomed to this. This is not the case in post-secondary school. At this level, you may go for weeks without getting any kind of feedback on how you are doing in the course. Extrinsic factors may not be very evident, so if you are not motivated from within to keep working, it becomes more and more difficult to summon the energy and interest to do all the work required. Non-traditional students (students who are returning to school after having been out for a while) have more intrinsic motivation than do traditional students (those who are attending post-secondary school right after graduating from high school), probably because they are no longer accustomed to or dependent on external rewards and punishments (Fazey & Fazey, 2001; Harju & Eppler, 1997; Walters, 2000).

There are other factors that seem to be related to extrinsic motivation. For example, the culture you live in plays a part in whether you have intrinsic or extrinsic motivation. Some cultures, such as those in North America, hold the belief that a job should be done well so that the worker may get extra pay, career advancement, attention or praise from supervisors, bonuses, special perks, etc. That is, North American culture favours an extrinsic motivation in the working world. Japan, on the other hand, favours an intrinsic motivation in the working world: in Japan, there is a greater emphasis on personal commitment to a job and integration into a group of workers labouring toward the same goals for the employer (England & Misumi, 1986). The differences are rooted in the ideals of the culture: individualism or collectivism, or which is given priority, the one individual person or the group to which the person belongs. In an individualistic culture, extrinsic motivation is more likely to be dominant, while in a collectivist culture, intrinsic motivation is more common.

There are some interesting effects of extrinsic motivation. For instance, we find that people who cheat academically are more likely to have extrinsic motivation (Jordan, 2001). This makes sense in the cases of people who are like Vernon, who desperately needs high grades, and like Bethany, who seems to be anxious to gain approval from others. They may rationalize their cheating as being justified, "the end justifies the means." Also, if they have no particular interest in the subject matter or value of learning, they may feel few qualms at accepting a mark that they haven't deserved. Similarly, people who procrastinate are more likely to have extrinsic motivation (Brownlow & Reasinger, 2001). Perhaps they procrastinate because they really have little interest in the subject matter and find studying the area to be unpleasant. Grades don't seem to be enough to motivate them to get started on their work before the last possible moment. We'll talk more about grades as motivators in a little while.

Another part of the expectancy–values model of motivation looks at how we feel about the task at hand. Does it make us angry that we have to do this work? If so, we might be less motivated to get at it. Do we feel pride that the work has been entrusted to us? This might be positively motivating in itself. Do we feel scared, with a case of test anxiety? This may make us procrastinate and feel even worse. When we do get to work, our negative self-statements may get in the way of studying effectively, as we saw in Chapter 4. People with test anxiety may internally be just as motivated to do schoolwork as people without test anxiety, but their anxiety may provide negative emotions that decrease their tendency to work, making it look like they have low motivation (Pintrich & DeGroot, 1990). In fact, high motivation increases the problem for people who already have test anxiety, making their performance even worse (Wolf & Smith, 1995). The more the anxious person wants to do well, the more he or she may be saying inside, "I have to do well. I just have to! If I don't, everything will fall apart, everything will be over. It will be a total catastrophe!" Thinking thoughts such as these will badly interfere with the ability to concentrate on the task at hand, and so the anxious person winds up sabotaging his or her own work, certainly without meaning to.

How we attribute our successes and failures often provokes an emotion in us. Thus, someone like Elizabeth, who attributes her low marks to her lack of ability, may feel depressed and insecure when she looks at the work she needs to do, whereas Wayne may feel satisfaction and eager anticipation because he believes he has the ability to do the task. Bethany, who has an external locus of control, may feel discouraged and find that even the most interesting material is burdensome for her because she thinks she has no control over the outcome of her work.

SCHOOLWORK AND GRADES

AREN'T GRADES MOTIVATORS?

Yes, we have seen that they are incentives in many cases, and they have a role in how much we value our work (e.g., which test do you think people are more likely to study hard for, the one that is marked as part of the final grade or the one that "doesn't count"?). External incentives such as grades do lead to increased motivation and better performance on a test (Wolf & Smith, 1995). But the precise effects of grades may depend on other factors (Hyde, Holschuh, & Nist, 2000). Take the following cases: Both Fayyez and Bethany received a mark of *D* on the first-term test in biology. Fayyez found this experience to be highly motivating, thinking, "I'd better study harder for next time or else I may fail or wind up with a mark that really pulls down my GPA." Bethany, on the other hand, found herself to be discouraged. She thought, "Why bother trying harder? I did my best and it got me nowhere." So she almost gave up trying. What was the difference between these two students that made them react so differently? The answer may lie in our discussion of self-efficacy and locus of control. Fayyez has the belief that he is competent and bright, and that he can master almost anything if he works hard enough. So a low mark is a wake-up call for him. But Bethany has the belief that she isn't very bright and that some subjects may be too difficult for her. She also feels that even if she works hard, the results may not be very good. She thinks that other factors, such as the instructor's "tricky" questions or imprecise instructions, may thwart her. A low mark for her is a sign to quit.

explanatory style
a person's way of explaining why events occurred

DOES IT MATTER WHETHER I'M AN OPTIMIST OR A PESSIMIST?

pessimistic explanatory style
a person's tendency to expect the worst outcomes and explain these events by blaming one's own inadequacy and/or believing that the environment is biased against one

In part, yes. Another related explanation for the differences in our reactions to grades lies within a concept known as **explanatory style** (Seligman, 1991). Bethany explains what happens in her life with pessimism: she believes that her low grades are her own fault for not being bright enough, that this sort of lack of success will be reflected in all areas of her life, and that this will never change. Her **pessimistic explanatory style** leads her to give up.

optimistic explanatory style
a person's tendency to expect the best outcomes and explain these events by taking credit for having ability and/or believing that the environment is changeable and problems can be overcome

Fayyez, however, has an **optimistic explanatory style**: he believes that he brings about his own success in getting high grades, and when he fails to excel, it is because of some environmental problem or a misguided strategy that he used; it is an isolated event that says nothing about how he will do on other tests, let alone the rest of his life; and he can change his strategy to bring him more success. Clearly, Fayyez is more inclined to keep working in the face of difficulties than Bethany is. And Fayyez will do better in school and in life in general because of this (Myers, 2000; Pajares, 2001; Peterson, 2000; Satterfield, 2000).

What about good marks, though? Aren't they positively reinforcing enough to make students keep working at a high level (i.e., to keep them motivated)? Again, it depends. Let's look at Edith and Franca. Both of them received *A*s on their first-term test in botany. Edith was elated and determined to work even harder for the next test, thinking, "I've got a great chance of getting an *A* in this course if I keep working." Franca, however, thought, "OK, that's cool. An *A* on this test means that I've got a good foundation, so I can slack off a bit for the next test and still probably get a *B* in the course." What makes these two women react so differently? To explain this, we probably need to know more about why Edith and Franca are taking botany and what grades mean to them. For example, if we learn that Edith is taking botany because she wants to major in it and go to graduate school in the area, and that her family always stressed the importance of getting good grades, we may not be surprised by Edith's reaction to her *A*. If we find that Franca is taking botany because she needed another credit and nothing else fit her schedule, and that her family stressed doing her personal best rather than relying on external criteria such as grades to measure effort, we may find her reaction understandable as well. It's important to note that neither woman is "right" or "wrong"; they simply have different priorities and motivations.

DOES NOT ATTENDING CLASSES MEAN A STUDENT IS NOT MOTIVATED?

This is another question whose answer is "It depends." When students were asked why they did or did not attend classes, they gave some interesting, and in some cases surprising, answers (Friedman, Rodriguez, & McComb, 2001; Wyatt, 1992). First, many people think that males are the ones who cut classes the most, but actually there is no large sex difference: both males and females cut classes equally often, and sometimes in first year, females seem to skip classes more than males do. Many people think that first-year students are the big class cutters, but this isn't so. Freshmen are getting maligned! It doesn't matter what year of post-secondary education one is in, there is no difference in the number of classes that are cut. Nor is it the case that holding a part-time job results in more class-cutting. Then there is the stereotypic notion that students don't cut classes if they are paying for it themselves: the ones whose parents are paying are thought to be the biggest offenders. Again, not true. Both groups of students are equally likely to cut classes. Another idea, particularly among instructors, is that the time at which the class is held makes a difference in whether or not students cut the class, with early morning and late afternoon classes being the ones most likely to be missed. But the research didn't substantiate this. There is also no difference in cutting classes between what is termed "traditional" and "non-traditional" students, that is, those students who entered post-secondary institutions right after high school as opposed to those who are returning to school after a period of time. However, among non-traditional students, the reasons for cutting classes often reflect the extra responsibilities (e.g., family) that they are carrying.

If so many of our assumptions and guesses about cutting classes aren't true, what is? Some of our expectations are true: first, the higher the student's GPA, the less likely it is that the student cut classes. We aren't sure whether this means that students get high marks because they attend classes, or that brighter, more studious students rarely cut classes. The research also determined, not surprisingly, that if students *wanted* to take the course (i.e., they were *motivated* to take the course), they were less likely to miss classes. Sadly for post-secondary classes, which tend to be large, students are more likely to skip large classes than small ones. Why? According to the students, their presence is more likely to be missed if they skip a small class, whereas no one is likely to notice their absence in a large class. Further, in a small class, there is more opportunity for the student to ask questions and interact with the instructor and the rest of the class, making the class more attractive for most students. Finally, students note that in small classes, attendance and participation are often components of the final grade, a state of affairs that is not present in large classes. The most common reasons given for attendance are shown in Box 8.2, and the most common reasons for missing a class are shown in Box 8.3. Note that most of the answers about attending a class reflect the desire to pass a course, although the most common answer does reflect an internal value. Interest in the course is mentioned, but only by a little over half of the students who responded to the questioning. While the most common reason for missing a class is a valid one ("I was sick"), the rest of the reasons clearly suggest a view that the students believe that the classes are not really important.

Students' Reasons for Attending Class   BOX 8.2

Below are the reasons students gave Friedman and his colleagues (2001) for attending classes, along with the percentages of students who gave each answer. The numbers do not total 100 because students were allowed to give more than one answer.

75.4%	I believe I should go (not going makes me feel guilty).
70.4%	Content is presented that I need to know (e.g., may be on a test).
65.7%	Information about course procedures and tests may be announced.
57.4%	I am interested in the course content.
57.0%	I want to take my own notes and not rely on anyone else.
55.7%	Hearing what's said in class helps me do my homework.
53.5%	I have to turn in an assignment.

Students' Reasons for Missing Class   BOX 8.3

Below are the reasons students gave Friedman and his colleagues (2001) for missing classes, along with the percentages of students who gave each answer. The numbers do not total 100 because students were allowed to give more than one answer.

38.1%	I was sick.
32.5%	I felt tired or overslept because I did schoolwork the night before.
32.0%	I felt tired or overslept because I had fun the night before.
22.0%	I had a personal task to do at this time.
21.6%	Attendance is not taken or does not influence my grade.
20.7%	I wanted to take a break during the time class was meeting.
20.1%	I was out of town or on my way out of (or back to) town.

NEED FOR ACHIEVEMENT

WHY DO SOME PEOPLE SEEM TO HAVE A HIGHER MOTIVATION TO SUCCEED THAN OTHERS?

When we were babies, we were eager to explore our world, even if that meant putting everything we could get hold of in our mouths. As we became toddlers, at the "terrible twos," we continued to get into every nook and cranny of our homes and manipulate every object—we were unstoppable, much to our parents' dismay. We demonstrated clearly that we wanted to do things for ourselves, from putting on our own clothes to feeding ourselves. It didn't matter to us if we put our T-shirts on inside out or got more food all over our faces and hands than in our mouths. The point for us was that we were trying to achieve. Even

need for achievement (nAch)
the need for accomplishment and success

though all of us showed this **need for achievement**, some of us developed a stronger need than others. For some of us, doing better, accomplishing more, and being more successful constitute a primary motive in our lives. We may experience this need in one area of our lives (e.g., our work), or in many areas (e.g., work, relationships, leisure activities, etc.).

Psychologists have measured need for achievement, which they abbreviate as **nAch**, by an interesting assessment device called the Thematic Apperception Test (TAT). This test consists of a number of pictures of a person or people engaging in some activity. The task is to write a story about what is happening in the picture, what one thinks might have happened in the past to bring the character to this point, and what may happen in the future. The stories are then examined for themes of achievement. Look at the picture in Figure 8.2 and read the story that Mavis wrote about it.

FIGURE 8.2 nAch Picture

The little boy is feeling very sad because he knows that no matter how much he practises the violin, he will never be good enough to be play in an orchestra. He has been taking lessons for three years and has given recitals but he isn't sure that he wants to continue. If he can't be the best at playing, he would rather try something else.

Mavis' story reveals her concentration on being successful and her belief that either one is the best at what one is doing, or it isn't worth doing it. Mavis would be scored as having a high nAch. Now read the story that Bethany wrote.

This little boy is looking at his father's violin and wishing his father would play with him as much as he plays with the instrument. He has been hearing his father play all his life, but he doesn't have much musical appreciation right now. He really wants his Dad to come outside and play ball with him, but he doubts that Dad will.

Bethany doesn't seem to be interested in achievement to the extent that Mavis is. Her interest seems to revolve more around relationships. Bethany would be scored as having a low nAch.

A great deal of research has been done to indicate that individuals like Mavis and Bethany behave differently in many ways (e.g., McClelland, 1985; Spangler, 1992; Winter & Carlson, 1988). Individuals with a high nAch like Mavis, for example, are more likely to be persistent and to take on moderate challenges that give immediate feedback regarding success or failure.

Mavis, like other high nAch individuals, is more efficient than those with low nAch like Bethany, but she sometimes takes the easy and not necessarily ethical way to maximize her performance. Individuals with low nAch like Bethany are more laid back and rooted in the present than those with high nAch. Mavis will not necessarily get higher marks than Bethany in post-secondary education, though, not unless she knows she needs the material in the course content for her future career. However, those like Mavis usually have more practicality than individuals like Bethany in their career goals (Mahone, 1960): Mavis is planning on being an accountant and Bethany really wants to be an astronaut. While we wish Bethany well, it is obvious that Mavis is more likely than Bethany is to achieve her career goal.

How did Mavis and Bethany get this way? We can't be sure, but it wouldn't surprise us if both biology and learning from the environment were responsible. Some babies are born more outgoing and ready to engage with the world (McCrae, 2005). If these children are then encouraged to do so, rewarded when they achieve a goal, and taught by their loved ones that their self-worth is dependent to a great extent on what and how much they achieve, they may well wind up with a high nAch. If they are born less inclined to be outgoing and if their caretakers have emphasized worth as a function of simply being instead of doing, these children may have a resulting low nAch. There is nothing to suggest that it is better to be one way or the other: each has its pluses and minuses. Mavis may achieve more in life than Bethany does, but she may not be happier. In fact, it is questionable whether Mavis will ever be happy with herself, or whether she will always desire to achieve more and more. She may burn out on this path. Bethany, however, may never realize her full potential in life; she could have had the talent of a great artist or the mind of an innovative research scientist or some other equally notable potential. But none of this may be realized if Bethany doesn't concentrate on achieving a little more. The healthiest state would probably be somewhere in between Mavis and Bethany, with a moderate nAch.

INCREASING MOTIVATION

HOW CAN I INCREASE MY MOTIVATION FOR SCHOOLWORK?

Since everyone is different and everyone's motivation comes from different sources, it follows that there is no one right way to increase your motivation for schoolwork. But given what we have seen in this chapter, we can make some suggestions. Let's do so by giving some advice to Bethany, whom we met at the beginning of the chapter. Hopefully, suggestions for her may be adaptable for you, too.

Advice for Bethany

▶ **B**ethany is experiencing a mid-term slump. It isn't uncommon, but that doesn't seem too reassuring to her. What suggestions can we make to help her get out of this slump?

WHAT TO DO	WHY
Hang around with people who are very studious.	We can increase our motivation by the process of imitating others (Middleton & Toluk 1999). That is, when we see others working hard, we are more likely to work hard ourselves. So, if Bethany spends her time with people who waste their time, she is more likely to keep doing so herself.

(continued)

WHAT TO DO	WHY
Find ways to become more personally engaged in courses. Bethany could join a study group, she could find ways to relate the course material to her daily life, she could get to know her instructors who may be able to infect her with some of their enthusiasm for the subject matter.	This will increase Bethany's intrinsic motivation, which will help keep her going when there are few immediate rewards from the outside world.
Examine her locus of control. Is she really taking responsibility for her own actions, or does she think that her lack of motivation is some external "virus" that has infected her? She could start to pay more attention to the statements she makes to herself. Do they indicate an irrational externalizing of responsibility? Do these self-statements suggest that effortful working is unpleasant or not worthwhile? If so, Bethany could use Ellis's *ABCD* technique, found in Chapter 3, to change these statements.	Bethany can change her negative, non-motivating, external locus of control statements to ones that would be more positive, reasonable, and motivating.
Bethany might start recognizing and appreciating how much she is learning and how the quality of her thinking is being enhanced by her education. She has a right to be proud of herself, but she may not be able to do this if she compares herself to others. Bethany needs to concentrate on doing her personal best. She needs to strive for excellence in maximizing her own potential. Getting the highest marks in the class is not relevant.	In these ways, Bethany may increase her mastery motivation, a benefit to keeping her on track since it seems that mastery goals are more motivating than performance goals in many situations.
Bethany should decide on small, achievable goals and reward herself for accomplishing them. She can use a self-modification program, such as that described in Chapter 3, to help her. Her rewards need to be extrinsic to begin with; as she accomplishes more and more, she will find that the internal reward of having accomplished her goal becomes the most important reward for her. This is a particularly good idea in dealing with her procrastination. Bethany also needs to make sure that her rewards are immediate for each task or part of a task that she completes, and long-term as she accumulates larger and larger blocks of work to make a finished whole. For example, in studying, she might reward herself with a cookie for reading her text for 20 minutes, with the overall goal of obtaining a larger reward, dinner and a movie, when she has completed all the reading she needs to do for the upcoming test.	Setting goals is also excellent means of increasing motivation. Bethany can increase her feeling of accomplishment by achieving these goals, which will increase her own feeling of self-efficacy and will reward her enough to keep her motivated to do her work and break out of her slump.
Be optimistic about her chance for success.	People who have an optimistic explanatory style increase their motivation to work hard by their belief in their own ability and that good outcomes will be achieved.
Allow some time for rest and having fun!	All work and no play is a very punishing state for most of us. We find that our motivation to work drops if we don't allow ourselves a little leisure recreation to regain our energy and our enthusiasm.

CHAPTER SUMMARY

■ Motivation is what makes us behave the way we do and keeps us performing. It's the "why" of behaviour. We often question why we perform certain activities (that we feel we shouldn't) and why we don't perform others (that we feel we should).

■ Arousal theory contends that we do what we do in order to maintain an optimal level of arousal or stimulation.

■ Incentive theory suggests that we do what we do because we think about the rewards or punishments that we will receive (incentives).

■ Abraham Maslow suggested that we have a hierarchy of needs. That is, we have needs at different levels that we must discharge in order to finally reach fulfillment in ourselves. The first level is physical needs, which are needs such as for food and water to keep our bodies alive. The second level is safety needs, or the need for a secure environment in which we have some degree of ability to predict what will happen. When we fulfill these needs, we progress to the level of love and belongingness needs, or the need to love and be loved; the need to feel that we are part of a group of other individuals. The next level, esteem needs, includes the need to feel respect from others and from ourselves. Finally, when the needs of all these levels have been satisfied, we move to the final level, self-actualization, encompassing the need to maximize our potentials, becoming the best that we can be.

■ We may not all reach the self-actualization level because of cultural or situational impediments, or because of the Jonah Complex (fear of our own potential).

■ Attribution theory looks specifically at how we account for our successes and our failures. It is highly dependent on our locus of control, whether we attribute the causes of our behaviour to factors outside of us or factors inside of us. People with an external locus of control believe that their lives are regulated by factors external to themselves, while people with an internal locus of control believe that they regulate their own lives. People with a realistic internal locus of control are more likely to persist in the face of problems and seem to be more motivated to continue their work.

■ The expectancy–value model of motivation looks at how much we expect to be successful at our work and how much we value the work. If we expect to do well and we value the work highly, we are motivated to continue working even when troubles plague us. For some people, the value of the work is determined by outside factors (extrinsic motivation), such as how much we will be paid for good work or how high our grades will be (performance goal). Or the extrinsic motivation may lead to a performance avoidant goal, such as avoiding punishment for not doing the task well. For some people, the value is determined by intrinsic motivation, or the inner joy of being successful (mastery goal). Note that we may have intrinsic motivation for some tasks and extrinsic motivation for others; probably a combination of both types of motivation will keep us working hardest and longest.

■ Grades may be motivating, depending on how we regard them. This depends largely on our explanatory style or the way we explain why events occurred. People with a pessimistic explanatory style expect the worst outcomes and explain these events by blaming their own inadequacy and/or believing that the environment is biased against them. There is little motivation for them to continue working in the face of problems. People with an optimistic explanatory style expect the best outcomes and explain these events by taking credit for having ability and/or believing that the environment is changeable and problems can be overcome. People with an optimistic explanatory style tend to persist at working longer and overcome obstacles more readily.

■ Not attending classes is related to lower marks and less enjoyment of post-secondary school.

■ Some people seem highly motivated to work because of their high need for achievement (nAch), or the need for accomplishment and success. People with a high nAch may accomplish more than people with low nAch, but they may never be satisfied with their accomplishments, always feeling that they need to do more. Having a moderate nAch seems to be optimal.

■ Motivation can be increased in a number of ways, such as becoming more optimistic about the chance of success, valuing the work for its intrinsic worth, and ridding ourselves of our belief that we have no control over how well we do on a task.

KEY TERMS

arousal theory	incentive	need for achievement (nAch)
attribution theory	incentive theory	optimistic explanatory style
esteem needs	internal locus of control	performance avoidant goal
expectancies	intrinsic motivation	performance goal
expectancy–value model	Jonah Complex	pessimistic explanatory style
explanatory style	locus of control	physical needs
external locus of control	love and belongingness needs	safety needs
extrinsic motivation	mastery goal	self-actualization need
hierarchy of needs	motivation	values

INDIVIDUAL ACTIVITIES

1. Why did you choose to pursue post-secondary education? List as many reasons as you can. Which are extrinsic and which are intrinsic? You might want to post this list over your desk to remind yourself when your motivation for work gets low.

2. Look at the hierarchy of needs that Maslow created. Where do you fit? Which needs have you satisfied and which needs are you still working on?

3. Who is your favourite character on television? in the movies? in literature? Who are your least favourite characters in these media? Do these characters have a high or low nAch? Do you think your likes and dislikes in these areas reveal anything about your need for achievement?

GROUP ACTIVITIES

1. In a group of four to six students, brainstorm ideas about what your instructor could (reasonably) do to increase the motivation of students in the class. Now brainstorm what the class could (reasonably) do to increase the motivation of your instructor to teach you. Share both these lists with your instructor.

2. In a group of four to six students, make a list of famous people (dead or alive) that you think are or were self-actualized. Read the following list of some of the people that Maslow regarded as self-actualized. Do you agree with him? Note that he has not included any spiritual teachers. Do you agree with this?

Albert Einstein   Abraham Lincoln

Aldous Huxley   Jane Addams

Baruch Spinoza   Albert Schweitzer

Eleanor Roosevelt   William James

3. In a group of three to four students, discuss reasons why you and other people you know decided to enter post-secondary schools. Which of these reasons comprise extrinsic motivation and which comprise intrinsic motivation? If you could program a human being with the kind of motivation that would maximize the chances of staying in school and being successful and satisfied with post-secondary education, what would you program?

4. In a group, discuss some of the reasons you or others have given for skipping classes. Which reasons are the most reasonable? Which are really the silliest?

REFERENCES

Amabile, T. M., Hill, K. G., Hennessey, B. A., & Tighe, E. M. (1994). The Work Preference Inventory: Assessing intrinsic and extrinsic motivational orientations. *Journal of Personality and Social Psychology, 66(5)*, 950–967.

Brownlow, S., & Reasinger, R. D. (2001). Putting off until tomorrow what is better done today: Academic procrastination as a function of motivation toward college work. *Journal of Social Behavior & Personality, 16(1)*, 15–34.

Butler, R. A. (1954). Curiosity in monkeys. *Scientific American,* February, 70–75.

Elton, L. (1996). Strategies to enhance student motivation: A conceptual analysis. *Studies in Higher Education, 21(1)*, 57–66.

England, G. W., & Misumi, J. (1986). Work centrality in Japan and the United States. *Journal of Cross-Cultural Psychology, 17*, 396–416.

Fazey, D. M. A., & Fazey, J. A. (2001). The potential for autonomy in learning: Perceptions of competence, motivation and locus of control in first-year undergraduate students. *Studies in Higher Education, 26(3)*, 345–361.

Friedman, P., Rodriguez, F., & McComb, J. (2001). Why students do and do not attend classes. *College Teaching, 49*, 124–133.

Greenberg, J. S. (2002). *Comprehensive stress management* (7th ed.). New York: McGraw-Hill.

Harju, B. L., & Eppler, M. A. (1997). Achievement motivation, flow and irrational beliefs in traditional and nontraditional college students. *Journal of Instructional Psychology, 24*, 147–157.

Heider, F. (1958). *The psychology of interpersonal relations.* New York: Wiley.

Hwang, Y. S., Echols, C., & Vrongistinos, K. (2002). Multidimensional academic motivation of high achieving African American students. *College Student Journal, 36(4)*, 544–554.

Hyde, C., Holschuh, J., & Nist, S. (2000). Learning complex information: Motivation theory and its relation to student perceptions. *Reading & Writing Quarterly, 16(1)*, 23–57.

Jordan, A. E. (2001). College student cheating: The role of motivation, perceived norms, attitudes, and knowledge of institutional policy. *Ethics & Behavior, 11(3)*, 233–247.

Mahone, C. H. (1960). Fear of failure and unrealistic vocational aspiration. *Journal of Abnormal and Social Psychology, 60*, 253–261.

Maslow, A. (1970). *Motivation and personality.* New York: Harper & Row.

McClelland, D. C. (1985). *Human motivation.* Glenview, IL: Scott Foresman.

McCrae, R. R. (2005). Personality structure. In V. J. Derlega, B. A. Winstead, & W. H. Jones (Eds.), *Personality: Contemporary theory and research* (3rd ed.). Belmont, CA: Thomson Wadsworth.

Middleton, J. A., & Toluk, Z. (1999). First steps in the development of an adaptive theory of motivation. *Educational Psychologist, 34(2)*, 99–122.

Midgley, C., Kaplan, A., Middleton, M., & Maehr, M. L. (1998). The development and validation of scales assessing students' achievement goal orientations. *Contemporary Educational Psychology, 23*, 113–131.

Myers, D. G. (2000). Hope and happiness. In J. E. Gillham (Ed.), *The science of optimism and hope: Research essays in honor of Martin E. P. Seligman.* Philadelphia, PA: Templeton Foundation Press, 323–336.

Pajares, F. (2001). Toward a positive psychology of academic motivation. *Journal of Educational Research, 95(1)*, 27–35.

Peterson, C. (2000). Optimistic explanatory style and health. In J. E. Gillham (Ed.), *The science of optimism and hope: Research essays in honor of Martin E. P. Seligman.* Philadelphia, PA: Templeton Foundation Press, 145–162.

Pintrich, P. R., & DeGroot, E. V. (1990). Motivational and self-regulated learning components of classroom academic performance. *Journal of Educational Psychology, 82(1)*, 33–40.

Satterfield, J. M. (2000). Optimism, culture, and history: The roles of explanatory style, integrative complexity, and pessimistic rumination. In J. E. Gillham (Ed.), *The science of optimism and hope: Research essays in honor of Martin E. P. Seligman.* Philadelphia, PA: Templeton Foundation Press, 349–378.

Seligman, M. E. P. (1991). *Learned optimism.* New York: Alfred A. Knopf Inc.

Spangler, W. D. (1992). Validity of questionnaire and TAT measures of need for achievement: Two meta-analyses. *Psychological Bulletin, 112*, 140–154.

Thompson, B. R., & Thornton, H. J. (2002). The transition from extrinsic to intrinsic motivation in the college classroom: A first-year experience. *Education, 122(4)*, 785–792.

Walters, M. (2000). The mature students' three *Rs. British Journal of Guidance and Counselling, 28(2)*, 267–278.

Winter, D. G., & Carlson, L. (1988). Using motive scores in the psychobiographical study of the individual: The case of Richard Nixon. *Journal of Personality, 56*, 75–103.

Wolf, L. F., & Smith, J. K. (1995). The consequence of consequence: Motivation, anxiety, and test performance. *Applied Measurement in Education, 8(3)*, 227–242.

Wyatt, G. (1992). Skipping class: An analysis of absenteeism among first-year college students. *Teaching Sociology, 20(3)*, 201–207.

READING AND INFORMATION LITERACY

The Case of Kisha

▶ Kisha has now been at school for six weeks. Truthfully, she has not kept up with her work. This has been her first time away from home and she spent far too many nights out with her new friends. She is now behind in her work and has to catch up on her reading. She has quite a few chapters to read in each of her classes and she has to begin to research a major paper for her anatomy class that is due next week. To start to catch up, she decided to read the three chapters of her physiology textbook in the afternoon and head to the library to research her paper in the evening. To her dismay, after reading for an hour she had only managed to get through eight pages. Even though she had reread them twice, she was still not sure if she understood them. To make matters worse, when she went to the library she was not sure how to use the library's computer system to search for books and articles. After speaking to another student who was working at the computer terminals, she learned that she needed to use keywords in the search engine. However, when she did this, the computer returned over 500 articles and none of them seemed to be exactly what she was looking for. Further, the articles that she did decide to use seem almost incomprehensible and she is pretty sure that one of them is not even relevant for her essay. Kisha wonders if there is a better way to conduct library research. She also wonders if there is some trick to reading academic material so that it is understandable.

Like Kisha, you will be required to read more than 150 pages of text and supplementary materials weekly. For most students this is a time-consuming and difficult process. You may have had no difficulties reading textbooks in high school. However, you, like many other students, might find post-secondary readings to be long, difficult to comprehend, and time consuming to read.

READING

HOW DO PEOPLE READ?

print characteristics
features of the written words, how the letters and words go together

Learning to read academic material is not unlike learning to read in general. Reading academic and non-academic material involves knowledge of **print characteristics** (words) and general knowledge. However, academic reading also requires knowledge and vocabulary specific to the topic.

When people read, their eyes do not smoothly move across the page; they seem to jump from word to word (Rayner, 1998). It turns out that, when reading, people do not look at each word. In fact, adult readers look briefly (less than 0.25 seconds) at parts of words, rather than whole words. They also skip some words altogether (Starr & Rayner, 2001).

When you look at only part of a word (as all adult readers do), the rest of that word falls into your peripheral vision. Readers are aware that letters are in the periphery but because of the poorer vision in the periphery, they may not be able to tell what all the letters are. Try the following demonstration. Look at the cross at the beginning of the line in Exercise 9.1 and see how many letters you can identify without moving your eyes away from the cross. You will find that as the letters move away from the cross you are able to identify fewer letters, even though you know they are there. Thus, in reading you can clearly see the letters that you look directly at and some, but not all, letters that you are not looking at. When we read, we don't look at every word or every letter of every word.

EXERCISE 9.1   ▶ *Visual Ability Demonstration*

+ A S R H J Y L O D C B M L N B F D X Z I U Y T R E C N K L G F D S A

There are differences in the way you read academic material and the way you read novels. Further, there are differences in the way skilled and poor readers read. Some of the problems that poor readers have also occur when you first start to read post-secondary academic material.

Poor readers and those reading post-secondary academic material for the first time (new academic readers) look at more words on the page and for longer periods of time than do skilled readers. Further, poor readers and new academic readers also look back to re-read previously read words more often than do skilled readers. We know that the odd reading patterns of these readers indicate that they are having difficulty processing/understanding the printed information (Sereno & Rayner, 2000; Starr & Rayner, 2001; Rayner, 1998). For example, people may re-read words that were previously read when they do not understand the vocabulary in a paragraph. People also spend more time looking at words that they do not understand. This is one reason why you are slower when reading academic material.

HOW DO PEOPLE KNOW WHAT THEY HAVE READ IF THEY DON'T LOOK AT ALL THE WORDS?

Since only some letters of words are viewed during reading and some words are skipped in reading altogether, it is likely that some words or parts of words are more important than others. It is possible that we can skip words or word parts that do not carry important information. It turns out that it is not necessary to read all the words on the page due to print characteristics (features of written words).

orthographics
knowledge of permissible word structure and sentence structure

One print characteristic is **orthographics**. That is, you are aware of how letters may be put together in your language. In English, it is permissible for some letters to sit beside one another but not others. For example, we often see a *P* followed by an *R* and that is permissible. However, we do not see a *P* followed by a *V*. Our knowledge of letter combinations, orthographic knowledge, helps us to predict what letters should come next. To fully understand this, try the demonstration in Exercise 9.2.

EXERCISE 9.2

▶ *Orthographic Knowledge Demonstration*

The following is an English message in which the letters of each word are scrambled. Read the message.

Tsdyunig rfo ym scalsse si nfu.

It likely did not take you very long to decipher the message. This is because you are aware of orthographics. You are aware of permissible letter orders. This knowledge can also help you guess words when you only view parts of them. For example, what is the last letter in the word *X-ra_*? You were able to quickly state that the last letter should be a *Y*. We could then argue that you do not need to see the *Y* in order to know what the word is. The first three letters carry enough information to tell you what the last letter should be. Try to read the following sentence in Exercise 9.3, in which only partial information of words is provided.

EXERCISE 9.3

▶ *Partial Word Reading*

Read the following sentence.

Whe_ I ent____ scho___ I did no_ kn__ h__ to rea_.

You likely found it quite easy to read this message. This is because you can determine words based on your knowledge of orthographics.

A second print characteristic is familiarity. Some words become so familiar to you that you read them as units rather than a group of single letters. To demonstrate this, count the number of *N*s when reading the sentence in Exercise 9.4.

EXERCISE 9.4

▶ *Count the Letter Ns*

Never has any man in the world had more of an interesting issue in the National Academy of Science.

You should have noticed 11 *N*s. However, many people would have missed the *N*s in some common words like *an*, *in*, and the ending *-ing*. This is because such words and endings become so familiar that we process them as single units instead of several letters. This type of single-unit processing is important because it allows us to speed up reading.

context
the story the words tell

A third print characteristic is **context.** At times we can guess the next word in a sentence without reading it. For example, fill in the blank in the following sentence. *After the man finished his T-bone steak he gave the _____ to his dog.* The context (story it tells) of the sentence suggests to the reader that the missing word should be *bone*. Thus, when reading, skilled readers monitor the context of the words on the page and this helps them to fill in missing information. Given that context helps us guess the proper words, it is not necessary to read every word (Rayner, 1998).

HOW DO PRINT CHARACTERISTICS HELP ME READ ACADEMIC MATERIAL?

If you have a strong comprehension of English, you likely have knowledge of orthographics in English. You are aware of appropriate letter combinations in English. However, as noted above, print characteristics go beyond orthographics. When reading academic material, it is essential for you to understand the vocabulary used (familiarity) and the context in which it is used. Reading becomes slower when you are not familiar with course-specific vocabulary. For example, if you were studying statistics, you might look at the letters *hete_____* *dis_____*. However, the first few letters of these words might not help you to know that you are discussing heterogeneous distributions. Thus, you may need more looking time, and you may have to go back to previous words when attempting to understand these words. A student who has studied statistics for many years could likely guess the remaining letters.

It is difficult to skip reading words if you are unsure of the context. Suppose you were studying Introduction to Anatomy. You read the following sentence: *The neurotransmitter dopamine helps the _____ _____ to cross the synaptic _____.* For an introductory student, the context of this sentence is not clear and it would be difficult to fill in the blanks. When context is not clear, reading is slowed.

You will improve reading speed and comprehension by learning course-specific vocabulary prior to reading text information. One such way, flash cards, was suggested in Chapter 6. In addition, you might highlight vocabulary in course lecture notes and in the text. In this way, you become familiar with topic vocabulary and how the vocabulary is used (context).

HOW DO I UNDERSTAND WHAT I HAVE READ?

Comprehension requires that you use your current knowledge base to understand reading material. Comprehension is linked to both the context of the material and your current knowledge. Even familiar ideas are difficult to decipher if context is not clear. Read Exercise 9.5 to see if you can recognize what the instructions are telling you to do.

EXERCISE 9.5   ▶ *Understanding Difficult Passages*

You will likely need to do this at least once each day. First scan the area, to ensure that the procedure is necessary. Sometimes a scan of the area is not enough so you might want to perform the procedure just in case. Next you need to choose the implement. There are many types, long and short. It is best to use one that suits your height but some prefer hand held ones. The ends of the implement differ so choosing the one that is right for you is important. Some have natural ends and others are synthetic. Once you choose, move the implement in a crosswise motion. You will need to move as well or the procedure will not work. Most people prefer to stand during the procedure but some do kneel. When you are completed, a small pile will be in one area. You need to address this pile and move it to the proper location.

This passage was talking about sweeping, however, unless you knew that prior to reading, you might have had difficulty with this. If you are not given the context of the passage (i.e., did not know it was about sweeping) before reading it, you may also have difficulties remembering details when tested later (Bransford & Johnson, 1973, as cited by Reed, 1996).

Prior knowledge of a topic can be helpful in comprehending textbooks and research articles, and it can also be a source of error (when knowledge is incomplete or inaccurate, Calisir & Gurel, 2003; Gaultney, 1995; Kim & Van Dusen, 1998). Your prior knowledge can clarify ideas in your textbook, help to emphasize what is important in the book, and help to categorize ideas for later recall. In fact, prior knowledge on the part of the reader allows authors to write about topics and concepts without having to describe them in detail. For example, if an author wrote a story in which a character entered a fast-food restaurant, likely the author would not explain that the restaurant has a counter where people order food, and a grill and a drink dispenser. The author could rely on the fact that the reader has prior knowledge of fast-food restaurants. The situation is similar in academic writing. When you are in your upper-level courses, readings may be assigned in which authors will assume you have background knowledge of many concepts and will not explain them in detail.

HOW DO I GAIN KNOWLEDGE IN ORDER TO BETTER UNDERSTAND MY TEXTBOOK?

Prior knowledge and context are difficult to achieve for students studying a new topic. As a result, reading is often slow. However, context and a knowledge base are provided to students through lectures, class discussions, and class demonstrations. If you participate in these activities, you will improve your reading because these activities add knowledge that you can use when reading your textbook later. Academic textbooks often include chapter outlines that emphasize important concepts. Many introductory-level books include chapter summaries. Reading these summaries and outlines prior to reading the chapter can help you to understand context and emphasize important concepts.

WHAT OTHER FACTORS HELP WHEN READING MY TEXTBOOK?

Reading quickly vs. speed-reading?

The goal of many students is to acquire the ability to read their required material within a reasonable amount of time. As you gain vocabulary and general knowledge in a field of study, your reading speed will improve. However, it is important to understand some interesting processes that take place, which help you during reading, and to warn you about the risks of speed-reading.

subvocal voice
the voice in your head when reading

When reading, you may notice that you hear a small voice inside your head that says the words to you. This voice is called your **subvocal voice**. When first learning to read, children read out loud, and as they become more skilled, they read silently, often moving their lips. Eventually, the skilled reader reads silently, but the subvocal voice remains for most readers. Subvocalizing during reading may help us remember what we have read. We can see the memory benefits by looking at the case of speed-readers. Most often, people learning to speed-read are asked to suppress or stop this subvocal voice while reading. This is because the subvocal voice limits speed of reading to about the speed of your spoken voice (for an interesting discussion of speed-reading, see Reed, 1996). The idea in speed-reading is to suppress this voice and thereby increase speed. Suppressing the subvocal voice is not an easy task. Usually you are advised to do something with your spoken voice while you read. It seems that we cannot easily subvocalize while we talk, so to suppress the subvocal voice, we can count, repeat a nonsense phrase, or repeat a chant such as 'ommm' while reading. In this way, the subvoice is suppressed and, with practice, reading is faster. Some speed-readers are able to process up to 700 words per minute (normally we read about 250 words per minute) but have difficulty in recalling details of what they read (Rayner, 1998). You might think of these speed-readers as skilled *skimmers*.

It seems that the subvocal voice is important in later recall of written material. It is possible that the subvocal voice provides a rehearsal of material so that it can be held in memory for a longer period of time. One problem with reading academic material is that we read it so slowly that the sentence we are reading fades from memory before we finish the paragraph. Academic material needs to be rehearsed and the subvoice can begin this rehearsal process.

WHAT DOES SUBVOCALIZATION HAVE TO DO WITH READING MY TEXTBOOK?

There are several lessons to be learned from literature on subvocalization. First, when reading, subvocalizing improves memory. This suggests that when studying academic textbooks (especially difficult material), reading aloud or subvocalizing may help to improve later recall of the material (De Haan, Appels, Aleman, & Postman, 2000). Reading speed will always be somewhat limited by this vocalization (though subvocalization rates can improve with practice). However, speed can still be improved by gaining background knowledge in a field and by learning the vocabulary of the subject area.

A second lesson learned from this literature is that speed-reading at the post-secondary level is not recommended. Speed-reading may give students a general idea of the content of the chapter but will not provide enough detail for examinations and theoretical analyses.

WHAT IS EFFECTIVE READING FOR POST-SECONDARY TEXTBOOKS?

effective reading
the ability to read and comprehend text materials in a reasonable time

The term **effective reading** means that you will read and comprehend text materials in a reasonable time. Effective reading involves a number of steps, which are summarized in Box 9.1.

Effective Reading   **BOX 9.1**

Requirement	Effect
1. Attend class	Instructors provide background knowledge in the area of study (even if they do not discuss the particular chapter you are reading). Knowledge speeds reading.
2. Learn vocabulary (perhaps use flash cards as discussed in Chapter 6)	Learning vocabulary results in better comprehension, recall, and increased speed of reading as you do not have to regress to parts of the text you do not understand.
3. Read the chapter summary if provided	The summary highlights important concepts and puts them in context, which helps with speed and comprehension.
4. Skim the chapter	Skimming it first helps you to understand the flow or organization of the chapter. It also helps you to better predict what is coming, thus improving reading speed.
5. Read a section of the chapter	This makes your workload seem smaller. It allows you to comprehend one section before moving on.
6. Read aloud difficult sections	Reading aloud helps to put material into memory.
7. Ask yourself questions about the section you completed (what did it say, why is it important, etc.)	This provides rehearsal, which aids in memory and comprehension.
8. Take a break	After you read a section, taking a short break acts as a reward and also helps you to reflect on what you read.
9. After the break, ask yourself what you read and how it relates to other topics in the course	This helps you to integrate lecture and text material so that exam answers will be complete.
10. Take notes when reading	Note taking highlights important points, and helps to integrate text and lecture material. Be sure you don't just copy out the book; rather, paraphrase and place the notes within your study notes as suggested in Chapter 5.
11. Ask yourself why this material is important and how it relates to you	This improves understanding of material.

INFORMATION LITERACY

WHAT IS INFORMATION LITERACY?

information literacy
recognizing when information
is needed, how to access
that information, and how
to evaluate and use the
information found

Information literacy exists when a person recognizes when information is needed, how to access that information, and how to evaluate and use the information found (The Association of College and Research Libraries, 2000; Bishop, 2003; Kinder, 2004). While this does not seem difficult on the surface, the standards for using information are quite different between high school and post-secondary school (Seamans, 2002). Most post-secondary schools follow strict standards for information use and expect you to recognize when and what type of information is appropriate for particular projects. The American Library Association has developed information literacy standards for post-secondary students, which, if followed, will help you prepare higher quality work.

WHAT ARE POST-SECONDARY STANDARDS FOR INFORMATION LITERACY?

The Association of College and Research Libraries (2000) has developed the five standards for information literacy listed in Box 9.2. The following is a discussion of each standard and how this standard might apply to projects you will receive at school.

Standard 1: Students recognize the type and amount of information that is needed for a project.

Information comes in many varieties. Most often students think of books, journal articles, and the Internet as sources of information. However, information can also be found through interviews, classes, discussions, life experiences, experiments, media, etc. In short, there are many types of information available for students to use, but not all information is appropriate for particular projects.

Take the case of Daphne, who was preparing a short essay for her sociology class on the community effects of divorce. Daphne's parents were divorced when she was young, so she felt she knew quite a bit about the topic. She had little difficulty adjusting when her parents split up and suggested in her essay, based on her own experience, that divorce does not have an impact on society. Her instructor wrote a note on Daphne's paper suggesting that Daphne's experiences were an inappropriate source for her essay. She received a grade of 55 percent. Daphne was concerned about the comments and made an appointment with the instructor, who explained to her that although at times her own experiences will be relevant

---

Information Literacy Standards   BOX 9.2

1. Students recognize the type and amount of information that is needed for a project.
2. Students know how to find the information that they need.
3. Students can evaluate the information they select.
4. Students can effectively use the information in their projects.
5. Students understand ethical issues surrounding information use.

Sources: The Association of College and Research Libraries (2000). Information literacy competency standards for higher education. Chicago: American Library Association. Information Power: Building Partnerships for Learning; Author: American Association of School Librarians and Association for Educational Communications and Technology; Publisher: ALA Editions/American Library Association; Date of publication: 1998. The Nine Information Literacy Standards for Student Learning excerpted from Chapter 2, "Information Literacy Standards for Student Learning," pages 8–9. Reprinted with permission.

(usually when the instructor asks the student to think about a personal experience and analyze it), they were not appropriate for this formal essay. Daphne needs to learn what type of information is appropriate for her different post-secondary topics.

Knowing what type of information is appropriate for a post-secondary project can be tricky. In many cases, the instructor will specify what are considered appropriate sources. The instructor may stipulate that students must find five primary source journal articles and further specify that Internet sources are not appropriate. By **primary source**, the instructor is suggesting that the students should use articles in which the author of the article is collecting his/her own data or developing his/her own theory. In other words, the author is writing about his/her own work rather than someone else's work (**secondary source**). In addition, this instructor does not want Internet sources. This is because, contrary to popular belief, information on the Internet can be very suspect (Darrow & MacDonald, 2004). Some information on the Internet is of high quality, but since anyone can post information on the Internet, some of it is simply not correct. You may have found while working on high school projects that different Internet sources contradict one another. It is then difficult for students to tell which source is correct. The problem with the Internet is that much of the material on it is not subjected to **peer review**. When authors write post-secondary textbooks and journal articles, most often, three to five other experts in the field review their work. In this way, we have more confidence that what the author is saying is acceptable in the field of study. This generally does not happen with Internet postings.

Sometimes the instructor does not specify the types of information needed. However, students can assess the needs by speaking to the instructor. Another way to determine information needed is to write out a research plan (it is a good idea to do this even if the instructor specifies the sources). A research plan includes the topic, the question the student plans to answer in the project, content areas needed to research to answer the question, the type of information needed, and, if library research is involved, **keywords** (content words to be used in the library search). Making a research plan prior to entering the library will speed up the search process because the search will be focused. Take the case of Jan, a journalism student who has to write a short essay about textbook costs at post-secondary schools. Jan decides to start with a research plan, which can be found in Box 9.3.

In Box 9.3, Jan first converted her topic to a topic question: "What is the effect of the high cost of textbooks on student performance?" She then identified key concepts/content areas for her journalism topic. She broke her article into three areas of interest. First, she decided to learn about the publishing industry costs. To learn about this area, she knew she would need to use some library books and possibly journal articles. Second, she wanted to know about the effect of the textbook costs on students. She decided to use some journal articles that discuss dropout rates for students in financial need, but augmented these articles with student interviews at her college. Third, she wanted to know about instructor expectations for students who cannot afford texts. She decided to interview some instructors on her campus and read some articles that examine the attitude of instructors to student financial burdens. The research plan helped Jan to decide what type of information best suits her project and how to organize the information.

It is also important to know how much information is required for a project. This is sometimes difficult to determine. However, after reviewing five articles about instructor opinion, Jan realized that they all came to the same conclusion. This helped Jan to determine that she had enough articles in this area. Jan also realized that some information would be time consuming to collect. For example, two of the articles Jan wanted must be obtained through interlibrary loan, and the reference librarian told her that the articles would not arrive for several weeks. She decided to use different articles so that she could meet the timeframe the instructor gave for the project. Knowing how much information is needed to stay within essay due dates can require changes in information gathering strategies.

primary source
usually a journal article in which the author is discussing the author's own work

secondary source
a book or article in which the author discusses others' work

peer review
written material is reviewed or read by other experts in the field

keywords
content words to be used in the library search

Project Plan for Jan	BOX 9.3

Topic: Publishing costs for post-secondary tests
Topic Question: What is the effect of the high cost of textbooks on school performance?
Content Areas:

1. Publishing industry costs

2. Effect of the cost on students

3. Instructor expectations for students who cannot afford texts

Type of information needed:

1. Publishing industry costs
   - Journal articles: Number of articles: Perhaps three, but may modify if they say really different things
   - Books: Perhaps a recent book on publishing will have all the information I need

   Searches
   Journal Articles
   - Which library database? I don't know so I will search the index by subject
   - Keywords: *publishing*, *costs*, *book publishing*
   - Initial search using *publishing*: I received over 1000 articles—too many!!!
   - Used: *publishing and costs*—still over 500 articles—too many to look through
   - Used: *book and publishing and costs*—23 articles: I looked at the titles and found seven that might be good
   - Read the abstracts (summaries) of the seven articles by clicking on them, found four that I will use. After reading them, they all seem to say the same thing, so I will use three.

   Books
   Database: Library Electronic Catalogue
   Keyword search:
   - Used the keywords: *books and publishing and costs*—two books came up and one looks excellent.
   - Wrote the call number down of the excellent one then went into the stacks (where books are shelved). Could not find the excellent book. Went back to the computer to figure out where it was and I noticed that the computer said the book was out for the next two weeks! By the time I got the book I would only have two days to finish the essay. Decided to use the other book, which, while not as good, is okay and AVAILABLE.

2. Effect of the cost on students

3. Instructor expectations for students who cannot afford texts

Standard 2: Students know how to find the information that they need.

Gathering information requires a number of skills because how you gather information depends on the type of information you need. Gathering books and articles requires knowledge of the post-secondary library system. Running experiments requires knowledge of research methods (see Chapter 11). Surveying and interviewing requires knowledge of observational research (see Chapter 11). Using the Internet requires knowledge of search engines. In other words, once you decide on the type of information required, you need to understand how to find that information. Your school reference librarian is a good source for learning different ways to access information. In this section, we will focus on using the post-secondary library.

How do I use a post-secondary library?
On the surface, using a library seems easy. After all, most students have been using a library since they were in kindergarten. However, the authors of this textbook have often given students assignments that require library research and the students have complained to us that finding appropriate information was time consuming and difficult. Kisha, the

student from the case study, had this problem. Library research does not have to be difficult or time consuming, but using an academic library takes practice. While we cannot tell you about your particular library, most academic libraries have commonalities that we will discuss here.

What can I find at a post-secondary library?

First, libraries contain many sources of information: books, journals, magazines, newspapers, videos, government documents, statistics, databases, etc. Your first job is to decide which type of information at your library is essential for your project. You will find it much easier to use the library if you have made a research plan prior to entering the library. Recall that Jan is to write a short essay about the effect of the high cost of textbooks on school performance. She made a plan prior to entering the library (Box 9.3) and can now use the plan to organize notes on her research progress.

Second, libraries are divided into numerous areas with specialized functions. To learn about these specialized areas, see Box 9.4. When entering your library for the first time, take the listed areas from Box 9.4 and try to find each. Knowing where these areas are will speed up your research in all your projects throughout your post-secondary career.

Third, the most important resource available to you at your library will be the reference librarian. These librarians have specialized training (holding a bachelor's degree, master's degree, and often a doctorate). They are experts in research and information gathering in academic settings and help both instructors and students with their projects. If you are having

---

Areas Found in Post-Secondary Libraries   BOX 9.4

Library Area	Function
Reference desk	This is the desk of the reference librarian, whose job it is to help instructors and students understand information sources and locations.
Computer databases	Usually computers are located throughout the library. These computers contain many sources of information, such as the library catalogue, indexes, user information, library policies, etc.
The stacks	These are the bookshelves. Books and print journals are kept here. These are organized by call numbers (each book is assigned a call number). Often in post-secondary libraries, there are many floors of stacks so you should find the call numbers you need prior to entering the stacks, and read (usually on the wall) the call numbers located on each floor. Each shelf will have a sign at the end telling you which call numbers are located on the shelf.
Current periodicals	There will be a section of the library in which recent magazines, journals, and newspapers are kept. Usually these are periodicals from the current year.
Media	In this section you can find videos and DVDs. Most libraries also offer viewing rooms where equipment for viewing is available.
Meeting rooms, classrooms, and study carrels	Throughout the library, there are rooms and desks for student use. Students can book meeting rooms for group projects. Study carrels do not have to be booked; if it is empty, use it.
Government documents	Documents included in this section are often reports and data released by the government for general use.
Archives and microfiche	In the archives, students can find older documents and books. Microfiche are slides that contain older articles, newspapers, and magazines that are no longer in the stacks.
Check-out area	You can check out your books in this area and also validate your library card (often your library card is your student card).

difficulty finding information, they are a valuable resource. They can help you determine the type of information you need and how much information is sufficient. They can also help you with keywords, if the ones you chose do not provide you with the information you need. Note that they will not find your articles for you, but rather, they will help you to find them. These librarians also offer free library orientation tours. Not only is the library orientation interesting and helpful, but most often students report that the librarians make it fun.

How do I find books at the library?

One of the most important resources to understand is the library catalogue, which is used to find books located in the stacks. In almost all libraries today the catalogue is on computer (some libraries let you access the computer system from home with your student card and a password) (see Figure 9.1). To access the online catalogue for books, you will click on "catalogue" on your library's home page. You will find you can search for a book by its title, by the author's name, or by a keyword (content/topic words).

Most often, students working on essays use the keyword search. In a keyword search, you enter one or more keywords, and the library book catalogue is searched for books that have that keyword as a content word. A list of books will come up on the computer screen and you can read their titles to decide if they are appropriate. Write down their call numbers and find the books in the stacks. The difficulty most students have with the search is in finding appropriate keywords for their topic. You can usually determine appropriate keywords by thinking about your research question. When you receive your topic, rephrase the topic as a question as Jan did in Box 9.3. Recall that Jan was to examine textbook cost at post-secondary schools. She rephrased this topic as a question: "What is the effect of the high cost of textbooks on school performance?" She then broke the topic into content areas and used the words in the content areas as her keywords. We will discuss more on keywords in finding journal articles.

FIGURE 9.1 The Electronic Card Catalogue

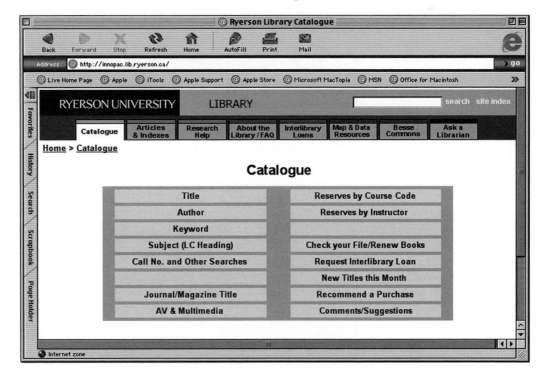

Source: Reprinted by permission of Ryerson University Library.

How can I find journal articles at the library?

Most online library computing systems have an area called "indexes" or "articles and indexes." An index is a sort of search engine, like Google, but for particular subject areas like psychology, sociology, English, engineering, etc. These indexes are used to search for journal articles. When you click on the index button on the library home page, you are sent to a screen that allows you to search the indexes by subject area (e.g., biology, English, etc.) (see Figure 9.2). Click on search indexes by subject and you will be sent to a page where different subject areas are listed.

Click on the subject area of your project (e.g. education, biology) and you will be taken to all indexes in that subject area. Once you open one of these indexes, you need to place keywords in the search line (see Figure 9.3).

Keyword searches can be tricky. Usually single word keyword searches result in too many articles being found (often over 1000). Look at the notes Jan made on her research plan about her keyword search in Box 9.3. She initially used a single keyword but there were too many articles for her to go through. She then modified her search using Boolean operators (words such as "and" and "or"). When she entered *publishing and costs*, she found fewer articles but still too many to go through. She modified her search again by adding a third keyword. Using the word "or" in a keyword search will have the computer look for either keyword in an article.

Once the keyword search is conducted, a list of articles will appear. If you click on the article title (or where the database says "abstract" under the article), you will get a summary of that article. This will help you determine whether this article is appropriate for your project. You will also notice that some articles are called **full text articles**. This means that if you click on the computer full text button, you can get the full article on computer. It is

full text article
an article that can be fully viewed on computer

FIGURE 9.2 Subject Area for Articles and Indexes

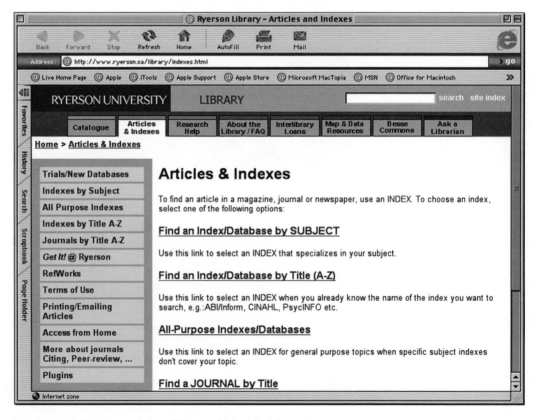

Source: Reprinted by permission of Ryerson University Library.

FIGURE 9.3 **Keyword Search in Proquest Index**

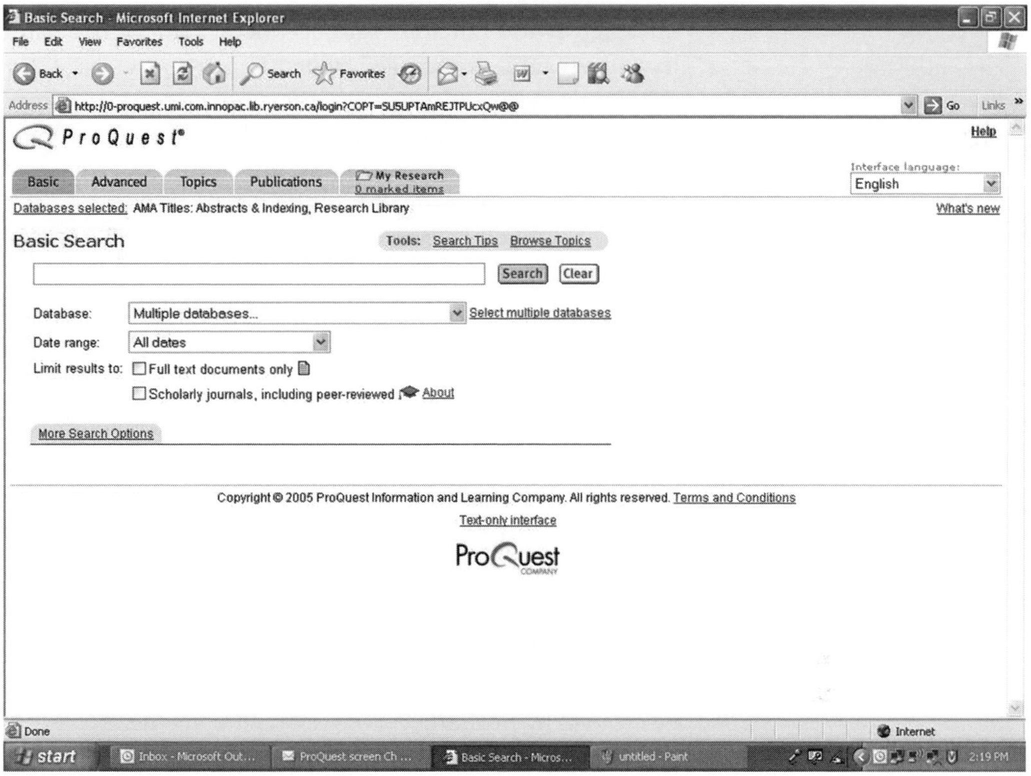

Source: Reprinted by permission of Ryerson University Library.

important to understand that these full text articles are exactly the same ones you would find if you went into the stacks and found the printed version of the journal. So having full text articles is a convenience, as it saves you going to the printed journal in the library to find the article.

Some articles listed provide only the abstract (summary) of the article. You cannot use just this summary for your project; you must find the full article in the stacks. Above the summary of the article (abstract) you will be given the title of the journal in which the article appears, the year it was published, and the pages it is on. You can then go back to the library catalogue to find where the journal is kept at your library. You then will need to go to the stacks, find the journal, and photocopy or read the article. Jan's plan (Box 9.3) describes some difficulties she had using the library databases and finding books. This required her to modify her plan. Once Jan has her information and has done some reading, she will be ready to create an essay plan. You can find how to prepare essay plans in Chapter 10. However, Jan must now evaluate the articles and books that she has found.

Standard 3: Students can evaluate the information they select.

Not all sources of information are appropriate for projects. You need to know whether the sources you are using are valid and reliable.

Valid information is an acceptable source for your project. That is, the evidence that is provided is acceptable as evidence in the field of study. There are several ways that you can evaluate the validity of information. First, if you are reading a book or an article, you can check to see if it is peer reviewed. Many libraries have databases that will check to see if a book or article is peer reviewed. Alternatively, if you go to the journal website or print version of the journal, this information will be provided. Second, when evaluating an article you need to check for bias (a full discussion of bias is in Chapter 7). Does the author fairly

valid information
information that is true, or acceptable, in a field of study

review previous material? Does the author ignore one side of an issue? Does the author back up opinion with evidence? Third, you might check to see if data presented are appropriately interpreted. You can also examine whether the author has used acceptable methods to collect information or provided evidence for opinion (see Chapter 11).

reliable information
information that can be demonstrated by a number of authors

You may also check whether it is **reliable information**. That is, do other authors seem to agree with the arguments made by this author? Do other articles you have found seem to support the conclusions made by this author? Or, given the information found in other articles, does the information in this article seem to be out in left field?

Finally, does the author acknowledge limitations of the study? You need to think of the possible limitations (problems that affect the interpretation of the information) of each source of information you collect and include these limitations in your discussion of the article (see Chapter 7).

Even if articles are valid and reliable, you need to determine if the information you found fits with your project. Recall that Kisha, the student in the opening case, is not sure that one of her articles is relevant. She was required to find ten articles for her anatomy essay. When she was collecting her papers, she did not really evaluate them at the library and has found that one likely is not relevant. She now has to decide whether she will use only the relevant nine articles or go back to the library to collect another article. Her decision will depend on the project due date. If her essay is due in two hours, her choices are limited. If the instructor required ten articles, and she has only nine, her grade will be reduced. If she places articles in her paper that are not relevant, her grade will also be reduced. Kisha needs to determine which course of action is best. Such problems can be avoided by planning essays well before due dates.

Standard 4: Students can effectively use the information in their projects.

Once information is gathered, it must be organized though an essay plan or project plan (these plans are described in Chapter 10). One of the greatest mistakes that students make in their essays and projects is in not integrating and organizing the information that they have found. Prior to making an essay/project plan, you need to read the articles and books you have found. When reading, it is a good idea to keep notes that briefly outline the main argument of each author, evidence that they provide for their argument, their conclusions, and biases in their papers. It is also a good idea to write down how the articles are limited in interpretation. For example, Jan, the student preparing an essay on textbook costs, read one article on the costs of publishing, but it was about publishing children's books. She realized that it is limited in its interpretation because publishing for children is quite different from publishing for adult students.

Once all articles have been reviewed, try to integrate the articles that are similar. For example, two of Jan's articles show that instructors are concerned about the cost of textbooks. In one, the number of complaints to publishing companies about costs was monitored, and in the second, a survey of instructor opinion was conducted. She decided to present both in the same paragraphs of her essay as they strongly support one another.

Standard 5: Students understand ethical issues surrounding information use.

When using information, citing sources within your essay or project is essential. When writing, if you do not cite, the reader assumes that all ideas presented were your ideas. When you forget to cite your sources or you cite inappropriately, we say that you have plagiarized (a most serious academic offence, see Chapter 10). Thus, learning when and how to cite is essential and this is presented in Chapter 10.

copyright
legal rights to written material held by the author and publisher

A second important ethical issue in information literacy is **copyright**. The copyright is protection for the author and publisher of the work and provides legal rights to the author and publisher. Copyright is broken when parts of the author's works are photocopied and distributed without permission. Most journals allow students to copy or print out articles from journals for personal use. Copying books is not permitted and is considered a violation of copyright.

Another ethical issue in information gathering is in confidentiality when conducting experiments, surveys, and interviews. If you are choosing to use these forms of information gathering, it is important that you discuss this with your instructor. Most post-secondary schools have an ethics committee that reviews projects to ensure that they follow strict ethical standards (e.g., the participants are treated fairly, humanely, confidentially, etc.). Your instructor will need to review what you intend to do and discuss details of your research.

Advice for Kisha

▶ It is unfortunate that Kisha waited for six weeks to begin her readings and essay. Kisha will need to spend considerable time catching up. There are a number of things that she can do to speed up both her reading and her library research; many of these actions can be found in Box 9.1. First, Kisha should review her class notes to ensure that she has some background knowledge in the topics covered in her textbook. Second, she should review the vocabulary used in the chapter. Using flash cards for this vocabulary will help with later reading and recall. Third, Kisha should read textbook chapter summaries and look over the headings in each chapter to help her understand the organization and important concepts that are about to be presented. Kisha should then start reading her chapters section by section with short breaks in between. During her reading she should take notes that can be placed into her study notes. After each chapter section, Kisha should ask herself questions about the reading. In general, these strategies will both speed up reading time and aid comprehension of the material.

Kisha's essay is another matter. Essays usually require more than one week to complete. However, Kisha will need to formulate a question for her research paper, decide the content areas of her paper, and figure out what type of information she needs to answer her question. If the library confuses Kisha, she needs to visit the reference librarian, who will help her become familiar with the library. Once Kisha finds her articles, she needs to evaluate them for validity, reliability, and bias. Finally, Kisha needs to organize her information into an essay plan and cite all studies appropriately. While this is a big task for Kisha because of the limited time (due to poor planning), it is not impossible. Kisha needs to remind herself that at school she needs to do the best she can within the limited time she has.

CHAPTER SUMMARY

■ In general, people read by understanding orthographics, having familiarity with words, and understanding the context of words. While students have orthographic knowledge, they sometimes are not familiar with the vocabulary and context of materials written in their academic textbooks. This slows down their reading.

■ Reading using a subvocal voice or reading out loud can help you to better understand academic material. These methods help by providing rehearsal of material and changing visual material into auditory material. Thus, students both see and hear the written words.

■ Information literacy means that students can access, evaluate, and use the information that they find. In post-secondary settings, students are expected to recognize appropriate sources for their work, know how to access these sources, know how to critically evaluate the information they find, effectively use the information, and understand ethical issues surrounding the use of information.

KEY TERMS

context
copyright
effective reading
full text article
information literacy

keyword
orthographics
peer review
primary source
print characteristics

reliable information
secondary source
subvocal voice
valid information

INDIVIDUAL ACTIVITIES

1. Below are three research topics. Based on each research question (or use a question from another class), create keywords to use in a library search. Go to your library and try these words in a search. Are you retrieving relevant articles? Are you retrieving too many articles? Try to modify your search to receive articles that seem more appropriate.

   Question 1. Can people understand words that fall into their peripheral vision?

   Question 2. Does speed-reading lead to poor comprehension?

   Question 3. Does understanding the context in reading lead to improved recall?

2. Write a research plan for an essay that you are required to write this term (use Box 9.3 as a guide). Be sure to note the types of information sources required for your paper and evaluate the methods needed to gather this information.

3. Using Box 9.4, go to the library to find the areas listed. Take notes on the types of information available in each area and suggest when such information would be most useful. Which areas do you anticipate that you will most often use for your assignments?

GROUP ACTIVITIES

1. Divide into groups. Designate one person as the tester. Have half of your group read a paragraph from your text in the usual way (remind them to subvocalize). The other half of the students should read the paragraph while counting from one to ten repeatedly (thus suppressing subvocalization). The tester should create and ask several types of questions. First ask students to write down the gist of the paragraph. Then ask the students detailed questions about the paragraph. How did the two groups do? How important is subvocalization? What types of tests and assignments require detailed and less detailed information?

2. As a group, write out a project plan to study whether creativity can be taught. Decide the content areas, the type of information you will be searching for, keywords to use in that search, etc. Once you have your plan, head to the library to test whether your keywords will result in appropriate books and articles. How can you refine your search?

3. Discuss with your group various forms of information and when each might be used. What are the advantages and disadvantages of each type of information?

REFERENCES

Association of College and Research Libraries (2000). *Information literacy competency standards for higher education.* Chicago: American Library Association.

Bishop, K. (2003). What in the world is happening with information literacy? *Knowledge Quest, 31(2),* 14–16.

Calisir, F., & Gurel, Z. (2003). Influence of text structure and prior knowledge of the learner on reading comprehension browsing and perceived control. *Computers in Human Behavior, 19,* 135–145.

Darrow, R., & MacDonald, C. (2004). What is information literacy in the digital age? *CSLA Journal, 27(2),* 21–23.

De Haan, E. H. F., Appels, B., Aleman, A., & Postma, A. (2000). Inter and intramodal encoding of auditory and visual presentation of material: Effects of memory performance. *Psychological Record, 50(3),* 577–586.

Gaultney, J. F. (1995). The effect of prior knowledge and metacognition on the acquisition of reading comprehension strategy. *Journal of Experimental Child Psychology, 59,* 142–163.

Kim, S., & Van Dusen, L. M. (1998). The role of prior knowledge and elaboration in text comprehension and memory: A comparison of self-generated elaboration and text-provided elaboration. *The American Journal of Psychology, 111(3),* 353–378.

Kinder, D. (2004). Information literacy: A key to success in the 21st century. *The Greet Exchange, Spring 2004,* 3–4.

Rayner, K. (1998). Eye movements in reading and information processing: 20 years of research. *Psychological Bulletin, 124(3),* 372–422.

Reed, S. K. (1996). *Cognition: Theory and Applications* (4th ed.). Pacific Grove: Books/Cole Publishing.

Seamans, N. H. (2002). Student perceptions of information literacy: Insights for librarians. *Reference Services Review, 30(2),* 112–123.

Sereno, S. C., & Rayner, K. (2000). The when and where of reading in the brain. *Brain and Cognition, 42,* 78–81.

Starr, M. S., & Rayner, K. Eye movements during reading: Some current controversies. *Trends in Cognitive Sciences, 5(4),* 156–163.

WRITING AN ESSAY

LEARNING OBJECTIVES

The Case of Marcel

▶ **M**arcel is a first-year student. He is taking five courses, all of which he enjoys (although some more than others). In three of his courses, he is required to write essays. Marcel has had very limited experience in writing essays. In high school he was required to write a few short papers but his teachers encouraged him to use the Internet for his sources (something that many of his post-secondary instructors clearly view as negative). Also, most of the papers he wrote in high school were for English class and the teacher had emphasized that the goal of the paper was creativity. His post-secondary teachers seem to be more concerned about the content of the paper than about creativity. In fact, he was told in one of his classes that the style of the paper had to be APA, something he knows nothing about. He did look up APA on the library website and feels that this style will limit his creativity. Marcel now worries that he does not even know how to begin to write his paper. His teachers have suggested that students need to choose a topic and, based on their research, create a thesis. They are then to support or refute this thesis. Marcel feels intimidated even before he starts. This worry about how to start his essays is leading him to procrastinate.

Marcel's problem is one faced by many students. The prospect of writing an essay strikes fear into the heart. Without knowledge of the mechanics of essay writing, students sometimes procrastinate, as we discussed in Chapter 4. They put off writing their essays until the last possible minute, a strategy that generally guarantees a poor grade. Essay writing takes time. Students need time to choose a topic and formulate a thesis, and to understand the mechanics of writing, how to use the library, how to read research papers, how to format their essay, and how to make proper conclusions on their essay topic. Some of these issues have been covered in other chapters of this book. However, since essay writing is a vital component of higher education, this chapter will remind students of topics covered in other chapters (e.g., reading research articles and critical thinking) and expand on these topics.

To Marcel, writing an essay looks like an enormous task, a mountain to climb. In Chapter 4, we saw that when faced with a mountain to climb, the best, most efficient, and least daunting technique is to break the mountain into a series of molehills. This technique will serve Marcel well in writing an essay. He is unsure of this, though; he feels that perhaps it would be a better idea to simply wait for a large block of time (e.g., a free weekend) to concentrate on doing nothing but one essay. Then, when one essay is out of the way, he can look for another large block of time to tackle the next essay, and so on. This is a big mistake. Marcel's idea is a gamble that (1) a large free block of time will emerge, and (2) he will be able to accomplish all the work he needs to do in that time. Large blocks of time can rarely be planned; Marcel may get sick, or he may find that other unexpected chores arise. Small blocks of time can always be found and taken advantage of, however. This is another good reason for breaking the mountain into a molehill: molehills fit very conveniently into small blocks of time.

THE PLANNING STAGE

HOW CAN I BREAK THE MOUNTAIN OF WRITING AN ESSAY INTO MOLEHILLS?

The first step in writing is to outline what must be done. This outline becomes the beginning of your essay plan. In general, the steps are:

1. Choose a topic.
2. Determine what questions need to be answered for this topic.
3. Determine what resources are needed to answer these questions.
4. Find the resources.
5. Make an outline of the structure of the essay, breaking it into segments.
6. Write one segment at a time.
7. Proofread the essay.

Let's examine each step, one at a time.

WHAT TOPIC SHALL I CHOOSE?

Marcel has been assigned 2000-word essays in three subjects. In economics, his instructor has given the students the choice of three specific questions to answer. In English literature, the instructor has asked the class to select one poem by either Byron or Tennyson, and demonstrate how the poet uses imagery. In psychology, the instructor has been very flexible, suggesting that the class choose a psychological disorder as the topic. What we see here is a variation in the directedness of the instructor, with one being very specific, another setting limits but allowing for some individual choice, and the third allowing freedom of choice within a topic area. Most likely, Marcel will enjoy the choice given by the psychology instructor best, but will find this the most difficult essay to write. The easiest essay will probably be the economics essay, which leaves students in no doubt as to what is required. In all cases, though, Marcel does have some decisions to make before he can move on to the next step.

The best topic is always the one you are most interested in. Let's look first at the options that Marcel's economics instructor has given him. Marcel must pick one of the following questions to answer:

1. Critically evaluate the statement that economics deals more with theory than with facts.

2. From the economic perspective, explain why a person who normally eats lightly may become a heavy eater if confronted with a buffet-style dinner.

3. "The job of the economist is to comfort the afflicted and afflict the comfortable," says Prof. Dimsdale. Do you agree or disagree? Why?

In all cases, Marcel is going to have to do some analytical thinking: it is unlikely that he is going to find the exact answer to any of these questions from any library source. So if Marcel is looking for the "easiest" question of the three, he's probably out of luck. But if he enjoys intellectually examining the nature of a subject, question 1 might be the one for him. If he has more fun applying theories and principles to real-life situations, question 2 looks like a good choice. If he enjoys debate, wherein there may be no right or wrong answer, but the logic of the argument is the important part, question 3 seems to be made for him. Marcel is going to have to know himself in order to make a good choice for his economics essay.

The English literature essay leaves Marcel with more choice. First, does he prefer Byron or Tennyson? These poets are very different, and it is likely that Marcel prefers one of the two. Clearly, that poet's work is the one Marcel should explore. But which poem should he choose? Obviously, if there is one poem that he particularly likes, that is the one he should work with. Then again, if he knows of one poem that is rich in imagery, perhaps this will give him more scope for his essay. One suggestion we can make to Marcel is that he choose a poem of short to moderate length: while many of these poets' longer poems are exquisite and inspiring, they may contain entirely too much imagery for Marcel to undertake in 2000 words.

Marcel's psychology instructor has given him the biggest problem. First, Marcel has to choose a psychological disorder to discuss. Hopefully, he has covered many disorders in class, so again his choice should be based on which one interested him the most. Let's say that Marcel is most interested in kleptomania, the recurring and persistent desire to steal. Having made this choice, the way is clear for Marcel to begin structuring his essay.

HOW CAN I DETERMINE WHAT QUESTIONS NEED TO BE ANSWERED FOR EACH TOPIC?

In the case of Marcel's economics essay, the major question has been given to him by his instructor. There may be other questions that should be answered as well, though. For example, if Marcel has chosen the first question ("Critically evaluate the statement that economics deals more with theory than with facts."), he needs to answer the further questions of how economics formulates theories and whether and how economics applies these theories to real life. In the case of the English literature essay, Marcel needs to answer further questions, such as, what is imagery and where in the poem does the poet use it? Then the questions of how it is used (i.e., to what purpose) and the effectiveness of its use can be explored. In the case of the psychology essay, more questions still should be posed: What is kleptomania? How often does it occur? What are its causes? How can it be treated? Marcel might also take note of the traditional journalistic questions as well: who? what? where? when? why? Once Marcel answers these smaller questions, he will want to create a question that will form the basis of an argument (rather than just to state everything he knows about kleptomania). For example, Marcel might decide to ask, "Is kleptomania just an excuse people use in court to justify bad behaviour?" Marcel then can use the body of the essay to argue for or against this statement.

HOW CAN I DETERMINE WHAT RESOURCES ARE NEEDED TO ANSWER THESE QUESTIONS AND HOW CAN I FIND THESE RESOURCES?

It's hoped that we have answered these questions for you in Chapter 9 on reading and information literacy. You may wish to briefly reread the suggestions in that chapter to help you design a project plan.

HOW DO I MAKE AN OUTLINE OF THE STRUCTURE OF THE ESSAY?

After finding and reading your references, you should have a clearer idea of the topic. Behind every successful essay is clear preparation and most of us benefit greatly from having a plan or outline written down. For some people, an outline of headings and sub-headings works well, while other people profit more from a visual approach. We will discuss several ways of making an outline: the best one is an individual choice. No matter which approach you choose, write down what the main idea/question/thesis of your essay is and keep this in front of you as you write. It's all too easy to get off track when one is writing, so it pays to keep yourself on track by whatever means you need. In Bill Clinton's first campaign for the presidency of the United States, he instructed all of his workers to post signs for themselves to keep them focused. In his case, the sign said, "It's about the economy, stupid!" We don't suggest you call yourself names, but the lesson is clear: keep on track.

If you favour a written plan, you will probably benefit from a written hierarchy. Essentially you are forming an essay plan with sub-goals, just as you did in problem-solving in Chapter 7. An essay plan involves stating your topic, reformulating your topic as a question to be answered in your essay, creating a project plan for library research (shown in Chapter 9), and breaking down the essay into an introduction, body, and conclusions. To create this plan, it is a good idea to briefly jot down all the major points you wish to make in this essay. What you should find is that the first sub-goal of your essay structure is to write an introduction. Your introduction should state what the main idea of the essay will be and what you plan to accomplish in this paper. Now take all the points you jotted down before, which will really encompass everything that you wish to accomplish in this paper, and give them headings. These are sub-goals as well. Put the sub-goals/headings in a reasonable order (this may change as you start writing). This will comprise the body of your essay. Your final sub-goal is your conclusion; this is where you summarize the arguments you make, draw a conclusion, note what limitations or exceptions there may be to your argument, and, if possible, make suggestions for further points of interest to explore in the future.

Box 10.1 provides a general format for an essay plan in a chart form and suggested essay plans for Marcel's papers.

Some people prefer to organize material visually. In Chapter 6, we discussed studying by the use of visual means such as mind maps. Mind maps can be used to organize an essay as well. They have the advantage of allowing you to see your organization

Written Essay Plans

BOX 10.1

General	Psychology	English	Economics
Introduction: a statement of the topic and why it is of interest, a statement of the thesis or main argument that is going to be made	Is kleptomania just an excuse people use in court to justify bad behaviour? This essay will examine what kleptomania is and how it differs from normal stealing in terms of why people steal.	Lord Byron suggests in his poem *The Maid of Athens* that the beauty and charms of a woman are best described through using the imagery of nature. This essay will examine his use of imagery in this poem, noting which elements of nature he finds particularly compelling in describing the maid.	Some people have contended that economics deals more with theory than facts. If this is so, it may be a severe criticism of the usefulness of this field. This essay will critically examine this argument, resulting in a refutation or agreement with the premise.
Body: development of arguments in support of the thesis, the points arranged in order of importance, with the weakest (but still important) coming first and the strongest coming last, so the body builds to a crescendo	• what kleptomania is • the feelings and anxieties kleptomaniacs have as opposed to normal thieves • treatment of kleptomaniacs and ordinary thieves by society—what works and what doesn't?	• types of nature imagery used: geographical, elemental, botanical, zoological • pick out each piece of imagery, categorizing it • determine which kind of imagery Byron uses the most in describing the maid	• implications of the argument • cases in which theories seem removed from real-world events • cases in which economic theory is derived from real-world events • evaluation of which side of the argument is stronger
Conclusion: a restatement of the main argument or thesis, implications of the argument, further questions to be asked	• kleptomania is different from ordinary theft • society needs to deal with it in a different manner • how can it be prevented? do we know?	• concluding that Byron uses little of botanical or zoological imagery to describe the maid, that he favours geographical imagery in this case • or does he mainly use geographical imagery in general? • suggest an examination of other Byronic works to answer this question	• concluding that economics is very much in contact with facts; that the formulation of theory is derived from factual events
Source citation	References (generally APA format)	Bibliography (generally MLA format)	References or bibliography (format should be specified by the instructor)

at a glance and of rearranging ideas to make your organization better. An example of a mind map can be seen in Figure 10.1. In this figure, we have used the psychology essay on kleptomania as an example, but the English essay and the economics essay can be diagrammed in this way as well.

FIGURE 10.1 **Mind Map Essay Plan**

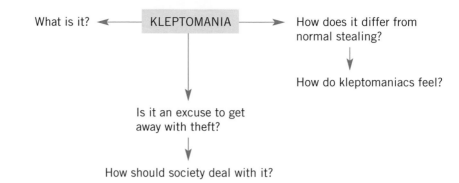

Another way of making a visual organization is by creating a flowchart. Flowcharts are particularly good for showing the sequence of what you will write, as well as determining headings and sub-headings. We will use the example of the psychology essay again in Figure 10.2 to illustrate this.

FIGURE 10.2 **Flowchart Essay Plan**

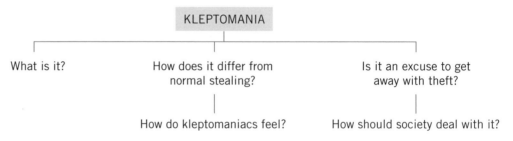

No matter which type of plan Marcel uses, each step is a sub-goal and can be tackled one at a time. In this way, Marcel does not have to feel quite so overwhelmed by the task at hand. Each step will take a small amount of time, so Marcel doesn't have to wait for a large block of time to materialize and gamble that nothing will disturb this large block of time. Once Marcel has created his plan, he is ready to start writing.

THE WRITING STAGE

IS GRAMMAR IMPORTANT?

Emphatically, yes! Your ideas may be wonderful, but if they can't be communicated to others, they are worth very little. The point of an essay is to communicate your ideas, but poor grammar, poor punctuation, incorrect word usage, and flawed sentence structure make communication very difficult. Remember that what is obvious to you, the writer, may not be so obvious to the reader. You must help the reader to understand your points, by presenting good arguments in a coherent fashion. Marcel, like most students in post-secondary schools, believes that he knows grammar well. But does he really? Do you? Exercise 10.1 presents sentences that have flaws in them. Can you correct them? Try to do this yourself and then check your answers in Box 10.2.

EXERCISE 10.1   ▶ *Check Your Grammar!*

All of the following sentences have errors in them. Can you make the appropriate corrections? See Box 10.2 for the correct answers.

1.   She overheard my mother and I talking.

2.   I would of done it, but I didn't know how.

3.   If the child knows their mother's voice, it feels secure.

4.   Data was gathered by several scientists.

5.   It was different than anything he had ever seen.

6.   Rereading this article, many contradictions appear.

7.   He had gotten a scolding from his mother for disobeying.

8.   The report was given to he and I for final approval.

9.   The judicial system is not tough enough. They should give longer sentences.

10.   End of story.

More grammar review can be found in this book's website: http://www.postsecondarylearning.nelson.com.

If you have further questions about grammar, it is worth investing in a small grammar book in which you can look up grammatical and punctuation formats quickly. Two excellent handbooks are *A Canadian Writer's Pocket Guide*, 2nd ed. by Jack Finnbogason and Al Valleau, and *The Bare Essentials Form B*, 5th ed. by Sarah Norton and Brian Green. You might also find the following website helpful in this regard: http://www.canadianwriterspocketguide2e.nelson.com.

Corrections to Sentences in Exercise 10.1   **BOX 10.2**

1.   She overheard my mother and *me* talking.

   The verb "overheard" takes the objective case.

2.   I would *have* done it, but I didn't know how.

   People often write "of" instead of "have" because in talking, we tend to slur our words and use contractions that can be misleading. In this example, we probably say "I would've done it," a contraction short for "would have." But in hearing this, we may mistake what we heard for "would of."

3.   If the child knows *his or her* mother's voice, *he or she* feels secure.

   The subject of this sentence is "child," a singular noun. Therefore, the pronoun referring to the child must be singular too. Also, a child is a human being, not an "it"!

4.   Data *were* gathered by several scientists.

   "Data," like "media," is a plural noun. The verb must be plural as well, then.

5.   It was different *from* anything he had ever seen.

   We often say "different than" in conversational speech, but the word "different" actually takes the preposition "from."

6.   *In* rereading this article, *he found* many contradictions.

   or

   When one rereads this article, many contradictions appear.

   In the original sentence, there is no indication of who is rereading the article.

7.   He *received* a scolding from his mother for disobeying.

   Even though we use it in conversation all the time, there is no such word as "gotten."

8.   The report was given to *him* and *me* for final approval.

   The preposition "to" takes the objective case.

9.   The judicial system is not tough enough. *It* should give longer sentences.

   The subject "judicial system" is singular and refers to a group. It must then be indicated by a singular, neutral pronoun.

10.   *This is the* end of *the* story.

   In its original form, this was not a complete sentence. A complete sentence must have a subject and a predicate (verb).

HOW CAN I GET 2000 WORDS OUT OF THIS TOPIC?

When Marcel was first told that his essays were to be about 2000 words long, he panicked, thinking that he would never be able to write that much. In fact, most students find that as they write, they need to be more concise. If Marcel finds that his finished essay contains far fewer than 2000 words, he will need to examine the points he made. Has he made enough points? Has he explained them adequately? If not, he must expand on what he has said, adding more ideas and/or explaining his ideas more fully.

Sometimes, when essays don't seem to be long enough, writers fill up their writing with extra words and phrases that don't need to be there. This kind of wordiness detracts from the message that the student is trying to send. Instead, it sends the instructor the message that the student is trying to "pad" the essay, making up for content that isn't there by putting in extra words to fulfill the word requirement. The suggestion is that the student doesn't know enough about the topic to write the essay adequately. Alternatively, this wordiness may indicate that the student is a poor writer. Marcel always thought that he needed to use words of many syllables and intricate sentence constructions to impress the instructor, but he's wrong. The instructor is impressed by clear communication. Often the multisyllabic words and intricate sentence structure obscure the message. Besides, often students such as Marcel use these words and sentence structures incorrectly, obscuring the message even further. Keep it simple. That's the technique that worked for Ernest Hemingway! Box 10.3 contains some phrases that we commonly use, but are really redundant; that is, more than one word is used when only one is required.

BOX 10.3

Eliminating the Tendency to Go On and On Using More Words Than Anyone Could Possibly Require in One Phrase or Sentence (i.e., Eliminating Wordiness)

Look at the following list of words. Can you see that they are redundant?

- past history—*have you ever known history that wasn't past?*

- true facts—*as opposed to true lies? or false facts? By definition, facts are true.*

- terrible tragedy—*this implies that some tragedies aren't terrible. Is that possible?*

- end result—*by definition, the result comes at the end of something*

- free gift—*if it isn't free, it isn't a gift, and if it's a gift, it is free*

- unexpected surprise—*if it isn't unexpected, it isn't a surprise*

- final outcome—*the outcome is always final, and if it's final, it's the outcome*

Try to eliminate wordiness by doing Exercise 10.2.

EXERCISE 10.2

▶ *Making Sentences Shorter*

While there is nothing grammatically wrong with these sentences, they are far longer than they need to be. Can you shorten them? See some answers in Box 10.4.

1. During that time period, many car buyers preferred cars that were pink in colour and shiny in appearance.

2. The microscope revealed a group of organisms that were round in shape and peculiar in nature.

3. The fundamental reason I'm doing this is to receive remuneration.

4. The need for food that he felt was extreme.

5. At that point in time, she was aware of the wet droplets falling all around her.

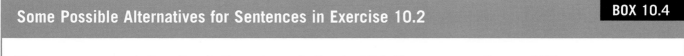

Some Possible Alternatives for Sentences in Exercise 10.2   BOX 10.4

These are some correct alternatives for the sentences in Exercise 10.2. There are many other possibilities.

1. At that time, many car buyers preferred pink and shiny cars.

2. Round, peculiar organisms were seen through the microscope.

3. I'm doing this for money.

4. He was very hungry.

5. Then she realized it was raining.

HOW CAN I GET OVER WRITER'S BLOCK?

Writer's block is that sorry state we reach when, no matter how hard we try, the words won't flow. It's puzzling why this happens; sometimes it seems to make no sense since we have done all the reading, our source material is at our fingertips, the plan is made, and the blank page sits before us. This is the point at which we may start to think, "Maybe I should do more research" or "Maybe I should re-think my plan" or "Maybe I should get a coffee first" or even "How do I get started?"

If this hits you (and it does hit most of us upon occasion), the remedy is to force yourself to start writing. Write anything, even if you think you're making no sense whatsoever. If you can't think of anything else, start with "I have no idea how to get going with this essay, but I want my instructor to know that my essay is going to be about . . ." and go on from there. Don't stop to check sources, although it will help in the long run if you put a note in the margin or a series of asterisks beside any point that you want to check or find a reference for. Don't answer the phone, don't get a coffee, don't take a break, just keep writing. Before too many minutes go by, some usable material will emerge. You can always edit out the nonsense and the poor grammar later, you can organize the material later, and you can look up the pertinent references afterwards. Once the words are flowing, don't stop the flow.

WHAT IS PLAGIARISM?

Plagiarism means presenting someone else's work as your own. This includes using their words without giving them credit, or using their ideas without giving them credit. In effect, it is theft. People who write academic textbooks typically don't make much money from this endeavour, and people are not paid at all for writing peer-reviewed journal articles. Why do they do it then? They do it for several reasons. The major reason is that they are interested in and knowledgeable about the area and want to share their enthusiasm and expertise. In addition, though, this is formally part of the job for most college and university instructors. It's in their contracts. Getting credit for their words and ideas is important to them both professionally and personally. The least we can do is to give them credit for freely sharing their ideas. After all, how would you feel if someone copied your work and passed it off as his or her own?

WHY DO STUDENTS PLAGIARIZE?

Many students plagiarize without even realizing it! Sometimes, when we do library research, we make notes on what we have read, forgetting to jot down whether we copied something straight from an original source or put the original source's ideas into our own words. Then, when it's time to write the whole essay, we may use the exact words in our notes without realizing that we are stealing. That's why it's important to indicate in our notes whether we are using someone else's words or our own.

In rarer cases, some students may actually be trying to get credit for something that isn't theirs, sometimes by copying from a book or article without acknowledging the source, or sometimes by using an essay that someone else wrote. Many students think that the chances of being caught are remote. This was always a questionable idea, but it is even more unlikely now. There are Internet programs (e.g., *turnitin*) that many schools are using to deal with the problems of catching plagiarism. With these programs, students submit their essays to the Internet program itself, which then compares the student's words against a database of hundreds of thousands of articles, books, websites, and other essays that have been submitted. The percentage of exact words that overlap with the student's essay is reported to the instructor of the class, along with the source of the words. Even instructors who do not use such resources check for plagiarism by comparing your work to Internet sources, papers by other students, journal articles, and passages in books.

Plagiarism is considered one of the most serious academic offences, and every college and university has policies for punishing the deed. These punishments can range from getting a mark of zero on the plagiarized piece of work, to failing the course, to expulsion from the institution. In some post-secondary institutions, a note is made on the student's transcript that the student has cheated in some way, and this transcript is permanent. It's what your prospective employer sees when you apply for a job, for example. The consequences of plagiarism can be so great that it simply isn't worth taking the chance. The ethical reasons for not plagiarizing, then, are not the only ones. Make sure that you know your school's policies. Note as well that at many schools, you are not allowed to submit the same paper (even if you wrote it) to more than one class. At Marcel's school, for example, if he takes a class in English poetry next year, he is not permitted to submit the same essay he wrote this year for his English class. (Of course, we wonder why he would want to—he won't get much education if he does this, and education is what it's all about.)

HOW CAN I MAKE SURE THAT I DON'T PLAGIARIZE?

First, when taking notes from original sources, make sure you clearly indicate which of your notes are direct quotes and which are your paraphrasing so that you never plagiarize by accident. Recall, however, that you need to cite your source even when you are paraphrasing. Paraphrasing is an important skill to learn. It means putting something in your own words. Not only do you avoid plagiarism by doing this (assuming you are still giving credit for ideas that are someone else's), but also, you demonstrate to your instructor that you have understood what you have read. Look at the following paragraph, taken from page 1 of a book entitled *Individuality, the impossible project*, by Carlo Strenger, printed in New York by Other Press in 2002:

> Children often fantasize that they could be whoever they want to be, or that one day they will be someone completely different. To some extent this fantasy accompanies us throughout life. The tension between what we want, or could be, and what we are, is one of the defining characteristics of our lives.

Paraphrased, this might read: Especially as children, we all recognize that we could change who and what we are.

If we were to use this in an essay, now, we would not need to put quotes around it, but we would need to give credit to Carlo Strenger. We shall see how to do this in a moment, but first, let's get some practice at paraphrasing in Exercise 10.3.

▶ *Using Your Own Words*

The following are quoted passages taken from indicated sources. Put these passages in your own words.

> A person who speaks too much—someone who describes too busily, who supplies too many details, who repeats and qualifies too many times—presumes without warrant on the right of hearers to build freely and creatively on the speaker's own depictions.

[This is taken from page 85 of a book entitled *Wisdom sits in spaces* by Keith H. Basso, published in Albuquerque, New Mexico, by the University of New Mexico Press in 1996.]

> With varying degrees of explicitness, multiple murderers see themselves as soldiers: small wonder then that they feel neither remorse for their victims, nor regret for launching their bloody crusades.

[This is taken from page 23 of a book entitled *Hunting Humans: The rise of the modern multiple murderer* by Elliott Leyton, published in Toronto, Ontario, by McClelland and Stewart in 1986.]

> Last week, in debt-free Alberta, Premier Ralph Klein made it clear that education would be a top priority this year. In a televised address, he unveiled a tuition freeze and a pledge for a new tuition policy, plus plans for 60,000 new post-secondary spaces by 2020. This is on top of the recently announced grants for education saving plans and a $500-million endowment for medical research.

[This is taken from page 45 of *Maclean's* in an article entitled *Driving a fresh agenda* by Ann Dowsett Johnston, published in Montreal, Quebec, by Rogers Publishing Limited on February 21, 2005.]

> This relationship between price and quantity demanded is true for most goods in the economy and, in fact, is so pervasive that economists call it the law of demand: Other things equal, when the price of a good rises, the quantity demanded of the good falls, and when the price falls, the quantity demanded rises.

[This is taken from pages 67–68 of *Principles of Microeconomics, Third Canadian Edition*, Mankiw, Kneebone, McKenzie, and Rowe, published in Toronto, Ontario, by Thomson Nelson, 2006.]

Compare the way you have paraphrased these segments with your classmates' answers. You will quickly see that there are several options, some of which might convey the ideas more accurately than others.

WHY CAN'T I JUST PUT QUOTATION MARKS AROUND THESE PASSAGES AND USE THEM AS THEY ARE?

Many students feel that using several quotations indicates that they have done the appropriate research and avoids any problems with plagiarism. Unfortunately, some students go overboard with this. The instructors are interested in your words, not solely the words of other authors. The overuse of quotations is often considered "lazy writing" and leaves the instructor wondering if the student really understood the topic. If you paraphrase (i.e., put it in your own words), it makes it clear that you comprehend the material.

WHEN SHOULD I USE QUOTATIONS?

Use quotations very sparingly, only to illustrate your point or when the original writer has phrased something so elegantly that paraphrasing can't do it justice. For example:

> Shakespeare uses small and sharp words to note the basic simplicity and power of the fundamental question of whether one will engage in life or not: "To be or not to be, that is the question . . ." (Hamlet 3.1, 1710)

In this case, the writer made a point about Shakespeare's literary style, and then followed it by an example that illustrated the point clearly.

Each academic discipline has different attitudes about how many quotes should be used. As a rule of thumb, take a look at the literature within the area in which you are writing an essay. Do these writers use any quotes, long quotes, or short quotes? Do they follow every point they make with a quote or only some? These are the general guides for your own writing in each particular subject matter. And, of course, when in doubt, ask your instructor.

REFERENCING AND CITING SOURCES IN THE ESSAY

WHEN AND HOW DO I USE REFERENCES?

Use references to give credit for someone else's idea. For example, you can't talk about evolution without giving credit to Charles Darwin. To do otherwise would be to imply that you thought up the theory of evolution yourself. If you use someone else's words, you must put the words in quotations and give credit to the person whose words these are. How this is done depends upon the subject of the essay. Different subject areas prefer different ways of referencing. In all cases, though, the idea is to give the reader enough information to be able to look up the source you used, to get more detail, to check your interpretation, or perhaps to find other points about the topic. The two most common ways of referencing are APA (American Psychological Association) and MLA (Modern Language Association). We can only briefly review these, but be sure to ask your instructor what form of referencing he or she prefers for the essay assigned, and get a more detailed guidebook or enter the suggested websites for more complete information.

1. APA FORMAT

APA stands for American Psychological Association. This format is used by most social sciences, such as psychology, sociology, economics, geography, political sciences, etc. We will only review some of the basics of the APA format here, but for more information, go to http://www.apastyle.org or consider buying the *Publication Manual of the American Psychological Association* if you are majoring in social sciences or taking several social science classes. Also, your school's library will undoubtedly have a copy of this publication, and may even have handouts for students.

The APA format puts emphasis on the author and the date of publication right in the body of the text, without using footnotes. For example, if you wanted to use this fact in your essay, you should give credit to the source from which you obtained the information. You might say:

According to Hadad and Reed (2006), the author and the date the author published his/her work are given prominence in APA format.

Or you could say:

APA format makes sure that the writer's name and the date of publication are stressed (Hadad & Reed, 2006).

Note that when the names were contained within the sentence, the word "and" was used to join the names: Hadad and Reed. But when the names appear in parentheses, an ampersand (&) is used instead of the word "and." When there is only one author, of course you don't have to worry about this. It gets a little trickier when there are three to five authors: then, the first time you cite them, you must use all their names. After that, you may use only the first author's name and the Latin words *et al.* (meaning "and others"). If you are citing six or more authors of one work, in all cases, you may use only the first author's name followed by *et al.* If the author's name is unknown, cite the name of the publication and the year. What if the author's name is unknown and the article is from the Internet? What if it's something that someone told you? Let's simplify this by using Box 10.5 to see all these possibilities. Box 10.6 demonstrates what the final page of references in APA might look like.

APA Format within the Body of the Essay

BOX 10.5

ONE AUTHOR

- Hadad (2004) claimed that liberal studies courses are highly valued by alumni, who recognize their value many years after graduation.

- Liberal studies courses are highly valued by alumni, who recognize their value many years after graduation (Hadad, 2004).

TWO AUTHORS

- According to Hadad and Reed (2006), the author and the date the author published his/her work are given prominence in APA format.

- APA format makes sure that the writer's name and the date of publication are stressed (Hadad & Reed, 2006).

THREE TO FIVE AUTHORS

- James, Watson, Davis, and Fredericks (1998) found a remarkable difference in the way some people viewed the landscape. It was seen as part of the natives' history, not merely their geography. James et al. (1998) wondered if this could be a part of their value of the land.

- Some people viewed the land as part of their native history, not merely as their geography (James, Watson, Davis, & Fredericks, 1998), leading to the speculation that this attitude might increase the individual's value of the land (James et al., 1998).

SIX OR MORE AUTHORS

- Bacon et al. (1986) claimed that unknown authorities reviewed all the work that had been done in planning for the upcoming festival within the city.

- All the work that had been done in planning for the upcoming festival within the city had been reviewed by unknown authorities (Bacon et al., 1986).

DIFFERENT STUDIES COME TO THE SAME CONCLUSION

- Reed (1999) and Astrabo (2001) both discovered significant effects of wearing prisms while playing the fiddle.

- Wearing prisms while playing the fiddle produces significant effects (Astrabo, 2001; Reed, 1999). [*Note that the authors are listed alphabetically.*]

PERSONAL COMMUNICATION

- It is possible that funding for more daycare will soon become available (P. Martin, personal communication, February 25, 2005).

- P. Martin (personal communication, February 25, 2005) informed the committee that it is possible that funding for more daycare will soon become available.

INFORMATION FROM THE INTERNET

- Eating chocolate is one way that many people cope with stress (Hadad, retrieved February 2005).

- Hadad (retrieved February 2005) says that eating chocolate is one way that many people cope with stress.

INFORMATION FROM THE INTERNET, AUTHOR UNKNOWN

- Sometimes it takes a sophisticated turn of mind to deduce how to take the necessary steps (*How to work miracles*, retrieved April 2005).

The APA Reference Page

BOX 10.6

The last page of your essay should be entitled References. List your references by alphabetical order. To show you how this is done, we will use the sources mentioned in Box 10.5. Note that personal communication is not listed in the reference page since it cannot be retrieved by anyone. Referencing for six or more authors is done the same way as referencing for three to five authors.

Hadad, M. *Website*. Retrieved February 25, 2005, from http://ryerson.ca/~mhadad.

Hadad, M. (2004). The role of liberal studies courses in post-secondary school. *Journal of Magical Psychology, 9³⁄₄,* 442–447.

Hadad, M., & Reed, M. (2006). *The post-secondary experience.* Toronto: Thomson Nelson.

How to work miracles. Retrieved April 1, 2005, from http://magicaljournals.edu.

James, K., Watson, F., Davis, B., & Fredericks, W. (1998). Understanding the land. *Journal of Dirt and Soil, 34,* 67–89.

Reed, M. (1999). Playing with prisms. In B. Spectacles (Ed.), *Understanding Vision* (pp. 121–147). Pittsburgh: University of the Mines Press.

Marcel is writing his psychology essay using APA format. In Box 10.7, we can see what part of the essay might look like.

Marcel's Introduction in APA Format   BOX 10.7

The act of stealing is usually associated with a need to acquire something without having the requisite money. Kleptomania, however, presents stealing in a different light. Kleptomania is an impulse control disorder that is characterized by an urge to steal even items that are not wanted (Barlow & Durand, 2005). This essay will examine what kleptomania is, how often it occurs, what its causes are, and how it can be treated.

"I just wanted to own it. I didn't need it. In fact, I have hundreds at home just like it that I have no use for. But I just had to take it." These are the compelling words of Jane Doe (cited by Haney & Whitside, 2004, 45). Jane Doe has been diagnosed with kleptomania, a disorder that is relatively uncommon and not to be confused with shoplifting: the difference is that shoplifters steal for necessary items for which they cannot pay or for fun, a dare. They are able to resist stealing though. The individual with kleptomania cannot resist so easily (Neille & Donovan, 2001).

---

2. MLA FORMAT

The MLA or Modern Language Association format is used mainly by the humanities, such as English literature and history. This is probably the one you are most familiar with since you probably learned whatever you know about referencing from your high school English teachers who used this style. Again, we can give you only a brief idea of how to use this format, but an excellent guidebook for this is *MLA Handbook for Writers of Research Papers*, 5th ed., by Joseph Gibaldi. A very useful website for this format is http://www.mla.org/style. Your school library or writing centre may have handouts for you that detail this format.

Similar to the APA format, the MLA format uses parentheses rather than footnotes to direct readers to the full citation of a source at the end of the essay. This format emphasizes the author's name and the page on which the quote or idea is to be found. Using MLA, you might say

According to Hadad and Reed (56), the author and the page number are given prominence in MLA format.

Or you could say:

MLA format makes sure that the writer's name and the page number are stressed (Hadad and Reed 56).

If there are more than three authors, only the name of the first author needs to be cited, followed by "et al." or the names of all the authors may be given. In Box 10.8 we'll use the sources that we examined in Box 10.5 to show MLA format.

As you can see, the main difference is that while APA notes the year of publication, MLA cites the page. Once more, the major idea is to direct the reader to a fuller citation where he or she can obtain the original source. In the MLA format, this is a page at the end of the essay entitled "Works Cited." For consistency, in Box 10.9 let's use the same references we used in Box 10.5 to see how MLA format will display the references.

MLA Format within the Body of the Essay

BOX 10.8

ONE AUTHOR

- Hadad (788) claimed that liberal studies courses are highly valued by alumni, who recognize their value many years after graduation.

- Liberal studies courses are highly valued by alumni, who recognize their value many years after graduation (Hadad 788).

TWO AUTHORS

- According to Hadad and Reed (56), the author and the page number are given prominence in MLA format.

- MLA format makes sure that the writer's name and the page number are stressed (Hadad and Reed 56).

THREE OR MORE AUTHORS

- James, Watson, Davis, and Fredericks (145) found a remarkable difference in the way some people viewed the landscape. It was seen as part of the natives' history, not merely their geography. James et al. (147) wondered if this could be a part of their value of the land.

- Some people viewed the land as part of their native history, not merely as their geography (James, Watson, Davis, and Fredericks 145), leading to the speculation that this attitude might increase the individual's value of the land (James et al. 147).

DIFFERENT AUTHORS COME TO THE SAME CONCLUSION

- Reed (65) and Astrabo (89) both discovered significant effects of wearing prisms while playing the fiddle.

- Wearing prisms while playing the fiddle produces significant effects (Astrabo 89; Reed 65). [*Note that the authors are listed alphabetically.*]

PERSONAL COMMUNICATION

- It is possible that funding for more daycare will soon become available (P. Martin, Letter to the author, 25 February 2005).

- P. Martin (Interview, 25 February 2005) informed the committee that it is possible that funding for more daycare will soon become available.

INFORMATION FROM THE INTERNET

- Eating chocolate is one way that many people cope with stress (Hadad, retrieved February 2005).

- Hadad (retrieved February 2005) says that eating chocolate is one way that many people cope with stress.

INFORMATION FROM THE INTERNET, AUTHOR UNKNOWN

- Sometimes it takes a sophisticated turn of mind to deduce how to take the necessary steps (*How to work miracles,* retrieved April 2005).

The MLA Works Cited Page

BOX 10.9

The last page of your essay should be entitled Works Cited. List your references in alphabetical order. To show you how this is done, we will use the sources mentioned in Box 10.5. Note that MLA format requires you to give the first names of the authors, if they are known.

Hadad, Marilyn. *Website.* Retrieved February 25, 2005, from http://ryerson.ca/~mhadad.

Hadad, Marilyn. "The role of liberal studies courses in post-secondary school." *Journal of Magical Psychology* 9¾, (2004): 442–447.

Hadad, Marilyn, and Maureen Reed. *The post-secondary experience.* Toronto: Thomson Nelson, 2006.

How to work miracles. Retrieved April 1, 2005, from http://magicaljournals.edu.

James, Kenneth, et al. "Understanding the land." *Journal of Dirt and Soil* 34, (1998): 67–89.

Reed, Maureen. "Playing with prisms." *Understanding Vision* Ed. Bertram Spectacles. Pittsburgh: University of the Mines Press, 1999. 121–147.

Now let's see what Marcel's essay introduction will look like in MLA format in Box 10.10.

Marcel's Introduction in MLA Format   **BOX 10.10**

The act of stealing is usually associated with a need to acquire something without having the requisite money. Kleptomania, however, presents stealing in a different light. Kleptomania is an impulse control disorder that is characterized by an urge to steal even items that are not wanted (Barlow and Durand 455). This essay will examine what kleptomania is, how often it occurs, what its causes are, and how it can be treated.

"I just wanted to own it. I didn't need it. In fact, I have hundreds at home just like it that I have no use for. But I just had to take it." These are the compelling words of Jane Doe (cited by Haney and Whitside 45). Jane Doe has been diagnosed with kleptomania, a disorder that is relatively uncommon and not to be confused with shoplifting: the difference is that shoplifters steal for necessary items for which they cannot pay or for fun, a dare. They are able to resist stealing though. The individual with kleptomania cannot resist so easily (Neille and Donovan 200).

A SPECIAL NOTE ON OTHER TYPES OF ACADEMIC WRITING

Writing essays for social science and humanities courses are different from writing science papers in some respects. While the same rules hold concerning plagiarism and the importance of planning, good grammar and punctuation, and proofreading, the format may be different. In many cases, a science paper is more like a laboratory report in which there are clearly defined sections with headings, such as Introduction, Apparatus, Subjects, Method, Results, Discussion, Conclusion, etc. It is best to ask your individual instructor of your science course as to how he or she would like the paper written. In the natural and physical sciences, the CBE style (Council of Biology Editors) is commonly used. See this website for details about this style: http://www.monroecc.edu/depts/library/cbe.htm.

At some point in your academic career, you may write a thesis or dissertation. This probably won't occur until you are an upper-year student or even in graduate school. A style that is commonly used—especially for humanities dissertations and papers—is called the Chicago or Turabian Style. It's possible that you may have an instructor who wishes you to use this style for the essay he or she assigns you, though. Details of this style may be found at http://writing.colostate.edu/guides/sources/chicago/.

THE FINISHING STAGE

AM I FINALLY THROUGH WITH MY ESSAY?

No. If you turn in your essay at this point, it is likely that your instructor will return it with a poor mark and numerous comments such as, "What do you mean by this?" "Expand on this point," or "Your argument isn't clear." Your essay needs to be reviewed and perhaps revised before you can hand it in.

If you have been wise enough not to put off writing your essay until close to the due date, you will have a great benefit: you will be able to give yourself a rest from it. Again remember that what is clear to the writer is not necessarily clear to the reader. You are so close to your essay at this point that your arguments may seem self-evident. This may well reflect the fact that you have been absorbed in the topic, not that you have written your arguments well. Put the essay away for a while, for a week at least. Then read it again. Now that you have not been absorbed in the topic for a time, does it still make as much sense and flow as logically as you thought it did? Did you really make the points you thought you made? Were your arguments as reasonable as they seemed to be a week ago? Did you contradict yourself at any point? Does rereading the essay with a fresh mind give you any more ideas or insights that you might want to include? If you have a friend who is willing to read your paper, take advantage of the offer. But stress to your friend that you do not want to be simply patted on the back for your work. A real friend, who wants what is best for you, will be honest with you, indicating areas that are unclear and/or seem contradictory. And if you are a real friend, you will value the honesty and recognize that realistic criticism is what makes us grow and develop. We will discuss more about how to give and take criticism in Chapter 12.

NOW AM I FINISHED?

No. You still need to proofread your essay. This is not the same as reading your paper. As we saw in Chapter 9, when we read, we read for content. For this reason, we may miss writing errors. For example, read this sentence:

At the top

of the world, there are

are many large trees.

Did you notice that the word "are" was repeated? If you read for content, this error would escape your notice. You can't allow such errors to remain in your essay or you may give your instructor the impression that you didn't care enough to proofread the paper properly, or you wrote the paper at the last minute and didn't have time to proofread properly. Neither possibility will make your instructor feel good about your work. Be aware that in many courses, marks are deducted for "literacy"; this means that you can get a lower grade for grammatical, punctuation, word usage, and other literary problems. It's a shame, and it's frustrating to lose marks because you haven't proofread carefully enough! If you have a word processing program that catches spelling and grammatical errors, take advantage of this technology. But note as well that you can't rely on a spellcheck program on your word processor to catch every error. For instance, a computer program will allow you to leave in the word "fist" when you really mean "first." Or you may wind up talking about "meditation" instead of "mediation."

In order to proofread properly, you need to be well rested: tired eyes make mistakes. You cannot proofread at the same speed at which you normally read. Proofreading involves reading every word, without missing any. Recall that when we read for content we do not view every word. Use a strategy such as using your finger to point at every word, sliding a blank piece of paper or a ruler down the page as you read, and/or reading aloud slowly. Become aware of what errors you make most often, then locate and correct these errors. Marcel, for example, found that he often forgot to put commas around "for example" in a sentence such as this one. He also found that the word "too" very often came out as "to." Knowing these characteristic problems made it easier for Marcel to ensure that he made the appropriate corrections before handing in his essays.

HOW WILL MY ESSAY GET GRADED?

Each instructor has his or her own methods of grading but it is highly likely that the elements included in Box 10.11 will be included.

It's hoped Marcel will receive some critical comments as well as a mark from his instructor on each essay. These comments will be very useful to him in the future. If he has any questions about how he could have made his essay better, he should ask the instructor for an appointment to discuss his work. (Hint to Marcel: the question to ask is "How can I improve?" not "Where did I lose marks?" For the most part in post-secondary school, you earn marks, starting from zero; you don't lose marks starting from 100.) Writing essays is a skill that improves with practice, and Marcel will probably become better and better with each essay he writes. So will you. Keep the essays you write in your first year, then re-read them in your last year. You will be amazed at how far you've come!

What Instructors Look For

BOX 10.11

This list includes some of the components that your instructors will be looking for in your essay. Remember that each instructor has his or her own preferences and weightings, though.

CONTENT

- Does this essay respond to the question or meet assignment criteria?
- Is there an adequate engagement with ideas/issues?
- Introduction (strong, weak, or absent)?
- Thesis (weak or absent)?
- Do sub-topics relate to the central thesis?
- Is the development of ideas repetitive or redundant?
- Conclusion (strong, abrupt, or absent)?

WRITING
Instructors will check for errors in:

- Spelling
- Capitalization
- Punctuation

- Word choice, form, and order
- Noun-pronoun agreement
- Subject-verb agreement
- Verb tense
- Sentence fragments, run-on sentences, comma splices
- Clarity of expression
- Paragraphing

PRESENTATION
Don't forget that your presentation of your paper will make a difference as well:

- Cover page
- Paragraph indentation
- Spacing
- Presentation of direct quotations
- Absent or incorrect in-text references
- Bibliography/Works Cited/References
- Page numbering

Advice for Marcel

WHAT TO DO	WHY
Pick a topic you are interested in.	It's hard to sustain interest and to develop an insightful essay on a topic you don't like or don't care about.
Pose questions that need to be answered for this topic.	This will start the search for information in a more focused manner.
Find references that will answer the questions. Find out from your instructor what referencing format he or she prefers.	Unless the essay is strictly a personal opinion piece, points will need to be backed by academic references, with appropriate credit given.
Decide on a major thrust (theme, thesis) for the paper and keep this in front of you as you write.	This will keep your paper focused and help prevent you from going off on tangents or straying from the topic.
Make an essay plan of the points you wish to make in the body of the paper. What do you want to say about the topic? What have you learned about the topic? Use an organization of headings and sub-headings, or a mind map, or a flowchart for the best organization.	This breaks the large body of work into smaller, more manageable sections and keeps you on track, in an orderly fashion. The order of the sections can be changed later, if you wish.

Write. Most people start by writing an introduction to outline where they are going in the essay, but if "getting on stage" is difficult, start anywhere. The introduction can be written later. Use sub-headings, if you like, to keep on track.	This is, after all, the point. Each section can be written in a brief period of time.
Put the sections together, making sure that each section flows from the one before and the order is coherent You may decide to omit the sub-headings at this point.	This puts the essay together and presents the points you wish to make in a clear, logical format that is easy to read.
Write a conclusion, summing up the points you made and suggesting new questions.	This gives more coherence to your paper, letting the reader reflect on whether you have made your case or not, and speculate on more areas of interest.
If possible, put your essay away for a while and reread it a week later.	This allows you to gain perspective on what you have written. Re-reading it when your mind is not immersed in the topic will help you determine whether you have said what you wished to say and may lead you to more insights that you might wish to include.
Ask a trusted friend to read the essay and make critical comments.	You know what you want to say, but having someone else read the essay will indicate whether you really have said it.
Proofread the essay.	Make sure you don't impair your communication and lose marks because of needless typographical, spelling, grammatical, or punctuation errors.

CHAPTER SUMMARY

- Essay writing takes time. Students need time to choose a topic and formulate a thesis, and to understand the mechanics of writing, how to use the library, how to read research papers, how to format their essay, and how to make proper conclusions on their essay topic.

- The first step in writing is to outline what must be done. This outline becomes the beginning of your essay plan. You need to choose a topic, determine what questions need to be answered for this topic, determine what resources are needed to answer these questions, find the resources, and make an outline of the structure of the essay, breaking it into segments.

- In general, the best topic is the one you are most interested in. The traditional journalistic questions of who? what? where? when? and why? can be used to help formulate questions that will guide the arguments and focus on the major point of your essay.

- The outline for your essay may be a written form using hierarchies of headings and sub-headings, or visual forms such as mind maps or flowcharts.

- The point of an essay is to communicate your ideas, but poor grammar, poor punctuation, incorrect word usage, and flawed sentence structure make communication very difficult. Remember that what is obvious to you, the writer, may not be so obvious to the reader. You must help the reader to understand your points, by presenting good arguments in a coherent fashion. Keep it simple.

- The remedy for getting over writer's block is to force yourself to start writing. Write anything, and don't stop, even if you think you're making no sense whatsoever. Before long, some usable material will emerge. Editing, organizing, proofreading, and checking sources can come later.

- Plagiarism means presenting someone else's work as your own. This includes using their words without giving them credit, or using their ideas without giving them credit. Many students plagiarize without even realizing it by making notes on what they have read but forgetting to jot down whether they copied something straight from an original source or put the original source's ideas into their own words. Plagiarism is considered one of the most serious academic offences, and every college and university has policies for punishing the deed.

- Plagiarism is avoided by paraphrasing what has been read and citing the source of the information. Quotations should be used sparingly.

- Referencing can be done using the APA style, the MLA style, the CBE style, or the Chicago style. Check with your instructor to find out which style he or she prefers.

- When you have finished, put the essay away for a few days and then reread it to make sure that your ideas are clearly conveyed and your arguments are logical. Proofread your paper carefully for spelling, grammar, and punctuation errors.

INDIVIDUAL ACTIVITIES

1. Pretend that you're the instructor for this course. How would you assign an essay to your students? Would you give directed questions? Would you leave the topic up to the student? If a student asked you where to start on an essay, what would you say?

2. Suppose you are asked by an instructor to write an essay on poverty. Without having done any research in this area, what information would you need to know? Make a list of questions to ask.

3. Take a personal topic such as "the happiest day of my life" and imagine that you are going to write an essay on it. Try making outlines for this essay in at least two different ways (e.g., chart, written hierarchy of headings and sub-headings, mind map, flow-chart). Which is the most useful and comfortable for you?

GROUP ACTIVITIES

1. As a group, think of redundant phrases that are common in the language. Find an easier way to say what is meant. For example, what is really being said when one says "a pair of twins"? Is this what the speaker means?

2. Take a paragraph from any book (this one will do) and let each person in a group rewrite the paragraph as briefly as possible while retaining its meaning. Look at each other's rewrites. Who has retained the most clarity in the fewest words?

3. As individuals, write one paragraph on "the meaning of life." Then, as a group, read each paragraph to see if the points are clear. In what places do the points made on this

highly abstract topic need to be expanded or made clearer? How often do members of the group say, "I don't see what you're getting at here"?

4. As individuals, write an essay plan on the topic of critical thinking at post-secondary school. Use written hierarchies with headings and sub-headings, or a chart such as the one in Box 10.1, or a mind map as in Figure 10.1 or a flowchart as in Figure 10.2. Compare your plans and discuss how each could be improved.

REFERENCES

Byron, G. (1960). The maid of Athens. in M. Martin (Ed.). *The world's love poetry*. New York: Bantam Books.

Dowler, M. (2002). *Help! With writing*. Toronto: Prentice-Hall.

Finnbogason, J., & Valleau, A. (2002). *A Canadian writer's pocket guide* (2nd ed.). Toronto: Thomson Nelson.

Norton, S., & Green, B. (2004). *The bare essentials Form B* (5th ed.). Toronto: Thomson Nelson.

UNDERSTANDING RESEARCH DATA

The Case of Brandon

▶ Brandon has just received an assignment in his Introduction to Environmental Science class requiring him to evaluate the effect of temperature change on sturgeon fish populations. The instructor has provided two articles on the topic and Brandon is to find a third article. Brandon must formulate an argument from these articles about the long-term effects of global warming on this fish population. Finding the article was not difficult since Brandon had attended a voluntary library orientation session in his first week at school. However, he has begun to read the articles and is having difficulties understanding them. First, each article cites statistics to support the author's viewpoint. One article presents the results of an expert survey, another article uses statistics to make some sort of prediction, and the article Brandon found seems to be an experiment. Brandon is not quite sure how to interpret the findings. He wonders if "expert" opinion can be flawed. He wonders about the probability of predictions made from statistics coming true. Finally, he wonders how to understand the statistics provided in the experiment he is reading.

One of the most difficult tasks you will face in post-secondary school is interpreting the value of the many research articles that you will be required to read. Learning to interpret the value of research articles is part of becoming a critical thinker (more on this in Chapter 7) and critical thinking is an important part of post-secondary success. It is not at all surprising that Brandon is having difficulty in interpreting the articles for his essay. Not all articles are equal; some give flawed evidence, some give opinion rather than evidence, and some show strong biases. In other words, not all evidence is equal. Evidence ranges from quotes from experts to anecdotal evidence, historical evidence, and statistical evidence. After a critical review of some articles, you may find that some lack appropriate support for opinion. For example, just because an "expert" claims that chewing gum makes you smarter does not mean it is true. While we will examine important aspects of interpreting research in this chapter, you could gain further insights into research methods by reading Minium and King (2003) and Kantowitz, Roediger, and Elmes (2001).

DATA

data
information that is presented in numerical or verbal/descriptive form

quantitative data
numerical information

qualitative data
non-numerical information

empirical article
an article containing data, which is either analyzed or collected by the author

literature review
a summary of studies on a particular topic

The word **data** simply means information. Information can be numerical, such as percentages or averages. Such data are called **quantitative data**. For example, Janice is the chair of the English Students' Council. She is interested in knowing how many students would like to have increased social activities. She surveys the students with a single yes/no question. She finds that 70 percent of the students surveyed want more social activities. Because Janice used a number to describe the desire for increased social activities, we say that Janice collected quantitative data. Data can also involve no numbers. Data can be people's verbal or written descriptions of an experience or event. This is called **qualitative data**. For example, John is the vice-chair of the English Students' Council. He too is interested in knowing if the students want increased social activities, so he interviews students. If the students say that they are interested in increased activities, John asks them what types of activities they would like. Some students would like more parties, some would like more speakers, some would like a pub night, and others would like "meet and greets" with their instructors. Note that the data John collected did not involve numbers but rather descriptions of events, so this is qualitative data. In many studies, both quantitative and qualitative data are collected. This is because quantitative data can tell you about how much support you have while the qualitative data can give you insight into what people want.

Articles in which data are collected and/or analyzed are often called **empirical**. In some empirical articles, the author collects and analyzes data; and in others, the author analyzes data from other sources, such as government databases. In the second case, while the author did not collect data, the raw or unanalyzed data was provided to the author to analyze.

Often instructors require their students to find empirical articles for their essays. This is true in Brandon's case. His instructor has asked the students to find only empirical articles for their essays. Brandon is not sure what this means so he asks the instructor in class. The instructor replies that she wants the students to use articles in which some form of data collection or analysis was performed, however, data collected could be either qualitative or quantitative. She says that she does not want the students to use articles where only secondary sources are cited, that is, where an author is talking about someone else's data or the author is presenting a **literature review** (a summary of studies on a particular topic). In addition, she reminds students to use proper sources found through an academic library and not through the Internet, newspapers, or magazines. Finally, she reminds students about the difference between opinion and evidence. She says that when an author states a theory or makes a statement without providing evidence, this is only an opinion and is not considered academic proof. To determine whether a theory is valid, some form of evidence should be provided in the article. She also tells her students that even opinions or theories that have supportive evidence do not result in proof of that theory or opinion. This is because evidence can be flawed, misinterpreted, or limited (i.e., true under only certain circumstances). She tells her students that it is their job to recognize situations in which evidence is not really providing support for a theory.

INTERPRETING EVIDENCE

HOW DO PEOPLE INTERPRET DATA?

observational studies
studies in which data are collected to describe an event, an individual, or groups of subjects

correlation studies
studies in which data collected are used to predict events

There are three types of research studies in which data are collected. These include observational studies, correlation studies, and experimental studies. In general, **observational studies** are meant to describe events, **correlation studies** are meant to predict events, and **experimental studies** are meant to explain events. Each type of study has both advantages and disadvantages, and each type of study has rules of interpretation.

OBSERVATIONAL STUDIES

experimental studies
studies in which data collected are used to explain events or behaviours

All observational studies have the same purpose: to describe. These studies can describe human and animal behaviour, individual opinion, events, and experiences. There are three types of observational studies: naturalistic observation, case studies, and surveys.

WHAT IS NATURALISTIC OBSERVATION?

naturalistic observation
an observational technique in which research subjects are studied in their natural setting

In **naturalistic observation**, the researcher observes the subjects of the investigation in their natural environment. For example, someone who is interested in describing the effects of non-governmental agencies in offering aid in a Costa Rican town may go to this town and observe citizens who live in that town. The subjects of naturalistic observation are persons, groups, or events. There have been many famous naturalistic observation studies, which have led to a better understanding of events and animals in their natural habitat. For example, the work of Jane Goodall in studying primates in the wild has led to greatly increased knowledge and social awareness of these fascinating creatures (Goodall, 1998).

operational definition
defining in terms of observable events or actions, e.g., *sad* is defined as crying, complaining, etc.

In a naturalistic observation study, the researcher defines what she/he will be studying, then studies the subjects by watching them and taking notes. For example, Eleanor Davis, a fourth-year early childhood education student, wonders if children from divorced families are aggressive and decides to use naturalistic observation to investigate. The first priority of this study would be to define what is meant by *aggressive*. In proper research all terms have an **operational definition**. This means that things are defined in terms of observable events. The problem with the word *aggressive* is that it could mean different things to different people. If someone told you that a child was aggressive, you might think that the child hits other people, or the child swears, or the child makes mean faces, or the child spits, etc. But to other people, the assumption might be simply that the child is disobedient. So, (in this example) the problem is that the word *aggressive* could mean different things to different people. Thus, Eleanor must operationally define *aggressive* in terms of actions so that her readers understand what she means. In the case of defining *aggressive*, actions could be yelling, punching, hitting, or poking. These are things that you see or hear and can therefore record. Actions cannot be things like feelings. You cannot see a feeling. For example, you cannot see "feeling annoyed." Yet, you can see and/or hear clenching fists, swearing, and talking curtly. Thus, when you define *annoyed*, you need to use observable, measurable, and verifiable behaviours such as fist clenching, swearing, and talking curtly. Try to operationally define the following words: *learn*, *stress*, and *forget*. Then see Exercise 11.1 to compare your definition to ours.

▶ *Operational Definitions*

Term	Operational Definition
Learn	The individual correctly identifies an event, correctly spells a word, etc. (Note you may have chosen different learning behaviours but they are correct only if they are observable.)
Stress	The individual is complaining, hand wringing, says "I am upset," etc. (As long as the behaviours you chose are observable they are correct.)
Forget	The person makes errors in retelling an event, does not arrive with required materials, etc. (You are correct if the behaviours are observable.)

Note that when defining a word, some people might not agree that what you chose represents the behaviour. For example, some might argue that hand wringing represents "worried" not "stressed." That might be true, and this is why in most studies a number of observable reactions are used to measure a feeling (e.g., high heart rate *and* hand wringing to measure "stress"). It is also why you need to carefully examine the operational definitions used in articles you read. If researchers defined "being anxious" as a heart rate increase, we could argue that the heart rate increases due to other emotions as well. Thus, we can argue that their definition of *anxious* is not appropriate, other factors (confounds) might have caused the heart rate increase.

In the study of aggression in children of divorce, Eleanor decided to define *aggression* as physical aggression and specified that aggression is when the children hit, punch, kick, slap, bite, push, or spit. Eleanor and her supervisor, Instructor Bellingham, arranged to go to a centre where children of divorced families have weekly activities. Eleanor plans to observe the children in 10-minute blocks of time and has brought an observation sheet, shown in Box 11.1, to record each aggressive event. Notice that the sheet consists of tick boxes where Eleanor simply makes a tick mark for every incident she sees.

When Eleanor arrives at the centre for the first day of observation, she finds that she cannot collect data because the children won't leave her alone. The children are not acting naturally because they are curious about her presence at the centre. This often happens in naturalistic observation studies. To combat this problem, Eleanor decides to come to the centre for several days, and just sit in the back of the room. She does not play with or speak to the children and eventually they get used to her being there and go back to playing with one another and ignoring Eleanor. On the third day, Eleanor starts to collect data, watching children in 10-minute blocks and making ticks when she sees aggressive behaviour. Eleanor collects data for one week. Afterwards, she analyzes her data and finds that on average there were five aggressive incidents every 10 minutes.

Example of a Naturalistic Observation Sheet   BOX 11.1

November 16, 2006
Day 3 Observations at the Living Centre
Playgroup *A*: 15 Children

Time	Hit	Punch	Kick	Slap	Bite	Push	Spit
9:00–9:10	✔✔		✔			✔✔✔✔✔	
9:11–9:20	✔	✔✔		✔	✔	✔✔✔✔✔✔	✔
9:21–9:30	✔✔✔	✔	✔✔	✔	✔✔	✔✔✔✔	

Each tick mark represents one incident of the behaviour in the group

confound
something that may affect the outcome of a study, which was not intended to be part of the study

limitation
something that precludes the researcher from generalizing the study results to those not included in the study

Eleanor uses these data to describe the aggressive tendencies in children of divorce. She notes that most often they push one another and they almost never spit. However, when she presents her data to Instructor Bellingham, he asks Eleanor to discuss confounds and limitations in her data. Eleanor is taken aback and asks Instructor Bellingham what he means. A **confound**, he explains, is something, an extra factor, that might affect the outcome of the study. For example, if their teacher punishes the children for aggression, they might not be aggressive in the playgroup but are aggressive at home. The punishment at school would be a confound. A **limitation** is something that limits the study results from being applied to children not in the study. For example if the children in the playgroup were all male, their results might not represent female children. Eleanor goes back to the library and sits down to think about possible things that could have affected her data. Well, there were equal numbers of boys and girls in the playgroup so it is possible that the outcome could have been different for only one gender. That is definitely a limitation. Also, the children in her playgroup were all five-year-olds. It is possible that children at older or younger ages show different levels of aggression, another limitation. In addition, in the playgroup, the playgroup teacher talked every day about feelings and that could have affected the study outcome. This seems to be a confound and a limitation. The talk about feelings might have reduced aggression and perhaps these children in the playgroup are not like other children of divorce who are not in playgroups. Eleanor makes a list of limitations and confounds in the study and discusses each in her research paper. She concludes that five-year-old children in playgroups where feelings are discussed show an average of five incidents of aggression every ten minutes as a group. However, she notes that there were limitations in her study and discusses each.

WHEN READING A NATURALISTIC OBSERVATION STUDY, WHAT SHOULD I LOOK FOR?

When reading a naturalistic observation study, you should look for several things.

First, look at the operational definitions provided in the study. Often the researcher will not give a definition, so you should look at what the researcher measured. For example, suppose you were reading a study in your economics class about how women have coped in Russia since the fall of communism. The researcher argues that women are coping poorly. As evidence, the researcher shows that live births per woman have fallen since communism ended. In other words, the researcher is suggesting that low birth rates mean poor coping. We could argue that low birth rate is not a good indicator of poor coping. Many factors affect birth rates. For example, if the researcher did not examine education rates of women in Russia since the fall of communism, we have discovered a confound. Women who become educated often put off having children and thus birth rates fall. If more women in Russia are becoming educated, this might represent good coping.

Second, along with examining the validity of operational definitions, you should think of possible confounds in the study you are reading. What factors could have affected the outcome of the study?

Third, you should also think of limitations of the study. If the Russian study only presents data from Moscow, these data may not well represent women from rural Russian communities.

Finally, you should look at the interpretation of the research. If this is an observational study, the researcher can only describe women's behaviour; he or she cannot explain why it happened; only that it did. If birth rates have declined, the researcher can only state that since the fall of communism, birth rates for women in Moscow have declined but cannot say why. Box 11.2 gives some guidelines for reading observational studies.

WHAT IS A CASE STUDY?

case study
an observational technique in which an individual or single event is studied

In a **case study**, observations are usually taken from a single event or individual. For example, sometimes a case study is made of a patient who has an unusual medical condition. The patient may be interviewed, medically monitored, or observed. Alternatively, a researcher might examine a single event that occurred in the world. For example, a researcher might look

What to Look for in Observational Articles

BOX 11.2

Naturalistic Observation

Operational definition	What is their definition for the study?
	What are they measuring?
	Is the measure appropriate (valid) to the definitional term (e.g., does low birth rate equal poor coping)?
	Should other things be included in their definition?
The subjects	Who are the subjects?
	How many subjects are there?
	What are the subject specifics (e.g., gender, age, location, etc.)?
	Do these represent the greater population (e.g., if the subjects are all five years old, can they represent all children)?
Confounds	Is anything happening in the study that might have affected the results?
Limitations	To whom can these results be generalized?
	Do the results represent a small group (e.g., all five-year-olds), the study group, or other people (all children)?
Interpretation	How did the researcher interpret the results (should be descriptive only)?

Case Study

Validity	Are the researchers measuring what they say they are measuring?
Interpretation	Is the interpretation only descriptive?
	Is the researcher claiming cause when cause cannot be claimed from a case study?

Survey Study

Sample	Who are the survey participants?
	Do they well represent the population of interest?
	Were they randomly selected?
	Is there a sufficient number of participants?
The questions	What types of questions were used?
	Did the questions show bias?
	Were response scales in rating questions balanced?
	Did each question use clear wording and ask only one thing?
The interpretation	Were the results descriptive?
	Did the author attempt to infer cause, and if so, on what basis (speculation, from combining two or more questions, etc.)?

at the spending habits of North Americans the week before New Year's Eve in the year 2006. Usually extensive qualitative and quantitative data are collected on the individual or event. For example, Ross, Olson, and Gore (2003) wondered if a blind musician with perfect pitch utilized different areas of the brain for music than do musicians with perfect pitch who are not blind. Such a person (blind, a musician, and having perfect pitch) would be rare and Ross et al. decided to conduct a case study on one such individual. They used magnetic resonance imaging (fMRI), a method to view active areas of the brain, to examine the workings of this individual's brain when he was analyzing music. They found that some unique areas of the brain were used by this individual that were not used in sighted musicians. Thus, this study showed particularly interesting findings about a blind musician and the researchers suggested that in blindness the brain might re-organize itself. While these results are intriguing, they are limited to description because this is a case study.

There are both advantages and disadvantages to case studies. The main advantages are that case studies offer a way to examine, in detail, individuals with rare conditions (a blind musician with perfect pitch) or rare events (attitudes of people to the millennium). In addition, in most other kinds of studies, only a limited amount of time is spent with the subjects, but in case studies, usually extensive observations are taken of the study subject over a much longer period of time. Thus, you can find out many things about the subject that you might not have known from a larger sample. For example, you could ask the subject how he processes pitch, watch him process, learn more about the subject's everyday life and his life as a musician, etc. In other words, you can learn things that in a larger study with many subjects (participants) you would not have the time or ability to learn. Therefore, the subjects in case studies can often provide you with insight.

On the other hand, there are some real disadvantages to case studies. First, data may not apply to other people. In the study above, we wonder if this single person represents other blind musicians with perfect pitch. Even if this musician's brain reorganized itself, does that mean *all* blind people have such re-organization? It is possible that this individual is unique and cannot represent others. Hence, the study has limited value in applying it to other blind people, but could become the basis for a larger study of people who are blind. In addition, while case studies provide much insight, like all observational studies they only provide descriptions of people or events and do not explain why things happen. For example, in the case of this musician, we do not know why his brain reorganized itself. It is possible the blindness caused the re-organization, but it is possible that his brain was different for other reasons that had nothing to do with blindness. To find out if blindness is the cause of brain re-organization, one would have to conduct a different type of study (experimental).

WHEN READING A CASE STUDY WHAT SHOULD I LOOK FOR?

survey
an observational technique where subjects (usually larger groups) are interviewed or given a questionnaire

sample
a small group meant to represent a larger group, for example, a small group of Canadians meant to represent all Canadians

As in any study, you need to review what data collection techniques were used: an interview, fMRI, physiological measures such as heart rate, etc? You should ask yourself if these measures seem to suit the question being asked in the study; in other words, are they valid? For example, if someone measured hat size and said it was a measure of intelligence, we would argue that this is not a valid measure of intelligence. Second, you might ask yourself if the collection techniques are reliable (could someone else use this method to produce similar results?). Third, in a case study you need to closely examine the interpretation of the results. Like all observational studies they should only be descriptive. Cases do not easily apply to the larger population as described above. These issues are outlined in Box 11.2.

WHAT ARE SURVEY STUDIES?

population
the larger group from which a sample is drawn, for example, all Canadians

The most popular of all observational methods is the survey. A **survey** is a questionnaire, usually given to groups of people to solicit opinions, experiences, personal information, etc. Usually the researcher wishes to apply the information from the survey group (**sample**) to the **population** (others of similar background). When conducting a survey, there are many important issues surrounding the sample, the questions, and the interpretation of the study results.

WHAT ISSUES SHOULD I BE AWARE OF WITH SURVEY SAMPLES?

representative sample
the chosen sample has the same characteristics as the population

random sample
sample is chosen such that every member of the population has an equal chance of being in the sample

In general, we say that the sample (survey group) must be representative, random, and sufficiently large. A **representative sample** must represent the population of interest. That is, if you were interested in knowing how first-year post-secondary students felt about student services, the sample should be first-year students. You would not include upper-year students in your sample.

Second, the sample should be random. A **random sample** is chosen in a random fashion. That is, we select students such that all first-year students have a chance of being included in the sample. We may do this by deciding that we will survey every third student on the full list of first-year students, or by taking all first-year student names, putting them in a hat and blindly selecting the students for the sample. The point is we do not choose our friends or people we know for our survey, as they are not a random selection. For example, if you decided to run a survey of first-year students' attitudes towards science and used the people in your introductory physics class, what you might find is that students who choose to take physics are not necessarily like students who do not choose to take physics. Students in your physics class would be expected to have much more positive attitudes towards science and might not well represent the students who do not take physics.

The third issue about a sample is complicated—how large should the sample be? This is a difficult question because in part it depends on the population. If your population is all voters in Ontario, your sample will need to be at least 400 individuals to ensure accuracy (Fowler, 1993). However, suppose that you have a questionnaire for students in your former grade 12 class. There are only 104 students in the class. In cases like this, it is a good idea to survey all students, if possible. In general, small samples are less accurate in representing populations than large ones. However, even small samples can be quite accurate if there are *high* levels of agreement among sample participants (Fowler, 1993). Yet, you need to be very cautious about the accuracy of a small sample in representing opinion of the population.

WHAT TYPES OF QUESTIONS SHOULD I INCLUDE ON A SURVEY?

open-ended question
a question in which no response options are given

choice-oriented question
a question in which some response options are provided

rating scale question
a question in which a numerical or verbal scale is used to represent opinion

Another area of importance in surveys is question design. The design of the questions can strongly influence the participant responses.

First, questions can be open-ended, choice-oriented, or rating scales. For example, if you were interested in learning about student attitudes towards your course instructor, you might design a survey question to poll the class. You could use an **open-ended question**, a question in which no response options are given and the students can write their own answers. You could use a **choice-oriented question** in which you provide some response options and the students choose the one that represents their opinion, or you could use a **rating scale question** in which the students could rate the professor on that scale (say from one to ten, where ten represents excellent). Box 11.3 shows some sample questions.

Survey Question Types   BOX 11.3

OPEN-ENDED QUESTIONS
How do you feel the instructor performed in the areas of course management, knowledge of material, fairness of tests, and sensitivity to students?

CHOICE QUESTIONS
Circle the items in which you feel the course instructor performed satisfactorily:

Course management

Knowledge of material

Test fairness

Sensitivity to students

RATING SCALE
Circle the number that best represents your opinion, where 1 = Disagree, 2 = Somewhat disagree, 3 = Somewhat agree, and 4 = Agree.
Do you agree that the instructor satisfactorily:

Managed the course?	1	2	3	4
Knew course material?	1	2	3	4
Gave fair tests?	1	2	3	4
Was sensitive to students?	1	2	3	4

Depending on the type of question given, very different responses will be made. Usually open-ended questions give more detailed answers but the answers are very descriptive so they can be difficult to summarize. Choice questions are easy to summarize (e.g., 90 percent of students were satisfied with course management), but they give very little descriptive information (why are they satisfied?). Rating scale questions allow the readers to show their level of satisfaction (20 percent of students are dissatisfied, 10 percent are somewhat dissatisfied, 50 percent are somewhat satisfied, and 20 percent are satisfied), however, they do not tell you why students might agree or disagree. Many researchers follow rating scale questions with open-ended questions to help them understand rating responses (e.g., If you disagree, why?).

WHAT BIASES SHOULD I LOOK FOR IN SURVEY QUESTIONS?

You can find numerous biases in survey questions. Most frequently, biases stem from unbalanced rating scales, wording, question misunderstanding, and failure to accurately predict one's own behaviour.

Rating scale question responses can show bias at times. A friend of the authors, Ron Collis, ran an experiment in his high school civics class in which students were asked to rate how satisfied they were growing up in Bowmanville, Ontario. He gave half the class the following scale choices: 1 = Extremely satisfied, 2 = Very satisfied, 3 = Satisfied, and 4 = Dissatisfied; the other half could choose from: 1 = Extremely dissatisfied, 2 = Very dissatisfied, 3 = Dissatisfied, and 4 = Satisfied. Note that the first scale emphasizes satisfaction and the second scale emphasizes dissatisfaction. The results indicated that students receiving the first scale were satisfied and the second were dissatisfied. Since students were reluctant to choose extremes on scales, these unbalanced scales (e.g., more negative than positive options) led to very different responses. Thus, to solicit accurate responses it is important to use balanced scales (equal positive and negative options).

The wording of the questions can also lead to bias in responses. For example, the authors recently watched a local government council meeting in which a community member was presenting survey results. The member had found that only a small number of townspeople supported a heritage designation for their town. However, it was later revealed that the question people were asked was something like "Do you support having a heritage designation that would allow council to control your property and reduce your property value?" Of course very few people would support this position, whether they agreed with a heritage designation or not. Thus, in any review of a survey study, it is important to examine the questions that were asked.

It is important that the reader easily understand the words in the survey questions. For example, if someone were asked "Do you feel town council did a good job and kept taxes low?" the reader would have difficulty clearly answering. First, no time frame was given. Did a good job when—forever, last year, last meeting? Second, the word *good* is difficult to interpret (were they polite, did they work many hours, did they answer their e-mail?). Third, two questions are asked here—one about the job of town council, and the other about taxes. It is possible to be happy about one and not the other.

Finally, it is important not to ask people to predict their future behaviour with survey questions. For example, someone might ask the question, "If the town built a dinner theatre, would you attend?" Likely, people would say yes but many would later not attend. It is best to judge people on their past behaviour, rather than on what they say they will do in the future.

In summary, when reading articles that contain surveys, questions need to be reviewed for bias. The review should be conducted to ensure that questions are simple, have a single meaning, use words readers understand, ask only a single question, and ask about the present/past, not the future. To ensure you understand what you are looking for in reviewing a survey within an article, review Box 11.4. This is a poorly written survey in which the survey errors are highlighted.

Common Survey Errors

BOX 11.4

Please answer the following questions about your experiences as a resident of Burkville.

1. What is your gender?
   a. Female
   b. Male

2. How often do you go out? ◄———— *"Go out" has multiple meanings*
   a. Every day/night of the week
   b. 5–6 times a week
   c. 3–4 times a week
   d. 1–2 times a week
   e. Rarely or never

3. Circle your *two* most favourite activities to do in Burkville.
   a. Go to the skateboard park ◄———— *Limited response options "Four corners" is jargon*
   b. Go to the movies
   c. Go to the firehouse
   d. Hang out at the four corners ◄
   e. Hang out at the Burkville Mall

4. If a great rock group were to put on a show at the Sports Complex would you attend?
   a. Yes ◄———— *Respondents are not reliable at predicting their behaviour*
   b. No

5. Since there are long delays between buses and it is often quicker to walk because the bus routes wind all over the place, do you think Burkville Transit is *not* very convenient?

   Biased wording, confusing

6. Do you think most store owners treat young people respectfully and have good reason to limit the number of teens that they allow in their store at one time.

   Two questions in one

Source: Reprinted by permission of Ronald Collis.

Like all observational research, the results of any survey are descriptive. They describe the opinions and experiences of the sample and that sample is used to represent the opinions and experiences of the population.

WHEN READING A SURVEY STUDY, WHAT SHOULD I LOOK FOR?

In general, when reading survey studies you should examine the sample, the questions, and the interpretation of results. Brandon, the student you met in the case study, is required to read an article that surveys expert opinion. Brandon will need to determine if the sample is representative of other experts, randomly selected, and large enough to represent the population of experts in this area. Further, Brandon needs to examine the types of questions asked and look for any possible biases in the questions asked. Brandon should be very skeptical of this expert survey if it reports more than a description of expert opinion. This is summarized in Box 11.2.

CORRELATION STUDIES

WHAT IS A CORRELATION STUDY?

variable
anything that can change, such as loudness, levels of aggression, amount of salt in water, etc.

The purpose of a correlation study is to predict an event or show a relationship between two items or variables. A **variable** is anything that can change, such as room lighting (high, low, medium), age, time to complete a problem (faster or slower time), etc. Correlation involves examining how two things relate to one another. For example, if you were writing an essay about the relationship between media violence and aggression in young adults, you might read an article by Uhlmann and Swanson (2004). This article shows that there is a significant correlation ($r = +0.35$) between exposure to violent video games and self-reported aggression. You might wonder what this means. In correlation, we first try to see if two variables are related and second, to see if one variable can predict change in the other variable. For example, you want first to see if there is any relationship between playing violent video games and aggression in young adults, and then to know if we can predict whether adults who play many violent video games will be more aggressive than those who play few violent video games.

While there are many different types of correlation, we will be discussing only one type, called the Pearson correlation, which is generally denoted by the letter r. Pearson correlation measures linear relationships. That is, the relationship between two variables can be described by a straight line: as one variable increases, the other increases or decreases. For example as people play more video games (one variable), aggression (the other variable) continues to increase. However, note that not all relationships between variables are linear. For example, the relationship between intelligence and creativity is not linear. People with low intelligence tend to be less creative than those with high intelligence. However, as intelligence continues to increase, creativity does not (Sternberg, 2003). Therefore the relationship between intelligence and creativity is not linear, but a relationship still exists.

scatterplot
a graph in which each dot represents a single score on each item of interest

Usually researchers graphically portray correlation by plotting a **scatterplot**, which is a graph in which each dot on the graph represents a single score on each item of interest. For example, suppose we were interested in the relationship between studying for an exam and the exam grades. We might ask students to report the number of hours they studied for the exam and then, once they have taken the exam, to record their grades. This is shown in Table 11.1. A scatterplot of these data is shown in Figure 11.1. For each student, the number of hours studied is plotted against the grade on the exam. For example, Mike studied for one hour and received a grade of 20, while Miranda studied for nine hours and received a grade of 90.

TABLE 11.1 **Student Hours Studied and Their Exam Grades**

STUDENT	HOURS STUDIED	GRADE RECEIVED
Kim	4	55
Phil	6	68
Ron	7	70
Miranda	9	90
Helen	2	25
Mike	1	20
George	9	75

FIGURE 11.1   Scatterplot of Hours Studied vs. Grades

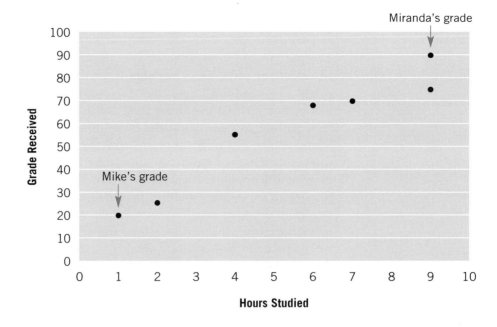

This relationship between the number of hours studied and the grade received can be expressed as a correlation number and it is this number that you will often encounter in your textbook, at work, in the media, and in articles you are required to read for your classes. The correlation number (r) can be calculated but this is beyond the scope of this book. Rather, we will describe the meaning of this number here. The correlation between hours studied and student grades as shown in Figure 11.1 is $r = +0.97$. Correlation (r) consists of two basic concepts: a statement of the relationship between the variables (study hours and exam grade), and a statement of predictability of this relationship (How well can you predict grades from hours studied?). Thus, there are two elements to any correlation: a sign (either + or −) that indicates the type of relationship and a number (varying between 0 and 1) that determines the strength of the relationship and the value of the prediction.

WHAT DOES THE POSITIVE OR NEGATIVE SIGN MEAN IN CORRELATION?

positive correlation
when two variables increase or decrease at the same time

negative correlation
when one variable increases while the other decreases

The sign in a correlation has no numeric value. It does *not* mean less than or greater than zero. The sign in correlation expresses a relationship between two items. A **positive correlation** sign (+) means that as one variable *increases*, the second variable *increases*. For example, you found $r = +0.97$ correlation between the number of hours studied for an exam and exam grade. The positive sign means that as the number of hours studied increases, the exam grade increases. A **negative correlation** sign (−) means that as one variable *increases*, the second item *decreases*. Suppose you had a negative correlation ($r = -0.97$) between number of hours watching television and exam grade. The negative correlation shows that as the number of hours watching television increases, the grade decreases.

In another example, Uhlmann and Swanson (2004) found a +0.35 correlation between playing violent video games and self-reported aggression. The positive sign means that as the number of violent video games played increased, the self-reported aggression also increased.

WHAT DOES THE NUMBER IN CORRELATION TELL YOU?

The number in correlation represents how strong the relationship is between the two variables and thus how well we can predict one variable from the other. The number in correlation can run from 0 to 1. The number 1 (+ or −) represents the best possible relationship between the two variables (you can predict changes in one variable from changes in the other). The number 0 represents the worst possible relationship (no linear relationship between the two variables, thus no ability to predict). The closer the correlation number is to 0, the weaker the relationship between the two variables and the poorer the prediction of one variable from the other. The closer the number is to 1 (+ or −) the stronger the relationship and the better the prediction. As a rule of thumb, correlations (both positive and negative) between 0 and 0.4 are considered weak relationships and thus poor accuracy predictors, correlations between 0.5 and 0.7 are considered moderate relationships and thus moderate accuracy predictors, and correlations of 0.8 or greater are considered strong relationships and thus good accuracy predictors. The correlation between study hours and grades is +0.97. The 0.97 shows us that there is a strong relationship between study hours and grades and we would say that we can accurately predict (good accuracy) grades from study hours. Uhlmann and Swanson have a correlation of +0.35 between playing violent video games and self-reported aggression. We would say that this is a weak relationship and thus the number of violent video games played will not accurately predict (poor accuracy) self-reported aggression.

WHEN READING A CORRELATION STUDY, WHAT SHOULD I LOOK FOR?

In general, what we discussed above about the sign and the number is the interpretation of correlation; however, there are a few other important factors that must be remembered. In summary, when viewing correlation you need to first interpret the sign (direction of the relationship), and second, interpret the number (the strength of the relationship and the accuracy of prediction). It is a good idea when reviewing media and articles that use correlation to first interpret their meaning. To ensure that you understand correlation, review Exercise 11.2. This box gives you four examples of correlations and asks you to interpret both the sign and the number. Once you have done so, look at the answer column and compare your answers. When you interpret correlation, try to use easy-to-understand words.

In interpreting correlation, there is one other factor that you need to consider: you cannot make causal statements about two variables based on correlation. For example, you might find a strong negative correlation between eating ice cream and the amount of clothing worn by people. This is interpreted that as the amount of ice cream eating increases, the amount of clothing worn decreases. This does *not* mean that eating ice cream causes people to wear fewer clothes. Certainly there are many other reasons why people might eat more ice cream and wear fewer clothes at the same time (hot weather, for example). This is also evident in the Uhlmann and Swanson paper. The study does show that as playing violent video games increases, so does self-reported aggression. However, you cannot say that the video games caused the aggression. It is possible that other factors cause the aggression. Perhaps people who are already aggressive play aggressive video games. These people may have been aggressive before they ever played a video game, and because they are aggressive, they like violent video games. Or perhaps these people have poor social skills, causing them both to self-report more aggression and to prefer violent video games. The point here is that correlations can help predict but they cannot explain cause. It is important when reading a correlation study that you examine the author's interpretation. Frequently, correlation is misinterpreted as causal.

EXERCISE 11.2   ▶ *Interpreting Correlation*

Explain in Easy-to-Understand Words	Answer
Dr. Jones has found an $r = -0.6$ correlation between taking vitamins and intelligence	The negative sign means that as the amount of vitamins increases, intelligence test scores decrease. The 0.6 means that this is a moderate relationship, meaning that it is a moderately accurate predictor. You can predict with moderate accuracy that those taking increased vitamins will show reduced intelligence scores.
Professor Hudson has found an $r = +0.8$ correlation between class attendance and exam grades	The positive sign means that as attendance increases, exam grades increase. The number 0.8 means that this is a strong relationship, meaning that there is good accuracy in predicting grades from class attendance.
Research assistant Dodds has found an $r = -0.2$ correlation between parental scolding and child academic success	The negative sign means that as scolding increases, academic success decreases. The number 0.2 indicates that this is a weak relationship and thus the prediction of poor academic success from scolding is poor in accuracy.
A researcher has found a correlation of 0 between eating hot dogs at a baseball game and getting sick	This shows that there is no relationship between eating hot dogs and getting sick. You cannot predict sickness from hot dog eating.

Brandon, the student you met in the case study, is reviewing an article that is a correlation study. In order to effectively evaluate this study, Brandon will need to first learn to interpret correlation, and then interpret the correlations presented in the article. In addition, Brandon will need to review the interpretation the authors have made to ensure that it has been limited to prediction. Brandon will have to be aware that cause cannot be inferred from correlation so that in his essay he considers the many factors that could have led to the relationship between changes in temperature and changes in the sturgeon fish population.

EXPERIMENTAL STUDIES

WHAT IS AN EXPERIMENTAL STUDY?

controlled conditions
in an experiment, the researcher controls and manipulates the environment

The purpose of an experimental study is to explain outcomes or events. This can be done because the researcher is usually conducting the work in **controlled conditions**, somehow changing the environment to see how that change affects outcomes. Experiments have at least two comparison groups or sets of observations. For example, in order to determine the effects of mercury levels on fish, a researcher might examine the behaviour of fish, then manipulate the mercury content of the water and re-examine the behaviour. Thus, there are two sets of observations, pre-mercury and post-mercury. Alternatively, a researcher might use two groups of fish. In one group, the researcher might look at behaviour of fish in low-mercury (natural levels) water and in a second group; examine behaviour in high-mercury water. What is important here is that in all experiments there are at least two sets of comparison observations and the observations are obtained under different conditions. We often call the group that receives an environmental change the **experimental group** (the fish receiving high mercury) and the group that does not is called the **control group** (the fish in the natural mercury level water).

experimental group
the group that receives the environmental change

control group
the group that does not receive an environmental change

In all experiments, the researcher makes a change between the experimental and control groups and then the outcome is measured. In the mercury level experiment above, the researcher measures the number of offspring fish have when living in low-mercury water and then measures the number of offspring fish have when living in high-mercury water.

control variables
factors held constant
between the groups studied
because of their potential
to affect the outcome of
the study

Other variables that should always be considered in an experiment are the **control variables**—items that could affect the outcome of the study, so the researcher controls or holds them steady. For example, in the fish study, a number of control variables need to be held steady. For example, both groups of fish (fish in the control and experimental groups) should be the same age, since age can affect breeding. If one group had older fish in it, likely these fish would have lower breeding rates and this would have nothing to do with mercury. Other important control variables are the type of fish (the groups should have the same fish species), the size of the tank, time of day when breeding rates are measured, etc. Experiments need to be well planned in order to achieve control.

Once data are collected in an experiment, they must be analyzed. The details of this analysis are beyond the scope of the book, however, when reading an article it is a good idea to know a few terms that will help you to decide whether the experiments truly showed differences between groups. In many articles you will encounter statistical tests such as t-tests, analysis of variance, chi-square tests, etc. Usually researchers have used special statistical computer programs such as SAS and SPSS to analyze their data. These programs run statistical tests such as t-tests, analysis of variance tests, and chi-square tests. You do not need to know how to perform these tests or use these computer programs to understand their meaning in an article. Usually, in the article you will see something like $t_{34} = 2.44$ or $F_{2,24} = 10.92$ or chi-square = 234. These numbers are interesting from a statistical standpoint, but for your purposes, it is the next set of numbers that is more interesting. Following these values you will encounter another value, which will look like this: $p = 0.01$.

Suppose in the fish study you read that the average number of offspring produced by fish in the low-mercury water was 10 and in the high mercury water was 3. Following these averages you see $t_{34} = 2.441$, $p = 0.01$. The p stands for the word *probability*. The p is telling you how rare an outcome like this would be if you were looking at any two groups of fish where mercury levels were not changed between groups. In other words, you would expect this outcome (this difference between the two groups) to happen by chance only one time in 100 experiments ($p = 0.01$). This means that it is very unlikely that you would see this result when making comparisons between groups of fish who had not had mercury levels changed. In other words, if it is unlikely that you would see this result without changing mercury levels, you can believe that the difference in breeding is due to the change in mercury levels. We therefore say that the experimental results are statistically significant, or that fish in high-mercury water have significantly lower breeding rates than those in low-mercury water. In general, if the p-value is less than 0.05 (happening five times out of 100 experiments by chance), then we are willing to believe that the experimental and control groups are performing at different levels. Check whether you understand this by testing yourself with Exercise 11.3. In each experiment, can we believe that the groups are performing at different levels?

EXERCISE 11.3

▶ *Interpreting Statistical Phrases*

Experiment

A nurse is interested in learning whether a certain drug reduces depression in clinically depressed patients. He tests three groups of people with depression. The first group receives no drug, the second receives 2 mg, and the third receives 4 mg. After six weeks, the patients rate their depression on a seven-point scale. After analysis he finds that the no-drug group rates their depression as a 3, the 2-mg group rates it as 3.3, and the 4-mg group rates it as a 3.6., $F_{2,54} = 1.1$, $p = 0.23$.

Answer

The probability tells us that the chance of getting these results by chance between groups is 23 times in 100 experiments, even if no drug were given to each group. Since you could get there results easily by chance, we will argue that there is no real difference in the ratings of these groups. In other words, the drug did not affect the rating of depression as you could have obtained the same result without the drug.

Experiment

An environmental scientist is interested in knowing the effect of crowding of tree growth following clear-cutting. To investigate, she takes two parcels of land that had been clear-cut. On the first parcel seedling trees are planted one metre apart, and on the second, seedlings are planted two metres apart. The number of centimetres of growth at the end of a six-month period is measured. The scientist finds that the trees grew 17 cm when planted one metre apart and 35 cm when planted two metres apart, $t_{98} = 2.63$, $p = 0.005$.

Answer

The probability statement shows that you could get these results by chance only five times in 1000 experiments. This is very rare, so we tend to believe that the growth levels between the two groups of trees are different and we interpret the difference as being due to the distance between the trees.

A social worker is interested in finding out if parenting style affects cooperative behaviour in children. He tests two groups of children. The first group has permissive parents and the second group has strict (authoritarian) parents. He measures the number of minutes it takes the children to stop playing and complete a chore at the command of the parent. The social worker finds that it takes the children of permissive parents 15 minutes on average to comply and the children of authoritarian parents 3 minutes to comply, $t_{31} = 2.04$, $p = 0.025$

The probability statement shows that you would only get these results by chance 2.5 times in 100 experiments. Thus we can say that the groups are different in their time to comply, and the difference is due to the parenting style.

WHEN READING AN EXPERIMENTAL STUDY, WHAT SHOULD I LOOK FOR?

When reading experimental studies, you need first to identify the stated purpose of the experiment. You will then need to determine what the researchers are changing and what they are measuring. You wish to know if what they are changing and measuring fits with the purpose of the experiment. For example, suppose researchers are claiming to study the effect of exercise during pregnancy on the activity level of the newborn. They have one group of pregnant women who exercise daily in the third trimester and the second group does not exercise. When the babies are born, the researchers measure the number of times they cry in a two-hour period. Here it is not clear how measuring crying relates to the purpose of the experiment. Does prenatal exercise increase activity levels in newborns? Does crying constitute an increased activity level? Thus, when reading experiments it is very important to examine the stated purpose and the measure. Sometimes the measures taken are not valid, that is, they do not really measure what they say they measure (e.g., activity level).

A second important aspect to examine in an experimental article is the experimental control. Did the researcher appropriately control the environment? For example, suppose you are reading an article about the effect of breakfast programs on student grades. In one school, children have a breakfast program and their grades are measured at the end of two months; in another school, no breakfast program exists and children's grades are measured after two months. The researcher concludes that breakfast programs do not lead to higher grades. However, upon reading the article you find that the school used for the no-breakfast program was an expensive private school where the children are from very wealthy homes and the school used for the breakfast program was a poorly funded public school, where the children were from families in poverty. It is likely that the children in the no-breakfast program had regular breakfasts since their families were wealthier. Consequently, since both groups ate breakfast, the conclusion that breakfast programs do not work is tainted by lack of control between the groups studied. A more appropriate study would have been to use two schools from poor neighbourhoods, one with a breakfast program and one without.

A third area to examine in an experimental article is the interpretation of the data analysis. When two groups are significantly different from one another, it is possible that they are not practically different. For example, suppose you read an experiment in which the researcher was studying athletics in school children. The researcher studied two groups of children: one group (the control group) simply performed a running task in which they were timed in running 100 metres, and the second group (the experimental group) was given a pep talk before running. The control group runs 100 metres, on average, in 35 seconds, and the pep talk group runs 100 metres, on average, in 34.6 seconds. Statistical analysis determines that this difference in running times is statistically significant. While it might be statistically significant, you need to ask yourself if it is practically significant. Does running 0.4 seconds faster represent an important improvement in the fitness of schoolchildren? Likely not. This might be a more important finding if these were Olympic athletes.

Brandon, the student from the case study, must review an experimental article that examines the effect of temperature on the sturgeon fish population. When reading this article, Brandon will need to review the purpose, the measures, the control, and the interpretation of the results, as outlined above.

LIMITATIONS OF STUDY METHODS

WHAT ARE SOME LIMITATIONS OF THE DIFFERENT STUDY METHODS?

Many researchers use more than one study technique in their research. You will find that some experimental articles will also present correlations, and some correlation articles will also present survey results. Combining techniques is a good way to overcome some limitations of each study method.

Observational methods provide insight into the study subjects but these insights are only descriptive. These studies cannot tell you why something happened, only that it did happen. Observational studies often suffer from difficulties in generalizing to the population and require clear operational definitions. Correlation provides insight into the relationship of one variable with another. These studies help to predict future outcome; however, these studies cannot tell you why variables are related. When variables increase or decrease together we can only say that they increase or decrease, not the cause of this increase or decrease. Experiments are advantageous in that they study cause. We can determine the cause of a change. However, often experiments suffer from lack of depth. The experiments often do not examine how the subjects feel about the change or cannot predict future outcomes.

Advice for Brandon

▶ **B**randon wonders how to interpret research findings in the articles he is reading. He has three articles to interpret. Clearly one article (which presented the results of an expert survey) was observational, one article (which used statistics to make a prediction) was a correlation study, and the article Brandon found was an experiment. First and foremost Brandon needs to recall that observational studies can only describe, correlation studies only predict, and experiments can explain cause. However, Brandon needs also to remember the following:

SURVEY STUDY

Sample	Who are the survey participants?
	Do they well represent the population of interest?
	Were they randomly selected?
	Is there a sufficient number of participants?
The questions	What types of questions were used?
	Did the questions show bias?
	Were response scales in rating questions balanced?
	Did each question use clear wording and ask only one thing?
The interpretation	Were the results descriptive?
	Did the author attempt to infer cause, and if so, on what basis (speculation, from combining two or more questions, etc.)?

CORRELATION STUDY

The sample	Who/what is the sample?
	Is the sample representative of a population?
	Is the sample in any way restricted?
Interpretation	Interpret the meaning of the correlation presented.
	Be sure to examine that the author's interpretation does NOT make causal statements.
	What other variables might be related to the prediction?

EXPERIMENTAL STUDY

Purpose	Do the measurements and the manipulations fit the study purpose?
	Is the measurement valid?
Method	Was proper control used in the experiment?
	What control variables were used?
	Was any control missing?
Interpretation	Were the results statistically significant?
	Were the results practically significant?

CHAPTER SUMMARY

- Qualitative data often provides insight into research problems. Quantitative data provides a numerical summary of the research question. Quantitative data allows for statistical comparisons between groups.

- Three types of research studies allow data to be collected. These are observational studies, correlation studies, and experimental studies.

- Observational studies are descriptive studies. They include naturalistic observation (in which the researcher observes the subjects of the investigation in their own environment), case studies (in which a single person or event is studied in detail), and surveys (in which groups of people are interviewed or asked to complete a questionnaire).

Each of these types of studies has its own limitations. The results of these three types of studies are only descriptive.

■ Correlation studies show relationships between two items. They are used to predict future events. If a relationship is found between two variables, it cannot be interpreted as causal.

■ An experiment is a study that can be used to interpret cause. Experiments are conducted under controlled conditions and the researcher compares two sets of data or two or more study groups. The experimental group(s) receives some sort of manipulation and the control group does not. These groups are then compared to see the effect of the manipulation. Statistical analyses are usually performed and estimates of probability are made to determine whether differences found between the groups are statistically significant. In other words, are these differences due to chance or due to the manipulation done by the experimenter?

KEY TERMS

case study
choice-oriented question
confound
control group
control variables
controlled conditions
correlation studies
data
empirical article
experimental group

experimental studies
limitation
literature review
naturalistic observation
negative correlation
observational studies
open-ended question
operational definition
population
positive correlation

qualitative data
quantitative data
random sample
rating scale question
representative sample
sample
scatterplot
survey
variable

INDIVIDUAL ACTIVITIES

1. When researching essays, you are required to find articles that relate to your topic of interest. However, as outlined in this chapter, different types of studies are used for different purposes. List where/when in an essay you might want to use these different types of studies (observational, correlation, or experimental). See the end of the chapter for our list.

2. Investigate biases in surveys by designing two similar surveys in which the questions on one have biases and the questions on the other do not. Ask students to answer the questions on the two surveys to see if the biases lead to differing responses.

3. Examine the results sections in two or three research experimental articles and attempt to interpret them. View the discussion sections of the same articles to determine if your interpretations are consistent with the authors'.

GROUP ACTIVITIES

1. In this activity, as a group, take observations of a campus activity. You will decide what campus activity to observe, define any terms, create an observation sheet, take observations, and report your findings. You could observe the number of students choosing healthy foods at the cafeteria (be sure to operationally define *healthy*). You could observe the number of students who are happy (define) when leaving a large lecture. You could observe the types of clothing worn on campus. You could observe the number of students

being disruptive (define) in a lecture. Your group should decide the topic, and after your instructor approves the topic, organize your observational study.

2. As a group, go to the library and find three articles, books, newspapers, or media stories that use correlation. Discuss how these correlations were used and whether there was any error in interpretation.

3. In your group, design an experiment to test whether meditation leads to lower stress (or choose another topic). Be sure to define terms clearly. Describe your control and experimental groups, control variables, and the experimental procedures.

ANSWERS TO INDIVIDUAL ACTIVITY 1

Use an observational study when:

- You want to describe a condition or a population
- You need insight into what individuals or groups might be thinking about an issue, task, or event

Use a correlation study when:

- You want to know if two things are related and the strength of that relationship
- You want to predict whether two things occur together or the likelihood of an event

Use an experimental study when:

- You want to provide evidence for cause
- You want to show the effect of an environmental change

REFERENCES

Fowler, F. J., Jr. (1993). *Survey research methods* (2nd ed.). Newbury Park, CA: Sage Publications.

Goodall, J. (1998). Essays on science and society: Learning from chimpanzees. A message humans can understand. *Science, 282(5397),* 2184–2185.

Kantowitz, B. H., Roediger, H. L., & Elmes D. G. (2001). *Experimental psychology* (7th ed.). St. Paul, MN: West Publishing Company.

Minium, E. W., & King, B. M. (2003). *Statistical reasoning in psychology and education.* New York: Wiley.

Ross, A. D., Olson, I. R., & Gore, J. C. (2003). Cortical plasticity in an early blind musician: An fMRI study. *Magnetic Resonance Imaging, 21,* 821–828.

Sternberg, R. J. (2003). *Wisdom, intelligence and creativity synthesized.* Cambridge, UK: Cambridge University Press.

Uhlmann, E., & Swanson, J. (2004). Exposure to violent video games increases automatic aggressiveness. *Journal of Adolescence, 27,* 41–52.

CHAPTER 12

COMMUNICATION: THE ART OF SPEAKING AND GIVING PRESENTATIONS

LEARNING OBJECTIVES

The Case of Lindsey

▶ Lindsey has always been a little shy. She usually goes along with what other people want to do. Sometimes her feelings are hurt by other people's careless comments or insensitivity to her, but she says nothing, feeling that the possibility of starting an argument would make her feel even worse. She participates little in class discussions, rarely raising her hand to make a comment or ask a question in class. She enjoys school, though, and likes to listen to other people. In her first year in a post-secondary journalism course, however, she finds that she is expected to give class presentations, give and take criticism from others, and defend her opinions. This is not going to be easy for her; as a matter of fact, she is strongly tempted to drop the course and take a class in which she can comfortably fade into the background.

Lindsey's feelings are common, but unfortunate for her. Her feelings may prevent her from taking a course that she would enjoy and profit from, and may prevent her from entering several possible careers. Former college students report that skills in oral communication and public speaking have been an important part of their successful career experiences (Zekeri, 2004). In fact, it's hard to imagine any career in which Lindsey will be sure that she never has to speak up, whether giving a presentation or working in a team, or in being evaluated on her performance or evaluating someone else. It's hard to imagine any situation in life that wouldn't be easier for Lindsey if she were able to present herself more confidently and forthrightly.

ASSERTIVENESS

WHAT DOES IT MEAN TO BE ASSERTIVE?

assertiveness
the ability to state our own needs and wants firmly, but without infringing on the rights of others; includes being able to satisfy your own needs without hurting others in the process

Let's start with assertiveness, because it is really at the root of presenting oneself well. **Assertiveness** is the ability to state your wants, needs, and feelings without infringing on the rights of others. It includes being able to satisfy your own needs without hurting others in the process (Greenberg, 2002). When you are assertive, you are perceived as more confident and more competent, qualities that would be highly beneficial in all situations, and especially in giving presentations or discussing matters in groups. People like Lindsey who feel uncomfortable about speaking up may need assertiveness training, a skills course that is offered widely, and probably at Lindsey's own school. There are other people who need this training too: those who act aggressively instead of assertively. For example, one of Lindsey's classmates, Merle, has a habit of leaning forward and pointing a finger at people while he shouts out his demands. He often gets what he wants, but his technique is that of a bully, and others avoid him whenever possible. Aggressiveness is generally rudeness and certainly infringes on the rights of others by acting as if no one else's feelings or thoughts matter. Are you assertive? Take the test in Exercise 12.1 to find out.

EXERCISE 12.1

▶ *Assessing Assertive Behaviour*

To determine your general pattern of behaviour, indicate how characteristic or descriptive of you each of the following statements is by using the code that follows:

+3 = Very characteristic of me, extremely descriptive

+2 = Rather characteristic of me, quite descriptive

+1 = Somewhat characteristic of me, slightly descriptive

−1 = Somewhat uncharacteristic of me, slightly nondescriptive

−2 = Rather uncharacteristic of me, quite nondescriptive

−3 = Very uncharacteristic of me, extremely nondescriptive

*1. Most people seem to be more aggressive and assertive than I am.

*2. I have hesitated to make or accept dates because of "shyness."

3. When the food served at a restaurant is not done to my satisfaction, I complain about it to the waiter or waitress.

*4. I am careful to avoid hurting other people's feelings, even when I feel that I have been injured.

*5. If a salesperson has gone to considerable trouble to show me merchandise that is not quite suitable, I have a difficult time in saying no.

6. When I am asked to do something, I insist upon knowing why.

7. There are times when I look for a good, vigorous argument.

8.   I strive to get ahead as well as most people in my position.

*9.   To be honest, people often take advantage of me.

10.   I enjoy starting conversations with new acquaintances and strangers.

*11.   I often don't know what to say to attractive persons of the opposite sex.

*12.   I will hesitate to make phone calls to business establishments and institutions.

*13.   I would rather apply for a job or for admission to a college by writing letters than by going through with personal interviews.

*14.   I find it embarrassing to return merchandise.

*15.   If a close and respected relative were annoying me, I would smother my feeling rather than express my annoyance.

*16.   I have avoided asking questions for fear of sounding stupid.

*17.   During an argument I am sometimes afraid that I will get so upset that I will shake all over.

18.   If a famed and respected lecturer makes a statement that I think is incorrect, I will have the audience hear my point of view.

*19.   I avoid arguing over prices with clerks and salespeople.

20.   When I have done something important or worthwhile, I manage to let others know about it.

21.   I am open and frank about my feelings.

22.   If someone has been spreading false or bad stories about me, I see him or her as soon as possible to "have a talk" about it.

*23.   I often have a hard time saying no.

*24.   I tend to bottle up my emotions rather than make a scene.

25.   I complain about poor service in a restaurant and elsewhere.

*26.   When I am given a compliment, I sometimes just don't know what to say.

27.   If a couple near me in a theatre or at a lecture were conversing rather loudly, I would ask them to be quiet or to take their conversation elsewhere.

28.   Anyone attempting to push ahead of me in a line is in for a good battle.

29.   I am quick to express an opinion.

*30.   There are times when I just can't say anything.

To score this scale, first change (reverse) the signs + or − for your scores on statements with an asterisk beside them. For example, if you gave yourself a +3, change it to −3, and if you gave yourself −3, change it to +3. Now total the plus (+) items, total the minus (−) items, and subtract the minus total from the plus total to obtain your score. The score can range from −90 through 0 to +90. The higher the score (closer to +90), the more assertively you usually behave. The lower the score (closer to −90), the more nonassertive is your typical behaviour. This particular scale does not measure aggressiveness.

If you are a female and you scored at about 8, you are right in the middle of the way most female post-secondary students score. That is, 50 percent of female students are more assertive than you are, and 50 percent are less assertive. If you scored 23, you are more assertive than 75 percent of female students, and if you scored −8, you are less assertive than 75 percent of female students.

Male students in general score higher on this test. If you are male and scored 11, you are right in the middle of the way most male post-secondary students score. That is, 50 percent of male students are more assertive than you are, and 50 percent are less assertive. If you scored 26, you are more assertive than 75 percent of male students, and if you scored −3, you are less assertive than 75 percent of male students.

When Lindsey took the test, she wasn't surprised to find that she scored −34. That makes her less assertive than 95 percent of other female post-secondary students. She knows she is unassertive, but she is a little afraid of changing this characteristic within herself. It might be helpful to look at the rights of the individual. In Box 12.1, there is a "bill of rights" relating to assertiveness. Are there elements of these rights that you find difficult upholding for yourself?

A Bill of Assertiveness Rights   BOX 12.1

1. You have the right to judge your own behaviour, thoughts, and emotions, and to take responsibility for their initiation and consequences upon yourself.

2. You have the right to offer no reasons or excuses for your behaviour.

3. You have the right to judge if you are responsible for finding solutions to other people's problems.

4. You have the right to change your mind.

5. You have the right to make mistakes—and be responsible for them.

6. You have the right to say, "I don't know."

7. You have the right to be independent of the goodwill of others before coping with them.

8. You have the right to be illogical in making decisions.

9. You have the right to say, "I don't understand."

10. You have the right to say, "I don't care."

Source: From *When I say no, I feel guilty*, by Manuel J. Smith, copyright © 1975 by Manuel J. Smith. Used by permission of Doubleday, a division of Random House Inc.

CAN I BECOME MORE ASSERTIVE?

Yes, absolutely. There are many strategies that can be used to increase assertiveness. If Lindsey practises these strategies, she will find that over time, she will become a more assertive person, enhancing her appearance as a confident and competent woman. The payoffs are many: she will see that with assertiveness, she will feel less hesitant about giving presentations, her presentations will be more successful, she will be able to give criticism more effectively and constructively, and she will be able to defend herself against unjust criticism.

WHAT ARE THE STRATEGIES TO INCREASE ASSERTIVENESS?

First, Lindsey needs to be aware of her own feelings. Sometimes she tells herself that it "doesn't matter" if she has to do things she doesn't want to do, and sometimes she tries to convince herself that other people have more rights than she does. The truth is that of course we all sometimes have to do things we don't want to do, and sometimes we all have to put ourselves second to other people. But not as often as Lindsey thinks. Lindsey needs to ask herself more often, "What is it that *I* want?" You have to know what you want before you can ask for it!

Next, Lindsey needs to observe her own nonverbal behaviour. Being assertive is easier if your posture is good and if you make eye contact with whomever you are talking. Lindsey was astonished when she observed herself in this interaction:

Todd (a friend): I'm not going to class today. Lend me your notes.

Lindsey (slouching over her books and looking down): I, er, yeah, I guess I can take notes, I mean if you, ah, need them.

Lindsey learned several things from this brief interaction: first, she learned that she was resentful and tired of taking notes for Todd, who habitually skipped classes and assumed she would cover for him. Second, she learned that she presented herself as a downtrodden submissive person, just by her body language. We might also point out to Lindsey that her behaviour has, in fact, been reinforcing Todd's treatment of her. If she presents herself as submissive and always acquiesces to Todd's requests, he will tend to continue treating her in a dismissive and exploitative manner.

In her brief interaction with Todd, Lindsey noted that her tone of voice when she agreed to take notes for Todd was low and rather mumbled, with hesitations and verbal fumbling. This indicates the next step in becoming assertive: Lindsey needs to cultivate a more assertive voice. This means speaking up, without shouting, and speaking clearly, with few pauses or hesitations. Even in agreeing to take notes for Todd, which of the following statements sounds more assertive and confident to you?

"I, er, yeah, I guess I can take notes, I mean if you, ah, need them."

"Yes, I'll take notes for you."

The answer is clear. What Lindsey says is important, but so is the way she says it.

Now Lindsey is clear that she wants to stop being Todd's secretary while he cuts classes, but she wants to do it in a way that won't alienate him entirely. She really wants him to see that he has been taking advantage of her and that she is hurt and resentful about this. Lindsey is doing well: she has identified her own feelings and what she wants, and she knows she wants to deal with Todd directly. Now Lindsey probably needs to "psych" herself up for talking with Todd. This is the time for her to remind herself of her assertiveness rights and to rehearse what she wants to say.

Lindsey's next step is to find the right environment in which to talk to Todd. She doesn't need to be told that it would be inappropriate for her to confront Todd in front of other people (this is something aggressive Merle would do, simply to embarrass Todd!). She needs to find a time when she can talk to Todd directly and alone. For example, she may have to say, "Todd, may I have a word with you privately?" or "Todd, may I talk with you privately after class?" What if Todd tries to put her off? Let's look at how this may play out.

Lindsey: Todd, may I have a word with you privately?

Todd (in a rather exasperated voice): What do you want, Lindsey?

Lindsey: I want to talk to you privately.

Todd: Tell me now.

Lindsey: No, I want to speak with you privately.

Todd: Why?

Lindsey: I'll tell you that privately.

Lindsey is already behaving assertively. She wants to talk to Todd privately and she is not backing down from this. If she is using a firm, steady voice, standing tall, and making eye contact with Todd, her persistence will probably pay off.

Once Lindsey and Todd are in a place where they will not be overheard, she can make her assertive statements to him and make sure that he has heard them. What are assertive statements like? Most importantly, assertive statements are not attacks on anyone's character; they are about behaviour, not personality. Therefore, Lindsey would not say, "You're an exploitative jerk!" Assertive statements state the facts about Todd's behaviour that are troubling Lindsey, her feelings about this behaviour, and what she would like Todd to do. They should be short and simple rather than long, rambling, and filled with qualifiers, such as "I know you don't mean it but. . . ." Lindsey's statements should use the word "I" rather than being accusations. That is, "When you skip class and expect me to take notes for you, I feel exploited," rather than "You always cut class and expect me to take notes for you." Examine the difference between these statements: the second is an accusation that Todd will resent and will dismiss as an exaggeration (after all, he probably doesn't "always" cut class). The first statement is an accurate reflection of Todd's behaviour and puts the emphasis on Lindsey's feelings about this behaviour. About the only response Todd can reasonably make to this is, "I didn't realize you felt that way." A good start, because most likely Todd *didn't* realize this—he's not a mind reader! Lindsey then follows up with a statement such as, "I thought so. I'm uncomfortable being responsible for your class notes. In the future, I'd like to be responsible for only my own notes." Now Lindsey has given Todd the benefit of the doubt that he didn't realize his effect on her, and she has indicated what she wants for the future. Again, there's not much Todd can say except, "Okay, I'm sorry." A smile and a "Thank you" from Lindsey is all that's needed now.

Lindsey is doubtful that this technique will work, though. It will, most of the time. "But what if Todd gets mad at me for it?" Lindsey asks anxiously. The answer is, "So what if he does?" If Todd gets angry at Lindsey's low-keyed assertiveness, expressed with respect for him and in private, does she really need to have him around? Todd's anger would mean a lack of respect for Lindsey, and none of us needs to be with people who don't respect us.

The scenario that we have used is a simple one, but one that occurs commonly in school and one that engenders a great deal of resentment from the person feeling exploited. Many situations are more complicated, and many people are not as open as the Todd of our scenario. In these situations, the same technique should be used, but with some additions. For example, you may need to keep repeating the message. Look at this scenario:

Lindsey: When you skip class and expect me to take notes for you, I feel exploited.

Todd: Oh, come on, don't be silly. No one's exploiting you.

Lindsey: I feel exploited under these conditions.

Todd: But I'm not exploiting you.

Lindsey: I feel exploited.

Todd: Okay, okay, you feel exploited. So?

Lindsey: I'm uncomfortable being responsible for your class notes. In the future, I'd like to be responsible for only my own notes.

Todd: Okay, okay. Let's get some coffee.

Lindsey: I'd like to be responsible for only my own notes. Do you understand what I'm saying?

Todd: Yeah. You think I'm an exploitative creep.

Lindsey: No, I'm only talking about being responsible for only my own notes in the future. Do you understand?

Todd: Yeah, you want me to take my own notes in the future. Now can we get some coffee?

Lindsey: Sure. Thanks.

In this scenario, Lindsey kept repeating her message in the same steady, firm voice until Todd finally "heard" her. She didn't accept his attempt at diversion, but brought the conversation back on course. She also required him to repeat back what she was requesting, to make sure there was no misunderstanding. When she found that Todd had misunderstood her, she had a chance to correct him and make sure he heard the correct message (i.e., that she wasn't objecting to *him,* but to his behaviour in one regard). Now that the conversation has ended, Lindsey should let the matter drop rather than reminding Todd over and over again. Many people feel tempted to "rub it in" but this only breeds resentment, painting a picture of a "victory." That's not necessary: this was not a victory, it was the resolution of a mutual problem. If Lindsey regards it in this way, she is showing respect for Todd and his rights. In the event that Todd lapses, asking for her notes again, then Lindsey can remind him of the conversation in which they agreed that she would only be responsible for her own notes. Box 12.2 summarizes the steps in being assertive.

Steps in Becoming More Assertive

BOX 12.2

1. Become aware of your own rights and your feelings.
2. Identify what it is you want.
3. Rehearse what you want to say and how you want to say it.
4. Find the right environment for being assertive.
5. Sit or stand straight and make eye contact.
6. Use short, simple sentences.
7. Use the word "I" rather than making "you" accusations.
8. State the facts of the troublesome situation. Don't exaggerate. Don't discuss the person, only the behaviour.
9. State how you feel about the situation.
10. State what you want to happen.

11. Repeat your message if you feel you are not being heard.
12. Avoid distractions and keep the conversation on topic.
13. Ask the person you're addressing to repeat your message back to you to make sure you have been heard correctly. Correct the person if necessary, and ask the person to repeat back what he or she has heard until you feel confident that he or she has it right.
14. Say "Thank you" and be gracious. Drop the matter unless the behaviour recurs.
15. If the behaviour recurs, firmly remind the person that this issue has been discussed already and an agreement has been reached

There are many situations that can come up in the life of a student in which assertiveness is the best option. Look at Exercise 12.2 for some examples. Work out what an assertive response would be to each.

EXERCISE 12.2

▶ *Scenarios That Require Assertiveness*

Work out what you feel the best assertive response to each scenario would be.

1. Your instructor has given you a low mark on your essay with no indication of why or how the essay might be improved.
2. Your roommate leaves his books and papers all over your desk.
3. The clerk at the bookstore has shortchanged you and won't admit it.
4. Your friend has used parts of your essay in her own without your permission or giving you credit.
5. Your brother borrows your car but doesn't refill it with gas.
6. Your best friend flirts with your boyfriend/girlfriend.

HOW WILL ASSERTIVENESS HELP ME GIVE PRESENTATIONS?

Assertiveness will help in several ways. First, you will come across as more competent and capable when you use an assertive approach in giving a presentation. Your manner of speaking will make your arguments clearer and more meaningful. You will feel more confident too because you know that your manner of presenting yourself is a strong one. With assertiveness as an underpinning, you are able to learn the techniques of giving a good presentation and become an effective public speaker. This will be especially helpful when you are required to speak without warning; for example, in your career you may well be asked to explain something or to give your opinion in a meeting with little or no notice beforehand. If you would like more information about assertiveness and tips for gaining assertiveness, the following websites might be helpful to you: http:// mentalhelp.net/psyhelp/chap13/chap13e.htm; http://www.tufts.edu/hr/tips/assert.html; and http://www.coun.uvic.ca/personal/assert.html.

PUBLIC SPEAKING

DOES LEARNING TO BE ASSERTIVE MEAN I WON'T FEAR PUBLIC SPEAKING?

performance anxiety
fear of not being able to perform adequately

Unfortunately no; it's only a first step. Lindsey may have learned how to be assertive, but she still has **performance anxiety**, or a fear of not being able to perform adequately in this area. The idea of giving a presentation still fills her with dread. She is in very good company; fear of public speaking is the most common performance anxiety there is (Barlow & Durand, 2005). What is it that people are afraid of? Why do so many people feel anxious about speaking in public? The reasons vary, but many people have a lack of confidence in themselves, feeling that others know more about the topic or are better speakers. Others fear looking foolish, imagining that the audience will laugh at them for stumbling over words or forgetting what to say. In Lindsey's case, one of the reasons stems from the fact that she will be evaluated by her instructor and by her fellow students. She is going to be judged by others in a very direct manner. It is understandable that she should feel some concern, but if her anxiety increases too much, she will wind up in a self-fulfilling prophecy. That is, she is anxious that she will make mistakes and her anxiety increases the possibility that she *will* make mistakes. What can she do?

HOW CAN I REDUCE MY FEAR OF PUBLIC SPEAKING?

This is a good time for Lindsey to review techniques for reducing stress that were covered in Chapter 3. She needs to be able to relax her body first of all. If her body is rigid when she is giving her presentation, her anxiety will be obvious and will increase. So we'll tell Lindsey to practise deep muscle relaxation and to take a few deep breaths, shaking out the tension from her arms, shoulders, and neck.

Next, Lindsey must become aware of the negative statements she is making to herself. The chances are great that she is saying something like this to herself, "I'm going to forget everything and look ridiculous. I'll get all tongue-tied and everyone will laugh at me and see how stupid I am. Someone will ask me a question I don't know the answer to and the instructor will think I'm a bad student and I haven't done my work. They're all going to think that I'm boring and dumb." These statements are enough to make anyone nervous! And they're not accurate. Remember the times that you have watched someone else give a presentation. Did you think the presenter was stupid because he or she fumbled over a word? If the presenter (even your instructor) is asked a question and answers, "I don't know," do you think that make makes the presenter a total failure? The point is that the audience is not as critical as Lindsey thinks. And she doesn't have to be perfect. Everyone stumbles over a word now and then, everyone momentarily forgets a point he or she wanted to make, and no one knows the answers to all the questions. Lindsey is putting a burden on herself that is out of proportion to the situation. She would be well advised to replace her negative self-statements with more realistic statements, such as "I don't have to be perfect. I have some interesting points to make that people will want to hear. Questions from the audience show their interest in what I've been saying. I've done my homework and I know the area better than most of the class. I'll be a success if I just make the audience aware of one or two points that they didn't know before."

A little situational reconstruction might be a good idea here as well: that is, interpreting the situation a little differently can make a world of difference. Lindsey has been regarding this situation as one of judgment upon her. There is undeniably truth in this, given that her presentation is for a grade, and there is truth in the statement that we are being judged whenever we are in the public eye. But the truth is also that no matter what we do, some people will love us and some will hate us. In Lindsey's case, most of her fellow students will feel empathy for her and be supportive, while a few others will take the opportunity to find anything they can to criticize. That's not pretty, but it is reality. Since this is the case, Lindsey might just as well concentrate on something else besides evaluation. In giving her presentation, Lindsey, by definition, is going to be teaching. This is a better focus for her: if she can concentrate on teaching her classmates, on imparting some interesting and important information, she will take her focus off herself and put it on the audience and their welfare. That is, Lindsey can reconstruct the situation as an opportunity for her to educate her class, and do the best job she can in this. She can recognize that success in her presentation doesn't necessarily have to come from a grade; it can come from causing people to think about things they have not thought about in the past, giving them information that they might not acquire in any other way. To this end, she can now prepare her best presentation to contribute to the education of her class.

HOW CAN I GIVE A GOOD PRESENTATION?

The first step in giving a good presentation is preparation. Just as in giving instructions for a written essay, Lindsey's instructor may have been very directive in letting her know what was expected of her (e.g., "Give a presentation on how the problem of homelessness has been made worse by the closing of mental institutions.") or very flexible (e.g., "Pick a topic in sociology and give a presentation on it."). Lindsey must decide on her topic and do the library research to make herself knowledgeable in the area. Again, as in a written essay, she needs to pick a topic that interests her. This is especially critical when giving a presentation: if the presenter is not enthusiastic about the topic, how likely is it that the audience will be?

Then Lindsey needs to decide what she wants to tell the class in her presentation. If her instructor has not given her a direct question to answer, she needs to pick one herself from her reading. It might be a good idea for her to brainstorm possibilities by jotting down on paper every idea that comes to her mind. It is likely that some interesting area with questions will pop out at her. Lindsey should note that while it may be very informative to give a presentation in which all the facts are present (e.g., how does a stickleback fish attract a mate?), her presentation will be more interesting to her and to her audience if it contains both information and questions. If the answers to the questions are controversial, that might be even better: Lindsey isn't required to answer controversial questions definitively, only to pose them and speculate on possible answers.

Let's take a concrete example: Lindsey is going to give a presentation on Martin Luther. She has choices concerning how she is going to approach this presentation. First option: She could simply give a biography of the Reformation monk and how he proposed changes within the Catholic church. Second option: She could reduce the amount of time she spends on the biography and pose the questions "Why did Luther think changes were necessary? What effects did he have on the church?" Third option: She could decide to become more controversial, asking perhaps, "Was Martin Luther being loyal to the true spirit of Catholicism, or was he a rebel trouble-maker?" Then she could present both sides of the argument and perhaps engender greater audience interest and participation. Other options are certainly possible, but let's work with only these three for the time being.

One thing Lindsey needs to remember in giving a presentation is that she needs to capture her audience's interest quickly. So no matter which option she chooses, she needs to start off with a "grabber." For option 1, for example, she might start out with, "He was a small man, and, many thought, an insignificant man who joined the church for the wrong reasons, but he changed the face of religion in the Western world forever. Martin Luther. . . ." For the second option, she might start with, "The Catholic church had changed from its traditional stance. Its practices were troubling many: Could souls really be saved by spending money to buy indulgences? Martin Luther thought not . . . ." For the third option, Lindsey might start by saying, "True son of the church or rebel monk? What Martin Luther was and why he acted as he did remain speculative. Martin Luther . . . ." Then the audience will have an idea of where Lindsey is going in her presentation and will be more ready to listen to the body of her presentation in which she presents the facts.

With the introduction of her presentation done, Lindsey now needs to present the informational content. What does she want the audience to know? What does the audience need to know to be able to speculate on the questions or premises that Lindsey has posed in her introduction? Lindsey's decision of what to include and how much to include will depend greatly on how much time her instructor is giving her for her presentation. If she is being given an hour with time for questions added on, she can obviously include more than if she is given half an hour, including time for questions. In any case, she can't include everything she has discovered about the topic. This is a mistake that many inexperienced presenters make: they think that because the instructor is evaluating them, they have to cram in every bit of information they can. The better technique is to be very discriminating about what you include, but provide an annotated bibliography for those who wish to explore the area more fully. Your instructor may ask for this, or even for a more inclusive essay to complement the presentation. In any case, the presentation itself must be briefer than the essay.

After delivering the body of the presentation, Lindsey must wrap it up; this is the time to summarize what has been said, going back to the premises and questions asked in the introduction. For example, Lindsey might end option 1 by noting that no one can be considered insignificant when he or she has made a lasting impression on the world, and reviewing the changes that came to religion in the Reformation. For option 2, Lindsey might end off by reviewing Luther's abhorrence of the practice of indulgences and discussing where the Catholic church stands on this issue today. For option 3, she might briefly review the arguments for Luther's devotion to Catholicism and the arguments for his wanting to be a rebel, ending by posing the question, "What do you think?"

The steps in creating a presentation are summarized in Box 12.3.

Steps in Creating a Presentation   BOX 12.3

1. Choose a topic that interests you.

2. Do your research in finding out all about the topic (see Chapter 9).

3. Pose questions about the topic based on what you have learned in your research.

4. Make notes of what points you want to communicate to the audience.

5. Start your presentation with an attention-grabber that asks questions and indicates to the audience the direction this presentation will be taking.

6. Give the body of the presentation, presenting select information that the audience will require in evaluating the questions you posed and premises you established in the introduction.

7. End the presentation by summarizing what you have said, by coming to a conclusion about the questions/ premises you posed, or pointing out the still speculative nature of the premises/questions.

HOW CAN I DELIVER MY PRESENTATION IN THE BEST MANNER POSSIBLE?

It's wise to be aware that a presentation depends just as much on how it is presented as on what it contains. Lindsey needs to make sure that the way she imparts her information is effective. There are several useful ideas to remember in this context.

First, Lindsey must know who her audience is. Is she presenting only to her own classmates and instructor? If so, it is likely that they will already have established a commonality of vocabulary. For example, when speaking to an economics class, it may not be necessary to explain the difference between macro- and microeconomics, but it might be necessary to explain the distinction to an audience that is more mixed and may not all have heard the terms.

Next, Lindsey must decide whether she needs visual aids in presenting her material. Many, if not most, presentations are enhanced by the use of visual aids. These may take the form of posters, overhead transparencies, or slides. Today, many people use computer software technology such as PowerPoint to help them make their presentations. These have the advantage of being easily prepared and stored, and they help to make the presenter look organized and professional. But sometimes visual aids can be overdone and can detract from the presentation. For example, it is possible to prepare slides that are so interesting or so comical that the audience pays more attention to them than to you! Visual aids should be used to enhance your presentation, not to take the place of you, the presenter.

If Lindsey decides to use visual aids, there are some points to consider. For example, her audience needs to be able to read or to understand what she is presenting visually. In general, slides are better than overhead transparencies or posters because they are more easily read, they can be transported and changed more easily, and they can be designed so that the lights don't have to be turned out in the room in which you are presenting. Why is that important? Because when the lights are out, some people have a tendency to fall asleep! It's also more difficult for them to take notes if they wish to do this. If she uses visual aids, such as overheads or computer slides, she must make sure that each slide or overhead complements what she is saying rather than giving the whole presentation for her. Tips for using visual aids are found in Box 12.4.

Depending upon the kind of presentation she is making, Lindsey might find that her audience would appreciate a hard copy handout of her slides/overheads to use as a guideline and perhaps to serve as paper with headings to take notes on how Lindsey expands on each point. At least, Lindsey needs to ensure that if her audience is taking notes, each slide remains visible long enough to allow audience members to copy whatever they wish.

Lindsey cannot read her presentation as if it were a speech. That's boring, and inefficient. Why give a presentation if all the presenter does is read aloud? The audience can do that for themselves! Lindsey needs to practise her material until she knows what to say, prompted only by index cards that contain key terms and points. In terms of the presentation itself, Lindsey's sentences should be short so that the audience does not have to struggle with a complex sentence construction. If Lindsey can inject a little humour that fits with the content of her presentation, this would be a plus in capturing attention and winning the audience's favour.

Now Lindsey has to concentrate on how she presents herself. Appearance does matter: Lindsey may not need to wear a business suit to give a presentation in her class, but this is not the time for torn jeans and a sweatshirt either. In any presentation, a neat, clean appearance is

---

Using Visual Aids

BOX 12.4

- Each slide/overhead/poster should make only one point. Crowding too much information on one visual confuses the audience and detracts from what you are saying while the audience tries to read everything. If the information you are presenting is complex, use a series of visuals rather than trying to cram everything on only one.

- In a similar fashion, this means that each visual should be uncluttered and clear. Use a font that is big enough to be read and is comprehensible.

- Make sure that the colours you use can be seen well by even those at the back of the room. For example, a light blue print on a slightly darker blue background may look nice to you as you make up the slide, but the print may not stand out enough for the whole audience to read. Light print on a dark background is usually easier for people at the back of the room to see. And by the way, about 10 percent of people have a degree of colour-blindness and will have problems with red and green in particular. These are good colours to avoid in general.

- Be consistent in your use of colour and font. It's fine to use underlining and italics to emphasize some words, but in general, when colours and fonts change a great deal, it seems more confusing than entertaining. A rule of thumb is "simple is better."

- Be sure to introduce each slide/overhead. The visual should reflect what you have just said so that your audience can see what they have just heard. If you present the visual before you verbally discuss it, your audience may tune you out in order to concentrate on reading and understanding your visual.

appropriate. A lectern is present in the class, and Lindsey would love to simply lean on it, reading her notes and grasping the sides as tightly as possible. Fortunately, she already knows that this would be a mistake. The lectern is not for leaning on, but for having a convenient place to put notes. A good presenter moves away from the lectern, at least occasionally. Gesturing is good since most of us talk with our hands at least to some extent, but Lindsey must be careful not to overdo it. She recalls a presentation she saw a classmate give once in which the classmate kept pointing her finger and waving her arms around. Now Lindsey can recall the gestures, but she was so mesmerized by these that the content of the presentation was lost.

Lindsey must remember to make eye contact with her audience: she is talking *to* them, not *at* them, and she must keep at least the feel of a two-way communication in her presentation. That won't happen if she never looks at them. Her gaze should sweep the room, resting on and making eye contact with several members of the audience, so that all the members feel included.

Finally, as nervous as Lindsey may feel herself to be, she needs to smile. No, she doesn't have to keep up a strange, idiotic-looking grin, but she must smile at her audience when she begins her presentation and when she gives some relatively light-hearted information or uses humour. Her face must mirror what she is saying; that is, when she talks of something unpleasant or tragic, she needs to look serious. When she poses a question, she needs to look curious. When an audience member makes a comment or asks a question, she needs to look interested. This sounds like a good presenter must be an actor, and there is a certain amount of truth in that. At least, a good presenter must look as if he or she is truly involved in what is being presented, and our body language, including our facial expressions, goes a long way in indicating our own level of involvement and interest.

This pertains to Lindsey's tone of voice as well. She must speak up so that her audience can hear her. If she naturally has a very soft voice, she should consult her instructor before the presentation about the possibility of obtaining a microphone to use. Also, her voice should vary in pitch, rising at some points and falling at others. The crucial idea here is not to use a monotone. She also has to watch how fast she speaks. The best rate is probably somewhat slower than she normally speaks in a conversation, and she should not be afraid to pause briefly between her points. A very good idea for Lindsey is to tape record or video-tape herself giving her presentation so that she can identify whether she speaks too fast or too slowly, whether her voice becomes too loud or too soft, whether her tone becomes shrill, and how her body language is. Becoming aware of how we look and sound is often a shock to us, but is a necessary part of becoming a good presenter.

Lindsey needs to practise and practise even more before giving her presentation. This is especially important for someone with performance anxiety like Lindsey's: the more she practises, the more comfortable she will feel with her material and the less anxiety she will feel. So it is important for Lindsey to practise even beyond the point where she feels comfortable. Practice and even more practice will serve her well.

If she can videotape herself, she can see how she comes across to her audience. If videotaping is not possible, she should practise in front of a large mirror, giving the presentation exactly as she will before her class. This will allow her to determine whether she is moving and gesturing appropriately, whether she is looking at her audience sufficiently, and whether she herself looks interested in her topic. She might also consider practising in front of some supportive friends or family members who will give her honest (but kindly phrased) feedback on how she is doing. This practice will also reduce her need for constant glancing at her notes on index cards and make her more confident that she is ready and able to present her class with something meaningful and educational.

WHAT IF THEY ASK ME QUESTIONS?

Let's hope they ask you questions! That means that the audience has heard you and has become involved in what you have been saying. Lindsey fears the questions, though; part of her public speaking anxiety has been based on the possibility that she will be asked questions she can't answer. When a question is asked, it is a good idea for her to pause. This gives her time to think, to make sure that she understands the question (and she should ask for clarification if she needs it). One of the authors of this book had the bad habit of blurting out an answer before a questioner was fully finished asking a question. Her professor in graduate school not-too-gently told her that by doing this, she gave the impression that the question was obvious and that the questioner was stupid! By pausing, he said, even if you know the answer to the question, it makes the questioner feel that the question was one that you need to reflect upon, and it makes sure that you don't answer a question that hasn't been asked. It was a mistake she learned not to make again!

If Lindsey knows the answer to the question (as she probably will), she can answer thoroughly. If she doesn't know the answer, it's perfectly fine to say, "I really don't know the answer to that question, but I'll look it up and get back to you on it" or, in other circumstances, "That question is a good one, and others have asked it, but no one has ever come up with a completely satisfactory answer." If the question is one that doesn't have a clear answer, but she has thought about it, she might say, "There isn't a clear answer to that, but if you allow me to speculate, one thing that I've been thinking is . . . ."

A summary of tips for presentations is given in Box 12.5.

Tips for Presenting Oral Information Effectively **BOX 12.5**

1. Know your audience so that you can adjust your language accordingly.

2. Condense your presentation into index card notes to prompt you rather than reading a speech. Use short sentences.

3. If you can think of a little context-related humour, use it.

4. Decide on whether visual displays are necessary or useful. If so, keep them simple and consider handing out hard copies for the audience to use for note taking.

5. Dress neatly and appropriately to the presentation.

6. Use a relaxed, upright posture. Move away from the lectern occasionally, gesture a little, smile.

7. Speak loudly enough to be heard and speak slowly enough to be understood. Don't use a monotone: vary the tone and pitch, as well as the rate of your voice. Listen to yourself on tape to determine whether you need to correct anything about your voice.

8. Practise in front of a mirror or by videotaping yourself so that you can adjust your movements, facial expressions, etc.

9. Listen to questions thoroughly and ask for clarification if you don't fully understand what is being asked. Pause a little before answering.

10. It's okay to say, "I don't know the answer to that." Don't try to bluff an answer.

 For more suggestions on effective public speaking, check out these websites: http://www.school-for-champions.com/speaking.htm; and http://wps.ablongman.com/ab_public_speaking_2.

CRITICISM

PART OF THE CLASS EXERCISE IS TO CRITICIZE EACH OTHER'S PRESENTATIONS. HOW CAN I COPE WITH THAT?

Many people say that they enjoy criticism, but the reality is that most of us enjoy praise! Hopefully, we learn to handle criticism and to improve ourselves and our performance by it. But it's never going to feel as nice as unqualified admiration. In order to learn to handle getting criticism, it might be best to first learn how to give constructive criticism.

HOW CAN I GIVE CRITICISM CONSTRUCTIVELY?

One of the tasks Lindsey will have in her class, and probably in her future career, will be to deliver criticism to others in a constructive manner. Criticism is meant to instruct, not to hurt. Yet most of us do feel hurt by criticism. We may feel personally attacked, or the person giving the criticism may be doing so in order to make himself or herself look superior or to compensate for his or her own bad mood. Learning how to give criticism constructively is an important task, and far too many supervisors, employers, and even instructors lack the skill. Learning to accept criticism is a little easier if one first learns how to give criticism in a manner that doesn't wound anyone else.

In Lindsey's course, the whole class is required to give feedback (i.e., criticism) to each person who gives a presentation. Hopefully, the instructor is sufficiently skilled in knowing how to give criticism that he or she will follow the general guidelines for giving constructive criticism.

The first element of giving criticism to consider is the timing of the criticism. For the most part, criticism, especially negative feedback, is uncomfortable and embarrassing when it is given in public. The best timing is in a private setting when the person giving the criticism and the person receiving it are in a relaxed frame of mind. In the classroom situation, written criticism for Lindsey to go over at her leisure and then discuss with her instructor and/or with the class might be the most constructive way of delivering the feedback. Lindsey might remember this for future situations she might be in: the object is not to hurt or embarrass the recipient of the criticism; it's to instruct and improve his or her behaviour or performance.

It's a good idea to start out with some positive statements. There is always something positive one can say about any presentation or performance. Starting with that will reassure the individual being criticized that he or she is not being judged as a complete failure, but that some of the things that he or she has done are valuable. For example, Lindsey's instructor might start out by saying something like, "Thank you, Lindsey, you've certainly put a lot of work into this and have given us all something to think about." It's a fair bet that a statement such as this is true, and recognition of it will help Lindsey feel better about herself and more receptive to negative statements that may follow.

Criticism should never be given when one is angry. For example, let's imagine that Lindsey's instructor believes that she has not done enough work for her presentation, or Lindsey believes that someone else's presentation is totally inadequate. In these cases, annoyance might be a reasonable feeling, but it is not reasonable to use that annoyance in giving feedback. After all, Lindsey's instructor really doesn't know whether Lindsey has done enough work or whether her performance is being affected by her anxiety. For that matter, Lindsey might be trying to give a presentation when she is very ill, and her illness, not the amount of work she has done, has made the presentation less than excellent. By the same token, Lindsey must remember when she gives criticism to anyone that she isn't a mind reader either, and there may be reasons for a less-than-optimal performance.

In future situations, Lindsey may become a supervisor or a leader of a group that is working on a task together. It is not unlikely that she will find one member of the group, or someone she is supervising, to be ineffective or not working up to the group's expectations. In this scenario, Lindsey will have the responsibility of delivering criticism to this individual. Her first act should be to outline the problem to the individual in very specific and neutral terms, and then ask the individual if he or she has an explanation for this. The individual may reveal problems in working that have not come to light before, and then perhaps Lindsey and other members of her group can work together to eliminate these problems so that whatever provoked the criticism disappears. This also ensures that Lindsey has her facts straight in delivering criticism. It may be that there has been a misunderstanding that has led to the problem. In this case, it is not criticism that is called for, but explanation and clarification.

Even if anger or annoyance is justified, criticizing someone in an angry or sarcastic or sneering tone is only going to make the recipient resentful and afraid to perform again. The tone that should be used in giving constructive criticism is one of specific, supportive objectivity; that is, the tone should reflect that what is being criticized is an element of the specific performance, not the individual nor the behaviour in general. It should be clear that the aim is to solve a problem together. That means that criticism should be focused on a specific behaviour, not on the individual. Will it help Lindsey to tell her that she doesn't have much charisma in giving a presentation? Or that her presentation was a huge yawn? Or will it be more helpful to say that her presentation could use more attention-grabbers and ways of involving the audience? Clearly, when the criticism is aimed at the individual, the individual feels diminished and doesn't really know what to do, except walk away, feeling like a lesser human being. When the behaviour in general is attacked, again, there is no indication to the individual of what to do about it. But when the criticism is aimed at the specific behaviour in a more supportive and positive manner, the individual doesn't feel so put down, and sees where he or she can improve in the future.

Making suggestions for improvement is a big part of giving constructive criticism. If Lindsey is only told that her presentation merits a mark of *C*, how will she ever know how to get a *B* or even an *A* in the future? When she gives criticism to others, she needs to keep in mind that without suggestions for improvement, her criticism is not constructive. Sometimes it's more effective to make suggestions by asking questions. For example, if Lindsey is evaluating someone else's presentation, she will find it more comfortable for herself and for the recipient of the criticism if she says, "Do you think a summary of your points at the end might have been useful?" rather than, "You should have given a summary of your points at the end." The technique of using questions makes the recipient of the criticism feel like more of a partner in a process aimed at improving performance, exactly what constructive criticism should do.

Finally, it is usually a good idea to ask the individual if he or she understands what is being said. For example, Lindsey might be asked to make a list of things she might change about her presentation, given the criticism she has received. If Lindsey is giving the criticism to someone, she would be well advised to ask the individual to repeat back what the problem seems to be and what might be done about it. This ensures that the recipient of the criticism really does see what the problem is and what to do about it, and makes sure that the recipient is not hearing a different (and usually more negative) message than was intended. If Lindsey, or whoever else is giving the criticism, detects that the recipient of the criticism is feeling badly, this is the point at which to reassure the person that the problem can be overcome and that help will be available.

Box 12.6 summarizes the steps in delivering constructive criticism.

Giving Criticism Constructively   BOX 12.6

In giving criticism, we must assume that you have good intentions and are not merely trying to "score points" by putting someone down, or criticizing as a result of your own bad mood of the day. It's always a good idea to examine our own motives first, asking ourselves if the criticism we are about to give is really justified. If the criticism is justified, the following steps should be considered in giving the criticism.

1. If possible, give criticism in private.
2. Start by saying something positive about the general performance.
3. Never give criticism when you are angry or annoyed.
4. Do not use sarcasm or sneering when delivering criticism.
5. Discuss the behaviour/performance, not the individual.
6. Be specific about what is being criticized; don't talk in generalities.
7. Outline the specific problem and ask if there is a reason that the problem is occurring. Make sure you have your facts straight and understand both sides of a problem.
8. Make suggestions for improving the behaviour/performance.
9. Phrase the suggestions in terms of questions (e.g., would it have been helpful to . . ., do you think it might have been more effective to . . .) if possible.
10. Ask the recipient of the criticism to repeat back what the problem is and what the possible solutions are.

HOW CAN I RECEIVE CRITICISM IN A MORE CONSTRUCTIVE MANNER?

Receiving criticism is never easy. We want people to point out the positive elements of what we have done; we want praise. But that's not how we learn. Like it or not, we learn better from our mistakes and from others' pointing out what we have done wrong or what we could have done better. When one receives criticism, one usually feels vulnerable and under attack. Some people feel this worse than others. If you feel very vulnerable when you are being criticized, ask yourself why. Are you, perhaps, playing out a scene from the past, the one where somebody sent you, as a child, the message that you weren't good enough? If so, take a deep breath and remember that you are not a child anymore; you are an adult, an intelligent, growing person who is ready to learn but who will not tolerate being abused.

We hope that whoever gives you, or Lindsey, criticism will follow the guidelines that we have just discussed, but even so, receiving the criticism might not be comfortable. This is a time to be thick-skinned. Lindsey is not a thick-skinned person; in fact, her skin tends to be thin and tender. We can try to help her toughen up a little though.

First of all, Lindsey needs to be in the right mindset. She has to realize that this is an opportunity to learn, a chance to find out how to improve. This is the point of education. After all, if she always did everything right, there wouldn't be much point in her going to school, would there? So as much as Lindsey feels that criticism is a threat, she has to make self-statements to the effect that this is a chance to get better, and nothing anyone says will make her a less intelligent, valuable human being. This is personal growth for her, not a diminishing of her spirit.

When listening to criticism, one is often in a nervous, rather emotional state, worrying about what will be said. Under these conditions, it is easy to misinterpret what is said. We all think that we listen, but do we really? How often have you talked to someone but not been sure whether that person actually "heard" you? In communicating with other people, and in the case of receiving criticism, it is most vital that we use *active listening*. **Active listening** involves more than the passive reception of what another person is saying; it involves direct questioning and clarifying of information. Active listening probes into the speaker's meanings and feelings, and it rephrases what has been said to make sure that the correct message has been transmitted and understood. Box 12.7 outlines the keys to active listening.

Lindsey must be careful to listen attentively and ask for clarification and more information. For example, if one classmate tells Lindsey that her visual presentation was not effective, Lindsey must first remind herself that this comment is about her visual presentation, not her whole presentation, and certainly not about her personally. Second, Lindsey should ask

active listening
involves direct questioning and clarifying of information, probing into the speaker's meanings and feelings, and rephrasing what has been said to make sure that the correct message has been transmitted and understood

---

Active Listening | BOX 12.7

1. Ask for clarification. Friendly and gentle questions—such as "Can you tell me more about this?" or "What's an example of that?"—encourage the speaker and make him or her feel that your attention is focused on what is being said and you are interested.

2. Paraphrase. Put what the speaker has said into your own words. This allows the speaker to correct any misapprehensions or to affirm that the correct message has been received.

3. Listen to the tone of voice as well as the content. Look at the body language of the speaker. Try to understand the feelings of the speaker and reflect what you ascertain. For example, you might test your empathy by saying, for example, "You seem disappointed by what happened" or "It

seems hard for you to tell me this." This lets the speaker know that you both hear the content of the message and understand the emotions underlying the message.

4. Summarize and reflect meaning. Restate in your own words what you have heard, both in content and in emotion. Try to interpret what has been said and put it in a larger context and meaning. For example, you might say, "You feel badly giving me a critical review, but you feel that for my own instruction, I need to know that my visual presentations were too crowded to be maximally effective." This helps you gain understanding and insight, and assures the speaker that his or her message has been understood with sensitivity.

Source: Schafer, 1996; Knippen & Green, 1994.

for more detail: was the visual presentation too short, too long, not specific enough, not colourful enough, too colourful? That is, Lindsey needs to know exactly what her critic means by "not effective" and how she can improve her presentations in the future.

Lindsey must also be aware at this time that most of what will be said to her will contain at least a hint of truth. She is not a perfect human being, no one is. There is always room for improvement in anything we do. But that doesn't mean that she has to blindly accept everything that she is being told. She needs to evaluate the source of the criticism: is the critic someone who genuinely does know more than she does? For example, it's wise to take your instructor's criticism seriously because he or she really does know more about the topic and how it should be presented than you do (that's why you're the student and he/she is the instructor!). But what about criticism from other people? When Lindsey receives criticism on her presentation from other people in her class, she needs to evaluate it carefully. It's unlikely that any of these people know more about the topic than she does, but they *do* know what it was like to be the audience while she gave her presentation. They know whether she made her points clear; they know whether she engaged their interest; they know whether she provoked them to think a little more about the topic. In these areas, their credibility is high, and Lindsey should listen to what they say. This is most especially true if she hears the same criticism from several sources. For instance, if three-quarters of the class indicated that they were unable to hear Lindsey's voice, Lindsey knows that she spoke too softly. But if only one person in the class indicated that he or she did not find the presentation clear, while the rest of the class found it very clear, Lindsey can safely disregard the one critic, knowing that the problem was with the critic, not her presentation. This is a place where Lindsey needs to remind herself that no one is universally liked, that no matter what you do, someone will find something wrong with it.

In receiving criticism, Lindsey must make sure that she does not become defensive. It's a natural reaction to want to defend oneself from threat, but when constructive criticism is being given, the situation is one of education, not threat. Defensiveness is inappropriate and impedes accurate listening. No one needs to be defensive constantly, and sometimes the best response to criticism is simply, "Thank you for taking the time to consider my work." If Lindsey feels that the criticism is unjustified, and her assertively asking for clarification doesn't seem to get her any reasonable information, she might respond with, "I'm sorry you feel that way about my work," and leave it at that—note that she does not have to give in to every critic's comments, nor does she have to explain herself and her choices continually. All she really has to do is respond politely and learn what she can from what is being said.

A summary of tips on receiving criticism is given in Box 12.8.

Receiving Criticism   BOX 12.8

1. Make sure you are in the mindset that the purpose of the criticism is to help you.

2. Take a deep breath and try to relax.

3. Listen attentively, asking for more detail and clarification of points. Make sure you understand exactly what the criticism is.

4. Don't become defensive. Arguing with a critic rarely changes his or her mind and tends to get in the way of your ability to listen.

5. Consider the source of the criticism. If the criticism comes from more than one person, and/or from people who are more knowledgeable about the topic than you, it should be taken seriously.

6. If you think the criticism has merit, thank the critic for taking the time to make his or her point. If you're not sure whether the criticism has merit or not, say something like, "That's an interesting point; I'll have to think about that" or "I'll have to give that point more thought."

7. If you feel that the criticism is unjustified or even hostile, maintain your cool: respond politely and assertively, "I'm sorry you feel that way. I understand your position, but I disagree. I think the criticism is stepping over the boundary of constructiveness. Can you tell me what to do to correct what you see as the flaws?"

More help in giving and receiving criticism can be found on the following websites: http://www.usu.edu/arc/idea_sheets/criticism.htm; and http://www.winstonbrill.com/bril001/html/article_index/articles/451-500/article454_body.html.

AM I READY TO GIVE PRESENTATIONS NOW?

Yes, you are, and so is Lindsey. A summary of advice to Lindsey is given below. And remember that public speaking is a skill: it gets better with practice. So don't shy away from giving presentations: learn to give them effectively so that others can benefit from the interesting things you have to say.

Advice for Lindsey

▶ The first piece of advice we have for Lindsey is to stay in the course! This course gives her a chance to (1) learn to give good presentations, and (2) learn valuable lessons about giving and receiving criticism. These are important skills that will stand her in good stead in the future.

WHAT TO DO	WHY
Learn to be assertive. (See Box 12.2.)	Assertive people feel more confident and are perceived as more confident and competent by others. By learning assertiveness, Lindsey will be able to give presentations, and give and receive criticism more effectively.
Prepare a presentation on a topic that interests you and that contains a few important points, with intriguing questions and attention-grabbers. (See Box 12.3.)	You have to feel enthusiasm and interest for a topic before you can impart that enthusiasm to others. Your audience doesn't know as much about the topic as you do, so find ways to challenge their thinking and keep their attention.
Check your manner of presentation. (See Box 12.5.)	The way you present information is almost as important as the information you present. The audience will learn more from your presentation and have their thinking challenged more if they feel engaged by your presentation style.
Learn to give criticism constructively. (See Box 12.6.)	You will be required to criticize others in classes, in careers, and in your personal life. It's important to know how to do this so that people are helped to better their performance, not hurt or devalued.
Learn to listen actively. (See Box 12.7.)	You are going to receive criticism in classes, in careers, and in your personal life. It's important to make sure that you hear what is being said accurately. At the same time, it's important that the person speaking to you knows that you have heard what he or she has said accurately and with insight.
Learn to receive criticism. (See Box 12.8.)	Since everyone is the recipient of criticism at some time (usually many times), it's vital to learn how to tell what is valid criticism and what is not, and how to respond to criticism in order to improve your performance in the future, rather than feeling resentful and diminished by the criticism.

CHAPTER SUMMARY

- Assertiveness is the ability to state your wants, needs, and feelings without infringing on the rights of others. It includes being able to satisfy your own needs without hurting others in the process. When you are assertive, you are perceived as more confident and more competent, qualities that would be highly beneficial in all situations, and especially in giving presentations or discussing matters in groups.

- Learning to be assertive includes knowing what you want, using direct verbal and nonverbal behaviour, focusing on actions, not the personalities of others, and repeating the message until you are sure that you have been accurately heard.

- Performance anxiety, or a fear of not being able to perform adequately, is a common problem that can be overcome by using relaxation techniques, changing negative self-statements to positive self-statements, and interpreting the public speaking situation as a chance to educate others, rather than as a situation in which you will be judged.

- Preparation and practice are vital to giving good presentations. The presentation should include enough information to be appropriate to the time allotted, with time to pose questions and to answer questions. Visual aids are often useful and interesting.

- In giving a presentation, you need to make sure your voice is heard and is not a monotone, and to use body language such as eye contact, gesturing, and appropriate facial expressions. Tape recording or, better still, videotaping a practice presentation will reveal how you appear to the audience and show you what to change, and will increase your confidence in your presentation.

- Criticism should be given only with the aim of helping someone to improve a facet of his/her performance. It should be specific, and include recommendations for improvement.

- Receiving criticism may be difficult, but it is important to use active listening, listen objectively, refrain from becoming defensive, and ask for specific examples of problem areas and specific recommendations for improvement. In deciding whether to act on the criticism, you need to evaluate the source of the criticism and how often this particular criticism has been given.

KEY TERMS

active listening   assertiveness   performance anxiety

INDIVIDUAL ACTIVITIES

1. Make a list of times when you felt you were not assertive enough or were aggressive. Knowing what you know now, how would you handle these situations?

2. If you have a fear of public speaking, try to ascertain why. What negative statements are you saying to yourself? How can you replace these statements with more reasonable, positive statements?

3. Practise giving criticism constructively in each of the following situations:

   a) Your friend's essay contains poor grammar and punctuation.
   b) Your younger brother's telephone manners are terrible.
   c) Your boyfriend/girlfriend chooses gifts that are completely inappropriate for his/her employer.

4. Practise responding to the following criticisms:

   a) "You never finish anything you start."
   b) "You didn't do enough work on this project."
   c) "Did you study at all for this test?"

5. Try active listening with someone with whom you don't normally have close conversations. It could be a parent or sibling, or a classmate you don't know very well. Does the active listening help the relationship?

GROUP ACTIVITIES

1. As a group, discuss whether you agree with all the "rights" listed in Box 12.1. Are there situations that you can think of in which these "rights" may not be appropriate? Think about this: part of learning to be assertive is to develop the discrimination to know when asserting these rights is appropriate. It's also important to find out from other group members where they feel assertiveness is appropriate and where it is not.

2. As a group, compare your answers to the scenarios in Exercise 12.2. Can you agree, as a group, on what the best assertive response would be?

3. Take a small topic (such as "What I did on the weekend") and let each member of the group simulate giving a presentation on this topic. Let the rest of the group evaluate the presenter on mannerisms, posture, eye contact, etc. Be constructive in letting each member know how he or she is seen by others. How does speaking without preparation differ from making a presentation that one has time to prepare?

REFERENCES

Barlow, D. H., & Durand, V. M. (2005). *Abnormal psychology: An integrative approach.* Belmont: Thomson Wadsworth.

Greenberg, J. S. (2002). *Comprehensive stress management* (7th ed.). New York: McGraw-Hill.

Knippen, J. T., & Green, T. B. (1994). How the manager can use active listening. *Public Personnel Management, 23(2),* 357–359.

Schafer, W. (1996). *Stress management for wellness* (3rd ed.). Toronto: Harcourt Brace.

Zekeri, A. A. (2004). College curriculum competencies and skills former students found essential to their careers. *College Student Journal, 38(3),* 412–422.

CHAPTER 13

WORKING IN GROUPS

The Case of Keiko

▶ "And for this project, you will work in groups of five," said Instructor Thomas, Keiko's urban planning instructor, on the first day of class. Many other people in the class looked happy, but Keiko's heart sank. Last year, she had watched her brother struggle to complete a project in a group, and he'd claimed it was the worst experience he had ever had in school. He'd said that other members of his group didn't cooperate or complete their work on time, which compromised everyone else's work. He had said that there was one person, Ralph, who hadn't done any work at all, but had coasted through on everyone else's work.

Keiko didn't want to face the same problems her brother had. "Is it inevitable that groups are like this? If it is, why does the instructor insist that we work this way?" she thought. Approaching him cautiously, Keiko asked Instructor Thomas, "Would it be all right if I did the project on my own? I don't know anyone in the class to form a group with."

"No," he replied. "I will assign people to groups randomly. Group projects and teamwork are mandatory today, not only in school, but in the working world. Get used to it, Keiko, and make the experience a good one."

Keiko would like to follow this advice, but she's unsure of what she might be facing in this group.

LEARNING OBJECTIVES

In this chapter, we will:

- Examine some of the particular phenomena that occur in groups that don't occur when one person works alone

- Take a brief look at the issue of diversity in groups

- Discuss the issue of leadership, when it is necessary in a group, and what kinds of leaders are best in particular situations

- Find ways to correct problems that may arise within a group

- Discover methods to keep a group on track and satisfied with their work

Keiko's instructor is right: working in groups is part of the normal experience of work today. Many people have found this part of work to be the best part. Sharing ideas, pulling together as a team, and accomplishing something bigger and better than any one of the group members could have done alone in the time allotted can be incredibly rewarding. But sometimes, as in the case of Keiko's brother, the group doesn't work as a team, things go wrong, and individual members may not know how to fix the problems.

THE ROLE OF GROUPS

WHY ARE GROUPS AND TEAMS SO POPULAR TODAY?

In today's fast-paced environment, many company executives believe that if groups of people, with different skills and different perspectives, work together to solve the problems, tasks can be completed efficiently and quickly. For example, teams are believed to save money, increase productivity, and arrive at better decisions. If this is true, they are the best use of resources (Robbins & Finley, 2000). Some of these beliefs are justified, but working in groups is complex. For example, it's not necessarily the case that a group of people will arrive at a better product than one person working alone. As we see in Chapter 14 on creativity, one individual, working alone, usually comes up with more and better ideas when brainstorming than when working with a group. Why might this be? The reason is that a group is more than just a collection of people: groups have specific dynamics of their own, and things occur in a group that are often unexpected.

Are you comfortable working in a group? Take the test in Exercise 13.1 to find out.

EXERCISE 13.1

▶ *Are You a Team Player?*

This quiz indicates your attitudes towards working on a team. Describe how well you agree with each of the following statements, using this scale:

> SD = Strongly disagree
>
> D = Disagree
>
> N = Neutral
>
> A = Agree
>
> SA = Strongly agree

		SD	D	N	A	SA
1.	I am at my best when working alone.	5	4	3	2	1
2.	I have belonged to clubs and teams ever since I was a child.	1	2	3	4	5
3.	It takes far too long to get work accomplished with a group.	5	4	3	2	1
4.	I like the friendship of working in a group.	1	2	3	4	5
5.	I would prefer to run a one-person business than to be a member of a large firm.	5	4	3	2	1
6.	It's difficult to trust others in a group on key assignments.	5	4	3	2	1
7.	Encouraging others comes to me naturally.	1	2	3	4	5
8.	I like the give-and-take of ideas that is possible in a group.	1	2	3	4	5
9.	It's fun for me to share responsibility with other group members.	1	2	3	4	5
10.	Much more can be accomplished by a team than by the same number of people working alone.	1	2	3	4	5

Total score

Scoring and interpretation:

Add the numbers you have circled to obtain your total score.

41–50: You have strong positive attitudes toward being a team member and working cooperatively with other members.

30–40: You have moderately favourable attitudes toward being a team member and working cooperatively with other members.

10–29: You much prefer working by yourself than being a team member.

Source: Dubrin, Andrew J., *Human Relations: Interpersonal, Job Oriented-Skills,* 6th Edition, © 1997. Reprinted by permission of Pearson Education, Inc., Upper Saddle River, NJ.

    Here's a website to check out if you want more information on how you might find working in groups: http://reviewing.co.uk/toolkit/teams-and-teamwork.htm.

THE BENEFITS OF GROUPS

WHAT GOOD THINGS CAN HAPPEN IN A GROUP?

social facilitation
refers to the way that people in a group motivate each other to do better work

Group members often influence each other in a positive way. This is called **social facilitation**. Strictly speaking, social facilitation refers to the way that the presence of other people in the group can either enhance or impede an individual's performance, but usually we talk about it only in its positive sense. In this chapter, we will examine how social facilitation can influence group members to do better work.

In the best of all possible worlds, people would come together in groups, bringing their different skills and ideas to work on some problem or task that was of interest to all of them. In Keiko's group, it would be wonderful if the group contained a person from an urban centre and a person from a rural location, so each could give a perspective on living in such different conditions. It would also be helpful if the group had individuals with experience in planning group activities and organizing events, and creative individuals. A group like this might discuss varying viewpoints, come up with some novel ideas and be able to implement them. By having **diversity** in the group, every member of the group is broadening the thinking of each other member. Sometimes this can be so marked that the group's output is actually greater than the sum of the individuals' contributions—this is termed **synergy**. This is more likely to happen if the group has high diversity.

diversity
refers to the mixture of people within a group

synergy
the group's output is actually greater than the sum of the individuals' contributions

WHAT IS DIVERSITY?

Diversity refers to the mixture of people within a group. An individual need not be from a different culture to be part of the diversity of the society. Differences among people come from many different sources, including:

- race
- sex or gender
- religion
- age
- education
- background
- abilities, both physical and mental
- values
- motivation

- sexual orientation

- marital status

- familial status (children? dependants? elderly?)

- weight

- habits (e.g., smoking, drinking)

- personality

- manner of dress

All of these factors, even if they seem minor, can make a difference in the way an individual will interact in a group and what the individual can bring to a group.

IS IT A GOOD THING TO HAVE DIVERSITY IN A GROUP?

cultural sensitivity
an awareness and willingness to acknowledge that people of different cultures act in different ways and have different norms and values from those of the country's dominant culture

cultural fluency
an understanding of what the differences are among cultures

The issue of diversity is one that has troubled some people and heartened others. As the society we live in becomes more and more culturally diverse, there are extra considerations to be aware of. First we must develop **cultural sensitivity**, that is, an awareness and willingness to acknowledge that people of different cultures and subcultures act in different ways and have different norms and values from those of the country's dominant culture. It is also useful to have **cultural fluency**, or an understanding of what the differences are among cultures. In Box 13.1, we can see some of the cultural differences between North American society and some other cultures. (Remember that Canadian and American cultures are not identical, though!)

You can see from some of these differences that misunderstandings can occur within a diverse group if there is not cultural fluency. For example, Keiko, whose background includes the view that lateness is rude, may be very upset by Marjorie's more laid-back attitude. To Marjorie, it doesn't really matter if the meeting starts at 10 A.M. or 10:20 A.M., as long as everyone is content to begin working. This example points out that it is most important that there exists a respect for all cultures and all forms of diversity. This is not only courtesy to others, but it is logical since no one of us has a lock on what the right or wrong way to behave or to think is.

There is an added benefit to diversity in groups: diversity is a great source of education. Researchers have consistently found that students exposed to diversity in their classes benefit greatly: they develop more commitment to multicultural understanding and tolerance, their

---

Cultural Differences between Countries   BOX 13.1

This is a list of differences that may exist in the way people in Canada and the United States view issues and the way people in many other countries view the same issues. There are no rules about these differences, and not all members of any culture adhere to all the listed norms. These are only generalities.

North American Culture	Other Countries
Time: promptness is valued	Time is fluid and promptness is not important
Informality: use of first name, assumed friendship and intimacy	Formality: use of first name is a privilege given only to those with whom one has established a friendship
Competition: this is a valued norm	Cooperation: competition may seem overly aggressive and even hostile
Emphasis on work	Emphasis on relationships
Individualism	Communalism (group orientation)
Direct speech: sometimes blunt	Indirect speech: courtesy and an attempt not to "shame" or embarrass another

Sources: DuBrin, 1997; Benton, 1998; Greenberg & Baron, 1995.

analytical and problem-solving skills are enhanced, and even their writing skills improve (Pascarella, Edison, Nora, Hagedorn, & Terenzini, 1996; Pascarella, Pierson, Wolniak, & Terenzini, 2004; Shuford, 1998). This is not surprising: with respect for the differences other people bring to the group, we all become more flexible in our thinking and open to possibilities that had, perhaps, not crossed our minds before.

Here are websites that discuss diversity in more detail, both for those who are members of the larger dominant culture of the area and for those of other cultures and subcultures: http://www.bambooweb.com/articles/d/i/Diversity.html; http://www.pch.gc.ca/progs/multi/respect_e.cfm; and http://DiversityInc.com.

ARE THERE OTHER BENEFITS TO WORKING IN A GROUP?

Yes, performance can be enhanced by other people in a number of ways. One way that group members can enhance the performance of the group is by evaluating each other's thinking. Sometimes two heads are better than one, and major errors that may escape one person are more likely to be caught by other members of the group. Of course, we must assume that one group member is not ridiculed for an error, nor discriminated against because of this. That's a big assumption.

It is more likely that there will be respect for each other's ideas and no ridicule for mistakes in groups of people that want to be together. In many ways, people often perform better in groups when the groups are *cohesive* (Greenberg & Baron, 1995). **Cohesiveness** refers to how much the group members want to be part of the group, share the group's goals, and work together in meeting the goals. In a cohesive group, we would not expect arguments, ridicule, or put-downs. Rather, we would expect a great deal of cooperation and respect for diversity and individual differences. If there is competition among the members, this could spur each one on to work to the best of his or her ability, but in the cohesive group, competition is for fun and is good-natured. It is not to "score" on someone else, nor to make oneself appear better than everyone else. We would expect that this kind of cohesiveness would make for the best possible group, and it often does. Later, however, we shall see the pitfalls of cohesiveness.

If a cohesive group generally works better, then fostering cohesiveness would seem to be a good thing. Keiko's instructor has made that a little difficult however. He has determined to put group members together randomly instead of letting students pick their own group members. Why has he done this? Not only does he want to encourage the learning that can come when a group is diverse, but he may fear that if only friends get together in a group, they will not be cohesive in regards to the goal, but they will concentrate on the social aspects of getting together. Furthermore, if they are not focused on the goal as much as they are focused on their enjoyment of each other, they may be reluctant to put forth divergent views, to criticize one member's work, or to catch the errors that one member may be making. Instructor Thomas is aware that these are potential problems when members of a group know each other well or the group is very cohesive.

On the other hand, there are advantages to allowing people to pick their own group members and allowing friends to work together. Instructor Thomas may have made gaining cohesiveness more difficult for the group members if they don't know each other and he has put them together randomly. For one thing, cohesiveness is fostered by the amount of time that group members spend together. It makes sense that if group members don't have much time to spend together, they may not develop cohesiveness. In randomly placing people in groups, Instructor Thomas may have inadvertently put people together who have very different timetables, who live far away from each other, etc. That is, it may not be easy for these people to meet as frequently as necessary to accomplish the goals of the group. In addition, while random placement suggests that each group will contain members who are different from each other and will bring different skills and perspectives to the group, this may not be the case. Of course, if students are allowed to pick their own group members,

cohesiveness
refers to how much the group members want to be part of the group, share the group's goals, and work together in meeting the goals

this may happen as well: they may pick people who are very similar to themselves, and so have little by way of differing perspectives to bring to the group. An even worse situation may come about if the people Instructor Thomas has placed together don't like each other, since this may lead to unpleasant conflict in the group.

Hopefully, Keiko's group does consist of people with different skills and perspectives, and hopefully they can find enough time to meet at school to work on their common goal of the class project. They don't have to become best friends, but if they find they can like and respect each other, their experience will probably be a good one. Nevertheless, this doesn't guarantee success for the group.

THE PROBLEMS WITH GROUPS

WHAT WENT WRONG IN THE GROUP KEIKO'S BROTHER WAS IN?

social loafing
the general finding that when people work in groups, they tend to do less work than when they are working alone

deindividuation
the finding that, when in groups, people tend to produce more behaviour that is against the norm or socially unacceptable because, in general, they cannot be as readily identified when they are in a group as when they are working alone

We would venture a guess that in Keiko's brother's group, the first thing that went wrong was that cohesiveness never developed. The group members didn't care about the project they were doing and didn't care enough about each other's welfare to do what was required of them for the group's success. Perhaps they didn't show respect for their group's diversity and different viewpoints. One of the problems that made life very difficult for Keiko's brother, and could have led to the ultimate failure of the group, was that one person did not do what he was required to do. This is called *social loafing*. **Social loafing** refers to the general finding that when some people work in groups, they do less work than when they are working alone (Guerin, 1999). Why does this happen?

The problem of social loafing comes from another aspect of groups called *deindividuation*. **Deindividuation** is the finding that, when in groups, people tend to produce more behaviour that is against the norm or socially unacceptable. They do this because, in general, they cannot be as readily identified when they are in a group as when they are working alone. Have you ever watched the actions of a mob on the TV news? People in the mob may have been looting stores, throwing bricks, punching each other, and generally acting in highly aggressive and reprehensible ways. We often make the assumption that these are just bad people who were looking for the chance to do harm. Yet this may not be the case: many people do things in situations when they know they can't be identified that they would not do if they knew they could be identified. Keiko's brother himself has done this: when he was about 10 years old, he and a friend made prank calls to strangers. Today, when so many telephones have "call display" showing where the call is coming from, Keiko's brother would be far less likely to do this! When we can be readily identified by others, especially those in authority, we are more likely to pull our weight and conform to the rules. In our example, in the group Keiko's brother was in, the instructor didn't know that one member of the group, Ralph, had not been pulling his weight. One reason Ralph loafed and let other people do his work was because the people in authority (the instructor) wouldn't know who did the work and who didn't.

The fact that the instructor could not identify him as the one not doing his share isn't the whole reason why Ralph loafed; after all, the rest of his group members could identify him. But in a group, he knew that someone else would pick up the slack. He knew that he might be inconveniencing others, but no one would really suffer because someone else would do the work that he was supposed to do in order to save the group's goal. Indeed, the rest of the group covered up for the social loafer, not because they liked him but because, if they didn't do his work for him, they all would have suffered. In addition, in most classes, there is little likelihood that the other group members will have any way to make the social loafer accountable: that is, they may dislike him and resent him, but they don't have the power to give him a failing grade or remove him from the group. So, from his perspective, why shouldn't the social loafer's philosophy be "Let someone else do it"?

It still seems amazing to most of us that some people would be irresponsible enough to let other people do the work that was properly theirs. But they have lots of excuses: "I didn't realize I was supposed to do that." "I couldn't get all the materials." "I thought someone else was going to tell me more about it." "I didn't have time." "I have personal problems that got in the way." Some of these excuses may be true, while others are merely rationalizations to get out of trouble.

WHAT CAN BE DONE ABOUT SOCIAL LOAFING?

It's a hard problem to solve sometimes, especially if there is no way to enforce a group member's compliance. Many instructors include an evaluation of each group member by the other group members as part of each student's overall mark. The social loafer, then, is exposed because the rest of the group will evaluate him negatively and his mark will suffer. If the instructor does not include this, it might be useful for the group members to suggest it. But if the instructor takes the attitude that students have to learn to solve their own problems with individuals in groups (not an unreasonable position), it's up to the group members to deal with the social loafer.

The best technique is to try to prevent social loafing in the first place. At some point in the early meetings of the group, responsibilities have to be assigned to each group member. This should be crystal clear and in writing. If Keiko takes on the responsibility of doing the library research for the project, she needs clear direction from the group regarding what kind of resources are needed, how many are needed, and by what date they are needed. Each group member should be sure of what he or she is required to do, and putting this organization in writing is the best way to make sure that all are clear on their functions. Let's say that Keiko's group is going to do a presentation to the class on green spaces within the city, their importance, and where they should be placed. An example of a group organization plan can be seen in Box 13.2.

Note that this organization stipulates what will happen if each member is late and what will happen if each group member doesn't do the job assigned to him or her. This kind of organization, clearly written down and in each group member's possession, should remove the excuse that the social loafer didn't complete his or her work because he or she was unclear about what to do. It also removes most of the deindividuation effect when it is so clear to all group members who is responsible for what. Another positive effect is that it shows clearly just how important each member's contribution is, another way of cutting down on social loafing (Greenberg & Baron, 1995).

To avoid the problems of the social loafer, it is also a good idea for the group to agree, right from the beginning, that if sickness, personal problems, or any other reverses beset any group member (i.e., anything that might get in the way of the group member's completing his or her work by the due date), the rest of the group must be informed *immediately*. It does the group no good to find out the day before the presentation is due that one group member couldn't complete the work because he or she had a cold!

As the group members do their work, they should check in with each other on a regular basis: this provides a little social pressure to keep working. At least, it may be possible to detect that a member of the group is not working up to par. The social loafer sometimes indicates that he or she is "planning on doing it this weekend." Maybe he or she will, or maybe this plan will fall through for unexpected reasons, or maybe the loafer said this just to get people to stop nagging! When the group recognizes that one member of the group is not doing the work assigned, the problem needs to be addressed. If there is a group leader (more about leadership later), the group leader needs to use a firm but assertive tone in confronting the loafer, saying something like, "We had all agreed to tasks and due dates, but we are very concerned that you will not have your part of the work done by the due date. This will badly compromise the work the rest of us are doing. Is there some problem that is getting in the way of your work? Do you need one of us to help you with it, and you can take on other duties later?" If the

Organizational Plans for Keiko's Group   BOX 13.2

Group Member	Task	Coordinate with	Due date	What happens if this member is a social loafer?
Keiko	Find six library articles on the effects of green spaces within urban centres.	Marjorie, Darrin	October 3 (if Keiko is late, Darrin may not have enough time to do his job)	The group will have no research or theoretical basis for any statements they make about green spaces.
Marjorie	Interview an urban planner, a social worker, and a teacher about the necessity of having green spaces in a city.	Keiko, Darrin	October 3 (if Marjorie is late, Darrin may not have time to do his job)	The group will have no practical input from members of the community who are concerned with green spaces.
Darrin	Write a summary of what Keiko and Marjorie have discovered.	Keiko, Marjorie	October 24 (if Darrin is late, the group may not have time to consult with Madison and the presentation may not be ready in time)	The group will have no summary of information to present.
Anwar	Make diagrams of locations of green spaces within the city, showing their connection to housing complexes and community centres.	Darrin, Marjorie	October 15 (if Anwar is late, the group may not have time to consult with Madison and the presentation may not be ready in time)	The group will have no visual display to indicate the significance of present placements or possibilities for future placements.
Madison	Make suggestions concerning placements of green spaces: are the existing ones in good places, what places would be better?	Keiko, Marjorie, Darrin, Anwar	November 5 (if Madison doesn't consult with other members of the group before this, she may not have time to integrate planning ideas and the presentation may not be ready in time)	The group will have no planning suggestions to present.

group has no leader, and there is no one in the group willing to be the speaker for all members, the group could consider sending the social loafer an e-mail signed by the whole group. It's important that the loafer not be attacked at this time. For one thing, there *may* be a legitimate reason why the work is not getting done. For another thing, while many of us hope that an attack will make the loafer feel guilty and get to work, the reality is that the loafer will feel resentful and be less likely to work. Social loafing is reduced in a cohesive group (Karau & Williams, 1997), so showing concern for the loafer is more likely to draw the loafer closer to the group (i.e., make the group more cohesive), thereby spurring the loafer to do more work.

If these techniques don't work with the social loafer, it may be time to ask the advice of the instructor. Even if the instructor is unwilling to intervene with the social loafer, he or she may have more suggestions for dealing with the problem, and at the very least, he or she will understand that a social loafing problem has been experienced by this group.

ARE THERE OTHER PROBLEMS THAT CAN OCCUR IN GROUPS?

group polarization
the tendency of groups to make more extreme final decisions than their initial positions indicated

Unfortunately, yes. Sometimes groups make decisions that are unwise simply because of the impact of the group. One of the decision-making problems that can arise is called *group polarization*. **Group polarization** refers to the tendency of groups to make more extreme final decisions than their initial positions indicated (Friedkin, 1999). Let's take an example of this.

The date of Keiko's group's presentation to the class is November 10. The group must decide on when they can have the presentation ready. Privately, Keiko thinks they could have it done by November 8. Privately, Marjorie thinks November 7. Darrin thinks November 9, while Anwar thinks November 7, and Madison thinks November 8. After discussing what to do and allotting tasks, the group starts discussing a date when they can have everything done. The final date they settle on is November 6. November 6?!? This is earlier than any of them anticipated until they had talked with each other. Having talked together, however, their final decision shifted to something more extreme (i.e., earlier) than anything anyone had contemplated before. Now in this case, there isn't much problem: it certainly is to the group's benefit to finish as early as they can so they have plenty of time to make corrections and iron out the wrinkles before the day they have to present their project to the instructor and class. But in some cases, group polarization can be a problem, and can lead the group to take risks or become more conservative (i.e., to become more polarized) than is warranted, possibly leading to bad decisions. Let's look at another example that has the potential for much more harm.

A group of students at Keiko's school gravitated together because they all live in the same, rather wealthy, neighbourhood. Coming from the same sort of background, many of their attitudes were already similar. One unfortunate attitude several of them held was that students from less well-off neighbourhoods were jealous of them and made fun of them. The more this group stayed together and talked, the more they became convinced that other students were ridiculing them. Their initial attitudes had become strengthened by their interactions with each other. They began to believe that other students were people who didn't understand them and they should stay away from them. This, of course, led the other students to assume that the students from the well-off neighbourhoods were snobbish. And the more these students talked among themselves about how the wealthy students were snobbish, the more they believed that the wealthier students were putting them down, and their attitudes became more negatively extreme against these students. This group polarization resulted in a split in the school: instead of students mixing freely with each other and sharing perspectives and ideas, they intensified and even created differences between them.

The phenomenon of group polarization is one that is of concern to many people in different walks of life. For example, lawyers worry that juries deciding on a sentence for a convicted criminal may settle on a sentence that is either much heavier or much lighter than may be warranted because of polarization. It has even been suggested that groups engaging in terrorism do so because their views have become polarized; that is, they commit acts as a group that they would never do if they had not been in the group because their attitudes become more extreme through their interactions with each other (Myers, 1999).

THIS SOUNDS SERIOUS. ARE THERE OTHER MAJOR PROBLEMS FOR GROUPS?

groupthink
deteriorated critical thinking that occurs when group members isolate themselves from other opinions and ideas from outside the group

Yes. Maybe the biggest problem is one that is connected with polarization. It's called **groupthink**. When group members don't want to rock the boat by disagreeing with each other, they isolate themselves from other opinions and ideas from outside the group and their critical thinking starts to deteriorate (Janis, 1982). A couple of real-life examples make this clear, and show how dangerous groupthink can be.

One of the most famous examples of groupthink occurred in 1961. American President John F. Kennedy and his close advisors were a very cohesive group who were often referred to as "The Best and the Brightest" (Halberstam, 1972). In those days of Cold War between the United States and the Communist countries, this young and somewhat inexperienced group followed plans that were designed (but never implemented) by the previous government to overthrow Fidel Castro in Cuba by an invasion at a place in Cuba called the Bay of Pigs. The invasion failed disastrously due to the poor planning and the erroneous assumptions made by the planners. Many lives were lost. Afterwards, the president and his advisors realized how very ill-conceived the plan had been, remembered that they had ignored other advisors who recognized that the plan was very ill-advised, and wondered how they had ever thought it could work or should even be attempted.

Another example is that of the decision to launch the space shuttle *Challenger* in 1986 when there were clearly structural problems with the spacecraft. The result, tragically, was the explosion of the *Challenger* and the loss of life of all those aboard.

These are dramatic examples, but they illustrate the impairment of decision-making processes that can occur in any group unless it is careful. In Keiko's group, let's suppose that the decision is made not to give the class handouts when the group gives the presentation. In fact, other groups have used handouts and the instructor has mentioned how useful they were. But Keiko's group ignores this information, as the members keep rationalizing to each other that the handouts are unnecessary. Privately, Keiko thinks that the handouts would be a good idea, but she doesn't want to be the lone dissenter, so she says nothing. Unbeknownst to her, Anwar and Marjorie are having the same thoughts, but they, too, say nothing. As it turns out, the handouts would have been a good idea, and Instructor Thomas mentions this as part of his criticism of the group's project. Keiko and her group then feel rather foolish because it would have been so easy to make handouts and now it seems obvious to them that it would have been beneficial.

Groupthink often occurs in highly cohesive groups because membership in the group seems more important than challenging the other members' thinking. But the group need not be cohesive for groupthink to occur (Hodson & Sorrentino, 1997). Box 13.3 outlines the symptoms of groupthink. Box 13.4 makes suggestions for preventing groupthink.

Symptoms of Groupthink   BOX 13.3

1. *The illusion of invulnerability.* Group members may become overly optimistic that their plans will work and they disregard and discredit information that suggests otherwise. In some cases, it is also seen that group members begin to assume that their viewpoints are morally and ethically right.

2. *Closed-mindedness.* Group members rationalize their positions by withholding dissenting opinions, and characterizing anyone who does disagree as being overly negativistic and unknowledgeable, therefore not worthy of regard.

3. *Desire for unanimity.* There is pressure within the group for unanimous decisions and an illusion that all group members agree. This is achieved by the group members themselves censoring their opinions and talking themselves into agreement with the group and by actively suppressing information that would call their viewpoint into question.

Sources: Benton, 1998; Myers, 1999; Greenberg & Baron, 1995.

How to Prevent Groupthink

BOX 13.4

1. Encourage questioning. Each group must make sure that no member is ever discouraged from bringing doubts or new information to the table. It is helpful to appoint a "devil's advocate," that is, someone whose job it is to poke holes in decisions and find fault with viewpoints.

2. Use sub-groups. Break up the group and have sub-groups or even two or three people talk about an issue apart from the whole group. Then, when the group comes together again, there has been opportunity for different views to emerge.

3. Seek outside information. Ask for opinions and information from sources outside the group. Do not discount

any out of hand, but remain impartial and critically evaluate *all* information.

4. Before any decision is implemented, have a "second chance" meeting: at this meeting, all group members are encouraged to air any doubts they may have and to bring up any new ideas. The point is to see if the decisions and ideas still seem good after group members have had a chance to leave the group and think about their positions for a while.

Sources: Myers, 1999; Greenberg & Baron, 1995.

ROLES IN GROUPS

MIGHT IT BE BEST TO HAVE A STRONG LEADER TO KEEP A GROUP ON TRACK?

task leader
this person is focused on the goal and serves to keep people on track with the project and to organize what is being done, when to meet, etc.

social leader
this person is more concerned with the feelings and well-being of the group members than with the job

Sometimes. But if a strong leader has a strong opinion, the rest of the group may not want to disagree with him or her, and so the potential for groupthink would arise again. Leaders do often arise in groups though. Sometimes they are appointed, sometimes they are elected, and sometimes, they just seem to appear. In an informal group like the one Keiko is in, it's unlikely that the members will choose to elect a leader. Nonetheless, as time goes on, it's likely that one person will emerge to keep people on track with the project and to organize what is being done, when to meet, etc. This person is generally referred to as a **task leader**. Task leaders are focused on the goal, but they may forget that groups are made up of people with feelings and needs. Sometimes task leaders seem to be rude or abrupt or insensitive to other group members. They really don't mean to be, but they are so focused on the job to be done that everything else fades into the background.

Often another kind of leader arises in a group, a **social leader**. This person is more concerned with the feelings and well-being of the group members than with the job. The task leader and the social leader may conflict at times because of their differing priorities, but both play a part in the functioning of the group. The task leader is better at motivating high achievement in the group (Locke & Latham, 1990), while social leaders are better at preventing groupthink (since they encourage everyone to express an opinion; Myers, 1999). In an ideal world, an individual could be both a task leader and a social leader; that is, the leader could be someone who keeps the group on track and gets the project done while also being sensitive to the group members' needs and feelings. Most leadership training programs try to promote this (Myers, 1999).

What are leadership skills? Box 13.5 describes the characteristics that successful leaders demonstrate.

Find out if you have leadership skills by taking the test in Exercise 13.2.

Characteristics of Successful Leaders

BOX 13.5

Successful leaders:

- have drive, the desire for achievement, high energy.

- stick with it, and don't give up until it's absolutely necessary. They are conscientious and follow through on work.

- have initiative. They don't wait around to be told what to do; they see work and they start doing it.

- have honesty and integrity. Leaders can be trusted by others to be reliable and open.

- enjoy influencing others to reach goals through their own enthusiasm and faith. They enable others to do their best work.

- have self-confidence and self-efficacy. They trust themselves to be able to do the job.

- are intelligent. They can analyze and integrate information and apply it to many situations.

- are creative, original, and flexible. They can adapt to the needs of the group members and to the requirements of the situation.

- are outgoing and emotionally stable.

- serve as role models for other members of the group.

Sources: Adapted from Benton, 1998; Myers, 1999; Greenberg & Baron, 1995.

EXERCISE 13.2   ▶ *Test Your Leadership Skills*

Rate yourself on basic leadership characteristics.

		Always	Sometimes	Rarely
1.	I'm a good listener.	❑	❑	❑
2.	I'm accessible.	❑	❑	❑
3.	I'm decisive.	❑	❑	❑
4.	I'm gracious.	❑	❑	❑
5.	I keep it simple.	❑	❑	❑
6.	I'm optimistic.	❑	❑	❑
7.	I give credit where due.	❑	❑	❑
8.	I confront problems.	❑	❑	❑
9.	I speak directly.	❑	❑	❑
10.	I acknowledge mistakes.	❑	❑	❑
11.	I have a can-do attitude.	❑	❑	❑
12.	I'm enthusiastic.	❑	❑	❑
13.	I seek strong subordinates/colleagues.	❑	❑	❑
14.	I have a positive attitude.	❑	❑	❑

Scoring:

Number of responses in the Always column x 5 = _____

Number of responses in the Sometimes column x 3 = _____

Number of responses in the Rarely column x 1 = _____

Total score (add the three totals): _____

Analyze your score:

More than 50: You have a great deal of natural leadership ability!

30–50: You have a good base of leadership skills.

Less than 30: Underdeveloped leadership skills may hamper you in your career. It may be useful for you to take a leadership development course.

DOES THERE HAVE TO BE A LEADER IN ALL GROUPS?

No there doesn't. Some groups, such as Keiko's, may not need a leader if the members of the group can agree on what needs to be done for the project and each person takes on responsibility for a particular part of the task. If the group members can be clear on what needs to be done and can exert the self-control to lead themselves (i.e., they do not need to be supervised), a formal leader is unnecessary. But it's important for the group to remember that they need to ensure that they all share information and any problems that arise, they make decisions together, and they all take responsibility for the work product (Benton, 1998).

ARE THERE OTHER ROLES THAT PEOPLE TAKE WITHIN A GROUP?

Yes. It's not at all uncommon to find that different members of the group show their individual interests and strengths by taking on roles such as being the cheerleader and the main source of encouragement and praise for the work of other members. Another role that is often taken is that of being the person who deflects conflicts that begin to arise and restores the harmony of the group. Still others may take on the role of being the one who keeps meticulous notes on what has been done, or the role of summarizing what people have said or what decisions have been made. What is important to note here is that many roles are available in every group, and each role—each person—is valuable to the success of the group.

 You can learn more about leadership at these websites: http://www.motivation-tools.com/workplace/index.htm; and http://www.nwlink.com/~donclark/leader/leader.html.

GROUP CONFLICT

ARE THERE ANY OTHER PROBLEMS THAT CAN OCCUR IN A GROUP?

Sadly, yes. Groups are made up of people, and sometimes people disagree. As alluded to earlier, sometimes conflict arises within a group. In Keiko's group, there could have been disagreement about who performed which chores, how many references were needed, what kinds of references were needed, how the information should be presented, and what conclusions could be reached. Countless other conflicts could have arisen based more on the personalities of the individuals than on the task itself. In Keiko's brother's group, conflict arose because one member did not pull his weight and the group members started to blame him, and each other, and became angry with their whole group situation.

In general, conflict arises because of:

- faulty communication: criticism is given inappropriately, and group members' feelings are hurt and they feel devalued.

attribution errors
errors in determining the causes of the behaviour of other members

- **attribution errors**: members make errors in determining the causes of the behaviour of other members. This can occur, for example, when one member doesn't complete his or her work and the other members jump to the conclusion that the reason for this was nothing more than irresponsibility. Maybe there was a good reason why that one member fell behind.

- mistrust: members do not trust each other due to poor communication, faulty attributions, or someone's lack of follow-through on obligations.

- grudges: members hold grudges when they feel they have been treated unfairly, when criticism has been given inappropriately, when there have been faulty attributions, or for other reasons; people become angry with each other and they sometimes nurse their anger and remain hostile rather than working through and resolving their anger and moving on.

■ personality clashes: this can occur when groups are put together randomly in particular. The styles of working differ with each member and in some cases, there may be a lack of fit among the members.

Conflict in a group doesn't have to mean that the group cannot function. In fact, if the conflict is handled well, it may actually help the group to function. People can grow and learn from conflict, especially if it can be resolved in a way that makes the group a winner, not in a way that makes one individual the loser. If the resolution involves all members of the group, regarding the conflict as a group problem rather than as one person's problem, the group cohesiveness may even be increased. Group conflicts should be dealt with because they can become destructive and divide the group (Benton, 1998).

There are many books and training programs for conflict management within working groups, but in a class group, it is hoped that less formal and more cooperative measures can be used to prevent conflict when possible, and resolve it when it does arise. How do you manage conflict? What is your particular style? Take the test in Exercise 13.3 to find out. Then look at Box 13.6 for some suggestions for conflict resolution.

EXERCISE 13.3

▶ *Styles of Conflict Management*

Check the alternative that most fits your typical reaction to the situation described.

1. When someone is overly hostile to me, I usually:
   a. ____ respond in kind.
   b. ____ persuade him or her to cool down.
   c. ____ hear the person out.
   d. ____ walk away.

2. When I walk in on a heated argument, I'm likely to:
   a. ____ jump in and take sides.
   b. ____ mediate.
   c. ____ keep quiet and observe.
   d. ____ leave the scene.

3. When I suspect that another person is taking advantage of me, I:
   a. ____ try to get the person to stop.
   b. ____ rely on persuasion and facts.
   c. ____ change how I relate to the person.
   d. ____ accept the situation.

4. When I don't see eye to eye with someone, I typically:
   a. ____ try to get him or her to see things my way.
   b. ____ consider the problem logically.
   c. ____ search for a workable compromise.
   d. ____ let the problem work itself out.

5. After a run-in with someone I care about a great deal, I:
   a. ____ try to make him or her see it my way.
   b. ____ try to work out our differences.

c. ____ wait before renewing contact.

d. ____ let it lie.

6. When I see conflict developing between two people I care about, I usually:

a. ____ express disappointment.

b. ____ try to mediate.

c. ____ watch to see what develops.

d. ____ leave the scene.

7. When I see conflict developing between two people who are relatively unimportant to me, I usually:

a. ____ express disappointment.

b. ____ try to mediate.

c. ____ watch to see what develops.

d. ____ leave the scene.

8. The feedback people give me indicates that I:

a. ____ push hard to get what I want.

b. ____ try to work out differences.

c. ____ take a conciliatory stance.

d. ____ sidestep conflict.

9. When having serious disagreements, I:

a. ____ talk until I've made my point.

b. ____ talk a little more than I listen.

c. ____ listen and make sure I understand.

d. ____ listen passively.

10. When someone does something that angers me, I generally:

a. ____ use strong, direct language.

b. ____ try to persuade him or her to stop.

c. ____ go easy, explaining how I feel.

d. ____ say and do nothing.

Scoring and analysis:

When you've completed the questions, add all the *A*s, *B*s, *C*s, and *D*s to find out where you collected the most responses. Then consider these profiles:

A. Competitive. If you picked mostly *A* responses, you feel best when you're able to direct and control others. Taken to extremes, you can be intimidating and judgmental. You are generally contemptuous of people who don't stand up for themselves, and you feel frustrated when you can't get through to someone.

B. Collaborative. If you scored high in this category, you may be from the "use your head to win" school of conflict management—strong-willed and ambitious, but not overbearing. You'll use persuasion, not intimidation, and are willing to compromise to end long-running conflicts.

C. Sharing. People who score high here don't get fired up. They listen to the opponent's point of view, analyze situations, and make a factual pitch for their case. But in the end, they will defer to opponents in the interest of harmony.

D. Accommodative. A high score suggests that you avoid conflict and confrontation at all costs, suppressing your feelings—strong as they may be—to keep peace.

Observation:

No one style of conflict management is better than another. Most people use all four, depending on the situation. But if you rely too much on one, start shifting your approach.

How to Resolve Conflicts

BOX 13.6

1. Deal with each conflict as it arises. Do not try to ignore it, hoping it will go away—it will probably fester and become worse if not dealt with. Let's use the example of one person in a group working at a very slow pace that is holding up the work of other group members.

2. Present the conflict as evidence that people are involved and excited about their work, that they are showing a passionate commitment to what they are doing. This may involve a little situational reconstruction (Chapter 3) to enable everyone to view what has been a negative situation as an opportunity for positive outcomes. For example, note that while the group may be frustrated with one member's slow work, the frustration reflects the enthusiasm of the group and the slowness may indicate the painstaking effort and care of the slow member.

3. Confront the issue as a problem to be solved. Focus on working together to solve the problem. In the example noted above, the issue would be how to enable the slow worker to be faster, providing what the rest of the group needs without losing the care that he or she has been taking.

4. Do not engage in blaming or character assassination. In the above example, blaming the slow worker or calling the slow worker derogatory names is strictly prohibited.

5. Be open-minded and fair, listening to all sides of the issue. Why does the slow worker say he or she is slow?

6. Insist on criticism being given appropriately and constructively. Explain the problems that slowness has been causing and how it is making the group members feel. (Review how to give and receive criticism in Chapter 12.)

7. As in dealing with criticism, make sure everyone in the group understands all sides of the issue by having them repeat or write down what they believe the arguments to be. Then check to make sure that everyone is correct in their understanding. Does the slow worker realize why the group is having problems with his or her slowness? Does the group understand why the slow worker is taking so much time?

8. Brainstorm to find solutions or compromises. Perhaps the slow worker's job is actually bigger than it seems and could be broken into sub-parts with another member helping. Perhaps the slow worker could filter parts of his or her work to the group as each part is ready, rather than waiting for the entire task to be done.

Sources: Parts are adapted from Benton, 1998; DuBrin, 1997.

THE BOTTOM LINE

DO I HAVE TO BE CONCERNED ABOUT GROUP WORK AFTER I LEAVE SCHOOL?

Most definitely, yes! Many employers today are particularly interested in potential employees' ability to work well with a group or team. With the complexity of tasks that are involved in so many jobs in the twenty-first century, the necessity of several people with different skills working together becomes clear. For the most part, the information presented in this chapter applies to all working groups, whether at school or in the workplace. In the workplace, there may be a delegated leader and less difficulty in finding meeting times and places, but the basic principles still apply. Learning how to work in groups while you are still in school is very valuable: at a job interview, the applicant who can say that he or she has had experience with teamwork on the post-secondary level, and can give some details about group projects that were successfully completed, may well have an edge in getting a job. The question "What did you learn about working in teams?" is one that is often asked at a job interview, and one that perhaps you would like to consider as you progress through your post-secondary academic career.

For more information about groups in the workplace, the following website is useful: http://web.cba.neu.edu/~ewertheim/teams/ovrvw2.htm.

WHAT CAN I DO TO BE A GOOD GROUP MEMBER?

To be a good and effective group member, Keiko has to strive to:

- be committed to the goals of the group, take a real interest in the project, and be determined to do her best work on it.

- pay attention to the other group members. What are their needs and wishes? How is their work going? What do they find to be the most satisfying? This will build cohesion, reduce individuation, and make the whole group happier in their work together.

- listen to others, and give and take criticism constructively.

- be open in sharing her own ideas, realizing that if her idea is adopted, it is no longer "hers"; it now belongs to the group.

- be open-minded and flexible in listening to the opinions of others. Appreciating the individual differences among members makes for greater respect in the group and more willingness to share ideas.

- take responsibility for the work she has promised to do, do it on time, and be ready to make changes as the work progresses.

- be ready to take on extra work without complaint if disaster hits (e.g., two group members get sick), recognizing that the task is a group effort, not simply a reflection of one person.

- give credit and praise where it is due, and learn to say "Thank you" when she is praised.

Keiko will hopefully find that working on projects with other people can be an exhilarating and enormously successful enterprise. Working on projects by yourself has its rewards too, but a good group experience can be the high point of a semester.

Advice for Keiko

WHAT TO DO	WHY
Go into the experience with a positive attitude. Don't let other group experiences of yours or anyone else's colour your expectations of this group.	This will start your own commitment to the group and encourage others to become committed; it may be a self-fulfilling prophecy: if you expect good things, you are more likely to get them.
Try to include a diverse cross-section of people in the group if you can.	This will increase the number of skills and perspectives that the group has access to.
Build cohesiveness in the group.	A cohesive group is less likely to have a problem with social loafing and is more likely to be committed to doing a good job.
Respect the different opinions of group members. Encourage all members to express their ideas.	In this way, no one will feel constrained not to put forward what may turn out to be a very valuable statement or idea. At least, statements from different perspectives can stimulate thinking in directions that would not have been followed otherwise.
Make up an organizational chart of duties, due dates, and consequences if the work is not done by the due date.	This ensures that everyone is clear on what his or her duties are, and who will be affected by slowness on the job or not doing the job. This makes the group run more efficiently and reduces the possibility of social loafing.
Follow the suggestions in Box 13.4 to reduce the possibility of groupthink.	These techniques will not only reduce the possibility of groupthink, but will also reduce group polarization and enhance the sharing of ideas.
Decide if a leader is needed in the group. If so, decide on whether a task leader or a social leader would be better.	A leader, even an informal one, may be helpful in keeping the group on track and increasing the satisfaction and enjoyment that the members of the group feel. This person may also be helpful in taking a lead role in resolving conflict.

(continued)

WHAT TO DO	WHY
If conflict among group members arises, follow the suggestions in Box 13.6.	Conflict can destroy a group, but if handled well, it can lead to growth and satisfaction for all members and to a better product in the long run.
Take responsibility for being a good group member yourself.	The group is only as good as the people in it. If you are a good group member, you may be a role model for others, and you will be a major benefit to task performance. Besides, you'll feel better about yourself and have more fun this way.

CHAPTER SUMMARY

- Working in groups is becoming a greater part of everyday school and work experience. Group members often influence each other in a positive way (social facilitation). By having diversity in the group, every member of the group is broadening the thinking of each other member. Sometimes this can be so marked that the group's output is actually greater than the sum of the individuals' contributions (synergy).

- As the society we live in becomes more and more culturally diverse, we must develop cultural sensitivity, that is, an awareness and willingness to acknowledge that people of different cultures and subcultures act in different ways and have different norms and values from those of the country's dominant culture. It is also useful to have cultural fluency, or an understanding of what the differences are among cultures. Students exposed to diversity in their classes benefit greatly: they develop more commitment to multicultural understanding and tolerance, their analytical and problem solving skills are enhanced, and even their writing skills improve.

- One way that group members can enhance the performance of the group is by evaluating each other's thinking. People often perform better in groups when the groups are cohesive, that is, the group members want to be part of the group, share the group's goals, and work together in meeting the goals.

- If only friends get together in a group, they may not be cohesive in regards to the goal, but they will concentrate on the social aspects of getting together. Furthermore, if they are not focused on the goal as much as they are focused on their enjoyment of each other, they may be reluctant to put forth divergent views, to criticize one member's work, or to catch the errors that one member may be making. Too much cohesiveness can be detrimental to group functioning, then.

- Social loafing occurs when people in groups do less work than when they are working alone. Part of the reason for this is deindividuation, the phenomenon that, when in groups, people tend to produce more behaviour that is against the norm or socially unacceptable. They do this because, in general, they cannot be as readily identified when they are in a group as when they are working alone. Techniques are available to prevent or deal with social loafing.

- Another problem that may arise in groups is called group polarization. Group polarization refers to the tendency of groups to make more extreme final decisions than their initial positions indicated. A related, more serious problem is groupthink. When group members don't want to rock the boat by disagreeing with each other, they isolate themselves from other opinions and ideas from outside the group and their critical thinking starts to deteriorate. This, too, can be prevented.

- Leaders often emerge in groups. The task leader is focused on the goal and serves to keep people on track with the project and to organize what is being done, when to meet, etc., while the social leader is more concerned with the feelings and well-being of the group members than with the job. Other roles, such as cheerleader or organizer, may also emerge in groups. All the roles are important.

■ Conflict may arise in groups because of faulty communication, attribution errors, mistrust, grudges, and personality clashes. While sometimes unpleasant, if conflicts are handled appropriately, the group may become strengthened and do better work.

■ Learning to work in groups and becoming a good group member are important skills to learn for both your post-secondary years and your working years thereafter.

KEY TERMS

attribution errors   diversity   social leader
cohesiveness   group polarization   social loafing
cultural fluency   groupthink   synergy
cultural sensitivity   social facilitation   task leader
deindividuation

INDIVIDUAL ACTIVITIES

1. What can you do to increase your exposure to the great diversity of people at your school? Think of three or four things you could do, and try at least one of them.

2. Imagine you are making a training manual for someone who is taking a leadership position in a group you belong to, your school residence, or a class. What would you include in the manual?

3. Think of three or four different assignments you have had at school, currently or in high school. Would the individual assignments have been different if they had been done with a group? Would they have been better? worse? Why? What about any group projects you have done? Would they have been better done individually? Why?

4. If you were the instructor of this course, what individual assignments would you give to students? What group assignments would you give? Would you let the students pick their own groups or assign people to groups? Why?

GROUP ACTIVITIES

1. In a group of three or four students, decide how you would handle problems with the following people:
   a) Janeesa always finds fault with anything anyone suggests.
   b) Cleo never says a word, although she does whatever is asked of her.
   c) Paul makes all the decisions by himself and then presents the group with the completed work.

2. In a group of four or five students, pretend that you have been given the assignment of presenting the key points in this chapter. Make up an organizational chart as in Box 13.2 indicating the division of labour, the due dates, the consequences of not completing the work, etc.

3. In a group of four or five students, pretend that you have to construct a group to make decisions on how to teach young children to stay away from criminal activities. What

sorts of people would you want in the group? Would you want a group leader? If so, what kind of leader?

4. In a group, discuss how to answer job interview questions such as the following:

   a) Do you enjoy working in a group? Why or why not?
   b) Have you had experiences with group work? Have they been successful? Why or why not?
   c) What would you do to build a good team to get a project done?
   d) What problems might you anticipate in a team and how would you handle them?

REFERENCES

Benton, D. A. (1998). *Applied human relations: An organizational and skill development approach* (6th ed.). Upper Saddle River, NJ: Prentice Hall.

DuBrin, A. J. (1997). *Human relations: Interpersonal, job-oriented skills* (6th ed.). Upper Saddle River, NJ: Prentice-Hall.

Friedkin, N. E. (1999). Choice shift and group polarization. *American Sociological Review, 64*, 856–875.

Greenberg, J., & Baron, R. A. (1995). *Behavior in organizations* (5th ed.). Englewood Cliffs, NJ: Prentice-Hall.

Guerin, B. (1999). Social behaviors as determined by different arrangements of social consequences: Social loafing, social facilitation, deindividuation, and a modified social loafing. *The Psychological Record, 49*, 565–578.

Halberstam, D. (1972). *The best and the brightest.* New York: Fawcett-Crest.

Hodson, G., & Sorrentino, R. M. (1997). Groupthink and uncertainty orientation: Personality differences in reactivity to the group situation. *Group Dynamics: Theory, Research, and Practice, 1(2),* 144–155.

Janis, I. L. (1982). *Groupthink: Psychological studies of policy decisions and fiascoes* (2nd ed.). Boston: Houghton-Mifflin.

Karau, S. J., & Williams, K. D. (1997). The effects of group cohesiveness on social loafing and social compensation. *Group dynamics: Theory, research, and practice, 1(2),* 156–168.

Locke, E. A., & Latham, G. P. (1990). Work motivation and satisfaction: Light at the end of the tunnel. *Psychological Science, 1*, 240–246.

Myers, D. G. (1999). *Social psychology* (6th ed.). Boston: McGraw-Hill.

Pascarella, E. T., Edison, M., Nora, A., Hagedorn, L. S., & Terenzini, P. T. (1996). Influences on students' openness to diversity and challenge in the first year of college. *The Journal of Higher Education, 67(2),* 174–195.

Pascarella, E. T., Pierson, C. T., Wolniak, G. C., & Terenzini, P. T. (2004). First-generation college students: Additional evidence on college experiences and outcomes. *The Journal of Higher Education, 75(3),* 249–284.

Robbins, H., & Finley, M. (2000). *The new why teams don't work* (2nd ed.). San Francisco: Berrett-Koehler Publishers.

Shuford, B. C. (1998). Recommendations for the future. *New Directions for Student Services, 83,* 71–78.

BEING CREATIVE

The Case of Issah

Issah has just received his assignment for his marketing class. It appears to be an interesting yet challenging group project. In this assignment, a group of five students (put in the group by the instructor) are to create a marketing plan for a new household product. In addition, the group is to develop an advertising plan. The most exciting thing about this project is that the assigned product is an actual newly developed product from a local company. The group will be required to present their plan and their campaign to the company's CEO, marketing executives, and staff, as well as to their instructor and classmates. Issah thinks that this is a real opportunity to get hands-on business experience, but at the same time, the project has the potential to fail in a very public way. Issah is hoping that his group (team) can come up with creative strategies that will wow the executives, but is not sure how to get his team moving in a creative direction.

Employers often show an interest in individuals who are creative. Creative employees and students can take problems and come up with unique solutions. In other words, these employees and students can think about problems in new ways. Creative approaches can lead to considerable success in post-secondary school and in the workplace.

Creativity is usually defined as going through a process in which the outcome is both unique and of value (Swede, 1993). Clearly, Issah is hoping that the marketing plan and advertising campaign his group creates will be both valuable and unique. However, the definition of creativity is a bit confusing. Most of us would agree that, to be creative, what you design should be unique. However, you might argue that an object does not have to be valuable to be creative. You might say that value is in the eye of the beholder. What you think is valuable, I might not find valuable. To deal with this difficulty, creativity has been further defined as personal creativity and universal creativity (Swede, 1993). Personal creativity occurs when the unique outcome is valued by the individual and perhaps a few others (such as coming up with a unique way to fix your broken pen), whereas universal creativity occurs when the creative effort is valued by many others (such as the invention of the personal computer).

INGREDIENTS FOR CREATIVITY: INDIVIDUAL CREATIVITY

WHAT INGREDIENTS DO I NEED TO BE CREATIVE?

Many researchers have thought about both inventions and art and wondered how it was that the creators were able to come up with the idea for their work (Sternberg, 2003; Swede, 1993). For example, how were scientists able to conceive of the idea of the personal computer? How were Banting and Best able to correctly develop insulin to aid individuals with diabetes? When we think about famous inventions and creative works, it is important to note that the creative individual is able to do two things: conceive of an idea, and implement the idea. It is also important to realize that creative works don't just happen. Most creativity takes work and happens because a number of important factors converge that allow the individual or group to be creative. Ingredients for creativity include a divergent or multi-contextual thinking style, intelligence, knowledge, motivation, particular personality characteristics, and a supportive environment (Mumford, 2003; Sternberg, 2003; Swede, 1993). These ingredients are discussed in more detail below.

DIVERGENT/MULTI-CONTEXTUAL THOUGHT

divergent thinking
thinking of a problem from more than one angle

Divergent thinking means thinking of a problem from more than one angle. This certainly is true of many creative works. The creator has thought of a new way to approach a problem. In a previous chapter, we noted that people who think of problems from only one angle often suffer from functional fixedness. That is, they have difficulty coming up with a solution to the problem because they only use old methods for solving the problem. One way that divergent thinking has been studied is by looking at the number and types of ideas that are generated by individuals to problems provided to them in tests. In these tests, you are given a problem or topic and asked to generate as many ideas as possible about this topic. The ideas are then evaluated for the number of ideas you have (**fluency**), the variety of different ideas you have from different categories (**flexibility**), and how unusual or original your ideas are (Guilford, 1967; as cited by Paulus, 2000).

fluency
evaluating the number of ideas you have

flexibility
the variety of different ideas you have from different categories

For example, you might be asked to think of as many uses as you can for a pen. You might suggest that a pen can be used to write, to scratch your back, to poke annoying people, etc. The number of ideas you have is tabulated and the variety of different ideas is also tabulated. For example, above you thought of three uses for a pen. If you had added that you can also scratch your foot with a pen, it would be counted as a new idea, but not a different idea (flexibility) because scratching your back and scratching your foot are in the same category. The idea of poking annoying people with a pen might be unusual when compared to other people's responses, so that idea might score for originality. In Exercise 14.1 we present a number of objects. Think of as many uses for each as you can. Your ideas should, however, be practical (don't suggest that robins should use the pen to learn to write). Ask a friend to do the same and compare your lists for number of ideas, variety of ideas (from different categories), and originality (are they different from your friend's ideas, do they seem to be really unusual).

EXERCISE 14.1

▶ *Unusual Uses*

Generate as many uses for the following items as you can think of and have a friend do the same. Then compare your lists based on fluency, flexibility, and originality.

1. Ruler
2. Tree
3. Portable pencil sharpener
4. Tissue box
5. Old tire

Source: Loosely based on Guilford, 1967; Torrance 1974.

Students often use divergent thinking in writing essays. Students will think of as many theories as possible to explain an issue. For example, you may be asked to determine how poverty and poor health are related. You could then generate as many theories as possible and explore some of these theories within the essay.

multi-contextual thought
the creator puts together previously unrelated ideas

Multi-contextual thought means that the creator puts together previously unrelated ideas to solve a problem (Swede, 1993). For example, in writing an essay about health outcomes for those in poverty, for your sociology class, you might use some theories from sociology class and relate them to theories from your nutrition and political science classes. Multi-contextual thought means that you associate things that were previously not associated. A number of tests have been developed to examine the ability to associate items. One popular test is the Remote Associates Test by Mednick and Mednick (1967). In this test, words are given to you to see if you can find a single word that will associate all items. For example, you might be given the words *rise*, *beam*, and *tan*. You need to find a word that is associated with these items. The word *sun* associates with all three (*sunrise*, *sunbeam*, *suntan*). Exercise 14.2 gives you an adapted version of this test. See if you can find the association between the items. Some researchers believe that your ability to associate items is related to your ability to create (Swede, 1993).

EXERCISE 14.2

▶ *Remote Associations*

Find a word that associates the two items.

1. work, run
2. period, piece
3. away, fetched
4. touch, under
5. child, storm

Answers can be found at the end of the chapter.

Source: Adapted from Mednick, S. A., & Mednick, M. T. (1967). *Examiner's manual: Remote Associates Test.* Boston: Houghton Mifflin.

INTELLIGENCE

Studies of creative people suggest that most creative people have above-average intelligence (an IQ greater than 120, where 100 is average intelligence; Sternberg, 2003). However, those with the highest intelligence scores (e.g., an IQ of 160) are not really more creative than those with above-average intelligence (e.g., an IQ of 120). Given that you are at university or college, you likely have above-average intelligence. So what intellectual abilities will help you to be creative? Some argue that certain intellectual skills lead to creativity (Sternberg, 2003). First, you need the intellectual ability to see problems from different viewpoints. Second, you need to recognize when your ideas are worth pursuing. For example, persistence in trying to make a hat from a slice of cheddar cheese doesn't really suggest creativity. Third, you need the intellectual ability to persuade others of the value of your idea (Mumford, 2003; Sternberg, 2003). Since people are often resistant to new ideas, this may take some keen mental work.

KNOWLEDGE

In general, people create in fields where they have a strong knowledge base (Swede, 1993). For example, Edward Jenner discovered a vaccination for smallpox in the eighteenth century. His discovery would not have been possible without his background knowledge as a physician and his knowledge that cow pox (a less lethal disease) was in some ways similar to smallpox and could thus be used to immunize people to smallpox. This suggests that, when writing papers, you should start with academic knowledge of the topic area—gained by visiting your post-secondary library—prior to building theories. Creativity requires knowledge, and a willingness to move beyond the conventions of the field that you are studying (Sternberg, 2003). However, it is important to note that creativity also requires that you recognize when it is appropriate to move beyond these conventions. This is especially true at post-secondary school. If your nursing instructor asks you to write a lab in APA format, it would be unwise to create a new format for your laboratory.

MOTIVATION

intrinsic motivation
internal reasons for behaviour

extrinsic motivation
external reasons for behaviour

Those who are creative need to be motivated. That is, people must *want* to create. Most argue that the motivation should be from within, or be **intrinsic motivation** (internal; Sternberg, 2003). This motivation means that the individual is curious, desires to see the limits of his/her own capabilities, wants to express him/herself, and hopes to be recognized by others (Mumford, 2003). However, **extrinsic motivation** (from things external to yourself) also influences creativity. For example, the types of assignments and projects you receive at school will affect your motivation to be creative. Assignments that are worth a large proportion of your grade, for instance, will enhance your desire to be creative and do well.

PERSONALITY CHARACTERISTICS

People who are creative often have a number of personality traits in common (see Sternberg, 2003; Swede, 1993). People who are creative are often more willing to take risks. Telling others of a novel idea is risky and takes courage. Others might refuse to listen or might even ridicule such ideas. Another trait often seen in creative people is self-confidence. These individuals are confident in their own abilities and knowledge. Likewise, these individuals are also independent in their judgment. They are able to realistically evaluate their own work. In addition, they often use negative feedback and failure as a learning opportunity, a chance to fix their mistakes. For example, when you receive a paper back from your instructor with comments, be sure to examine these comments closely. Some of this feedback may feel negative to you. However, remember that feedback is meant to help you improve and you should try to view this feedback as an opportunity for you to correct past mistakes in future papers. Creative individuals stay committed to their work even when faced with negative comments from others. Finally, creative people tend to be focused on their creative endeavour. They show commitment to their work and are able to concentrate on it for long periods of time.

SUPPORTIVE ENVIRONMENT

In order to promote creative ideas, the environment must support creativity. In many cases creativity is valued, however, you need to evaluate whether creativity is supported in all your environments. Original ideas are typically encouraged in art class, but if your police foundations instructor teaches you a standard interview technique, then asks you, as an assignment, to interview a classmate, changing the technique in a creative fashion would not be supported. Thus, as a student, you need to recognize when and where creativity would be considered appropriate. Sometimes students feel that they should not be creative when working on essays and assignments. Usually it is okay to come up with original hypotheses, if you can support them. It is okay to write in a more creative way. However, when instructors require that you write in a strict format or you are asked to evaluate a particular theory, it is necessary to follow task instructions. If you plan to take a creative approach with an assignment, it is a good idea to check with your instructor before investing time in your creative process.

To further understand the ingredients of creativity, you might complete Individual Activity 2 located at the end of this chapter.

HOW IS CREATIVITY ASSESSED IN INDIVIDUALS?

Numerous tests of creativity have been developed. However, the tests used to assess creativity depend very much on the working definition of creativity. We saw above that many believe that creative individuals have the ability to think both divergently and in a multi-contextual manner. The goal of some tests, then, is to explore your ability to think in these ways. Two tests described in Exercises 14.1 and 14.2 (Guilford's Unusual Uses Test and Mednick and Mednick's Remote Associates Test) assess how many different ideas you have and how well you associate unrelated items. Another test that examines your ability to form associations is the Barron Symbolic Equivalence Test. In this test, individuals are asked to come up with metaphors, or symbolic comparisons, for common objects and state three ways in which the metaphor is like the common object (Swede, 1993). For example, you might be asked to come up with a metaphor for a ticking clock. You might say that a marching band is like a ticking clock because they both keep a beat, move forward, and signal events. Your answers are then evaluated for originality and acceptability by a rater (Swede, 1993). In Exercise 14.3 a list of common objects is given. Try to state a metaphor and three reasons this metaphor fits with each common object.

EXERCISE 14.3 ▶ *Metaphor Equivalents*

Give a metaphor (a symbolic comparison) and three reasons why the metaphor fits each of the following images.

1. A steaming cup of coffee
2. An old running shoe
3. A fallen tree
4. A broken violin
5. A computer

Source: Loosely based on Barron, 1988.

The responses to these tests are usually scored by a rater for originality and/or acceptability. However, there is no hard and fast way to score most of these tests. Raters use their own opinion when scoring. This is called subjective scoring. The problem is that one scorer might rate the outcomes differently from other scorers (Swede, 1993).

Other creativity tests allow you to use your imagination and the outcome is scored for originality. Tests such as the Thematic Apperception Test, the Mosaic Test, the Rorschach, and drawing completion tests ask you to create a product from your imagination. In the Thematic Apperception Test you create a story based on pictures presented to you. In the Mosaic Construction Test you are asked to create a picture from mosaic tiles presented to you. In the Rorschach you are asked to view ink blots and describe an image you see within each ink blot, and in the drawing completion tests you are asked to complete a drawing based on a partial drawing that is presented to you. These tests are usually evaluated subjectively by raters who score them for complexity and originality. Once again, these tests suffer from problems related to the rater's opinion. One rater may view a product as original whereas another may not. Regardless of these problems, it is important to note that creativity tests are not intended to be used alone. That is, when you assess your creativity, you will get a better idea of your creative strengths by taking a number of tests. Single creativity tests do not really tell us much about creativity in individuals (Swede, 1993).

To ensure that you understand assessments of creative try Group Activity 1 and compare your activity to other students. What are the benefits and limitations of your assessment activity?

HOW CAN I BECOME MORE CREATIVE?

Developing creativity in yourself involves a number of steps, which are summarized in Box 14.1.

Whether you are interested in creativity in the sciences, the social sciences, or the workplace, etc., you first need to generate ideas. To do so, you must begin to view situations and problems from new perspectives (Sternberg, 2003). For example, when you see your classmate shouting in a class, think of what reasons there might be for this action. Think of as many different possibilities as you can. Maybe the classmate is demonstrating projective voice techniques. Maybe your classmate is in a terrible mood. Maybe the professor is hard of hearing and has asked that the class raise their voices. Likewise, when faced with a problem, such as an essay question or a project, think of new ways to approach it and solve it, and try to see how other issues and academic areas relate to your problem. See if you can come up with more than one method to solve this problem. For example, if you are working on a project on zebra mussels in your biology class, you might think of how concepts from environmental science fit into your project by helping to explain the ecological threats posed by these small creatures. Once you come up with an idea, you need to question it (Sternberg, 2003). Could this idea be improved? Do you have your facts right? Be

Steps to Creativity	BOX 14.1
Step 1: Generate ideas	Brainstorm, think of ideas from more than one side, examine old ideas, use knowledge from other classes to help with this class
Step 2: Evaluate ideas	What biases are evident in your ideas? Are the ideas objective? Are the ideas practical? Could these ideas be implemented?
Step 3: Sell your ideas	List the value of your ideas, be aware of the limitations of your ideas, practise communication and presentation skills

sure that you use your knowledge in many areas to help improve your creativity, but be sure to remember these areas accurately (Swede, 1993). Review information from these areas to ensure that you do recall this academic information accurately. You might find it helpful to make a diagram or mind map (as shown in Chapter 7) of your problem to get a better understanding of each part of the problem (Swede, 1993). Finally, you will need to learn to tolerate ambiguity because there is often no one correct answer or approach that is guaranteed to give you success. All ideas do not solve your problem immediately. They are steps towards a creative product and all creative products develop over time, with much rethinking and reworking (Sternberg, 2003).

A second step in developing creativity is to evaluate your ideas (Sternberg, 2003). Since your ideas are subjective (internal), you will need to critically evaluate them. What assumptions did you make? For example, when seeing your classmate shout in class, did you just assume that the classmate must be doing something wrong since shouting in class is not the norm? Are you looking at this problem in an objective way? Or have your own biases coloured your thinking? Think of possible obstacles to your idea and ways to overcome them (Sternberg, 2003). Sometimes just being aware of your need to overcome preconceived notions is enough to help you do it. You will also find it useful to look at others who you think are creative when attempting to overcome obstacles. Study their creative methods and adopt those that seem to fit with your project (James, Clark, & Cropanzano, 1999; Swede, 1993). Also, note that creative people often fail many times before they succeed. They learn from their failures (Swede, 1993).

A third step towards developing creativity is the ability to sell your ideas. Because creativity involves value, it is important that others (such as your professor) see the value in your creative idea or work. It is your job to show them this value, not their job to see it. Learning presentation and communication skills (as taught earlier in this book) will help you to sell your ideas.

GROUP CREATIVITY

CAN MY GROUP BE CREATIVE?

Group creativity contains many of the ingredients of individual creativity noted above. Certainly, groups need to demonstrate divergent and multi-contextual thought, have appropriate background knowledge, be motivated, be willing to take risks, and have a supportive working environment. However, the method to achieve these ingredients may differ when working within a group.

DIVERGENT AND MULTI-CONTEXTUAL THOUGHT IN GROUPS (BRAINSTORMING)

brainstorming
listing as many ideas as possible on a topic

Groups are frequently asked to brainstorm, that is, to generate ideas and solutions to problems. Interestingly, groups tend to generate fewer ideas than do individuals when they **brainstorm** and group ideas tend to be of lower quality than individual ideas (Paulus, 2000). This may be due to a number of factors that were discussed in our previous chapter on working in groups. Group members may not generate ideas because they feel their ideas have been presented before, are not relevant, or will be viewed by the group as silly (Paulus, 2000). In addition, some members may choose to coast on the ideas of others or may feel their ideas to be less important than other group members', or group members may go off on tangents, talking about irrelevant matters (Paulus, 2000). To counteract these difficulties, some researchers have suggested that when brainstorming, groups should have rules (Osborn, 1957; as cited by Paulus, 2000). Members should be allowed to generate ideas without evaluation: no one is allowed to judge any idea prematurely. Other members may build on ideas that someone else has presented. In addition, members should be encouraged to contribute ideas prior to the group meeting. For example, individual group members could be asked to come up with as many ideas as possible and e-mail them to the rest of the group, or submit them anonymously to a bulletin board that tracks which group members submitted ideas, but does not identify which idea is from which member. In this way, all ideas are put forward with less social pressure and because a member who doesn't participate is readily identified, the tendency to coast on the group effort is reduced (Paulus, 2000).

GROUP KNOWLEDGE

The type and scope of knowledge of individual group members can affect the creative product. Most researchers believe that group members should vary in their areas of expertise because if all group members have the same backgrounds, few ideas will be generated. In other words, members who have differing backgrounds will likely have differing ideas and it is more likely that members will then associate these ideas in new ways (Paulus, 2000). However, it is best to have group members with overlapping areas of expertise, rather than members who are not familiar with each other's areas of expertise. For example, if group members include a philosopher and a chemist, these two group members may not understand each other's areas well enough to evaluate each other's ideas. However, a chemist and a biologist have some overlapping scientific background and would more likely be able to evaluate and associate ideas put forward. One of the challenges Issah, the student from the introduction, will face in his group is in finding where group members' expertise lies. Luckily, since all of his group's members are from his marketing class, they do share some expertise. However, Issah will want to establish what areas of business each group member is from (what is the student's major and what business courses have been taken). If members have different business experiences—such as retail, advertising, business development, and accounting—the group is likely to generate more different ideas about the marketing plan than if the students were all accounting majors.

GROUP MOTIVATIONS

Groups are motivated to perform by the consequences associated with the task, the responsibility each member carries for the task, and task feedback (Paulus, 2000). Your group will be more highly motivated when the task goals are made clear to everyone. Factors such as competition between groups can increase creativity, especially when the groups cannot see each other's outcomes prior to submitting their work (Shalley & Oldham, 1997). That is, if your group has no information about how other competing groups are approaching the problem, your group's creativity will be enhanced. Further, group motivation for creativity is increased when each member of your group has to account for his or her individual contribution to the group and is given feedback about his or her contribution by the group (Paulus, 2000). In other words, if you want your group to be motivated to be more creative, you need to ensure that your group understands the task involved and feels competitive with other class groups, and that each member has to present his or her contribution to the entire group for feedback. Group members will need to understand that what they create may be changed or enhanced by the group. This is in no way a criticism of their contribution: rather, it is group action at its best, with one member having the knowledge that he or she has spurred the group on by making the original suggestion.

CREATIVE RISK TAKING

You may recall that we previously discussed that groups often take higher risks than do individuals. Not all risk taking results in creativity, but usually creativity involves risk taking. In general, groups have more creative potential when they explore ideas that are undeveloped (higher risk) than ideas that have already been developed (lower risk) and accepted (Paulus,

2000). In other words, if Issah's group develops new advertising techniques or methods for the product, rather than modelling their advertising after other product advertising, they will likely end with a more creative advertising plan.

THE GROUP ENVIRONMENT

One strong influence on group creativity is the institutional environment. For example, your environment might be a classroom. If you plan to be creative on a project within that classroom you will need to assess the attitude of the instructor toward creativity, the time given for the project (creativity is difficult overnight), the resources (i.e., information technology, PowerPoint, etc.) available (if you plan to create Web-based advertising, you need to have a server and space available), and freedom of choice (you are allowed to choose creative options; Paulus, 2000). If the instructor discourages creativity (as might be the case on some assignments) and resources needed to be creative are not available, then it would be difficult to design a creative project. You might also find that your group will be more creative if you have a group leader who is supportive and outgoing (Mumford, 2003). In this way, your group leader can track creativity and delegate responsibilities to the most able members in each area of the project. Finally, group members who feel a strong sense of commitment to the project will more likely foster more creativity (James et al., 1999).

HOW CAN MY GROUP BECOME MORE CREATIVE?

Developing creativity in groups will be affected by group leadership, group procedures, group make-up, and the group environment. A number of steps can help to make the group more creative. First, the group should select a leader who is supportive of creativity and will help other members see the value in individual ideas. This individual will be responsible for ensuring that the group remains on task and for delegating work.

Second, the group needs to establish procedures for having and evaluating ideas. More ideas will be generated if each group member is to submit a list of individual ideas to a group leader, who then itemizes these ideas and shares them with the group. Creativity will be better fostered if members are asked to listen to each idea prior to evaluating it. Evaluation of each idea should include both positives and negatives of the idea and how this idea fits with other ideas that have been submitted.

Once an idea has been selected, the group should brainstorm on obstacles in achieving the goal (finishing the project) using this idea. Are resources available; does this idea move the group closer to the goal of the project; will this idea be well received by the instructor?

At this point, the group leader should begin implementation of the idea by dividing the project into sub-goals based on member ability and background. Once each member has achieved his or her sub-goal (his or her part of the project), the group should meet to evaluate each part. Be aware that membership may not be entirely satisfied with your part of the project, and the group should feel free to discuss each part and make suggestions for improvement. In fact, the membership should brainstorm on each submitted part of the project to suggest ideas that might improve this part or make this part of the project more creative. When evaluating others' work, try to avoid personal criticisms. Group conflict can lead to poor creativity. Part of the job of the group leader is to control these conflicts.

Next, the group should brainstorm on methods to present their ideas and project to others (classmates, instructor, etc.). Once methods are chosen, the group should work together to perfect the presentation (see Chapter 12), anticipating criticisms that often follow creative endeavours and planning how to deal with these criticisms. To further understand group creativity, try Individual Activity 3 presented at the end of this chapter.

IS CREATIVITY REALLY NECESSARY AT THE POST-SECONDARY LEVEL?

Creativity will be an important aspect of some but not all of your projects. Knowing when to be creative is as important as being creative. In some classes, your instructor will be teaching you accepted methods of producing results, for example, appropriate times to apply certain interview techniques, certain ways of negotiating, and certain styles of writing. The instructor expects that these procedures will be followed. Your instructors do not want or expect you to come up with new methods to do these standard procedures. On the other hand, at times your instructors will desire that you develop an idea, create a theory, or design a presentation. In these cases, your instructor may want you to show some creativity. The trick is to read your assignment carefully and ensure that all requirements of the instructor are met. Often creative aspects of your project go beyond the basic assignment. However, it is important that you run some of your ideas by your instructor if you plan to do more than is required of you in the assignment, to ensure that your instructor finds this acceptable.

Advice for Issah

▶ Issah is required to work in a group setting to create a marketing plan for a new household product. The group is also to develop an advertising plan and to present the plan and the campaign to the company's CEO, marketing executives, and staff, as well as to their instructor and classmates. Issah realizes that his group's plans must be both practical and creative. The following table shows some steps Issah and his group should take to ensure that their plan is both functional and creative.

LEVEL	STEP	OUTCOME ADVANTAGE
Individual members	Read through the assignment and list sub-goals needed to reach the goal. Submit your list to the group.	Begin understanding the requirements.
Group	Examine each member's sub-goal list and complete a list that includes all sub-goals identified by individual members.	This ensures that all areas of the project are addressed.
Group	Choose a group leader who is supportive of creativity and responsible to ensure that all sub-goals are addressed.	One individual will ensure that all areas of the project are complete, offering support to individual members and directing members when some sub-goals are not met.
Individual	Examine creative models (professionals who show creativity in marketing and advertising).	This helps to start initial thoughts on the project.
Individual	Brainstorm. Come up with ideas for the project sub-goals. Try to have more than one idea about each sub-goal and also think about how other areas (economics, accounting, finance, etc.) are important to consider in this plan. Submit all ideas to the leader.	This allows for divergent and multi-contextual thought within the group. All members are required to participate.
Group	Review the list of ideas compiled by the leader. Give constructive feedback on all	This allows ideas to be improved and expanded upon. The group can then

	ideas and examine how many of these ideas might fit together.	recognize obstacles to proceeding with some ideas (e.g., limited resources) and discard ideas that are not worth pursuing.
Group	Define areas of expertise of members.	This allows members to be assigned to sub-goals that use their strengths.
Group and individual	Examine motivation issues such as group rewards (grades), exposure to professionals, and competition with other groups.	Rewards motivate group members to meet deadlines and focus on their task.
Group	Evaluate each member's product (once the member meets the sub-goal).	This helps to improve the product, expand on the product, and integrate other areas of expertise into the product.
Group	Discuss presentation of the product (market and advertising plan) to sell the product.	This allows for input from many points of view. Ideas to sell the product to the audience can be enhanced through group input.
Group	Practise presentation of the product.	This allows for critical feedback to improve the presentation.

CHAPTER SUMMARY

- Becoming creative involves a number of ingredients: thinking about problems from more than one angle (divergent thinking), putting together previously unrelated ideas (multi-contextual thought), having above-average intelligence, having a knowledge base, having motivation, having certain personality characteristics, and having a supportive environment.

- Creativity is assessed subjectively by examining a person's ability to make unique associations and think divergently. In addition, tests often examine the originality of thoughts and stories.

- Becoming creative involves the ability to generate ideas, evaluate ideas, and sell ideas.

- Group creativity involves many of the same ingredients as individual creativity, including multi-contextual and divergent thought, knowledge, motivation, group personality (risk taking), and a supportive group environment. However, in group creativity members must learn to constructively criticize all ideas and expand/improve upon them.

KEY TERMS

brainstorming
divergent thinking
extrinsic motivation

flexibility
fluency

intrinsic motivation
multi-contextual thought

INDIVIDUAL ACTIVITIES

1. List three courses that you have taken in your last year of high school or in post-secondary school. Write out the main themes that were discussed in each of these classes. Think of ways in which the main themes for each of these classes relate to one another. When you consider how different areas/topics relate, you are using multi-contextual thought.

2. Think of three individuals whom you consider to be creative. List things about these individuals that you believe relate to their ability to create. Are these consistent with the ingredients for creativity presented in this chapter? How do they differ?

3. If you were chosen as a group leader, list five things that you could do to increase the creativity within your group.

GROUP ACTIVITIES

1. As a group, create one or two creativity tests that attempt to show at least two aspects of creativity. Try your test on different individuals who state that they are or are not creative. Does your test distinguish between these people? Why or why not?

2. As a group, consider Exercises 14.1 and 14.2, which attempt to assess divergent and multi-contextual thought as part of creativity. Do you think that doing well on these tests would result in higher creativity? Why or why not? What is the value of these tests?

3. As a group, discuss times when creativity is appropriate and times when it is not appropriate. Also discuss how you can increase your creativity in essays, assignments, and group projects.

ANSWERS TO EXERCISE 14.2

1. home
2. time
3. far
4. down
5. brain

REFERENCES

Barron, F. (1988). Putting creativity to work. In R. J. Sternberg (Ed.), *The nature of creativity: Contemporary psychological perspectives*, pp. 76–98. Cambridge: Cambridge University Press.

Guilford, J. P. (1967). *The nature of human intelligence*. New York: McGraw Hill.

James, K., Clark, K., & Cropanzano, R. (1999). Positive and negative creativity in groups, institutions and organizations: A model and theoretical extension. *Creativity Research Journal, 12*, 211–226.

Mednick, S. A., & Mednick, M. T. (1967). *Examiner's manual: Remote Associates Test*. Boston: Houghton Mifflin.

Mumford, M. D. (2003). Where have we been, where are we going? Taking stock of creativity research. *Creativity Research Journal, 15*, 107–120.

Paulus, P. B. (2000). Groups, teams and creativity: The creative potential of idea-generating groups. *Applied Psychology: An International Review, 49*, 237–262.

Shalley, C. E., & Oldham, G. R. (1997). Competition and creative performance: Effects of competitor presence and visibility. *Creative Research Journal, 10*, 337–345.

Sternberg, R. J. (2003). *Wisdom, intelligence and creativity synthesized*. Cambridge: Cambridge University Press.

Swede, G. (1993). *Creativity a new psychology*. Toronto: Wall & Emerson, Inc.

Torrance, E. P. (1974). *Torrance tests of creative thinking*. Lexington, MA: Personnel Press.

WHAT HAVE I LEARNED AND WHERE CAN I USE IT IN THE FUTURE?

We've come to the end of the book, and the chances are, you have come to the end of the semester. We feel a sense of accomplishment, and we hope you do too. Throughout the preceding chapters, we have tried to help you gain knowledge and skills to make your post-secondary school life more successful and more enjoyable. In some cases, perhaps we taught you things you were unaware of, and in some cases, we may have told you what you already knew. In all cases, though, we tried to concentrate on areas that would be useful not only in your school life but also in your life after you leave school.

In Chapter 1, we told you the differences between high school and post-secondary institutions, to expect something new, and where to go for help. No matter where you go after school is over, the same basic principles still apply: you will be facing something new, so don't expect all the old rules to hold, but there will be places for you to go for help if you need it.

Chapter 2 dealt with your self-concept and your feelings of self-efficacy. This concern will go on for the rest of your life. We all change our self-concepts as we grow and develop, and we all run the risk of having our self-esteem lowered when we meet with failure and disappointment, as we all do. And every new task we encounter (new job, new relationship, parenting!) involves our feelings of general self-efficacy, and building a new self-efficacy specific to the task.

Chapters 3 and 4 on stress management, we hope, gave you a basis for coping with the inevitable stress that life will hand you. With general stress management techniques and with specific techniques for areas such as time management, procrastination, and financial planning, we hope that you will be able to confront your new challenges with confidence and ability. Again, self-efficacy is important!

In whatever career and life path you enter, you will be learning for the rest of your life, so we hope that knowing more about learning (Chapter 5) and memory (Chapter 6) will be beneficial to you. We believe that Chapter 7, on critical thinking and problem-solving, may be one of the most important to you in the long run. No matter what walk of life you will be in, you will be called upon to make major decisions. This starts immediately, with your choice of new courses and programs of study, to your choice of a career, to the important choices you will make in your personal life regarding relationships and involvement in your community. Perhaps we have given you some tools that you can use to analyze the information you have and make your decisions more wisely and with more confidence than before. With the education you are obtaining, it is likely that you will be asked to make or at least participate in decision making that will affect large numbers of people and perhaps, a great deal of money. We hope that Chapter 7 has helped equip you for this.

We all get tired. Not just physically, but emotionally and cognitively too. No matter how much we enjoy our work, our motivation to keep going sometimes slips. Increasing your own motivation was the thrust of Chapter 8, but remember in the future that the same principles can be used to motivate others, such as people whom you work with, or indeed, who work under you.

Being sophisticated in reading and evaluating what you read are skills that you also will use for the rest of your lives. Every time you pick up a newspaper, we hope that you use the information we have given you to make your own judgments about what you read. The content of Chapters 9 and 11 should be particularly useful in this.

Like it or not, you will undoubtedly be called upon to write reports, and perhaps some of the tips in Chapter 10 will help you do this. You may also be in the position, one day, of reading the reports of your subordinates. With the information in Chapter 10, maybe you can help them write better reports too. Similarly, you will no doubt be called upon at some time to give presentations to groups of people. This may be formally in your work, or it may be in the context of community work that you will be volunteering to do, or it may even be in making a point at your child's school association meeting. In whatever context, your presentation style will matter. Knowing how to communicate with others verbally, giving and receiving criticism, and being assertive are skills that you will use almost every day of your life (Chapter 12).

As a human being, you are a social animal, and you will live and work in groups. From Chapter 13, knowing more about the growing diversity of our culture, the dynamics of groups, and the role of a leader will, we hope, make your group work more successful and satisfying. Overall, your creativity (Chapter 14) will be utilized in whatever you do.

WHAT COMES NEXT?

In the near future, you will have to make some decisions about a career path, if you haven't done so already. With a clear view of your values, you need to match what you value in life to whatever occupation you will pursue. Without this kind of congruence, you may find your working life (where you will spend almost 30 percent of your time) to be unsatisfying and unproductive. Making the decision about what career to choose can be difficult, but again, there is help available for you if you need it. Your school's career counsellors can help you explore your options and provide you with aptitude and interest tests and literature on different occupations. It's a good idea to tap these knowledgeable sources: there are careers available that you might not have even thought of, and these sources can show you a broader array of options than you may have been aware of. Career counsellors can help you to discover what careers will have the greatest employment opportunities and the best pay and benefits in the next 10 years. They can also be of great assistance in your decisions of what further courses to take and where to take them. After all, there is little point in deciding on a career if there will be no real job opportunities available (what happens to someone who wants to be a blacksmith today?). Similarly, it can be frustrating and even heart-breaking to decide upon a career and find that you don't have the courses or training that employers in the field want from their potential employees.

You can do a great deal of the work in finding out about potential careers on your own too. There are several books available to help you decide what kind of a career would be good for you. For example, the book *What color is my parachute?* by Richard Nelson Bolles has gone through several updated editions because it has been found to be so useful for people deciding on a career or career change. Another good resource for finding out about jobs is the Internet. Most companies and professional organizations maintain a website that will give you up-to-date information about careers and career opportunities. And don't forget about one of the very best ways to connect with a career that fits you: networking. Do you or your family or friends know people who have careers that pique your interest? Ask them. In most cases they will be happy to put you in touch with people who can give you the inside story about particular careers and how to prepare for them. If possible, spend a day or two shadowing them in their jobs so that you can see first-hand what the job entails. If you get an opportunity to shadow someone in a career that you have never really thought about, take it! You may find that this career is more interesting than you thought, or you may meet more people who can also be valuable sources of information for you. At the very least, you may start thinking about categories different from those you have previously explored.

A survey of employers (Collins, 1996) found that the following are the skills they look for in potential employees:

■ Proficiency in the field of study

■ Analytical skills

■ Speaking skills

■ Teamwork skills

■ Interpersonal skills

■ Flexibility

■ Leadership skills

■ Writing skills

■ Computer skills

These are all skills that you can learn directly or pick up from your experiences in post-secondary school. If you are not taking a course that directly teaches some of these skills, think about becoming involved in extracurricular activities that will help you acquire these skills. For example, taking part in athletic teams will help in acquiring interpersonal skills and teamwork; working on the school newspaper or yearbook can help with these skills too, as well as contributing to your flexibility, your writing skills, and your computer skills. A debating team is very effective in enhancing speaking skills and analytical skills as well. Becoming involved in extracurricular activities also shows potential employers that you have a broader range of interests than only your field of specialty, again indicating your flexibility. Be careful not to get involved in extracurricular activities to such an extent that your grades drop, though! Employers look for good grades as well!

IS THERE ANYTHING ELSE?

We have one final concept to teach you: optimism. Some of us seem to naturally be optimistic, expecting good outcomes from whatever we endeavour to do. On the other hand, some of us expect bad outcomes; these are the pessimists. We often think that we are one or the other, or we are optimistic or pessimistic depending on the situation and our experiences in similar situations. If you are optimistic, you seem to be a magnet for good outcomes. Perhaps it's a self-fulfilling prophecy, but good things generally do come to people who expect good things to happen. This book has included several techniques, all of which feed into the development of optimism. For example, you can defuse negativity and become more optimistic by dealing with stress better, by learning to be assertive, by thinking critically, and by knowing yourself. Being able to read and evaluate what you have read, being able to write effectively and talk to groups in a persuasive way, and being able to remember what you have learned are all factors that contribute to an individual's optimism. If you can do these things, you have reason to be optimistic. If you have read this book and been affected by anything in it, you have reason to be more optimistic than you were.

The choices are yours now. You have the tips and the underlying principles of the tips for many areas now. You are able, if you choose, to use the suggestions or to adapt them to fit you better. Only you can determine what works for you. We believe that you have grown and developed perhaps more than you realize in the last semester. Take the same tests that you took in Chapter 2 and compare your answers to your answers the first time you took the test. In particular, take the test on the next page again. How did you describe yourself at the beginning of the semester? And how do you see yourself now? Maybe, for fun, you could keep these records and try the test again when you have graduated. Have you changed even more?

▶ **What Describes You?**

Which of these words apply to you the most? Which apply the least?

sincere	stubborn	prejudiced	independent
pessimistic	naïve	friendly	courageous
broad-minded	sloppy	impulsive	diplomatic
distrustful	grouchy	shy	loyal
patient	trustworthy	short-tempered	unreliable
anxious	influential	obsessive	charming
helpful	nervous	sarcastic	responsible
neat	clumsy	respectful	persistent
logical	rebellious	imaginative	neat
vain	studious	superstitious	energetic
sociable	accepting	industrious	modest
oversensitive	daring	proud	smart
cheerful	immature	optimistic	kind
honest	cynical	caring	easygoing
sensible	efficient	courteous	selfless
forgetful	capable	straightforward	generous
shrewd	insightful	idealistic	boastful
methodical	punctual	warm	

We hope that you will have happy, fulfilled, productive lives. We hope that you will have the knowledge and skills to create meaning for yourselves. We hope that your talents are used to their fullest potential. And, we hope that we have helped just a little bit on your journey.

All the best,
Marilyn and Maureen

REFERENCES

Bolles, R. N. (2002). *What color is your parachute? 2003: A practical manual for job-hunters and career changers*. Berkeley, CA: Ten Speed Press.

Collins, M. (1996). The job outlook for '96 grads. *Journal of Career Planning, 56(2)*, 51–54.

a priori beliefs beliefs do not need evidence to show that they are true

ABCD technique a self-help method designed by Albert Ellis to change irrational thinking in ourselves by learning to replace negative self-statements with more realistic positive self-statements

abstract conceptualizer someone who prefers to understand by hearing theories and creating theories to explain experiences

active experimenter someone who prefers to learn by doing or experimenting

active listening involves direct questioning and clarifying of information, probing into the speaker's meanings and feelings, and rephrasing what has been said to make sure that the correct message has been transmitted and understood

algorithm testing all possible solutions

analogy heuristic occurs when someone uses a previously learned solution to help solve a new problem

analysis level in Bloom's Taxonomy, the level at which the student is required to see patterns in the material, to organize elements into a new and meaningful whole, and to catch subtle meanings and nuances

application level in Bloom's Taxonomy, the level at which the student is required to demonstrate that he/she can use basic information

appraisal-focused coping modifying our appraisal or evaluation of the situation and our own abilities in order to recognize that the stress is manageable

approach-approach conflict both options are positive, or ones that one would like to approach

approach-avoidance conflict there are pluses and minuses to the option—elements that one would like to approach, and elements that one would like to avoid

arousal theory a theory of motivation that says we perform actions in order to maintain a sufficiently high level of arousal in ourselves

assertiveness the ability to state our own needs and wants firmly, but without infringing on the rights of others; includes being able to satisfy your own needs without hurting others in the process

associative learning learning that takes place when two events are linked; creates expectations

attribution errors errors in determining the causes of the behaviour of other members

attribution theory a theory of motivation that looks specifically at how we account for our successes and our failures

auditory learning style preference for learning and understanding by listening

authority ranking people often silently rank group members as those of high status and those of low status

availability bias people adopt beliefs based on how easily they can recall instances of something

avoidability of physical harm people believe that undesirable outcomes are avoidable

avoidance-avoidance conflict both options have elements that one would like to avoid

belief a statement that is deemed true by the individual who holds it

belief in a just world people believe that the world is a just place and we get what we deserve

Bloom's Taxonomy a classification system of levels of learning

brainstorming listing as many ideas as possible on a topic

case study an observational technique in which an individual or single event is studied

causal theories in this bias, the individual inappropriately believes that things that happen together cause one another

change alterations in one's life requiring one to make adjustments and adaptations

choice-oriented question a question in which some response options are provided

chunking grouping material into meaningful units

coding a mnemonic method in which phrases represent to-be-remembered items

cognitive biases assumptions that result from inappropriate analysis of the information provided

cognitive learning styles preferences for the way in which one best understands and learns information; based on thought processes

cohesiveness refers to how much the group members want to be part of the group, share the group's goals, and work together in meeting the goals

communal sharing the group shares the stress of the decision outcome and the responsibility for the decision

comprehension level in Bloom's Taxonomy, the level at which the student is expected to show understanding of terms, concepts, theories, etc.

conceptual knowledge how the elements fit together in concepts, theories, categories, etc.

concrete experiencer someone who understands by actively experiencing information, by working on examples

conditioned emotional response (CER) an emotional response that is largely involuntary but is learned originally through classical conditioning

conflict the uncertainty we may feel when we have to make a decision or choose between two options

confound something that may affect the outcome of a study, which was not intended to be part of the study

consequential learning learning that takes place because voluntary behaviour is attached to a consequence

context the story the words tell

control group the group that does not receive an environmental change

control variables factors held constant between the groups studied because of their potential to affect the outcome of the study

controlled conditions in an experiment, the researcher controls and manipulates the environment

copyright legal rights to written material held by the author and publisher

correlation studies studies in which data collected are used to predict events

covariation bias people assume that certain things exist together

cultural fluency an understanding of what the differences are among cultures

cultural sensitivity an awareness and willingness to acknowledge that people of different cultures act in different ways and have different norms and values from those of the country's dominant culture

daily hassles the problems that come up in day-to-day life that the individual must cope with

data information that is presented in numerical or verbal/descriptive form

decay theory memory fades over time

deductive methods a theory is proposed, then evidence is gathered to support or refute that theory

deep muscle relaxation a method of inducing a heightened state of relaxation in the body

deindividuation the finding that, when in groups, people tend to produce more behaviour that is against the norm or socially unacceptable because, in general, they cannot be as readily identified when they are in a group as when they are working alone

discrimination in associative learning, showing a response to an original stimulus, but not to a stimulus similar to the original stimulus; in consequential learning, not responding to a situation that is similar, but not identical, to one in which reward has been given

displacement placing feelings about one person or situation onto a different unrelated person or situation

divergent thinking thinking of a problem from more than one angle

diversity refers to the mixture of people within a group

effective reading the ability to read and comprehend text materials in a reasonable time

elaboration or deep processing studying by understanding meaning or providing examples for the to-be-remembered item

emotion-focused coping coping techniques that target calming a general emotional state

empirical article an article containing data, which is either analyzed or collected by the author

encoding entering information into the mind

esteem needs in Maslow's hierarchy of needs, the need to feel respect from others and from ourselves

evaluation level in Bloom's Taxonomy, the level at which the student is asked to be critical of what has been learned, and is asked for educated opinions

expectancies in the expectancy–value model of motivation, this refers to our sense of self-efficacy or how much we believe that we are able to do a particular task

expectancy–value model of motivation a model suggesting that several components affect motivation; they are the expectancies we have of a situation and our values, or our beliefs about how important the situation is, and how interested we are in it

expected utility taking into account the value you place on the decision

experimental group the group that receives the environmental change

experimental studies studies in which data collected are used to explain events or behaviours

explanatory style a person's way of explaining why events occurred

external locus of control the belief that our lives are regulated by factors external to ourselves

extinction in associative learning, the removal or reduction of the response when the two events are no longer paired or associated; in consequential learning, the removal or reduction of behaviour because the behaviour is no longer followed by a reward

extrinsic motivation motivation that is derived from factors outside oneself; external reasons for behaviour

extrovert someone who is very outgoing and sociable

factual knowledge terminology and the basic factors within the area of study

failure of organization a memory is stored but not accessed because it has not been properly categorized

failure to discount in this bias, people fail to consider alternatives to their belief or theory

false consensus bias people believe that their own theories and beliefs are common

fear of failure the fear of catastrophic consequences if one should not be successful at some task

feeler someone who is very emotional and empathic in his/her approach to life

flexibility the variety of different ideas you have from different categories

fluency evaluating the number of ideas you have

foreclosure an identity state in which we have committed to actions and a code of behaviour without having experienced an identity crisis or questioned our identities

frustration the feeling experienced when we are kept from meeting some goal because of an obstacle in our way

full text article an article that can be fully viewed on computer

functional fixedness having difficulty seeing new uses for old objects and ideas

fundamental attribution error overemphasizing internal causes of others' behaviour

generalization in associative learning, showing a response to a stimulus similar, but not identical, to the original stimulus; in consequential learning, responding to a situation

similar, but not identical, to one in which reward has been given

group polarization the tendency of groups to make more extreme final decisions than their initial positions indicated

groupthink when group members isolate themselves from other opinions and ideas from outside the group and their critical thinking starts to deteriorate

heuristic a shortcut solution

hierarchy of needs Abraham Maslow's formulation of levels of needs, the satisfaction of which drives our behaviour

hypothesis a possible suggested solution

ideal self Karen Horney's term for the ideas we have about what we want to be, the self we aspire to be

identity a sense of who we are, especially in our relationship with the outside world

identity achieved a sense of who one is, after having struggled with an identity crisis and having committed oneself to personal values and a code of behaviour

identity conflict a state in which two or more parts of ourselves are inconsistent with each other

identity crisis a problem in forming a stable sense of self, a difficulty in answering the question "Who am I?"

identity deficit having little of our own identity, which makes major decisions in life very difficult

identity diffusion an identity state in which we have never had an identity crisis, nor have we formed any commitment to a career or a set of values or code of behaviour

incentive reward that is anticipated and/or received that causes our behaviour

incentive theory a theory of motivation that says we perform actions in order to achieve certain outcomes as a result of our behaviour, to gain favourable outcomes and avoid unfavourable outcomes

inductive methods information (studies, experience, surveys, interviews) is first gathered, then a solution or theory is determined

information literacy recognizing when information is needed, how to access that information, and how to evaluate and use the information found

information processing the study of how information moves through the human mind

insight occurs when one discovers the solution to a problem without having made an effort to solve the problem

interference theory old or new memories interfere with current memory

internal locus of control the belief that we regulate our own lives

intrinsic motivation motivation that is derived from factors inside oneself; internal reasons for behaviour

introvert someone who is quiet, shy, and prefers to be alone

intuitor someone who is very creative and imaginative in his/her approach to life

Jonah Complex Maslow's name for the fear of being one's best, leading to non-actualization

judger someone who makes decisions quickly and is task-oriented

keyword method a mnemonic method for learning foreign-language words

keywords content words to be used in the library search

knowledge level in Bloom's Taxonomy, the level at which the student learns basic information

learned helplessness occurs when people are rarely or never reinforced, when nothing they do can affect whether they are rewarded

limitation something that precludes the researcher from generalizing the study results to those not included in the study

literature review a summary of studies on a particular topic

locus of control refers to whether we attribute the causes of our behaviour to factors outside of us or factors inside of us

long-term memory a memory system that can store information indefinitely

love and belongingness needs in Maslow's hierarchy of needs, the need to love and be loved; the need to feel that we are part of a group of other individuals

mastery goal the object of behaviour is in the inherent worth of the behaviour

meditation a method of using focused attention to calm the mind

metacognitive knowledge understanding of oneself in terms of what one knows; knowing what one knows

method of loci a mnemonic method in which to-be-remembered items are attached to locations

mind map a diagram of how concepts are linked together

mindfulness meditation a form of meditation that concentrates on being fully aware of the body's sensations

mnemonic method to improve memory

moratorium an identity state in which we are having an identity crisis and we have not

been able to form the commitments that would solve the crisis

motivation what makes us behave the way we do and keeps us performing a certain behaviour; the "why" of behaviour

motivational biases assumptions that help the individual hold to a belief that meets individual needs

multi-contextual thought the creator puts together previously unrelated ideas

naturalistic observation an observational technique in which research subjects are studied in their natural setting

need for achievement (nAch) the need for accomplishment and success

negative correlation when one variable increases while the other decreases

observational learning an indirect method of learning in which the learner learns by watching a model perform a behaviour

observational studies studies in which data are collected to describe an event, an individual, or groups of subjects

open-ended question a question in which no response options are given

operational definition defining in terms of observable events or actions, e.g., *sad* is defined as crying, complaining, etc.

optimistic explanatory style a person's tendency to expect the best outcomes and explain these events by taking credit for having ability and/or believing that the environment is changeable and problems can be overcome

orthographics knowledge of permissible word structure and sentence structure

peer review written material is reviewed or read by other experts in the field

perceiver someone who gathers a great deal of information before making a decision

performance anxiety fear of not being able to perform adequately

performance avoidant goal the object of behaviour is to avoid some undesirable external outcome

performance goal the object of behaviour is in external validation, such as grades, awards, etc.

personality-based learning styles preferences for learning that are unique to your personality type

personal learning plan a summary of personal learning objectives, self-assessments, and suggestions to meet objectives

pessimistic explanatory style a person's tendency to expect the worst outcomes and explain these events by blaming one's own inadequacy and/or believing that the environment is biased against one

physical needs in Maslow's hierarchy of needs, the most basic level at which we have needs to keep our bodies alive

population the larger group from which a sample is drawn, for example, all Canadians

positive correlation when two variables increase or decrease at the same time

positive reinforcement any behaviour that is rewarded is likely to occur again in the future

premise a statement that is deemed true

pressure what we feel when there are many expectations placed upon us

primary source usually a journal article in which the author is discussing the author's own work

print characteristics features of the written words, how the letters and words go together

problem-focused coping solving the specific problem that is causing stress

procedural knowledge the skill of how to do something

procedural learning learning how to perform an action

qualitative data non-numerical information

quantitative data numerical information

random sample sample is chosen such that every member of the population has an equal chance of being in the sample

rating scale question a question in which a numerical or verbal scale is used to represent opinion

real self Karen Horney's term for the ideas we have about ourselves as we really are

reciprocal interaction the environment affects your behaviour and your behaviour also affects the environment

reflective observer someone who prefers to learn by watching others and reflecting on experience

reliable the source provides information that is generally accepted or has consensus and can be replicated

reliable information information that can be demonstrated by a number of authors

representative sample the chosen sample has the same characteristics as the population

representativeness bias people judge based on how many features one thing has in common with a prototype

retrieval pulling into awareness information that has been previously stored

safety needs in Maslow's hierarchy of needs, our need to live in a stable, secure environment in which we have some degree of ability to predict what will happen

sample a small group meant to represent a larger group, for example, a small group of Canadians meant to represent all Canadians

sample bias people adopt beliefs based on their own experience or experiences of a few others

scatterplot a graph in which each dot represents a single score on each item of interest

secondary source a book or article in which the author discusses others' work

selective attention the process of attending to some information while ignoring other information

selective attention biases people pay attention to information that is most prominently presented

self-actualization need in Maslow's hierarchy of needs, the highest level of needs, encompassing the need to maximize our potentials, becoming the best that we can be

self-awareness the extent to which we know ourselves, including what we are like, what we think, and what we feel

self-concept the total of what we think and feel, how we behave, what attitudes we have, everything we believe about ourselves

self-control procedure the application of learning principles to change one's behaviour

self-efficacy Albert Bandura's term for our judgment regarding how well we can do a certain action or task or how well we think we can handle a task

self-esteem the way we feel about ourselves; the emotional level of self-concept that measures how much we like or dislike ourselves, whether we think we are worthwhile or not, whether we value ourselves or not

self-serving bias people see themselves in a more positive light than other people see them

sensor someone who is very logical and detailed in his/her approach to life

sensory memory a memory system that gathers vast amounts of information from the senses (vision, hearing, touch, smell, taste) and holds it only briefly

short-term memory a memory system that analyzes current information and selects it for further processing

situational reconstruction changing one's thoughts about a situation by questioning one's interpretation of the situation, leading one to see it from a different perspective

social facilitation refers to the way that people in a group motivate each other to do better work

social leader this person is more concerned with the feelings and well-being of the group members than with the job

social loafing the general finding that when people work in groups, they tend to do less work than when they are working alone

storage holding information in the mind

stress any circumstances that threaten or are perceived to threaten one's well-being and thereby tax one's coping abilities[1]

sub-goals small components of a problem created by dividing the problem

subvocal voice the voice in your head when reading

surface characteristics studying print such as looking at words rather than understanding the words

survey an observational technique where subjects (usually larger groups) are interviewed or given a questionnaire

synergy the group's output is actually greater than the sum of the individuals' contributions

synthesis level in Bloom's Taxonomy, the level at which the student is required to create something new derived from analysis of the material

tactile learning style preference for using touch when learning; learning best by doing or manipulating objects

task leader this person is focused on the goal and serves to keep people on track with the project and to organize what is being done, when to meet, etc.

theory a set of statements that may be true, usually a theory will be argued or tested

thinker someone who is very analytical and objective in his/her approach to life

tyranny of the shoulds Karen Horney's term for the pressure created by expectations placed upon us

uphill practice moving in the direction of a goal

valid information information that is true, or acceptable, in a field of study

values that which is important to us; in the expectancy–value model of motivation, this refers to your goal in attempting the task, your belief about how important the work is, and how interested you are in it

variable anything that can change, such as loudness, levels of aggression, amount of salt in water, etc.

visual learning style preference for using visual imagery when reading, studying, or listening to lectures

[1] Weiten, W., & Lloyd, M. A. (2003). *Psychology applied to modern life: Adjustment in the 21st century* (7th ed.). Belmont, CA: Wadsworth.